T0327452

MIDAS
TECHNICAL
ANALYSIS

MIDAS TECHNICAL ANALYSIS

A VWAP Approach to Trading and Investing in Today's Markets

Andrew Coles and David G. Hawkins

BLOOMBERG PRESS
An Imprint of
WILEY

Published by John Wiley & Sons, Inc., Hoboken, New Jersey.
Published simultaneously in Canada.

For general information on our other products and services or for technical support, please contact our Customer Care Department within the United States at (800) 762-2974, outside the United States at (317) 572-3993 or fax (317) 572-4002.

Wiley also publishes its books in a variety of electronic formats. Some content that appears in print may not be available in electronic books. For more information about Wiley products, visit our web site at www.wiley.com.

Library of Congress Cataloging-in-Publication Data:

Coles, Andrew.
  Midas technical analysis : a VWAP approach to trading and investing in today's markets / Andrew Coles, David Hawkins.
      p. cm.
    Includes index.
    ISBN 978-1-57660-372-7 (hardback)
1. Investments–Mathematics   I. Hawkins, David (David G.)   II. Title.
    HG4515.3.C65 2011
    332.63'2042–dc22

                                                                                                    2010047237

10   9   8   7   6   5   4   3   2   1

To my mother and the memory of my grandmother
—Andrew Coles

Contents

Introduction   xiii
Andrew Coles

Biographical Sketch, Paul H. Levine   xix
David G. Hawkins

Acknowledgments   xxi

**PART I: STANDARD MIDAS SUPPORT AND
RESISTANCE CURVES**

**CHAPTER 1
MIDAS and Its Core Constituents: The Volume Weighted
Average Price (VWAP) and Fractal Market Analysis**   3
Andrew Coles
MIDAS and Its Two Key Backdrops: VWAP and Fractal Market Analysis   4
The MIDAS Approach as a Genuine Standalone Trading System   20
Summary   26

**CHAPTER 2
Applying Standard MIDAS Curves to the Investor Timeframes**   29
David G. Hawkins
Definitions of Timeframes—The Triple Screen Trading Methodology   29
MIDAS Curves within the Triple Screen System   31
The Basic Behavior of the MIDAS Support/Resistance Curves   31
Equivolume Charting   32
What Price Should Be Used?   35
Support/Resistance Becomes Resistance/Support   35
Distinguishing an Uptrend from a Trading Range   39
The Foothill Pattern   40
A Trading Range Turning into a Downtrend   41
Tracking a Trend with a Hierarchy of MIDAS Curves   43
MIDAS S/R Curves for Entry Setups and Triggers   46
Same Launch Point, Different Timeframes   48
Special Start Points—The Left Side   50
Special Start Points—The Initial Public Offering (IPO)   53
Special Starting Points—The Down Gap and Its Dead Cat Bounce   55
Special Starting Points—The Highest R and the Lowest S   57
Summary   59

CHAPTER 3
MIDAS Support and Resistance (S/R) Curves and Day Trading   **61**
Andrew Coles
Multiple Trend and Timeframe Analysis   62
Part One: The MIDAS System as a Standalone Day Trading System   68
Part Two: Using the MIDAS System alongside Other Technical Indicators   82
Capturing Today's High and Low with Standard MIDAS S/R Curves   119
Summary   120

PART II: THE MIDAS TOPFINDER/BOTTOMFINDER

CHAPTER 4
The MIDAS Topfinder/Bottomfinder on Intraday Charts   **125**
Andrew Coles
Levine's Two Insights Governing the MIDAS Methodology   126
Part One: The Quantitative Features of the TB-F Algorithm   126
Part Two: The Engineering Aspect of TB-F Curves   135
Summary   159

CHAPTER 5
Applying the Topfinder/Bottomfinder to the
Investor Timeframes   **161**
David G. Hawkins
A Most Unusual Indicator   161
The Basic Program of the TB-F   162
What is an Accelerated Trend?   162
Discovering the Topfinder/Bottomfinder   163
Using the TB-F   165
An Interesting Mathematical Observation   166
Fitting the TB-F Curve in Chart Views Other than Equivolume   167
Fitting to More than One Pullback   170
Nested TB-Fs: The Fractal Nature of the Market   178
TB-F Curves on Different Timeframes   180
Bottomfinders Are Sometimes Problematic   185
What Comes after a TB-F Ends?   187
Summary   188

PART III: THE LONGER-TERM HORIZON, OTHER VOLUME
INDICATORS, AND BROADER PERSPECTIVES

CHAPTER 6
Applying MIDAS to Market Averages, ETFs, and Very
Long-Term Timeframes   **193**
David G. Hawkins
Using MIDAS with the Indices—The S/R Curves   195
The Validity of Volume Data   198
Using MIDAS with the Indices—The TB-F   201

Using Exchange-Traded Funds Instead of Market Indices   202
MIDAS Applied to Long- and Very Long-Term Timeframes   205
Back to 1871   209
Inflation Adjustment   209
A Closer Look at the Very Long-Term   211
The Very Long-Term Horizontal S/R Levels   213
The Bavarian Deer Herd   214
What Can Be Said about the Very Long-Term Future?   215
Summary   218

CHAPTER 7
EquiVolume, MIDAS and Float Analysis   **219**
David G. Hawkins

The Basic Principle—"Volume Leads to Volume"   219
Why Does Price Projection Work?   221
The Connection between Price Projection and the Topfinder/Bottomfinder 223
Using Price Projection   224
Steve Woods' Float Analysis   227
Volume Periodicity   230
Summary   237

CHAPTER 8
Putting It All Together   **239**
David G. Hawkins

Trend Following   239
Calling Bottoms   249
Base Breakouts   251
Summary   254

PART IV: NEW DEPARTURES

CHAPTER 9
Standard and Calibrated Curves   **257**
David G. Hawkins

Discovering the Calibrated Curves   257
Examples   258
Summary   267

CHAPTER 10
Applying the MIDAS Method to Price Charts without
Volume: A Study in the Cash Foreign Exchange Markets   **269**
Andrew Coles

MIDAS and Cash Foreign Exchange Markets   269
A Comparison of the MIDAS S/R Curves Using Cash FX Intraday Tick Data and
     Intraday Futures Volume Data   270
A Comparison of the MIDAS Topfinder/Bottomfinder Curves Using Cash FX
     Intraday Tick Data and Intraday Futures Volume Data   273
Options in the Cash Foreign Exchange Markets for Higher Timeframe Charts 275

Options 1 and 3—Replacing Cash Forex Markets with Futures Markets or
    Currency ETFs/ETNs   276
Using MIDAS S/R Curves in Markets without Volume: The Daily and Weekly
    Cash FX Charts   277
Using MIDAS Topfinder/ Bottomfinder Curves in Markets without Volume: The
    Daily and Weekly Cash FX Charts   280
Summary   283

CHAPTER 11
Four Relationships between Price and Volume and Their
Impact on the Plotting of MIDAS Curves   285
Andrew Coles
Relationships between Price and Volume Trends and the Four Rules Affecting the
    Plotting of MIDAS Curves   286
Applying the Rules to Applications of Standard and Nominal MIDAS S/R Curves 290
Using Relative Strength or Ratio Analysis   294
Summary   296

CHAPTER 12
MIDAS and the CFTC Commitments of Traders Report:
Using MIDAS with Open Interest Data   297
Andrew Coles
An Overview of Open Interest and Open Interest Data Options   298
The Orthodox Interpretation of Changes in Open Interest   299
A First Look at Standard MIDAS Support/Resistance Curves with Open Interest 300
Pursuing MIDAS and Open Interest More Deeply   302
Concise Overview of the Commitment of Traders (COT) Report   302
Understanding the Main Players in the Legacy Report   303
Identifying the Key Players in the COT Report   304
Choosing the Appropriate Category of Open Interest   307
MIDAS and Total Open Interest   308
Choosing between Commercial and Noncommercial Positioning Data   312
Measuring the Market with Commercial Net Positioning Data   315
MIDAS and COT Report Timing   318
Comparing the Commercial Net Positioning Indicators with MIDAS using
    Noncommercial Net Positioning Data   319
Additional Reading   327
Summary   328

CHAPTER 13
Price Porosity and Price Suspension: The Causes of these
Phenomena and Several Partial Solutions   331
Andrew Coles
Porosity and Suspension Illustrated   332
Identifying the Cause of the Two Phenomena   333
Solving the Problem of the Two Phenomena   334
Summary   342

CHAPTER 14
A MIDAS Displacement Channel for Congested Markets 345
Andrew Coles

The Problem: Mean Reversion in Sideways Markets 346
The Solution: Applying a Displacement Channel to Sideways Markets 348
MIDAS Displacement Channel Methodology 349
Trading Implications of the MDC 349
Additional Forecasting Implications 349
Additional Benefit: Applying the MDC to Trending Markets to Capture Swing
   Highs in Uptrends and Swing Lows in Downtrends 350
Second Benefit: Applying the MDC to the Problem of Price Porosity 353
Comparing the MDC with the Moving Average Envelope 355
The MDC in Relation to Topfinder/Bottomfinder (TB-F) Curves 356
The MDC in Relation to the MIDAS Standard Deviation Bands 356
Features of the MDC in Relation to other Boundary Indicators 356
Summary 357

CHAPTER 15
MIDAS and Standard Deviation Bands 359
Andrew Coles

The MIDAS Standard Deviation Bands in Sideways Markets 360
The MIDAS Standard Deviation Bands in Uptrends and Downtrends 361
Band Adjustment for Shorter Timeframe Analysis 363
The MSDBs and Narrowing Volatility 363
Comparing the MSD with the MIDAS Displacement Channel 364
Alternatives to Standard Deviation 365
Trading with the MIDAS Standard Deviation Bands 368
Summary 370

CHAPTER 16
Nominal–On Balance Volume Curves (N-OBVs) and Volume–On Balance Curves (V-OBVs) 371
Andrew Coles

On Balance Volume for the Uninitiated 371
Nominal–On Balance Volume Curves 373
The Dipper Setup 377
Volume–On Balance Volume Curves 377
Further Chart Illustrations 378
Summary 381

CHAPTER 17
Extensions, Insights, and New Departures in MIDAS Studies 383
Andrew Coles

MIDAS Curves and Volume-Based Oscillators 384
Correlation Analysis as an Effective Overbought/Oversold Oscillator 389
The Contributions of Bob English 391
Summary 400

APPENDIX A
Programming the TB-F   **403**
David G. Hawkins

APPENDIX B
MetaStock Code for the Standard MIDAS S/R Curves   **411**
Andrew Coles

APPENDIX C
TradeStation Code for the MIDAS Topfinder/Bottomfinder
Curves   **413**
Bob English

Notes   **417**

About the Authors   **433**

Index   **435**

Introduction

Andrew Coles

This book is a study of the MIDAS method of technical analysis based on work that the physicist and technical analyst Paul Levine, PhD, published online in 1995. MIDAS is an acronym for Market Interpretation/Data Analysis System, and although mathematically and conceptually distinct, is a unique development of a market methodology known as Volume Weighted Average Price (VWAP). The latter is an approach to establishing price levels in today's markets that has a variety of uses, from applications in the brokerage industry to trade-management benchmarking and latterly to a growing number of trading strategies and forecasting systems.

Although the MIDAS method uses the volume weighted average price, MIDAS algorithms are distinct from standard VWAP formulations and the more sophisticated techniques for applying MIDAS curves also differ fundamentally from standard VWAP applications. Accordingly, although this book title correctly describes MIDAS as a VWAP approach, it would be quite incorrect to conflate the two.

The aim of this book is twofold. On the one hand, regardless of the reader's experience in technical analysis, one prevalent theme is to teach the basic principles of the MIDAS method as they were originally conceived of by Paul Levine in 1995. However, in many respects the technological changes that have affected the markets since that time on the hardware and software fronts mean that approaches to using the MIDAS method have inevitably evolved too, especially for contexts such as day trading and new markets.[1] It has therefore been important to retain the basic authenticity of Levine's teachings while allowing the approach sufficient flexibility to apply to these new areas, including the development of new MIDAS-based indicators.

Beyond remaining true to Levine's teachings, the book extends them in two ways. On the one hand, with years of experience of applying the curves comes the inevitability of new insights and new methods of working with them. Wherever possible, this book discusses these factors in the context of new markets and timeframes as well as in relation to traditional areas of application. On the other, the book extends the original MIDAS teachings by some distance in relation to genuinely new innovations. These are gathered in the nine chapters that comprise the fourth part of this book.

The MIDAS method is based on the idea that there's a hidden and continually evolving relationship between chart-based areas of support and resistance and trader/investor psychology known as accumulation and distribution. This evolving dynamic was for Levine the ultimate factor in price development and one that could be made apparent by the curves created by the MIDAS indicators. As a consequence, Levine believed that this dynamic relationship could be seen for what it is, an ordered and progressive structure to price development and not a random jumble of trader and investor impulses. Furthermore, Levine believed that this underlying structure could be detected by the curves at all degrees of trend on the daily charts on which his ideas were originally conceived. Because this orderly price movement was evident on larger as well as on smaller trends, Levine referred to the markets as fractal systems and to the MIDAS approach itself as a fractal method of price analysis. This is why the MIDAS approach can be transferred so successfully to other chart timeframes relevant to the very long-term investor as much as to the swing trader and day trader. Moreover, the approach is serviceable on a range of markets beyond stock prices, including the futures markets and even—with certain adjustments to be made clear in Chapter 10—to the volumeless cash FX markets. Indeed, as will be shown in later chapters, even volume substitutes such as open interest and On Balance Volume curves can work successfully with MIDAS. Since Paul Levine's passing in 1998, the online availability of his lectures has ebbed and flowed in relation to the fluctuation of interest in his work. When I first discovered David Hawkins' interest in the MIDAS approach in December 2008 through the Boston Chapter of the American Association of Individual Investors, it took me some time to track down even a single working link to Levine's notes. However, as I write this introduction in the summer of 2010 I can readily find a number of working links on web-hosting domains as well as credible investment-management and technical analysis web sites. We are delighted by this development but are still disappointed that not a single anthology of technical analysis studies over the past decade has included Levine's lectures.

There is no question that in the years after Levine's passing there was a sharp decline in interest in his work, a factor exacerbated by only a small circle of people ever having become acquainted with it and indeed the man himself (in Hawkins' case) as he published his MIDAS notes online over the months of 1995. During the latter stages of this online publication, Levine developed with Dr Stokes Fishburne Associates a program he called WinMIDAS. A web site was subsequently developed to host the software which was available in a 30-day demo with an option to purchase for $95. Levine transferred his MIDAS notes to the WinMIDAS web site, and there were also ongoing MIDAS analyses of various markets similar to those on our own web site, www.midasmarketanalysis.com. In 1998 version 2.1 of the WinMIDAS program was favorably reviewed by John Sweeny, the then editor of *Technical Analysis of Stocks & Commodities*,[2] and there was every reason to believe that the MIDAS method would flourish. Sadly, Paul Levine passed away in 1998 and with his passing the MIDAS method declined in popularity. By the end of the 1990s the WinMIDAS web site was taken offline. By 2001 Dr. Fishburne was still making trial copies of the WinMIDAS program available through a web-hosting site, but this was only on a trial basis and there was no longer product support. WinMIDAS 2.1 was programmed to receive daily data in Worden TeleChart 2000 and Metastock and ASCII formats, but the charting software was soon made obsolete by the introduction of Windows XP in August 2001. There were a number of incompatibilities with the new Windows operating system and there was no technical backup to upgrade the program. As a result, when George Reyna published his article on VWAP and the MIDAS method in the May 2001 edition of *Technical Analysis of Stocks & Commodities*, all of his chart illustrations of the MIDAS method were in Excel and there was no discussion of the more complex MIDAS topfinder/bottomfinder indicator.[3] Behind the scenes, Hawkins had programmed the topfinder/bottomfinder into Excel as early as 1995 even while Levine was publishing his lectures online, and Hawkins continued to work with it in this format right through to 2009 when we were able to develop intraday and higher timeframe versions of the indicator as an external DLL for eSignal and Metastock, our preferred charting platform. Around 2002 Hawkins also had a coded version of the standard MIDAS S/R curves for intraday use in Metastock. In 2005 Hawkins had successfully urged StockShare Publishing LLC to code the standard MIDAS S/R curves for its higher timeframe charts, and in 2009 he also persuaded the company to code the topfinder/bottomfinder for the same chart timeframes. The result is that its charting software StockShareV2 uniquely has both indicators functioning on its charts. Unfortunately, the topfinder/bottomfinder is impervious to a number of charting platform languages due to its complexity, hence the need for an external DLL. Months before becoming acquainted with Hawkins in 2008, I had coded the standard MIDAS S/R curves for intraday use in Metastock and the results were published in the September 2008 edition of *Technical Analysis of Stocks & Commodities*. In that same issue, most of the other leading trading platforms also submitted code for the indicator so it is now extensively available to most traders and investors. Unfortunately this is still less true of the topfinder/bottomfinder, though many trading platforms, including TradeStation and eSignal, do have the resources to code it.

At the time of this writing, there has been a resurgence of interest not just in the MIDAS method but also in the Volume Weighted Average Price (VWAP) more generally. However, as indicated earlier, MIDAS and VWAP are not to be conflated and, this being so, this book is neither about VWAP generally nor about recent developments in related volume-based research. Rather, the book's focus is on the development of MIDAS-based studies and we have had no interest in extending its remit beyond them to include broader VWAP approaches.

Another related point is that while this book will take the reader on an introductory tour of MIDAS through to advanced themes and ideas, it is not an introduction to technical analysis, nor has there been the space available to offer detailed explanations of other indicators when they are introduced. Accordingly, by reading the recommended literature it will be the reader's own responsibility to raise his knowledge to levels necessary to work with other approaches discussed.

The only exceptions to this are Chapters 7, 10, and 12. In Chapter 7 Hawkins provides an introduction to the Float Analysis approach to stock trading as well as a selective introduction to the volume techniques of Richard Arms Jr. in relation to MIDAS approaches. He also works extensively with the equivolume style of charting throughout the book. All of these techniques complement the MIDAS method extremely well. Chapter 10 on the cash foreign exchange markets was a necessary feature of this book because it is to be expected that an approach to the markets that supposedly relies so heavily on volume would be met with a significant degree of skepticism when it's claimed that it can also be applied to the volumeless cash foreign exchange markets. Accordingly, Chapter 10 explains how to apply the MIDAS method to the cash FX markets and what can be expected from the approach. These concerns are also duplicated in Chapter 6 where the focus is on longer-term chart environments. As for Chapter 12, in the past decade there have been considerable advances in technical applications of open interest data available through resources such as the Commitments of Traders (COT) report. Chapter 12 is of additional benefit in providing a short introduction to open interest as well as summarizing every development in COT report research over the past decade while discussing how the MIDAS approach can utilize open interest over longer-term horizons in the futures markets. It's hoped that readers will appreciate this succinct knowledge resource as much as the MIDAS applications that go with it.

Another point that needs stressing is how this book addresses one of the main weaknesses in Levine's lectures, namely his exclusive emphasis on the forecasting implications of MIDAS analysis at the expense of trade-management criteria in their application. The trading implications of using MIDAS curves are addressed most thoroughly in Chapter 8, the second half of Chapter 1 and the first half of Chapter 3, where detailed implementations of the curves are illustrated alongside trading system criteria. Indeed, the first half of Chapter 3 is motivated by the hope that this book will get traders to use MIDAS curves immediately in their trading, whatever their prior level of skill and experience. With this in mind, the discussion is aimed at newer to intermediate-level traders interested in how MIDAS could be used to create a relatively simple, limited-stress day trading or short-term swing trading system. As such, it should also be of interest to the large number of part-time traders with limited time for complex chart analysis and who require a fairly straightforward but robust standalone system.

Importantly, it's an obvious implication of this book not being a general introduction to technical analysis that there are certain foundational skills that a reader new to technical analysis will need to have in place before getting everything he should from this book. This is an important point, since unlike other areas of technical analysis there are certain key aspects to the MIDAS approach that can be acquired prior to learning it and indeed are highly recommended before a relatively inexperienced trader in technical analysis thinks about utilizing the MIDAS method. For the inexperienced trader, it will be helpful to add to this introduction a brief breakdown of these foundational areas.

1. *A basic grasp of trends and at least the basic ability to analyze them using linear trend lines.* Since MIDAS curves are essentially nonlinear trend lines, it's important that a relatively inexperienced trader new to MIDAS possess a solid understanding of price trends. MIDAS curves interact in certain critical ways with the directional bias of the market through the peaks and troughs that define trends and other areas of support and resistance, and it's crucial therefore that a trader using MIDAS for

the first time possess a prior understanding of trends, how they change, and the key areas of support and resistance that define them.

2. *Appropriate peak and trough analysis.* Technical analysts conventionally refer to the peaks and troughs of trends as areas of support and resistance. These concepts are fundamental in MIDAS analysis because for Levine they objectively identify areas of accumulation and distribution that are the ultimate determinants of price behavior.

3. *Chart timeframe and trend size relationships.* In addition to their direction, trends are also classified according to their size and the corresponding chart timeframe best suited to analyze them. For example, the intermediate-term trend lasts from six weeks to nine months and is typically viewed on a daily chart. In addition, there are higher and lower trend lengths influencing price simultaneously in virtue of what Levine called the dynamic interplay of support and resistance, and accumulation and distribution. This means that at any one time a market can be broken down into various trend lengths and can be simultaneously described as moving up, down, or sideways in relation to them. MIDAS curves can play a corresponding role in analyzing relative trend lengths but not in the hands of those inexperienced in trend analysis.

Since MIDAS curves measure price movement at all degree of trend, traders new to MIDAS analysis should be able to articulate trend sizes with ease. Indeed, the more proficient a trader is at this skill, the more his MIDAS curves will be able to tell him about trend direction and its implications for forecasting. These implications will be discussed thoroughly in Chapter 3 and similar concerns are addressed in Hawkins' Chapters 2, 6, and 8.

4. *Fractal market analysis.* Quite simply, to describe the markets as fractal is to say that they're self-similar at all degrees of trend. Levine felt strongly that the markets are fractal, and it was another reason for him to believe that the same principles of MIDAS could be applied at all degrees of trend. Given this assumption, it's another reason why traders new to technical analysis and MIDAS should ensure that their skill at trend analysis covers trend magnitude as well as directional bias. The fractal nature of financial markets has a further consequence for MIDAS analysis, namely the tendency of MIDAS curves to displace from price. Without anticipating later discussions, the displacement of a MIDAS curve from price means that it is drifting away from immediate price action only for price to return to it later during a much larger pullback. Since displacement is related to trend size, there is further reason for an inexperienced trader new to MIDAS to appreciate the significance of the size of the trend in relation to pullbacks and displaced MIDAS support and resistance curves.

5. *Moving averages.* Since the MIDAS approach is based on (but isn't identical with) the volume weighted average price, it's important that an inexperienced trader new to MIDAS possess some understanding of moving averages. The first reason is that moving averages are, like linear trendlines , another method of highlighting a trend. They can also confirm that an old trend has ended and a new one has begun. Thus, some experience with moving averages is of additional benefit in building the skills

necessary to work with trends. Second, MIDAS curves are a form of "anchored" moving average with cumulative volume. Hence, the nonlinear nature of moving averages is an ideal starting point for working with MIDAS curves. Third, many users of moving averages today don't look for moving average crossover signals; instead, they look for price pullbacks to the averages for trading setups.[4] Since the latter is an important component of MIDAS analysis, prior experience of these setups with moving averages will be of benefit. Finally, regular users of moving averages will have probably worked with various length moving averages, especially the 20, 40(50), 100, and 200 moving averages. In so doing they will already have a prior understanding of displacement in the longer-term moving averages such as the 100 and 200.

6. *Volume*. Volume is usually regarded as the next-most-important factor in technical analysis in its role as confirming price activity. The VWAP component in MIDAS is cumulative volume, and it is important when working at a more advanced stage with MIDAS curves to be able to appreciate the influence that cumulative volume plays in their creation in relation to increasing and decreasing levels of volume in ongoing trends.

7. *Candlesticks*. It was noted earlier that the absence of practical trading rules and criteria is a significant weakness in Levine's lectures, and the careful use of candlesticks alongside MIDAS analysis helps to remove this weakness. For example, Japanese candlestick reversal patterns in particular are of considerable help when working with MIDAS techniques.

As a final point in this introduction, David Hawkins and I decided to collaborate on this book without writing it jointly partly because of the inconvenience of the distance between us, but more importantly because it was felt that there were sufficiently large divergences in our interests for it to be more effective for us—and the reader—if we discussed these areas individually rather than as collaborators in jointly-written chapters. At its best, technical analysis captures what happens in the markets only for the most part. Because of this, it's a well-known cliché that technical analysis is as much of an art as a science and this in turn means that no two traders are likely to work with the same methods and indicators in the same way. This is certainly true in our case and hopefully another advantage of our writing chapters individually rather than jointly is that the reader will gain additional insights from each of us and will hopefully be better served by this in the longer run.

In the meantime, the reader is invited to visit our web site, www.midasmarketanalysis.com, to pick up on timely market analysis using the MIDAS method as well as to take advantage of other free resources such as indicator code.

Biographical Sketch, Paul H. Levine

David G. Hawkins

The founder of the MIDAS Method of Technical Analysis was Paul H. Levine, born in New York City on September 27, 1935. He grew up in upstate New York, and attended MIT, graduating with his BS in Physics in 1956. He did his graduate work at California Institute of Technology, where he blossomed as a theoretical physicist, earning his PhD in 1963. The title of his thesis was, "Phase Space Formulation of the Quantum Many-Body Problem."

In July of 1963, he married Burgess Lea Hughes in Copenhagen.

He joined Astrophysics Research Corporation in 1965 as their Chief Scientist. Then, in 1972, he and three colleagues left and founded Megatek Corp. in San Diego, CA, which started primarily as a consulting house, doing contract work for various government and military agencies. Most of Levine's work was on radio propagation, communications, and navigation problems, resulting, over the years, in dozens of publications. Megatek grew to become more than a consultancy, developing and selling imaging hardware and software. In 1981, the founders sold Megatek to United Telecom, after which Paul did freelance consulting for the rest of his life.

Paul's interest in trading and the markets started when he was an undergraduate, and grew and stayed with him for the rest of his life. He was always keen on applying his insights from theoretical physics to trading in the stock market. Over the years, the concepts of the MIDAS method grew in his mind, and, with the help of the computing technology that was available at the time, he put them to use in his trading, with considerable success. In 1995 he wrote, and self-published on the web, 18 articles describing the MIDAS method. He worked with a friend, Stokes Fishburne, to have a computer program written for use by the general public that would apply MIDAS to trading. The program was called WinMIDAS, which Fishburne managed, sold, and maintained. They established a web site where one could access the articles, the WinMIDAS program, and other related goodies, and where people could communicate with Paul. This was before the formal establishment of web blogs, but their site essentially functioned as what we would now call a blog, where Paul made postings of his views roughly every week, and people responded. I (Hawkins) was one of those who corresponded with him during that time.

Tragically, Paul succumbed to cancer, and passed away in March of 1998 at age 62. After his passing, Fishburne took down the web site, and ceased selling and supporting the WinMIDAS program.

Paul Levine was a superb theoretical physicist and market trader, but he was also a lot more. He was something of a mystic, deeply involved with Transcendental Meditation. He and Lea traveled to Switzerland and India to live and work with others in the movement. They also enjoyed other travels around the globe, and were especially fond of their place in Hawaii. It may truly be said that he was a polymath.

We are deeply grateful to Lea Levine for her assistance with biographical material.

Acknowledgments

Thanks are due initially to Stephen Isaacs of Bloomberg Press for suggesting a significant broadening of the book's initial scope and latterly to the team at John Wiley, especially Laura Walsh and Judy Howarth, for managing the earliest stages of the editorial process.

Thanks are also due to Bob English of Precision Capital Management for agreeing to supply TradeStation code for the topfinder/bottomfinder in the third appendix to this book. Due to an interpolation requirement that requires looping, the programming languages of a number of trading platforms cannot program the topfinder/bottomfinder. This includes Metastock, our current platform. While it is possible to create an external DLL written in a language such as C++ for platforms such as Metastock, it was felt that the topfinder/bottomfinder should be coded for the book in at least one accessible script and Bob kindly stepped in with a version of his own code. A number of Bob's ideas concerning the MIDAS approach crop up in this book, especially in the final chapter.

A final word of thanks should go to Satyajit Roy who was responsible for programming the topfinder/bottomfinder in C++ for an external DLL application for both Metastock and eSignal.

Standard MIDAS Support and Resistance Curves

CHAPTER 1

MIDAS and Its Core Constituents

The Volume Weighted Average Price (VWAP) and Fractal Market Analysis

Andrew Coles

It was emphasized in the introduction that this book is not about Volume Weighted Average Price (VWAP) but a particular development of it in the MIDAS approach of Paul Levine. This point requires re-emphasis at the start of the book because at the time of writing there's a lively surge of interest in VWAP. As a result, it's becoming harder for newcomers to this area to differentiate between what lies within the ambit of Levine's contributions and what lies outside of it. A timely first aim of this chapter therefore will be to highlight a number of boundaries to the MIDAS approach in relation to its VWAP background.

A second theme will be to look at the main ideas underlying Levine's philosophy of price movement, especially his fractal conception of the markets and the application of multiple hierarchies of curves. This application adds a powerful ubiquitous forecasting capability to the curves and requires separate attention. The discussion will be partly academic in tone in its brief outline of the fractal conception of the markets that was becoming popular when Levine was working on his approach in the early 1990s.

A final theme lays the groundwork for the practical emphasis throughout this book on trading with MIDAS curves. One of the major shortcomings in Levine's lectures is his emphasis purely on the forecasting implications of the MIDAS method. Never at any time did he consider the trade-management implications of using the curves. The final theme of this chapter begins a trend in this book that focuses heavily on using the curves in practical trading contexts.

This chapter is more theoretical than other discussions in this book in outlining Levine's debt to fractal interpretations of the markets and various approaches to VWAP.

3

However, these deeper perspectives are helpful in understanding the MIDAS method historically as a product of two unique and very different approaches in the markets, which were just beginning to be felt in the early 1990s.

MIDAS and Its Two Key Backdrops: VWAP and Fractal Market Analysis

The MIDAS approach consists of two primary indicators, the basic MIDAS support and resistance (S/R) curves and the more complex topfinder/bottomfinder curves. Let's make a start by considering very generally the relationship these two indicators have to the broader VWAP background prior to their development and that are still very much a part of the professional market trading context today.

Before MIDAS: Initial Motivations for VWAP

There have been several motivations behind the application of VWAP to the financial markets which emerged prior to Levine's development of the MIDAS method. None of them initially involved technical market forecasting, but since they're still very much a part of today's market environment it will be worth outlining them briefly.

Distortion and Price Manipulation

One motivation has stemmed from a closing price free of distortion due to unusual transactions or even intentional price manipulation. An anomalous transaction could be caused by a large accidental buy or sell at a very high or low price level prior to market close.

As an extreme illustration, while this section is being written $1 trillion was temporarily wiped off the market value of U.S. equities on Thursday May 6, 2010, in the so-called 2010 Flash Crash. During a six-minute period the S&P 500 fell nearly 5 percent and the crash was the largest one-day point decline (998 points) in Dow Jones Industrial Average (DJIA) history. By the day's close the markets had recovered to a degree, but the S&P 500 was still 3.2 percent lower. Various reasons have been put forward for the crash, including an errant "fat fingered typo" sell order that set off a chain reaction, a sudden movement in JPY/USD, and even market manipulation.[1] Eventually, in a formal statement published in October 2010, the SEC and CFTC blamed the crash on a liquidity crisis caused by a computer trading algorithm.[2]

Circuit breakers are now being tested to halt such anomalies in the future, but one motivation for calculating the VWAP would be to remove very unusual distortions from the closing price, even if such distortions involve complex intermarket relationships in the currencies and bonds markets through sophisticated computer networks.

Alternatively, direct market manipulation may involve the intentional placing of orders during late market hours at various extreme prices. Again the reasons could be various. For example, closing prices are used for formal statements of the value of a portfolio in a company's annual report and are also occasionally used to calculate directors' remuneration as well as the settlement values of derivatives.[3] Again the VWAP is said to help prevent such skewing of market data.

Guaranteed VWAP Executions

A second motivation for VWAP calculations has emerged from the brokerage industry and bears on the ever-demanding relationship between broker and client. Many brokers will now guarantee their clients that orders are executed at the VWAP (so-called guaranteed VWAP execution) in "targeted VWAP" trading. For example, Euronext, the pan-European stock and derivatives exchange, has available what it calls a "VWAP transaction," based on an average price weighted by security volumes traded in a central order book. A large number of brokerage firms will also guarantee the VWAP for large domains of stocks, especially large caps. Due to the growing popularity of VWAP executions data, vendors such as Bloomberg will also display VWAP prices after market close.

The Minimization of Market Impact and Trader Assessment

A third and fourth motivation have arisen from the very heavy volume trading under-taken in the mutual and pensions industry. Here large investors aim to be as passive as possible in their executions and use the VWAP to ensure that they are entering the market in line with typical market volume. This minimizes market impact, which in turn reduces transaction costs. Thus, a final related motivation would be the actual assessment of trading performance: a large institutional trade entry beyond the VWAP may be criticized in light of higher transaction costs; similarly, an order filled above the daily VWAP would be regarded negatively in view of the slippage implications.

Standard VWAP Calculations

Now that the nontrading motivations for VWAP are understood, it would be helpful before turning to Levine's MIDAS approach to obtain a basic understanding of how the VWAP is calculated and how basic VWAP curves appear on a chart. In part, this discussion should also alleviate some of the confusion that has arisen around the relationship between VWAP and the MIDAS approach.

The VWAP is calculated by multiplying the volume at each price level with the respective price and then dividing by the total volume. The more volume traded at a certain price level, the more impact it has on the VWAP.[4] Here is the basic formula for VWAP calculations:

$$\Sigma(Pn * Vn) / \Sigma(Vn)$$

where

P = price of instrument traded
V = volume traded
n = number of trades (i.e., each individual trade that takes place over the selected
    time period)

There are variations on the basic formula. For example, George Reyna finds the following version more useful:[5]

$$(((Hc * Lc)/2) * Vc)/(Vc - V(c - s))$$

where

H = high price
L = low price
V = volume
c = current bar
s = launch point[6]

As a simple illustration of calculating the VWAP, we can go back to the original VWAP formula and calculate the VWAP over 15 minutes on a 5m chart of the DAX March 2010 futures. We'll use the closing price of three 5m bars:

Bar #1: 5,827 with a volume of 2,856 contracts
Bar #2: 5,819.5 with a volume of 1,729 contracts
Bar #3: 5,816.5 with a volume of 2,271 contracts

The average price over this 15-minute period is the total number of contracts divided by 3, or 5,821 contracts. But let's calculate the VWAP. The result obtained will depend on which method of utilizing the formula we choose. Day trading software firms will probably use one of two algorithmic procedures to derive it.

The first, usually assumed to be the more accurate method, is known as "cumulative VWAP." The first step would be to multiply the closing price with the volume for each of the three bars, arriving at the following numbers:

16,641,912
10,061,915.5
13,209,271.5

The next step would be to add them together to arrive at 39,913,099. To arrive at the denominator, the volume numbers would be summed to get 6,856 contracts. With the division, the cumulative VWAP would therefore be 5,821.630 (this method is usually calculated to three decimal places).

A second method of arriving at the VWAP is known as "iterative VWAP." It uses the last value of the VWAP as the basis for calculating the VWAP on the next trade.

This is an example of the procedure:

First iteration: (5,827 ∗ 2,856) / 2,856 = 5,827

Second iteration: 5,827 + [(5,819.5 − 5,827) ∗ 1,729] / (2,856 + 1,729) = 5,824.172

Third iteration: 5,824.172 + [(5,816.5 − 5,824.172) ∗ 2,271] / (2,271 + 2,856 + 1,729) = 5,821.830

Thus, the iterated VWAP for this same time period is 5,821.830, as opposed to 5,821.630 in the cumulative VWAP approach. As more trades (iterations) are made, the closer the two VWAP calculations will become.[7]

Aside from there being variations of the VWAP formula and calculation differences, another potential source of confusion is that the basic VWAP formula is identical to the one for the volume weighted moving average (VWMA).[8] The two differ only indirectly in terms of the calculation procedure in trading platforms, with the VWMA relying on the "sum" (summation) function and the VWAP utilizing the "cum" (cumulative) function. The difference this makes will be illustrated in a moment in Figure 1.1. It's also worth pointing out that some platforms additionally calculate the Volume Adjusted Moving Average (VAMA), a slightly different curve that's based on the "mov" (moving average) function and that results in a variation of the VWMA

FIGURE 1.1   5m chart of Eurex DAX September 2010 futures showing the DAX as a basic line plot (heavy black).

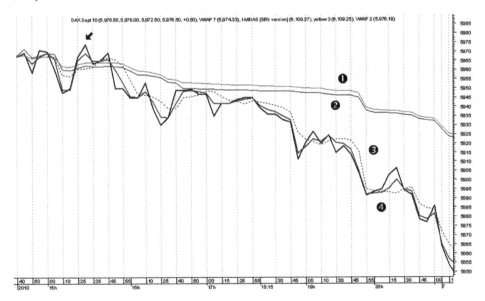

Plot (1) (gray) = standard VWAP; plot (2) (black) = MIDAS; plot (3) (dotted) = VWMA; and plot (4) (heavy gray) = VAMA.

Source: eSignal and Metastock. www.esignal.com and www.equis.com.

plot. Figure 1.1 is a 5m chart of the German DAX September 2010 futures illustrating four curves alongside the dark black line plot of the DAX. Plot (1) (gray) is a standard VWAP curve anchored to the start of the chart. Plot (2) (black) is a basic MIDAS curve. Plot (3) (dotted) is the VWMA, and plot (4) (heavy gray) is the VAMA. We'll come to the discussion of MIDAS curves shortly, but the purpose of this chart is to illustrate how different these curves appear on a chart even though there is so much conflation over the use of the terms used to describe them.

The conflation is at its worse with regard to the terms "VWAP" and "MIDAS." Indeed, many traders who use MIDAS analysis techniques are actually using VWAP curves without realizing it. Yet there are four reasons why traders who deploy MIDAS techniques should ensure that they're using the MIDAS formula (see below) and not the standard VWAP formula:

1. As illustrated in Figure 1.1, the first plot (standard VWAP) is quite different from the second (basic MIDAS).
2. There are variations of the basic VWAP formula (Reyna's version is a good illustration). There's the potential therefore for an even greater difference between VWAP and MIDAS curves.
3. There are even alternatives to the way the standard VWAP formula is calculated, as illustrated in the difference between the cumulative and iterative methods. These methods can give rise to further variations between a standard VWAP and MIDAS plot.
4. VWAP utilizes the average price whereas many who use MIDAS curves use the low price in uptrends and the high in downtrends (Hawkins is an example). This again will create significant differences between a standard VWAP plot and a MIDAS curve.

Trading Applications of VWAP

As already noted, the earliest motivations for establishing the VWAP were not related to technical market forecasting. The first published use as a market entry criterion appears to be trader Kevin Haggerty's in a 1999 interview. Haggerty stated that he favored a simple methodology of choosing long positions when price is above its daily VWAP and short positions when it's below.[9] However, in the past few years there has been a blossoming of interest in VWAP and now there are seemingly as many ways of utilizing it for trading purposes as there are traders taking an interest. As noted, the problem is that many traders use the term "VWAP" erroneously to refer also to MIDAS curves, so when trading ideas are being discussed it's often hard to know which particular curve a trader has in mind.

Bob English, of The Precision Report, has argued that the previous day's closing VWAP is a powerful support and resistance pivot for the current day, often determining the absolute high and low.[10] The trader Brett Steenbarger, PhD, plots the VWAP from the start of the new day's futures session and views its direction as giving a sense to the intraday trend. In trending market conditions, he'll stay to one side of the VWAP, whereas if the market is in a trading range he'll consider trading both sides of it.[11] Participants in the trader forums are also busy with new ideas. For example, one long and influential thread on the Traders Laboratory web site outlines a trading system based on combining the daily VWAP with a volume distribution histogram similar to market profile.[12]

VWAP and Paul Levine's MIDAS System

In relation to the VWAP backdrop there are two main aspects to MIDAS support/resistance curves that differentiate them from it.

The Formula Difference

First, there's Levine's variation of the basic VWAP formula. Second, which we'll come to below, there's his view of how to launch MIDAS curves. As for the variation, in his twelfth lecture he gave the formula for his MIDAS S/R curves as follows:

$$\Sigma(Pn * Vn) - \Sigma(Ps * Vs) / \Sigma(Vn) - \Sigma(Vs)$$

where

> Pn and Vn are the current cumulative price and volume
> Ps and Vs are the cumulative price and volume at the MIDAS curve launch
> Vn is the current cumulative volume
> Vs is the cumulative volume at the MIDAS curve launch

In plain English the formula reads: (cumulative average price)(volume at a given instant) − (cumulative average price)(volume at a period d units of cumulative volume earlier), all divided by d, where d is the cumulative volume displacement measured from the launch point to the given instant.

We've already seen from Figure 1.1 that Levine's variation of the VWAP formula results in a curve that differs from a standard VWAP curve. The question is why Levine felt it necessary to introduce this minor modification to the original VWAP formula. He never tells us in his lectures, but it's possible to speculate accurately as to his reason. To do so, we need to look at an important theoretical idea that distinguishes the MIDAS method from more basic approaches involving VWAP.

Paul Levine's Philosophy of How Market Prices Evolve

This theoretical idea lies in two factors that were of fundamental importance to Levine:

(i) The critical choice of where to launch MIDAS curves, and
(ii) The multiple applications of MIDAS S/R curves based on a fractal conception of price movement

It's the combination of (i) and (ii) that turns the MIDAS approach into a genuine trading system as opposed to a set of indicators on a chart.

We can better understand these two features by reducing Levine's philosophy of price movement implicit in his lectures to five key tenets:

1. The underlying order of price behavior is a fractal hierarchy of support and resistance levels.
2. This interplay between support and resistance is a coaction between accumulation and distribution.
3. This coaction, when considered quantitatively from raw price and volume data, reveals a mathematical symmetry between support and resistance.
4. This mathematical symmetry can be used to predict market tops and bottoms in advance.
5. Price and volume data—the volume weighted average price (VWAP)—subsequent to a reversal in trend, and thus to a major change in market (trader) sentiment, is key to this process of chart prediction.

The Critical Choice of Where to Launch VWAP Support/Resistance Curves

According to factor (i), Levine believed that when charted all price behavior can be reduced to multiple hierarchies of support and resistance. What this means is that as price moves forward at all degrees of trend, it is either testing existing support or resistance or breaking out from them to create new hierarchies. Accumulation therefore amounts to price respecting existing support, breaking out of overhead resistance, and moving up the chart to create new levels of resistance and support. Distribution amounts to its opposite. According to tenet (4), this repetitive price behavior can be captured using the MIDAS support and resistance curves with the same formula. In other words, it makes no difference to the algorithm whether price is rising (accumulation) or falling (distribution).

With tenet (4) in mind, the question is how MIDAS can be used maximally to highlight these hierarchies of support and resistance. This is where tenet (5) assumes importance. It's this tenet that marks the main distinction between standard applications of VWAP and Levine's specialized use. It's also why these MIDAS support and resistance curves have come to be known as "anchored VWAP" curves. Levine focuses on this topic in lecture eight. He ends lecture seven with the following remark:

> We have not yet specified the interval over which the averages are to be taken. In fact, it is this *choice of averaging interval which uniquely distinguishes the MIDAS method*.[13]

In lecture eight he first identifies and then justifies this averaging interval. He argues that where price finds subsequent support or resistance is directly associated with where there was a change in the underlying psychology, otherwise there'd be no change in trend. This is where the averaging must start and hence where a MIDAS curve should be launched, or "anchored."

With this information, we can now answer a question left unanswered earlier, namely why Levine felt it necessary to introduce a minor modification to the original VWAP formula. As we've just seen, Levine believed that the launch bar of a MIDAS curve was the last bar—and hence the bottom—of the previous trend. Since for him the VWAP subsequent to a reversal in trend is the critical data, he subtracted the VWAP of the launch bar from subsequent data because he believed that the launch bar VWAP was a part of the previous market psychology before it changed direction and thus marked a new change in sentiment. He might have omitted the VWAP of the launch bar from the equation entirely instead of subtracting it from the subsequent VWAP. Or he might instead have launched MIDAS curves from the price bar subsequent to the last bar of the previous trend and simply used the original VWAP formula. For reasons he doesn't specify, he does neither, and opts for the approach that underlies the MIDAS formula provided earlier. Possibly Levine had done research on these alternatives and found them wanting. He never tells us one way or the other.

When it comes to the actual plotting of the curves, subsequent reversals in trend, which the MIDAS S/R curves are intended to capture, are connected mathematically to this change in sentiment, since subsequent trader mood is intimately linked to it. Here is Levine again:

> Our "message" is that instead of "moving" averages, one should take fixed or "anchored" averages, where the anchoring point is the point of trend reversal.[14]

The implication for trading is this. If I know that certain points on a chart are trend reversals and that the corresponding changes in psychology are associated with subsequent levels of support and resistance, I can use this information to trade these subsequent levels, provided I have the right tool—in this case, a MIDAS curve—to identify these subsequent levels. By contrast, nothing this precise is implied by the VWAP itself.

Compare, for example, Figure 1.2 with Figure 1.3. Figure 1.2 is a 5m chart of the March 2010 Xetra DAX futures and has a standard anchored VWAP curve plotted throughout the day from the market opening. As noted earlier, some traders will start what is actually an anchored VWAP curve from the market open and stay to one side of it in trending days or trade both sides of it in rangebound conditions. Now there's nothing wrong with these suggestions, but they're not MIDAS strategies. For one thing, the curves are standard VWAP curves not MIDAS curves. For another, today's open (or yesterday's close) would figure in MIDAS thinking only if it represented a change in market psychology. Where it doesn't, I showed in a previous article that plotting a MIDAS curve from the previous day's close or today's open is ineffectual in relation to the MIDAS method.[15] Figure 1.2 is a case in point. Here there's no significant swing high or low involving the open; as a result, the MIDAS curve drifts through the opening hours of trading and then displaces as prices make a sharp upside move. The two pullbacks circled represent good opportunities to join the ongoing trend. However, it's clear that the MIDAS curve has displaced far too much to be of any help and we get little aid from indicators, such as the stochastic, which is already

FIGURE 1.2   5m chart of Xetra DAX March 2010 futures with a standard VWAP curve plotting from the open.

Source: eSignal and Metastock. www.esignal.com and www.equis.com.

FIGURE 1.3   The same 5m chart with an anchored MIDAS support curve accurately capturing the two pullbacks.

Source: eSignal and Metastock. www.esignal.com and www.equis.com.

overbought. The best we could do is trade basic breakouts while the MIDAS curve itself is irrelevant.

By contrast, Figure 1.3 is the same chart with a MIDAS support curve meaningfully anchored to the start of the new phase of the uptrend highlighted by the gray arrow and interacting directly with its pullbacks. By a judicious use of Japanese candlesticks, both to gauge reversals and to set stops, a properly anchored MIDAS curve checks every box a trader requires, including trend direction, trade timing and entry, plus trade-management in clear risk levels.[16] In Figure 1.3 the On Balance Volume indicator also significantly enhances the MIDAS signals in virtue of its trend line properties, as can be seen at the arrow highlights (see also Chapter 3).

Multiple Applications of MIDAS S/R Curves Based on a Fractal Conception of Price Movement

Moving on to factor (ii), anchoring MIDAS curves to clear points on a chart where there's a change in psychology isn't the only theoretical element that distinguishes the MIDAS system from basic VWAP. The other major determinant is Levine's insistence on the application of multiple curves to the same chart. In his lectures, Levine maintained that support and resistance levels connected with earlier points of trend reversal should be associated with a hierarchy of theoretical curves. I summarized this idea in terms of the first of the five tenets earlier. This is one of the factors that truly establish the MIDAS approach as a genuine standalone trading system, since the concept of hierarchy presupposes multiple levels of price action, none of which are beyond the analytical reach of the anchored MIDAS curves. The concept of the market as a hierarchy of support and resistance levels presupposes in turn that price formations are fractal. Levine uses the term "fractal" four times in his lecture series, with the main passage being this:

> The foregoing properties [namely, similar zigzags in price behavior at all degrees of trend] of *self-similarity* and *scale-independence* are characteristics of *fractal* behavior. *The fractal nature of stock price fluctuations has been recognized for some time on purely empirical grounds.* What has been missing is an understanding of why markets should behave fractally (i.e., beyond the obvious fact that they are *complex non-linear dynamic systems*). In the Midas method, we have seen that the complex zigzags in price behavior can be (to quote article #8) "understood with respect to a single algorithmic prescription: support (or resistance) will be found at the VWAP taken over an interval subsequent to a reversal in trend." The psychological elements of greed and fear, whose quantification led to this algorithm, *apply to investors/traders across all time scales* (my italics throughout).[17]

What is meant by "fractal" in this context, and how precisely is it linked to the notion of a hierarchy of support and resistance levels? This is an important question because without its fractal capabilities MIDAS would be a shadow of its true forecasting potential. Consequently, we'll complete the first half of this chapter by focusing on the crucial role that fractal market analysis plays in the MIDAS method.

Levine refers to the fractal nature of markets as a self-similar, scale-independent, nonlinear dynamic system, and of this fractal nature as being proven empirically. As a research physicist publishing his lectures online in 1995, Levine would not have been deferring to Elliott Wave theory in claiming that the fractal market hypothesis had been proven empirically. He would have been referring to a particular statistical method affirming this hypothesis. It is worth spending a section or two on this topic, not only to enlighten the role played by the fractal market hypothesis in Levine's thinking but also to allow other relevant discussions of it in later chapters.

MIDAS and Fractal Market Analysis

The empirical grounds Levine refers to have their origin in the pioneering work of the British hydrologist H. E. Hurst (1880–1978) and subsequently in the applications of Hurst's ideas to the financial markets by Benoit Mandelbrot. From 1913 Hurst had spent his early career as head of the Meteorological Service working on the Nile River Dam Project with its focus on the control and conservation of Nile waters. Working with vast records of contemporary and historical rainfall and river flow patterns in the Nile and its network of tributaries, Hurst came to believe that the Nile's overflows weren't random and that there was evidence of nonperiodic cycles (one of several hallmarks of a fractal process (see below)). As a result, Hurst developed his own statistical methodology to test this assumption known as Rescaled/Range (R/S) analysis. His work was formally published in 1951[18] and was subsequently refined by Mandelbrot and others when it began to be applied extensively to financial market time series.[19] As a practicing physicist with an abiding interest in the financial markets, it's possible that by the 1990s Levine was familiar with some of this work. However, it's more likely that he was drawing on the recently published books of Edgar Peters in 1991 and 1994,[20] although there was also other material on fractals discussing the financial markets in more or less detail of which Levine might have been aware.[21] Much of this work describes R/S analysis as proving empirically that the financial markets are fractal time series. For reasons that will emerge later in the book, it will be worth explaining the nature of this empirical evidence in a little more detail as well as linking it to several core ideas in Levine's market philosophy.

R/S analysis claims to show that the financial markets are fractal because it is a statistical methodology for distinguishing between random and nonrandom (fractal) time series. When Einstein looked at the random path followed by a particle in a fluid (Brownian motion), he discovered that the distance covered increases with the square root of time used to measure it ($R = T^{0.50}$, or the "T to one-half rule," where R = distance covered and T = a time index).[22] This equation is now commonly used in finance to annualize volatility by standard deviation. For example, the standard deviation of monthly returns is multiplied by the square root of 12 on the assumption that the returns increase by the square root of time. Here markets are assumed to follow a random walk (i.e., exhibit Brownian motion). By adapting the T to one-half rule and embedding it within a larger statistical procedure,[23] Hurst arrived at the R/S methodology that produces an exponent he called the K exponent and which has since been labeled the Hurst exponent by Mandelbrot in honor of Hurst. It's the Hurst exponent, then, that estimates the degree of nonrandomness in time series to which it is applied.[24] A vast amount of recent work has focused on the international financial markets using this technique,[25] albeit with varying results in regard to the actual Hurst exponent for each market.[26]

If the R/S analysis applied to a given time series results in a Hurst exponent of 0.5, it means that the time series is a pure random walk; in other words, it increases with the square root of time as Brownian motion. However, if $0.50 < H < 1.00$, it implies a "persistent" time series covering a greater distance in the same timespan than a random walk—hence the term "fractional Brownian motion"—and it is characterized by a long-term memory effect. In other words, what happens today affects what happens tomorrow, and the changes are correlated. This means that there is sensitivity to initial conditions (another hallmark of a chaotic system) and that this long-term memory effect affects changes at all degrees of trend (daily changes are correlated to later daily changes, weekly changes to weekly ones, and so on). There is thus no characteristic timescale, yet another hallmark of a fractal time series.[27] If $H < 0.5$, it implies that the time series is antipersistent, meaning that it covers less distance than a random walk because it is reversing itself far more frequently. In the financial markets antipersistent price activity would be typically found in tight congested (rangebound) markets.

If $0.50 < H < 1.00$ (that is, a persistent time series with long-term memory), it also means that H is scaling according to a power law as there is a shift from smaller to larger increments of time in the time series. Power laws are common to all fractal time series as well as to fractals in the natural world as diverse as city population size, earthquake magnitudes, clouds, coastlines, word frequency in languages, in addition to thousands of other natural phenomena. In virtue of these power laws, all fractals have in common the fact that they don't scale up or down according to the same ratio, hence the term "scale invariant" which Levine refers to in the passage quoted. For example, trees and coastlines are well-known fractal systems because although they scale up and down, each scaling level is similar to but not identical with the others. Trees have branches that resemble one another (global determinism), but none are identical close up (local randomness).[28] Applied to examples such as these, and also to time series such as the financial markets, the term "qualitative self-similarity" is used. As we have seen, the power law that explains this is related to the Hurst exponent. This power law scaling feature is also sometimes called the fractal dimension. The fractal dimension is related to the Hurst exponent by the equation $D = 2 - H$. Thus, a Hurst exponent of 0.7 is equivalent to a fractal dimension of 1.3. The fractal dimension is often used as a means of describing how fractal objects, such as coastlines, fill the space around them and how they scale in relation to it. Fractal time series, on the other hand, scale statistically in time,[29] and so the fractal dimension of a time series measures how jagged or rough it is ("statistical self-similarity"). A straight line would have a fractal dimension of 1, while a random time series would have a fractal dimension of 1.50. A fractal

FIGURE 1.4   Dietmar Saupe's illustration of time series ranging from antipersistence to a time series exhibiting clear long-term memory processes (the lines added to the final time series are my own).

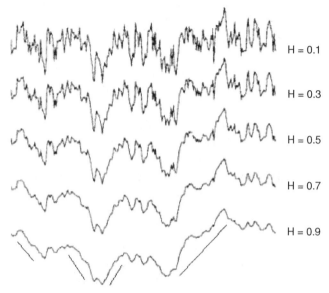

Source: Adapted from D. Saupe, "Random Fractal Algorithms," Chapter 2, in *The Science of Fractal Images*, ed. D. Saupe and Heinz-Otto Peitgen (New York: Springer Inc, 1988).

time series would therefore always have a fractal dimension between 1 (indicating a pure deterministic process) and 1.50 (indicating a random walk or Brownian motion). Thus, a fractal time series increases at a faster rate than the square root of time ($= H = 0.5$). Anything between 1.50 and 2 would imply the antipersistence mentioned earlier.

In the remainder of this section, let's highlight more clearly the relationship between the fractal interpretation of time series and the notion of "anchoring" MIDAS curves and how the latter depend critically on the former to work at all. A very helpful visual appreciation of statistical self-similarity can be seen in Figure 1.4, which is derived from an illustration by Dietmar Saupe in his chapter "Random Fractal Algorithms" in Saupe and Peitgen.[30]

From a MIDAS viewpoint, what is interesting about the first of these two time series is that they're both antipersistent ($H < 0.5$) and not particularly amenable to MIDAS curves. The middle time series, with a Hurst exponent of 0.5 ($D = 1.50$), is a pure random walk. Here we begin to see opportunities to launch MIDAS curves from certain highs and lows. However, the last two time series are fractal ($D = 1.3$ and 1.1 respectively). It can be seen straightaway how inviting they are to MIDAS analysis. The second of the two, with a fractal dimension of 1.1, gets close at certain points to being a deterministic straight line (hence the high Hurst exponent), especially in the four areas highlighted. Here, because of the high Hurst exponent, the trends are showing distinct signs of acceleration and as such are suitable for the launch of the topfinder/bottomfinder indicator. This is an important point (see Chapter 4 where this indicator is examined in relation to the fractal characteristics of time series components to which it should be applied).

The Real-Time Fractal Dimension and MIDAS Curves

In the meantime, we round off this discussion by looking at an actual time series in relation to Figure 1.4 that illustrates a full application of standard MIDAS S/R curves. Figure 1.5 is a 15m chart of the September 2010 Eurex DAX futures spanning nearly six trading days from July 5 to July 12. This entire period has a Hurst exponent of 0.526138 and thus a fractal dimension of 1.473862. The Hurst exponent is graphically illustrated in Figure 1.6, a common way of presenting the Hurst exponent in the financial markets as discussed in Peters (1991 and 1994).

With a fractal dimension of 1.473862, the DAX futures are barely more than a random walk over this timeframe and should be compared with the third time series in Saupe's illustration in Figure 1.4. Yet as Figure 1.5 reveals, it's still easy to apply standard MIDAS support and resistance curves to this chart as well as three topfinder/bottomfinder curves (points (1), (2) and (3), even though the latter function correctly only when the market is exhibiting a very high degree of persistence. In fact, the overall Hurst exponent in Figure 1.5 is misleading, since the price series

FIGURE 1.5 15m chart of DAX September 2010 futures showing six trading days with a Hurst exponent of 0.526138 and hence a fractal dimension of 1.473862.

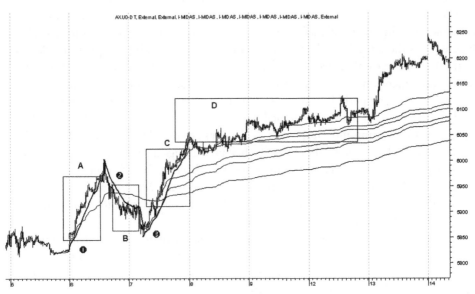

Source: eSignal and Metastock. www.esignal.com and www.equis.com.

FIGURE 1.6   R/S chart of the DAX 15m September 2010 futures over six trading days.

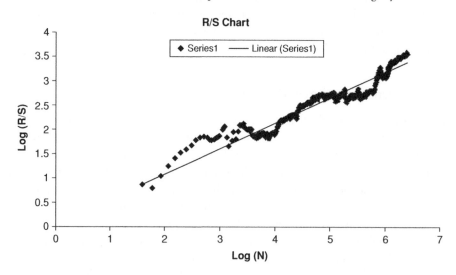

Source: Xlpert. www.elpert.com.

clearly shows signs of acceleration in the trend portions highlighted by rectangles A, B, and C where the three topfinder/bottomfinder curves have been launched successfully.

To get a more accurate real-time perspective on the fractal dimension of the market, and hence an accurate mathematical context in which to use MIDAS, it's now possible to obtain real-time Hurst estimates[31] and the corresponding fractal dimension in virtue of indicators such as the Fractal Dimension Index (FDI). Figure 1.7 is the same 15m chart with the FDI programmed into eSignal. In relation to the 1.5 random walk level, the real-time fluctuation of the indicator clearly shows the fractal dimension decreasing during trending periods and increasing into antipersistent levels during periods of deceleration and rangebound conditions. In her 2007 study of the FDI, Radha Panini argued that the indicator is a much better filter than other trend-measuring indicators such as Wilder's Average Directional Index (ADX) and the Vertical Horizontal Filter (VHF) when used alongside moving average systems, breakout systems, and oscillator trading systems such as the RSI.[32] If this is true, there is undoubtedly an even better theoretical synergy between MIDAS and an indicator that actually measures the fractal dimension of markets in relation to which MIDAS was primarily developed.

Since, as Saupe's diagram in Figure 1.4 illustrates, there's a critical relationship between the fractal dimension of a market and the successful application of MIDAS curves, a real-time fractal measuring device such as the FDI would prove to be a much better fit with MIDAS than would any other technical tool. I suspect that Paul Levine would have approved strongly of it, given his tendency to choose other indicators selectively to work alongside MIDAS.

FIGURE 1.7 Same 15m chart of the DAX futures covering the same trading period with the Fractal Dimension Index plotting in real-time in the lower pane.

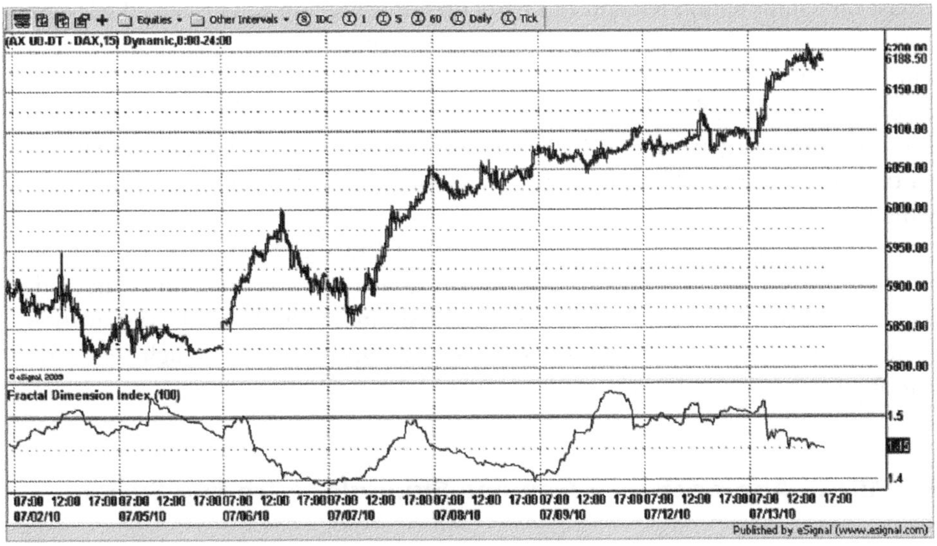

Source: eSignal. www.eSignal.com.

The Background Influence on Levine

Finally, on a point of pure academic interest I've suggested that Levine's view that trader emotions are fractal probably has its origins in Peters's fractal market hypothesis. First, let's remind ourselves of what Levine said:

> The psychological elements of greed and fear, whose quantification led to this algorithm, apply to investors/traders *across all time scales* (my italics).[33]

In so far as fractal market activity is assumed to be linked in the MIDAS approach by means of predictable human emotion, it's the opposite of what has come to be known as the Efficient Market Hypothesis, and it's very tempting to see it as a radically foreshortened statement of the Fractal Market Hypothesis put forward by Peters in *Fractal Market Analysis*.

In the Efficient Market Hypothesis (EMH) price changes are noncorrelated (serially independent) from period to period and timeframe to timeframe, with the semistrong version stating that the market's random walk is due to a rational dissemination of all known news and fundamental information uniformly across timeframes. This is radically unlike the fractally dispersed emotional psychology Levine believed in.[34] Moreover, it's certain that he would have seen the mathematics of MIDAS as being inconsistent with standard deviation and the normal distribution curves of the EMH.[35]

In putting forward his Fractal Market Hypothesis in his book *Fractal Market Analysis* Peters[36] argued that prices aren't interpreted univocally across timeframes because only information relevant to a particular time horizon will be judged relevant. In general, technical information will be weighted much more highly in the shorter term. When markets occasionally do weight information equally across timeframes the consequence is a loss of market liquidity, resulting in a market crisis, since longer-term investors either stop participating in the market or else lose faith in fundamental data and trade short-term.[37] Thus, liquidity and market stability cannot be accounted for by the EMH.

Levine was relating the mathematics of VWAP to the fractal ideas inherent in distinctive multi-timeframe market psychology in virtue of the "anchoring" methodology implicit in his hierarchies of support and resistance. Ultimately the formulation of these ideas goes back to Peters's book *Fractal Market Analysis*, though they have their origin too in several earlier studies.

The MIDAS Approach as a Genuine Standalone Trading System

In the introduction to this chapter, I observed that a major weakness in Levine's presentation of the MIDAS approach is his lack of attention to the practical implications of trading with MIDAS curves, whereas the emphasis in this book is very much on practical trading implications. With this in mind, the second half of this chapter lays a little groundwork for what is to come by discussing how the MIDAS approach can be converted into a practical trading system.

In the following discussion, trading system criteria will be outlined alongside a brief discussion of how the fractal nature of MIDAS meets each one. This discussion can also be read alongside the discussion in Chapter 3 of how standard MIDAS S/R curves could be used with relative ease by an advanced beginner or an intermediate-level trader as a standalone day trading system.

Van K. Tharp, PhD,[38] defines a trading system in terms of the following eight components:

1. A market filter
2. Setup conditions
3. An entry signal
4. A worst-case stop loss
5. Re-entry when it is appropriate
6. Profit-taking exits
7. A position-sizing algorithm
8. The possibility of multiple systems for different market conditions

We can omit criterion (7) because it's not so relevant to the present discussion and replace it with the requirement that a system (especially in a context such as day trading) generate sufficient signals throughout the trading day (or timeframe of interest) to ensure that the system is self-reliant; that is, that it doesn't require the input of outside elements to generate an appropriate number of signals. Criterion (7) can be reframed as follows:

7. That the system be capable of generating sufficient signals over the timeframe of interest

A Market Filter

This criterion has to do with how a market is moving (i.e., trending up, down, or sideways) and whether the system works adequately in relation to it. Volatility will also play a role here insofar as markets can be more or less volatile, regardless of their direction.

Detailed studies of how the standard MIDAS S/R curves and the topfinder/ bottomfinder algorithm work in various market environments is discussed in forthcoming chapters, while Chapter 14 specifically explores conditions in congested markets and increased volatility. For now, however, we have seen in Figures 1.5 and 1.6 that any market with a Hurst exponent above 0.5 will provide maximum opportunities for MIDAS curves. Figure 1.8 is a 5m chart of the Xetra DAX March 2010 futures illustrating this point. The majority of the movement is captured by the standard S/R curves, while accelerated portions of the trend where the fractal dimension is reduced

FIGURE 1.8   5m chart of Xetra DAX March 2010 futures showing one trading day (March 9) and extensive applications of MIDAS with Granville's OBV in the top pane.

Source: eSignal and Metastock. www.esignal.com and www.equis.com.

to a minimum are captured by the two topfinder/bottomfinder indicators. The top pane contains Granville's On Balance Volume indicator, which was favored by Levine as providing a background indication (in the form of divergences) of whether standard S/R curves are likely to continue holding price.

The trading opportunities illustrated in Figure 1.8 should again be compared with the single VWAP curve in Figure 1.2 and how it must be bolstered by additional analysis in order to generate a timely market filter. No such additions are required with the MIDAS method.

Setup Conditions

As noted, it's a very significant weakness in the original MIDAS method that Levine never discussed trade-management issues. Typically, a setup would occur with respect to a standard MIDAS curve when price pulls back to it and we establish a pure support/resistance-based contrarian play. For example, if we look again at Figure 1.8 we can see a variety of instances where this occurs. In the case of the topfinder/bottomfinder curves, a setup would be when the curve is launched and it provides a certain cumulative volume prediction while price is trending above or below the curve respectively. The trade-management implications relating to the topfinder/bottomfinder curves are discussed in Chapter 4. As discussed earlier, no comparable setup conditions are available in the case of a standard VWAP curve unless additional indicators and/or chart analysis are brought in.

The Entry Signal

This is another important topic that is discussed in more detail in Chapter 3, but for now it's necessary to concede that Levine fails to meet this criterion in his discussion of the MIDAS method. My own view is that Japanese candlesticks are ideally suited to MIDAS setups insofar as one can use the well-known candlestick reversal signals as filters for price reversals off standard MIDAS S/R curves. Readers should consult Steve Nison's book *Japanese Candlestick Charting Techniques*,[39] especially Chapter 11 ("Candlesticks with Trend lines") and Chapter 12 ("Candlesticks with Retracement Levels"), as a primer for what is being proposed here.[40]

Figure 1.9 is a 3m chart of the same DAX March 2010 contract. A standard MIDAS support curve is already running on the chart from an earlier time, and our interest is in boxes (1) and (2).

In box (1) price reverses on the support curve in a hammer candlestick. By the time of this reversal, it has also been possible to draw a trend line from the low at the arrow, thus strengthening the MIDAS support. An entry signal is subsequently produced when price breaks above the hammer's high. This also coincides with the breaking of the small downtrend line. Where the downtrend line is above the break of the high of the reversal bar, a trader could wait until the trend line has been broken at the cost of a later entry.

FIGURE 1.9 The two boxes highlight how combining MIDAS with Japanese candlesticks produces robust criteria for entry signals.

Source: eSignal and Metastock. www.esignal.com and www.equis.com.

In the box marked (2), we have another hammer candlestick with a longish lower shadow. Here the entry signal is the same: price breaks above the hammer's high at the same time as it breaks the downtrend line, thus triggering the entry. For uptrend reversals, of course, the conditions would be reversed.

The topfinder/bottomfinder curves require a more subtle approach as regards an entry signal (see Chapter 4).

The Protective Stop

Again Levine never discussed stop-losses in relation to the MIDAS approach, but I believe that Japanese candlesticks provide the solution. If we go back to the two boxes in Figure 1.9, we see that stop-losses are placed at the low of each hammer reversal candlestick. We can't tighten them further because, as we can see, candlesticks often penetrate MIDAS curves marginally as they respond to them. This also happens when combining Japanese candlesticks with standard trend lines and support and resistance as well as with Fibonacci retracement levels, so it's a common phenomenon a trader must get used to. Again the topfinder/bottomfinder curves require a more subtle approach as regards an entry signal (see Chapter 4).

The Re-Entry Strategy

One of the topics discussed further in Chapter 13 is a phenomenon Levine labeled "porosity." This occurs when price marginally penetrates a MIDAS curve before responding to it. Porosity can be very misleading because once price breaks a MIDAS S/R curve the expectation is that it will move to the next most proximate curve. Consequently it can be very easy for a trader to be caught on the wrong side of the market when price does belatedly respond. Figure 1.10 illustrates this phenomenon. At the area circled, price has penetrated the curve while in a steep downtrend. Below the curve, it pulls back very marginally and then forms a doji candlestick before price very slightly turns down. Here a short position might have been taken before price reacts to the curve. If so, the short would have been stopped out on price crossing back through the curve. The first re-entry point is either at the first trend line break above the curve or in the first box when price breaks away after finding support on the curve for several bars. Another re-entry point comes at the second box when, after a long black candlestick, price creates a doji candlestick on the curve and then moves away. In both cases, the entry point and stop-loss follow the same strategy outlined earlier.

As we see later, whether porosity is actually taking place should always be considered alongside a confirming indicator such as Granville's On Balance Volume. In Figure 1.10, for example, porosity, rather than a breakdown, is virtually guaranteed by the fact that the OBV line started diverging positively from price at 9.44am (vertical line), some two hours before the porosity occurred. It's highly likely in such circumstances that the MIDAS support curve will hold price and that the downtrend line will be broken.

FIGURE 1.10   3m chart of DAX March 2010 futures with the trading implications of price porosity.

Source: eSignal and Metastock. www.esignal.com and www.equis.com.

Profit-Taking Exits

There are two primary ways that the MIDAS system provides price targets, though it's also perfectly compatible with techniques such as trailing stops or other indicator-based approaches. The first is that, by its very definition, a MIDAS support/resistance curve will confirm the price direction until it is broken. Price also has a tendency to move between MIDAS support and resistance curves once they've been penetrated. These phenomena will be illustrated thoroughly in forthcoming chapters. The topfinder/bottomfinder curves also support and resist price in addition, uniquely, to establishing cumulative volume targets, which are easily converted into price targets. These again are features of the topfinder/bottomfinder curves to be discussed in Chapters 4 and 5.

Sufficient Signals over the Timeframe of Interest

This is an important, if underappreciated, criterion of any system. If we go back to Figure 1.2, we can quickly appreciate that a single VWAP curve running indiscriminately from the start of the day fails to provide anything beyond a superficial idea of market direction and provides little by way of trading opportunities satisfying the criteria we've been considering here. By contrast, as we've seen in Figure 1.8, the fundamental relationship between the fractal nature of the financial markets and the notion of "anchored VWAP" means that MIDAS curves can be launched at all degrees of trend and need to be if MIDAS is to provide a clear perspective on current market direction. The higher resolution analysis of Figure 1.8 can be contrasted with the broader sweep afforded by the curves in Figure 1.11. This is another 5m chart, with MIDAS curves spanning days of price activity as they pick up most of the broader price movement.

In comparing these two charts, the true scale invariance Levine referred to becomes evident; yet because the fractal dimension is less than 1.50 (the Hurst exponent on these several days of data is 0.62 (= 1.38)) MIDAS curves are highly effective. Both Figures 1.11 and 1.8 can be usefully compared with Figure 1.4, especially the last two time series with Hurst exponents above 0.5.

The Occasional Need for More than One Trading System

Obviously the more robust the system, the less this need will arise. Provided markets are trending, MIDAS curves will be applicable according to the criteria already discussed. When trends are accelerating, the topfinder/bottomfinder curves take precedence, as discussed in Chapters 4 and 5. One of the main drawbacks with the MIDAS system is that it was never designed for sideways markets and it would also be useful if a curve could be created to capture the VWAP highs in uptrends and the lows in downtrends. Chapter 14 discusses an indicator to meet these requirements.

FIGURE 1.11   5m chart of the DAX March 2010 futures with lower resolution multiday price activity captured by the broad sweep of the curves.

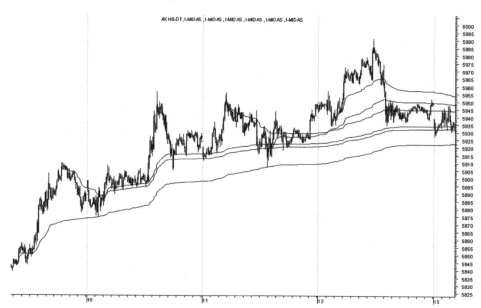

Source: eSignal and Metastock. www.esignal.com and www.equis.com.

Summary

- With a growing interest in VWAP among the trading community, the boundary between the MIDAS approach and the broader VWAP backdrop is becoming very unclear, especially in the labeling and use of curves. Clarity is required both on the mathematical differences between basic VWAP formulae and the MIDAS formula as well as on the theoretical differences.
- The five main tenets that define Paul Levine's market philosophy help accentuate two theoretical factors that separate MIDAS from mainstream VWAP analysis: (i) the critical choice of where to launch MIDAS curves, and (ii) the use of multiple MIDAS curves.
- The latter is based on the notion of a hierarchy of support and resistance that assumes a fractal interpretation of the financial markets that has in turn been supported by a growing body of empirical statistical studies.
- These studies do indeed show that persistent time series with a Hurst exponent higher than that signified by a pure random walk ($H > 0.5$) are best suited for MIDAS curve analysis. Indeed, the topfinder/bottomfinder curves only work if the fractal dimension of the markets is significantly less than 1.5. See also Chapter 4.

- It's likely that Levine's fractal market hypothesis owes much to the work of Edgar Peters, which in turn is derived from other academic interpretations of price movement in the early 1990s that were incompatible with the Efficient Market Hypothesis.
- Despite the absence of trade-management considerations in practical trading contexts by Levine, the fractal nature of MIDAS justifies the claim that MIDAS (alongside a robust charting method such as Japanese candlesticks) can be elevated to the status of a genuine trading system.

CHAPTER 2

Applying Standard MIDAS Curves to the Investor Timeframes

David G. Hawkins

This chapter explores the basic properties of the MIDAS support/resistance curves, and their applications to trading in timeframes longer than either intraday or short-term swing trading. This means I do not use intraday charts, but instead show charts of daily, weekly, monthly, and quarterly price bars. Later chapters cover charts of yearly price bars.

Definitions of Timeframes—The Triple Screen Trading Methodology

The fractal nature of the markets is such a fundamental characteristic that it has to be dealt with right up front in the definitions of terms, and then must always be handled with a consistent methodology. People often talk about "short term," "intermediate term," and "long term" as if there were some fixed meanings for those three terms. However, they are relative terms, and should be defined before using them. In this and subsequent chapters, I deal with multiple timeframes in accordance with the Triple Screen Trading System described by Dr. Alexander Elder in his several publications.[1] Here is a brief summary of this method.

The first step is to identify which timeframe chart will be your primary one, and then designate it to be the intermediate term chart. This will be the chart that will cover a time period long enough to show both your entry and your exit trades on one chart, and yet detailed enough to allow the application and development of your favorite indicators so that you can manage your trade as it unfolds. This means that for a trade typical of how you operate, the entry will appear early in the chart, and the exit in the later part of the same chart. For most indicators to operate properly, one needs at least a few dozen bars on the chart, so let's say that the minimum number of bars on your chart should be, very approximately, 50. The maximum number produces a chart on which separate bars are still discernible, approximately a few hundred. For example, let's assume you want to take advantage of the tax law that gives a lower tax rate for trades of at least 12 months' duration, and that your trading style is based on this minimum holding period. Then, typically, your trades will last somewhat longer than a year, perhaps much longer. So, for you, the weekly bars chart will be your primary one, since it will have at least 52 bars between your entry and exit and, with a couple of hundred bars, would cover up to about four years. The tax law defines your holding period as "long term," but that is not how "long term" is defined in the Triple Screen Trading Methodology. In this example, the weekly bars chart is your primary chart, and it is defined as the intermediate-term chart, not the long-term one.

The second step is to define two other charts, the short-term chart and the long-term chart. The bars on the short-term chart are one timeframe shorter than your primary one, and the long-term is one timeframe longer. Thus, continuing with this example where your primary chart is of weekly bars, your short-term chart will be daily bars, and the long-term, monthly bars. This set of three charts is the Triple Screen of the methodology.

Next, you observe what the direction of the market is on the long-term chart, and only trade in that direction. If the market is in an uptrend on your long-term chart, then you will buy the security ("go long"), but if the trend is down, you will initiate a short sale. Again, terminology can be confusing, as my use of the terms "going long" and "going short" in this discussion has nothing to do with timeframes, but rather refers to whether the security is purchased, or is borrowed and then sold.

After defining the trend, you watch your primary chart, the intermediate term, looking for a trade setup. Elder recommends looking for a pullback against the trend, which then stops, and just begins to turn around and resume the trend. This is the setup.

The trigger for the entry is found on your short-term chart, where a price bar moves beyond an important close-in support or resistance level. Some people call this a "breakout entry system." But notice that this is only a breakout on the short-term chart. On the intermediate-term chart, it's not a breakout, but rather a pullback against the main trend. And on the long-term chart, this entry is simply called "trend following."

In the foregoing example, where the desired holding period is at least a year, the triple screen is the set of daily-weekly-monthly bar charts. If your investing timeframe is much longer, you might choose to use the weekly-monthly-quarterly bars charts as your set. But what about holding periods that are shorter than a year, but longer than what a swing trader uses? There are many traders whose typical holding period is anywhere from as short as a few weeks to as long as several quarters, but usually not longer than a year. Much of my own trading is of this type. I have found that the daily-weekly-monthly bars set of charts usually works well for this holding period. On a few rare occasions, I've found it necessary to look at an hourly bars chart. Swing traders, whose holding periods are a couple of days to a week or more, have to go to something like an hourly-daily-weekly bars triplet set.

MIDAS Curves within the Triple Screen System

Each chart of the triplet set has its own primary function. The long-term chart is the trend follower. The intermediate-term chart watches for pullbacks against the trend, and on the short-term chart we're primarily interested in breakthroughs of support or resistance. MIDAS curves address each of these functions very well. I take up each one of these, but before that, let's closely examine the basic properties and behaviors of the MIDAS curves.

The Basic Behavior of the MIDAS Support/Resistance Curves

A MIDAS support/resistance (S/R) curve marks a place on the chart where the collective aspirations, fears, and greed of all those who have traded since the beginning of the curve are expressed within the curve by giving price a tendency to reverse direction there. If price has been in an uptrend, riding some ways above a support curve, and then turns down and approaches that curve, when it touches (or gets very close to) the curve, there is a tendency for price to reverse direction and move up again, thus resuming the original uptrend. Similarly, if price is in a down trend, moving along below a resistance curve, and then turns up towards the curve, once price gets (near) there, it tends to reverse direction and move down again. The key word here is "tendency," not "certainty." If there's been nothing of significance going on with the security in question, no news or other change in major external driving sentiment, then it's likely that price will reverse direction upon coming to an S/R curve, and whatever trend had been in effect will resume, the approach to the curve having been just a relatively minor pullback from an ongoing trend. But, if there is some major sentiment change among traders, perhaps driven by news or by overall market conditions, such factors may provide enough force to penetrate the S/R curve and keep on moving in the direction counter to the original trend that was in effect.

A MIDAS S/R curve, therefore, identifies a "fight or flight" place on the chart. When price comes to such a curve, it either turns around and retreats, or it definitively moves on through the curve. What price does not do is meander around an S/R curve as if the curve were not there. Price responds to the curve by either moving away from it or clearly forcing through it. This is what makes the MIDAS S/R curves so significant; they identify these fight-or-flight places on the chart, places you can see on the chart before price gets there.

A MIDAS curve does not predict what price will do there; rather, it identifies the place on the chart where price will have this fight-or-flight behavior. The skeptic might ask, *If it can't predict what will happen, what good is it?* After all, it's always true that price may go one way or the other. And during any extended price move, there usually are pullbacks and fluctuations that occur on smaller timeframes than that of the overall move. One answer to the skeptic is that if what starts out to be a minor turnaround in price happens to occur upon coming to a MIDAS S/R curve, you can have reasonable confidence that this turnaround is significant, unlike other fluctuations that occur elsewhere. You can trade this turnaround where you would have no reason to trade a small fluctuation that happens somewhere else. The second answer to the skeptic is that if you see price move straight on through a MIDAS curve, this signals that there is strong sentiment driving this move, and that's important information you may want to trade on. For example, a good place for a stop-loss order would be a short distance below a support curve, because if price breaks the curve, it's very likely to continue considerably further. Absent the MIDAS curve, you wouldn't necessarily know that (an exception to this rule is explained later in this chapter).

Equivolume Charting

Before showing examples of the properties of the MIDAS curves, let's consider what method of charting provides the most comfortable home for the MIDAS curves. In the first of his 18 articles on the MIDAS method, Paul Levine shows a typical, time-based chart of a stock, with price in the upper pane and volume in the lower, and with the horizontal axis marked off with equally spaced dates. But that's essentially the last time-based chart he shows. For his second chart, he says: ". . . we plot the prices vs. CUMULATIVE VOLUME rather than time."[2] And virtually all of the rest of the charts in his articles are done that way. The horizontal axis is linear in cumulative volume, and he labels it that way, without any reference to date or time. Each data point on a chart of his is located to the right of the previous point by a horizontal distance proportional to the volume traded during the time of that data point. He plots just the mean price, (H+L)/2, as his data point, and then connects the points with straight line segments. About this method of charting, he goes on to say: "This has the effect of giving less visual weight to periods of relative inactivity . . . since the lower cumulative volume increase during such a period compresses the daily points into a smaller space."[3] (We will see later on why it is important to de-emphasize periods where there is little alteration of the ownership profile of the people holding the stock.)

Plotting price versus cumulative volume did not originate with Paul Levine. It was first introduced by Edward S. Quinn in the late 1940s, but it didn't gain any traction then. Richard W. Arms Jr. rediscovered this charting method, and fully developed it in his 1971 book *Profits in Volume*, subtitled, *Equivolume Charting*.[4] In a typical time-based chart, each data point is actually not a point, but rather a vertical bar, referred to as the "price bar," where the height of the top of the bar is the high price for that period, the bottom of the bar is the low, and where a tick mark for the level of the close is placed on the right side of the bar (and sometimes also one for the open on the left side). What Arms did was replace the bar with a rectangular box whose top and bottom levels are the same high and low prices, but where each box has a finite width proportional to the volume traded in that period. In his charts, these price boxes are adjacent to each other, so the horizontal axis of the chart becomes proportional to cumulative volume. This type of plotting he named Equivolume Charting.

Figure 2.1 here is a typical time-based daily bars chart of General Electric, ticker GE, from November 2008 through May 2009. The first dotted line is a trend line started from the December 8, 2008, high and fitted to the January 5, 2009, high. Then, as is usually done with trend line analysis, a second one is launched from January 5, 2009, and fitted to the February 9, 2009, high, and finally the third one is launched from February 9, 2009, and fitted to the February 26, 2009, high. That last trend line was broken by the second price bar to rise up out of the vicinity of the March low. The break of this third line would've been an entry signal to those using trend line analysis.

The solid curve in Figure 2.1 is a MIDAS resistance curve launched from the December 8, 2009, high. Notice that the price pullback in mid-December turned around at the MIDAS R curve and headed down again. The same thing happened at the January 5, 2009, high, and again at the March 19, 2009, high. Finally, price definitively broke above the R curve on April 13, 2009, and, after consolidating above the curve for a week or so, price took off on a new uptrend.

FIGURE 2.1   GE, daily bars, with trend lines and a MIDAS R curve, on a time based chart.

Data Source: Reuters DataLink.

Notice the general appearance of the MIDAS R curve in Figure 2.2, an Equivolume chart, as compared to Figure 2.1. In Figure 2.1, the curve appears to be lumpy and erratic in its general shape, without suggestiveness in the way it moves. But in Figure 2.2, for the most part, it's very smoothly monotonic. It's exactly the same curve in both charts, with the same vertical height at each bar or box, just displaying differently. The smoother appearance on an Equivolume display happens because a MIDAS S/R curve is a volume weighted average, not time weighted. If I had put a time weighted moving average, such as the Simple Moving Average or the Exponential Moving Average, on these two charts, it would have looked smooth on the time-based display (Figure 2.1), and lumpily erratic on the Equivolume display (Figure 2.2). So, the MIDAS curves reside naturally—smoothly and with a pleasing appearance—on an Equivolume display. This is one of the reasons that Paul Levine[5] chose this display for his MIDAS system. There are additional reasons that I'll discuss in later chapters.

Displaying prices as boxes is what Arms did in his 1971 book[6] and in all of his subsequent books. But often, a modern charting software package that offers the Equivolume option will also have the option of displaying a Japanese candlestick instead of a box for each price period. In that option, which I often use in this book, as in Figure 2.4, the width of each candle is adjusted the same way as Arms does with the width of each price box. This kind of display is called Candlevolume, and

FIGURE 2.2   Same as Figure 2.1, but as an Equivolume chart.

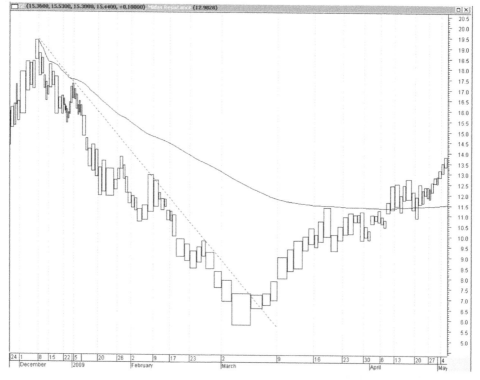

Data Source: Reuters DataLink.

the MIDAS S/R curves look the same on it as on the original Equivolume charts. Chapter 5 discusses a problem that Candlevolume displays have when used with the MIDAS topfinder/bottomfinder curves, but for now, we can assume the two displays are equivalent.

Levine never referred to his charts as Equivolume, and he never mentioned Arms or Quinn. Maybe he didn't think it was necessary to credit anyone for something that, to Levine, probably seemed like such an obvious and natural thing to do. Arms' full body of work[7] is very well worth studying along with the MIDAS methods, since there are many synergies between the two, which are discussed in chapter 7.

What Price Should Be Used?

Since Paul Levine[8] always used the mean price, $(H+L)/2$, of each data point in his calculations of the MIDAS curves, and since mean prices were what he plotted on his charts, when a MIDAS curve provided support or resistance to price, it appeared on his charts as the price coming to and touching (or nearly touching) the curve and then turning away from it. But, in this book, we're using modern technical analysis charting software, which usually shows a price bar, or box, or candlestick, not just one price point. If, in Figure 2.1, I had calculated that resistance curve with the mean prices instead of the highs, the curve would have started at the middle of the December 18, 2009, bar, and then passed well within the January 15, 2009, February 9, 2009, and February 26, 2009, bars. This is shown in Figure 2.3.

Such an appearance—the price bars poking out beyond the curve, sometimes called porosity—would not have looked like successful resistance at those points. But since the curve came reasonably close to the midpoints of those three bars that poked out, it was successful resistance. So, I used the high prices of the boxes in calculating the curve in Figure 2.1, which very nicely displayed those resistances. A similar situation arises with support curves; when price comes down to and bounces up from a support curve, we'd like to see the low of the bar (or box or candlestick) just touch the curve, then rise up. So, for support curves, we always use the low prices in their calculations, and that works very nicely, as you can see in the subsequent illustrations. This means that, where Levine had only one formula for an S/R curve, which was sufficient for his type of charting, we now need two forms of the formula, one using the low prices for a support curve, and the other using the high prices for a resistance curve. This small increase in complication allows the MIDAS S and R curves to lie very nicely on today's charts.

Henceforth, I'm using the word "bar" generically, referring to price bars, boxes, and candlesticks.

Support/Resistance Becomes Resistance/Support

The foregoing section is all well and good, and works as described. However, a serious question arises when using two different formulas, one for S and the other for R curves,

FIGURE 2.3   Same as Figure 2.1, but R curve calculated with mean prices.

Data Source: Reuters DataLink.

a question that Levine never had to face. Since the MIDAS S/R curves are a subset of all of the support/resistance methodologies within technical analysis, we should expect that they would behave as the other methods do. Specifically, I'm referring to the principle that once price breaches a support level, and then later comes back up to it, that level then acts as a resistance level. And similarly, once resistance is breached and later approached, it acts like support. This is a very well-known and documented phenomenon when S/R is provided by horizontal lines or trend lines. And if MIDAS S/R curves are to take their rightful place in the pantheon of S/R methodologies, we'd expect them to behave the same way. And indeed, when they're calculated and displayed the way Levine did, they do behave that way.

But, what happens now that we're using two different formulas, one for S and the other for R? A MIDAS S curve is calculated with the low prices, and a price bar's bottom bounces up off the S curve. Now, if price breaks down through the S curve, and later comes back up to it, what we'd like to see happen is for the *top* of a price bar to bounce down off the curve, since the curve should now be acting as an R curve. However, it's not an R curve; it's an S curve, since it's still being calculated with the low prices. Will we see some awkward-looking thing happen, like the *bottom* of the price bar bouncing down from the curve, while the rest of the bar is still sticking out above the curve? In order to make things work right, do we have to modify the formulas for the curves so that, when a curve is breached, it changes from being calculated with lows to highs, or vice versa?

I faced this question very early in my involvement with MIDAS, during 1995, while Levine was still in the process of publishing his 18 articles on the Internet, one per week, and I was following him.[9] I very quickly saw the need for the two formulas, one for S and one for R, programmed them into a standard technical analysis software package that plotted price bars, and was very pleased to see how well they worked. However, I worried about the above-described problem of S becoming R, and R becoming S. Then, I made a most amazing discovery; the answer to the problem turns out to be breathtakingly simple! (See Figure 2.4.)

Figure 2.4 is the weekly bars chart of GE from late 1998 through early 2002, in CandleVolume display. The curve is an S curve, launched from that low of December 19, 1998. Even though that low was a minor one, the curve turns out to be very significant since it provided such good support on multiple occasions during 1999.

FIGURE 2.4   GE weekly bars, 1998–2002. The S curve becomes an R curve.

Data Source: Reuters DataLink.

Therefore, it is a very important curve, which should be kept on the chart. Price went on to crash down through the curve twice in 2001. But look at what happened at the beginning of March 2002—*perfect resistance!* The curve is still being calculated as an S curve, using low prices, yet now it's acting as an R curve, just the way you would want it to work, without having to change the formula or do anything else. It just simply works.

Could this capture of the March 2002 high by this curve be just a random coincidence? Very unlikely. The high of that bar is $41.84, which is the highest high since that huge spike low in September 2001. And the level of the curve at that high is only 4 cents higher, a difference so small as to be utterly insignificant. Even though I've seen this kind of thing happen countless times over these many years, every time I see it, it's awe-inspiring.

Another good example of support becoming resistance is shown in Figure 2.17.

Now, let's see an example of a resistance curve becoming support. Figure 2.5 is the monthly bars chart of Johnson & Johnson, ticker JNJ, from 1999 through 2007. The curve is an R curve launched from the major high in late 1999. Price went back and forth over this curve many times in the succeeding years. Then, in early 2006, after 10 months of a relentless downtrend, price came to a screeching halt exactly at this curve, and turned up. The price difference between the low of that bar and the

FIGURE 2.5   JNJ monthly bars, 1999–2007. Resistance becomes support.

Data Source: Reuters DataLink.

level of the curve was an insignificant 6 cents—another awe-inspiring performance by a MIDAS curve.

Another example of resistance becoming support appears in Figure 2.18.

Distinguishing an Uptrend from a Trading Range

As previously mentioned, in the Triple Screen method of dealing with the fractal nature of the market, the long-term chart is where you look to discern what the trend of the market is. Now let's see how MIDAS curves can distinguish a trading range from an uptrend. Later in this chapter, I show how MIDAS curves are used to track a trend to its end.

Let's very carefully examine the daily bars chart of Corning, GLW, Figure 2.6. There are five MIDAS S curves here, launched from each of the major lows. At the beginning of each curve, as price lifts up, it looks at first as though an uptrend may be starting. But each of those first four starts fails, and price comes far back down again. However, long before price gets all the way down it breaks through the MIDAS S curve.

FIGURE 2.6 GLW, Aug. 2004 through June 2005. Five MIDAS S curves.

Data Source: Reuters DataLink.

That break is the signal that the nascent uptrend has failed, and that this is not a trending market, but rather price is in a trading range.

Notice that right after curve 2 was broken by falling price, along came curve 1, which provided support, and price started up again for its third attempt at an uptrend. But that attempt also failed, price coming down and breaking curves 3, 2, and 1.

Now look at the fifth curve. Yes, one minor bar did perforate it a bit in early April, but there was no follow-through to that break (more on how to deal with such a perforation later in this chapter). Instead, price roared on up. In mid-May, there was a substantial pullback, one of comparable depth to the prior pullbacks that lead to breaks of the earlier curves. But this time, the pullback didn't come down anywhere near its MIDAS S curve. *The fact that the pullback didn't get down to the S curve means that this truly is an uptrend.*

The Foothill Pattern

Now look at the weekly bars chart of GLW over a wider timeframe, October 2004 through November 2005, shown in Figure 2.7. Support curves 1 and 2 behave in a

FIGURE 2.7   The Foothill Pattern, defined by S curve 3.

Data Source: Reuters DataLink.

way similar to the first several curves in Figure 2.6, both being broken shortly after prices started to rise. But in this example, we see something new with curve 3. Look at the region from the start of curve 3 on through March of 2005. This is the same date region that was covered in the daily bars chart in Figure 2.6, but on the weekly chart, the S curve, 3, behaves differently (more about that later in this chapter). Without putting MIDAS curves on this chart, this region wouldn't look particularly different from what preceded it. But curve 3 reveals a significant new pattern. Price rises and then falls back on three successive occasions, but each fallback comes down to the support curve and turns up again. Curve 3 is never broken; therefore, even though it may not look like it, this *is* an uptrend.

This particular uptrend pattern above curve 3 is what Paul Levine called the Foothill Pattern, which he considered to be of great importance. In his fourth article he said:

> This Foothill Pattern has proven to be the most useful tool for spotting low risk/high reward entry points.... It is noteworthy that without reference to the support levels, very little seems to be going on in the foothills.... Price is confined to a very narrow range, and it is only if one is trained to look for a pattern of repeated bounces from a theoretical support level that the situation can be recognized. Imprint this graph firmly in your mind, for we will see this behavior over and over again.[10]

The reason this pattern is so important is that it is usually followed by a very powerful new uptrend, as we see here in Figure 2.7. Price took off above curve 4, and the first pullback never came close to the support curve under it.

Recognizing a Foothill Pattern as it is unfolding can put you in position to enter for the coming strong uptrend, and one more MIDAS curve on this chart will provide you with an entry signal. That curve is the resistance curve marked R, launched from the high in November. The point where R was definitively broken by that large white candle in late March was an entry signal. Without curves 3 and R, you would have no reason to think that this candle is an entry point, but with the insight provided by the MIDAS curves, you can enter with confidence.

In the preceding paragraph, I've shown an entry method using an R curve on the same chart as we were using, which would have been our primary chart, the intermediate term chart, in the Triple Screen method. However, the Triple Screen method calls for dropping down one timeframe, to the short-term chart, for getting the breakout entry signal. But for now, since I'm primarily illustrating how MIDAS curves follow a trend, I'm not going to show that entry on the short-term chart, and will hold it for a later section of this chapter.

A Trading Range Turning into a Downtrend

The previous two examples both show how support curves are used to distinguish a trading range from an uptrend. On the complementary opposite side of things, one can use MIDAS resistance curves to look for the change from a trading range to a downtrend. Figure 2.8 is an example of this, where this chart is a continuation of Figure 2.7. On the left side of this chart, you can see the uptrend that started in Figure 2.7 at around a price of 12, going all the way up to a peak of 29.61. Curves 3 and 4 are the continuations of the same named curves from Figure 2.7. With hindsight, we can look at the whole of Figure 2.8 and see that price went into a consolidation for over two years, and then started a major new downtrend. But, of course, as it's unfolding, you don't know what's going to happen next, so let me walk you through this chart, left to right, event by event, using only the insight provided by MIDAS curves at each event. At each point, imagine that you are at the hard right edge of the chart and can't see what comes next.

From our previous examples, we know that as long as price remains above curve 4, we're still in the major uptrend that started at the beginning of curve 4. In early 2006, price came down sharply from its peak and broke curve 4, so that's confirmation that the uptrend is over. Yes, that is quite a large drop from the high of 29.61 down to 19.5 where it hit curve 4, so if you had bought this stock down at about 12.5 as shown

FIGURE 2.8   The continuation of Figure 2.7, testing for the beginning of a downtrend.

Data Source: Reuters DataLink.

in Figure 2.7 where price broke above curve R, you certainly wouldn't want to wait for the break of curve 4 on Figure 2.8 to get out, as that would make you give up a huge amount of the profit gained from the uptrend. Later, I show other methods of identifying the top and getting you out long before price comes all the way down to the first support curve. But for now, all I'm doing is using this chart to illustrate how MIDAS resistance curves can be used to distinguish a trading range from a downtrend.

As the fall from the high of 29.61 develops, we want to test if this fall is the beginning of a new downtrend, so we launch a MIDAS resistance curve, R1, at the high. Shortly after breaking curve 4, price approached curve 3 and turned up again. This is your first hint that maybe the fall from the peak is not the beginning of a new downtrend. Sure enough, price came up and broke up through R1, telling us that we're in a trading range, not a new downtrend. In late 2006, price peaks and turns down again, so we launch R2 to test if this is the start of a downtrend. Then, price goes down to curve 3, bounces up and breaks not only R2 but also R1, so for sure, this is still just a trading range. The same scenario repeats again, starting at the peak in mid-2007, another resistance curve R3, and in early 2008 the break of that curve, so again, no new downtrend.

Price peaked once more in May 2008, and then started down very sharply, so we track it with R4. But this time, price comes down, pauses at support curve 3, tries to rise but barely does, and finally breaks below curve 3 in a big way. The feeble rise in price just before the break didn't come anywhere close to R4. That failure to reach R4 is the signal that we're now in a new downtrend.

Tracking a Trend with a Hierarchy of MIDAS Curves

MIDAS support and resistance curves are, in the first instance, a means of showing support and resistance areas on a chart. However, these same curves can also do much more for the trader. We've already seen how they can determine if a market is trending or just in a trading range. But more important than that, they can be used to track a trend, giving a good indication of when the trend has ended, which is the topic of this section.

Trends virtually never go in straight lines. Almost always, there are fluctuations on timeframes shorter than that of the trend, and often those fluctuations are large enough to be seen as significant pullbacks against the trend. Most commonly, a trend has three or four such significant pullbacks, assuming there are enough bars in the chart of the trend to allow such pullbacks to develop and be seen. Somewhat less frequently it will have two or five pullbacks, and on rare occasions, one or six. Only on extremely rare occasions does a trend have no significant pullbacks (assuming again that there are enough bars in the trend to see any pullback), or more than six pullbacks.

The way to track a trend with MIDAS curves is to launch a curve from the beginning of the trend, and a new curve from the extremum of each one of the pullbacks. The set of curves thus produced is called the Hierarchy of MIDAS Curves. *When price pulls back and breaks through the latest curve in the hierarchy, that's the signal that the trend has ended*. Thereafter, price will go on to do something else—maybe a consolidation, maybe a trend in the opposite direction, or maybe even a new trend in the same direction as the old one.

For our first example, let's apply this methodology to the uptrend that started in Figure 2.7 and finished in Figure 2.8. Figure 2.9 is a chart that includes the whole trend, from before the beginning of the foothill pattern to substantially after the peak. In this chart, I've relabeled curve 3 as S foothill, curve R as R foothill, and curve 4 as S1. After S1 starts, there are four significant pullbacks in the trend before its peak, and the S curves that are launched from them are labeled successively S2, S3, S4 and S5. Just four bars after S5 is launched, price comes crashing down through it, indicating that the trend is over.

Let's look at how well a trader could have done in this example, using what we've learned here about the foothill pattern and the hierarchy of curves. In late March 2005, that white candle broke the R foothill curve and closed significantly above it. These are weekly candles, so a trader who was watching to enter on this breakout

FIGURE 2.9   The MIDAS hierarchy of curves following the uptrend.

Data Source: Reuters DataLink.

would probably have entered around the close of that week's bar, which was at 12.32. After entering, the way to manage the trade is to trail a stop-loss order under the S curves, the first such order just under where S1 starts, and trailing just under it as that curve rises. I would have put the stop about 30 cents below the curve, down at 10.47 (see Figure 2.12). After S2 is launched, the stop should be trailed under S2, and then similarly with S3, S4, and S5, each time 30 cents below the latest curve and trailing up as the curve rises. Price broke down through S5 at 26.68, so, if one had been carefully trailing the stop, the exit would have been at 26.38. Therefore, with the entry at 12.32 and the exit at 26.38, the profit would have been 14.06. More important than the actual value of the gain is how it compares to the total extent of the trend. That trend started at 10.77, the low where S1 starts, and ran up to 29.61, the high at the peak, for a total extent of 18.84. The trader' profit of 14.06 was 75 percent of the total extent of the move, which is quite good compared to any other method of trading a trend.

If, in the preceding paragraph, the trader was using the full Triple Screen method, and dropped down to the short-term chart for the entry signal, that would have provided an even better entry. This is shown in a later section of this chapter.

Look at the portion of the trend in Figure 2.9 from its beginning in March up to that peak in September. That's a very steep price rise, riding far above S1. As that rise was developing, a trader may not want to wait for it to come all the way back down towards S1; in other words the trader, after a few months into that trend, may want to treat this portion of it as the main trend, and to get out when this very steep move ends. Thus, the trader would want to apply a hierarchy of MIDAS curves to this steep rise, and get out near its top. But, looking at this chart, the rise is almost a straight line, with no pullbacks, so there are no places to launch more curves. As mentioned earlier in this section, most commonly, a trend has three or four such significant pullbacks, *assuming there are enough bars in the trend to allow for such pullbacks to develop and be seen.* What's happening in this particular very steep rise is that there aren't enough bars in its display. The solution is to drop down to the next lower timeframe chart, which here would be the daily bars chart, and that's what Figure 2.10 is.

Figure 2.10 gives a much clearer picture of the situation with this very steep price rise. There are three obvious price pullbacks (ignoring that little close-in one in early April) from which we launch S2, S3 and S4. When S4 is broken, that's your exit signal.

In the early portion of Figure 2.10, from mid-April through mid-May, we see another region where there's a very steep trend with no pullbacks and not enough bars. So, if the trader wanted to trade that little trend, the trader would have to drop down one more timeframe to an hourly bars chart and apply a hierarchy of MIDAS curves to that chart. Also in Figure 2.10, look at the steep rise from early July to early August. That one does have enough bars, and it shows three pullbacks to which a hierarchy could be fitted, so a trader could trade that little trend. These are beautiful examples of the fractal nature of the market—trends within trends within trends.

So far in this section, all of the examples have been of uptrends. But, of course, this trend-following methodology applies equally well to downtrends, where one would apply a hierarchy of resistance curves. For an example of this, Figure 2.11 is of this same ticker, GLW, daily bars, moved forward in time to the period from August 2008

FIGURE 2.10 Expanded view of Figure 2.9 with daily bars.

Data Source: Reuters DataLink.

through March of 2009, covering the great crash of 2008. The crash produced a downtrend from August through November of 2008, which is nicely tracked by this fivefold hierarchy of resistance curves. Although it's rather hard to see here, shortly after R5 was launched, it was broken to the upside, indicating the end of that downtrend. Notice our old friend, the foothill pattern that started in mid-November. In early March, price blasted off into a new, powerful uptrend, being followed by a new S1. And we know that that new uptrend turned out to be a very strong one, another testament to the importance of recognizing the foothill pattern.

MIDAS S/R Curves for Entry Setups and Triggers

The Triple Screen methodology calls for identifying an entry setup on your intermediate-term chart as a pullback against the overall trend, and the very beginning of a turnaround and resumption of the trend. As you can see in many of the foregoing charts, a MIDAS S/R curve is ideal for identifying such a setup. When

FIGURE 2.11 GLW with a hierarchy of resistance curves.

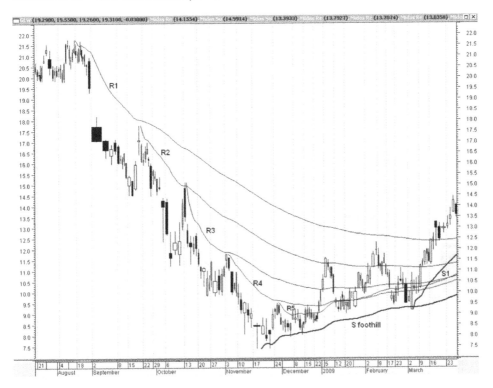

Data Source: Reuters DataLink.

you see a countertrend pullback stop and turn around at a MIDAS curve, that's a very nice setup for a trade entry, since you can have reasonable confidence that this turnaround is robust and unlikely to go back through the curve. A good example of this is on Figure 2.9, during March 2005, as price again came down to the S foothill curve and started to turn up. By that point, the trader should have recognized that this is a foothill pattern, and be looking for an entry.

The next step is to drop down to the short-term chart, the daily bars chart, and look for a breakout above the closest-in resistance. See Figure 2.12, the daily bars chart from late January to late April of 2005.

Here I've applied a hierarchy of MIDAS resistance curves to the downtrend that started in early February. The closest-in curve is R3, and the clear breakout above R3 is that white candle marked as Breakout. The three days previous to that all poked above R3 somewhat, and then the next day, price opened above R3 and kept moving up. If I had been the trader here, I probably would have entered an hour or so after the open of that day, probably getting in around $11.35, between R3 and R2, 88 cents above the stop-loss level, a pretty good entry. The trader can have reasonably good confidence entering here, since the break of R3 means that the downtrend that started in February is now over. If our trader had used the $11.35 entry instead of the $12.32

FIGURE 2.12   GLW daily bars, showing the breakout entry.

Data Source: Reuters DataLink.

one showed earlier, then the profit for the overall trade would have been $15.03, a capture of 80 percent of the total range of the trend.

Same Launch Point, Different Timeframes

If MIDAS curves are started from the same date on two different timeframe charts, for instance a daily bars chart and a weekly bars chart, are they the same curve? To illustrate this question, let's see how it illuminates what at first seems like a problem. Figure 2.13 is the daily bars chart of Aetna, ticker AET, as it came up from the March 2009 low. The curve is the S curve launched from that low. Notice how that large black candle in late April forcefully breaks through the curve, but thereafter price goes no lower. This seemingly contradicts one of the basic principles of MIDAS S/R curves, which is that when price definitively penetrates a curve, it shows a lot of force behind that move, and price is very likely to go much further. Yet here, after a huge one-bar penetration, the move stops dead in its tracks and reverses direction. Price seems to be acting as if it hit some hitherto unseen support level below where this S curve is.

Now let's see what this situation looks like in Figure 2.14, a weekly bars chart covering the same time period, and with an S curve launched from the same low. Amazingly, the weekly chart's S curve exactly captures the late-April low and in fact

FIGURE 2.13 Price breaks through a support curve, but then reverses direction.

Data Source: Reuters DataLink.

goes on to capture the mid-June low, which was also problematic on the daily bars chart. So, in fact, that big black candle of late April on the daily bars chart had indeed found support, but that support didn't come from the S curve on the daily bars chart; rather; it came from the S curve on the weekly bars chart.

This is but one illustration of a very common occurrence, namely, when a MIDAS S/R curve seems to fail—shows porosity—on the chart of one timeframe, often the curve launched from the same turning point on the next longer timeframe will work very well. Curves launched from the same dates on different timeframe charts are indeed different, and need to be considered separately.

This is a very important fact that the trader needs to keep track of. While watching things develop on, say, your primary screen, your intermediate-term chart, you should also watch the curves launched from the same price turning points on the long-term chart. In fact, it's useful to mark the locations of those long-term curves on your intermediate-term chart.

MIDAS S/R curves on charts of even longer timeframes than your long-term chart can also be important. In Chapter 6, I show that the market's sharp V-bottom in March 2009 was actually captured by a major resistance-turned-support curve that was launched many decades earlier from an important market top on a quarterly bars chart.

FIGURE 2.14   Same as Figure 2.13 but on a weekly bars display.

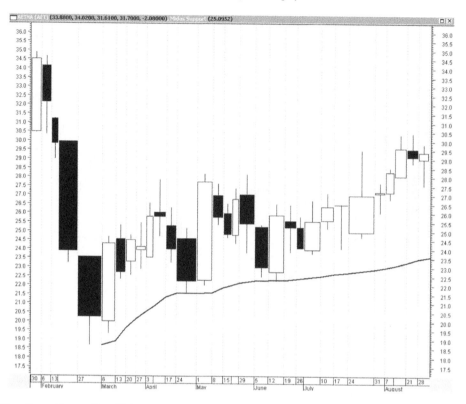

Data Source: Reuters DataLink.

The phenomenon described in this section, that a MIDAS S/R curve separates further from the price bars when one switches to a longer timeframe chart, results from using High prices to calculate R curves and Low prices for S curves. It does not occur if one were to calculate all S and R curves with mean prices, (H+L)/2; in that case a MIDAS curve remains virtually unchanged when one switches the timeframe of the chart. Having this behavior of greater separation on longer timeframes when using H for R curves and L for S curves is a big advantage, for two reasons. One is that it often allows us to solve porosity issues as in Figures 2.13 and 2.14. The other is that it provides us with multiple, robust support and resistance levels that can be carried over to lower timeframe charts. I explain this in detail in Chapter 8.

Special Start Points—The Left Side

Over the 15 years that I have been working with the MIDAS method, I've identified a number of situations where it is beneficial to start a MIDAS S/R curve at a point other than a price turning point. One of these, called Calibrated Curves, is so important that I'm devoting a whole chapter to it. But for the rest of this chapter, I'm showing you some other such special situations. The first of these is called the Left Side.

The standard, default starting point for an S/R curve is from a price extremum, a low or a high. Sometimes, though, an extremum is not just one price bar, but is a relatively flat consolidation region of the chart with a number of bars in it, all at approximately the same level, or where there may be two or more bars sticking out, any one of which could be identified as the extremum. When that happens, where should the curve be started—from the beginning, middle, or end of the flat area? The answer is the beginning, the Left Side. The reason for doing this is that it usually works better that way, generating an S/R curve that is more likely to capture pullbacks in price going forward.

Figure 2.15, the daily bars chart of Exxon Mobil (XOM) from August 2006 through February 2007, shows two examples of the Left Side giving better-behaved support curves. The low in September is a broad, uneven consolidation, which shows three separate bars that are lows, one on the left side, the middle and the right. The solid curve is launched from the left one, and the dotted curves from the other two. The solid curve supports pullbacks at three different locations, marked by the arrows, whereas the dotted curves exhibit serious porosity. In November there is another flat low area with two low bars, on the left and right sides. The S curve launched from the

FIGURE 2.15   XOM on daily bar. S curves launched from the leading edges of pullbacks work better.

Data Source: Reuters DataLink.

left one provides excellent support for the mid-December pullback, whereas the one from the right has porosity.

There was already an example of this earlier in this chapter, in Figure 2.6. There, curve 2 was launched from the left side of a very broad low in October 2004. Notice that this curve went on to provide support at that little spike low in early January 2005. If the curve had been started further to the right, it would have missed that capture.

By launching from the leading edge of a relatively flat extremum, it is inevitable that the curve will intersect price bars within the rest of the flat area. This should not be construed as breaking the curve, since the curve really doesn't get going until it clears out of the flat area.

Of course, the same holds true for R curves as for S. Figure 2.16 shows the daily bars chart of Hewlett Packard (HPQ) in the second half of 1991. In this case, the top could be considered to be more of a double top instead of a flat one. In such cases,

FIGURE 2.16 HPQ daily bars, with two R curves.

Data Source: Yahoo! Finance.

you should always try an R curve from each top. Notice that the left top is actually a flat itself, and the R curve from its left is the one that works so well in capturing the pullbacks in late August and late October.

Special Start Points—The Initial Public Offering (IPO)

A major feature of the MIDAS curves is that they are fixed starting point moving averages, so every point on an S/R curve captures the sentiment of all the traders who acted since the fixed date of the start of the curve. Extending this concept of including all trades, it makes sense to launch an S and/or R curve from the date of the stock's initial public offering (IPO), a truly unique date in the history of the stock. I have found that keeping such curves on your charts can be very beneficial many years after the IPO.

Figure 2.17 is the monthly bars chart of Vermont Pure Holdings, ticker VPS, since its May 1999 IPO, along with the MIDAS S curve launched at the IPO. You

FIGURE 2.17 VPO an S curve since its IPO.

Data Source: Yahoo! Finance.

can see the very dramatic captures of the spike highs of 2005 and 2007. There are other curves that will capture one or the other of these two highs, but not both. The IPO curve is obviously both unique and very significant.

Notice also that Figure 2.17 is an example of a support curve, once breached, going on to become resistance. This raises the question—which curve, S or R, should be launched from the IPO? Although I only showed S in Figure 2.17, I recommend that you launch both, and keep both on your chart.

Figure 2.18 is a good example of why one should do this. It's the quarterly bars chart of Staples, ticker SPLS, since its 1989 IPO, where both the S and R curves, launched from the IPO date, are shown. Notice that even though the high and low prices from which these two are launched are quite close together, over time these two diverge significantly, becoming very different curves. Looking at that chart before launching any curves, you might think that, since the IPO was very near the all-time low, and since the stock has risen greatly since the IPO, that only the S curve would be useful. But notice what happens. It's the R curve, not the S curve, which in 2008, 19 years after the IPO, provided perfect support for the spike low of that year. If you

FIGURE 2.18   SPLS quarterly bars chart since its 1989 IPO.

Data Source: Reuters DataLink.

had been closely watching SPLS during 2008, knowing that curve was there would certainly have been very useful information. So, you need to keep both curves on your chart.

My recommendation is that if a stock's IPO is within the data file of the stock that you're working with, plot both the S and the R curve from that IPO on both your monthly and quarterly bars charts. And, if the IPO happened fairly recently, put these curves on both the daily and weekly bars charts as well.

Special Starting Points—The Down Gap and Its Dead Cat Bounce

A stock that is hit with major negative news, and suffers a large down gap on the next daily price bar, will often experience an attempted recovery over the next few days. How do we know if the recovery is to be trusted and may be traded, or if it's just a "dead cat bounce," meaning that price still has a lot further to go to the downside? I've found that there is a special MIDAS resistance curve to answer this question. It's the curve started from the bar immediately prior to the down gap. If the recovery breaks up above this curve, then it's real, and can be traded; but if the recovery doesn't break the curve, but rolls over and starts to head down again, then it was just a dead cat bounce.

Figure 2.19 shows Axcelis Technologies, ACLS, daily bars, in 2008. Before the open on September 15, Sumitomo Heavy Industries announced it was abandoning its hostile takeover bid for Axcelis, and the stock opened gap down 50 percent, and headed down another 50 percent during that day on extremely heavy volume. To track this, we launch Rg, the MIDAS R curve starting from the bar before the gap. Over the next few days, price attempted a rally, going from a September 15 low of 1.25 up to the September 22 high of 2.00, but then started to roll over. The height of the Rg curve on September 22 was 2.12; therefore, we declare that this little price recovery was only a dead cat bounce, and we don't want to buy this stock here. And sure enough, over the succeeding months, price sank deep into penny stock territory. Many months later, in late 2009, price did finally break above Rg, and thereafter went into a significant new uptrend.

Now, here's an example which turned out not to be a dead cat bounce. On February 28, 2007, Bitstream Inc., BITS, gapped down 30 percent on extremely heavy volume (see Figure 2.20). We launch Rg from the day earlier and see that, seven days after the down gap, price came up to Rg and paused a bit, as if it might be going to roll over, but then broke strongly above Rg, indicating that this is a good, new uptrend. Notice how Rg went on to become support in April, an illustration of the validity of the Rg curve.

Figure 2.21 is an example that lies somewhere between the previous two. It's Bruker Bioscience, ticker BRKR, from April through August 2008.

After the huge down gap, there were two attempted recoveries that remained below Rg, then in mid-June, price definitively broke above Rg. But in mid-July, price

FIGURE 2.19   ACLS in a gap down, holding below Rg.

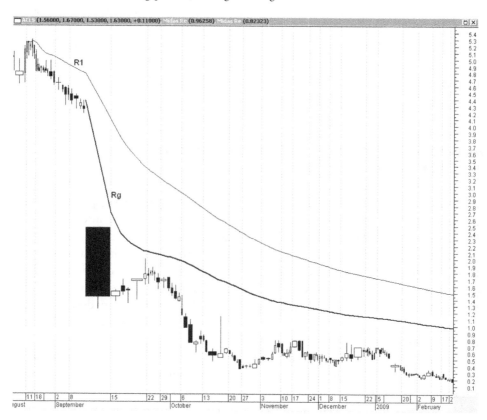

Data Source: Reuters DataLink.

sank back down below Rg, going down almost as far as the previous low, before finally launching into a strong new uptrend. Had you entered on the breakout in mid-June, you might have been shaken out during the mid-July fall. This situation is better understood in conjunction with another MIDAS curve, the calibrated S curve that appears on the weekly bars chart, whose position I have drawn in on this chart. Prior to the June breakout, we see price in a trading range between Rg and the S curve. This is telling us that price is being supported from below. With the June breakout, we understand that the sentiment behind the stock has changed to that of a real up move. Had you entered at the breakout, perhaps seeing the S curve down there, and knowing that price had honored it twice before, would have kept you in the stock.

The advantage to using Rg to test for a dead cat bounce after a down gap is that it isn't based on any absolute price levels, but rather on the simple and robust behavior of a MIDAS R curve. It isn't the price level of a bounce after a down gap that tells you whether it's a dead cat bounce; rather, it's whether price breaks above Rg. My trading rule in these situations is to avoid going long in these stocks unless and until such a break occurs.

FIGURE 2.20   BITS with no dead cat bounce after a down gap.

Data Source: Reuters DataLink.

Special Starting Points—The Highest R and the Lowest S

When you launch an R curve from a high, the level of that curve will always be above any R curve launched from a later, lower price point. But that R curve, which we call the Primary Curve, is not the highest R curve associated with that price high. If you move the starting point somewhat back in time, the curve generated will soon break above the primary curve and remain above it thereafter. If you keep sliding the starting point further and further back in time, you'll be generating higher and higher R curves, until, eventually, by going back far enough, you'll start generating lower ones. So there is one launch point that generates the highest high R curve, and that's a significant curve, which you should keep on your chart.

Figure 2.22 shows Intel, INTC, weekly bars, from 1998 through 2004. Let's say we're in early 2004, and wondering if there is an R curve to capture the high at that time. The thin solid curve is the Primary curve launched from the all-time high, and it's clearly too low to be of any use. So we start sliding the launch point back in time, trying various locations, shown by the dotted curves. The launch point of each curve

FIGURE 2.21   BRKR with two dead cat bounces, then a breakout.

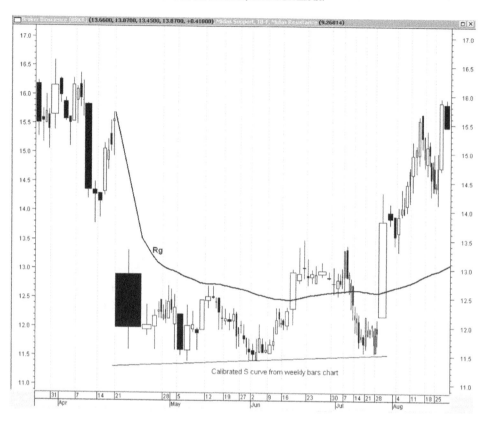

Data Source: Reuters DataLink.

is marked with a little square. Finally, we arrive at one launch point, July 30, 1999, which generates the thick solid curve; thereafter, curves launched from earlier points end up, in early 1994, being lower. So, we have found the highest R curve for 2004, and it does capture that high, so it's a very important curve.

If you follow these curves in Figure 2.22, you can see that they do cross each other from time to time. At any one time, you may have located the highest R curve, but as time goes on, you may have to adjust the location of its starting point to keep it at the highest level.

A similar situation happens with S curves. If you launch a Primary S curve from a major low, you may then slide the start point back in time until you find the curve that is the lowest S curve; earlier launches than that will bring the curve up.

In general, if the present point on your chart comes after a very significant high (or low), then you should locate the highest R (or lowest S) curve that's associated with that high (low), and keep that curve on your chart, adjusting the launch point periodically to make sure you still have the highest (lowest) curve.

FIGURE 2.22 INTC and its highest R curve.

Data Source: Yahoo! Finance.

Summary

In this chapter, I've described:

- The Triple Screen method of coping with the fractal nature of market.
- The basic behavior of MIDAS S/R curves.
- Equivolume charting.
- Using low prices to calculate support curves and high prices for resistance curves.
- Trend following with MIDAS S/R curves.
- Special launch points for MIDAS S/R curves other than extrema.

CHAPTER 3

MIDAS Support and Resistance (S/R) Curves and Day Trading

Andrew Coles

As someone who predominantly works intraday, I have come to see the value of the MIDAS system as a standalone approach to technical trading as well as a method that can be implemented alongside other technical indicators. The aim of the present chapter is to discuss these two factors while expanding on previous observations on using the MIDAS S/R curves intraday.[1] Throughout the discussion there is a practical focus on trading with MIDAS curves, since, as observed, the main weakness in Levine's work was the absence of direction on how MIDAS curves should be traded aside from their obvious role in forecasting market direction.

This chapter is a long and often detailed examination of how MIDAS S/R curves perform in relation to price and indeed other technical indicators. It contains a considerable number of charts and several sections of in-depth chart commentary. The chapter has two halves: the first focuses on how MIDAS curves can be used to create a relatively simple day trading system I call the "multimarket" approach. This section is included because the book isn't merely about explaining the MIDAS method while introducing new insights and ideas. It's also about getting traders to use it and, with this in mind, there'll be traders reading this book with a wide range of prior skills and experience. The first part of this chapter is particularly directed towards newer to intermediate-level traders interested in how MIDAS could be used to create a relatively simple, low-stress day trading or short-term swing trading system. It's also directed towards the large number of traders who trade part-time and who don't have opportunities to spend long periods analyzing the markets.

The focus of the second half of the chapter is on the relationship between MIDAS and various technical indicators that I believe work extremely well alongside it. This again consists of another detailed discussion. It isn't expected that readers will be interested in every technical indicator discussed. Rather, traders are free to pick and choose between various discussions depending on prior interests. In general in this section I'll be arguing for a mutually beneficial relationship between MIDAS and other forecasting tools. For example, in the discussion of Market Profile I'll suggest that whereas the curves create superior price and time trading parameters to Market Profile, the latter will often provide information on the underlying directional bias of the market that the curves cannot supply.

Preliminary Note. Before exploring the creation of a basic day trading system from MIDAS, it's essential to obtain a clear understanding of the relationship between intraday trend lengths, intraday chart timeframes, and the corresponding size of the intraday pivot from which an S/R curve is launched. These relationships are important because understanding them is key in turn to understanding the displacement phenomenon in MIDAS analysis. The latter is crucial because it bears on two basic issues, especially for a day trader and short-term swing trader, namely:

1. The size of the move off a given MIDAS curve
2. The number of trading signals that can be expected from a given MIDAS curve

Accordingly, in the first discussion that follows I look at typical intraday trend lengths and chart timeframes before returning to the implications for day trading and short-term swing trading. The basic logic also applies to higher timeframe analysis when using MIDAS.

Multiple Trend and Timeframe Analysis

To use the MIDAS approach effectively for day trading and short-term swing trading, it's essential first of all to possess the prior skill of understanding trend relationships between timeframes and then of seeing how these relationships can generate signals when analyzed with MIDAS S/R curves.

Let's briefly explore these two skills, illustrating their importance briefly in Figure 3.1 with the more familiar longer-term trend lengths as they're defined in standard technical analysis textbooks:

- Secular-term trend = 10 years to as long as 25 years and constructed from a number of primary-term trends.
- Primary-term trend = nine months to two years, reflecting investors' attitudes to unfolding market fundamentals and closely associated with the three-to-four-year business cycle.
- Intermediate-term trend = roughly six weeks to as long as nine months, though sometimes longer but rarely shorter.
- Short-term trend = two to four weeks, though it can be slightly shorter or slightly longer.[2]

To these four technically-defined trend lengths, I'll shortly be adding three much shorter-term trends (two of them intraday) as a result of recognizing consistent price moves in relation to active and displacing MIDAS curves. Identification of these three trend sizes is very important for the MIDAS day trader, as we'll shortly see. They include:

- The One to Two day trend on the 15m chart
- The Two to Six Hour trend on the 5m chart
- The 15m to 60m trend on the 1m chart

Figure 3.1 is a weekly chart of the euro FX continuous futures illustrating a secular, primary, and intermediate trend identified by the trend lines labeled S, P, and I respectively. The resolution of this chart is too low to include the short-term trend. Although a simplified chart technically, it clearly illustrates the forecasting implications of price movement in relation to trends of different durations. In short, in simple trend line analysis identifying the appropriate trend line in question as well as appreciating its magnitude is key to establishing an overall perspective on market direction, both in price and time. Similarly, to work with MIDAS S/R curves effectively intraday, and to understand their implications for price forecasting and the number of intraday trading signals they're likely to generate, it's vitally important that we establish a similar framework for chart and timeframe relationships. This will be our first obligation. We'll work our way through it by using the DAX futures from the intermediate-term trend down to the smallest meaningful intraday trend capable of analysis by a MIDAS curve, namely the One to Two Day trend on the 15m chart, the Two to Six Hour trend on the 5m chart, and the 15m to 60m trend on the 1m chart.

FIGURE 3.1   Euro FX continuous weekly futures with secular, primary, and intermediate trend line and support and resistance analysis.

Source: eSignal and Metastock. www.esignal.com and www.equis.com.

FIGURE 3.2   Daily chart of DAX June 2010 futures showing the short-term trend MIDAS
S/R curves.

Source: eSignal and Metastock. www.esignal.com and www.equis.com.

The Intermediate-Term Trend on Daily Charts

In my view day traders, especially those using MIDAS, should always start by monitoring the intermediate-term trend. This is not because MIDAS curves appended to
this trend are going to generate a significant number of signals for the day trader.
Rather, they create an understanding of the broader price direction that is still a required backdrop for intraday analysis. As the resolution of Figure 3.2 illustrates, S/R
curves of intermediate duration are best analyzed on the daily chart. Figure 3.2 is a
daily chart of the Xetra DAX June 2010 futures with the intermediate-term trend
highlighted by the three-month gray trend line. Each MIDAS S/R curve is analyzing
trend changes of roughly a month in duration, putting them at the very long end
of the short-term trend or the start of the intermediate-term trend. In terms of the
most recent price action, price has been resisted by R1* and has just broken S1* and
pulled back, forming a doji candlestick with a small body. This is an obvious sign of
indecision in the short-term trend.

The Short-Term Trend on 60m Charts

Some day traders will begin their analysis of trend direction using moving averages on
the daily charts and then move directly down to a timeframe such as the five-minute
to look for intraday signals.[3] This to my mind is far too large a timeframe gap if a day
trader wishes to combine pure intraday analysis with higher timeframe insight into
the broader trend direction, especially when applying the MIDAS method. The 60m
or 120m is the next timeframe to look at when identifying the short-term trend.

The short-term trend is illustrated in Figure 3.3, a 60m chart of the same DAX futures contract. The period covered equates with the portion of the trend highlighted by the rectangle in Figure 3.2. The heavy gray trend line in Figure 3.3 represents the short-term trend and longer curves such as S1 and S2 capture the pullbacks associated with this trend. Longer curves in this chart, such as S1 and S2, typically range from 8 to 14 days, putting them at the lower end of the short-term trend.

However, as Figure 3.3 highlights, these curves are still missing the smaller displacements in the trend such as those highlighted in the rectangles. Indeed, following the logic of the displacement phenomenon in the last two charts we can formulate an obvious recommendation I'll call "D = LT," short for "Displacement equals Lower Timeframe":

> Whenever price displaces at a given trend magnitude, it creates a smaller contiguous segment of the trend that is probably best analyzed on a lower timeframe resolution with another MIDAS curve.

The "D = LT" recommendation is illustrated in the rectangles in the previous two charts.

The One- to Two-Day Trend on the 15m Chart

My research suggests that trend segments such as those highlighted by the two rectangles in Figure 3.3 are best highlighted on the 15m chart. Attempts to create curves related to trend segments of this size on lower chart timeframes will result in confusion

FIGURE 3.3   60m chart of the same DAX futures revealing the short-term trend in the gray trend line and longer MIDAS support curves such as S1 and S2.

Source: eSignal and Metastock. www.esignal.com and www.equis.com.

in respect to the all-important displacement phenomenon, which in turn will affect two critical factors highlighted earlier, namely:

1. The size of the move off a given MIDAS curve
2. The number of trading signals that can be expected from it

Figure 3.4 is a 15m chart showing the period highlighted in Figure 3.3 by the first rectangle. The trading day March 25, 2010, which this chart captures, is characterized by a strong uptrend with a continually displacing price movement until 5.00 P.M. in the afternoon. From here until the close, it sharply retraces the trend from the open by a Fibonacci 38.2 percent. As we can see, the finer resolution allows the launching of at least three additional S/R curves (S2 and S3 plus R1) which would have been difficult to launch on the 60m.

If the 60m chart typically catches the lower end of the short-term trend, running from 8 to roughly 14 days, the 15m chart is ideally suited for trends that are typically one to two days in duration. This information is summarized in Table 3.1 on page 70. In Figure 3.4 there is a two-day (gray) trend line with MIDAS curves clearly supporting the intraday trend and, in the case of S1 and S2, continuing to support it into the second day (26th) as the upwardly displaced price corrects the trend by 38.2 percent. For further projections we'd need to step back up a timeframe to the 60m chart.

Figure 3.3 contained a second rectangle and this is also seen on a higher resolution 15m chart in Figure 3.5. Here the higher resolution immediately reveals opportunities for the launch of additional curves, including four support curves and one resistance curve.

FIGURE 3.4   15m resolution of the first rectangle in Figure 3.3.

Source: eSignal and Metastock. www.esignal.com and www.equis.com.

FIGURE 3.5   Same 15m chart highlighting at higher resolution the second rectangle in Figure 3.3.

Source: eSignal and Metastock. www.esignal.com and www.equis.com.

It's clear that there are still further opportunities on this chart to launch additional curves, but for that we require an even higher resolution.

The Two- to Six-Hour Trend on the 5m or 3m/2m Chart

To sum up, it's been suggested that a day trader should be monitoring the intermediate and short-term trends using MIDAS S/R curves and that the ideal chart timeframes for them are the daily and 60m/120m charts respectively. The 60m chart reveals that price consistently displaces over an average two-day window (sometimes a little longer) and that the best timeframe to analyze these movements using MIDAS S/R curves is the 15m chart.

However, for pure intraday price activity on shorter-term trend displacements the resolution of the 15m chart again falls short. In particular, it fails to clarify a fairly consistent trend length ranging from two to six hours. My research suggests that the 5m chart is an ideal timeframe for this trend, though there's no reason why a 3m chart cannot also be used.

Figure 3.6 is a 5m chart with a number of trends highlighted between the vertical lines of the typical duration of two to six hours. The first uptrend of five hours is analyzed by three support curves, S1, S2, and S3. Thereafter, other potential launch points for S/R curves are highlighted by the black arrows. Again we can note that curves such as S1, launched from the start of trends, will support or resist the largest pullbacks, as we can see here when the subsequent two-hour downtrend finds support on S1 at the 38.2 percent level.[4] On the other hand, curves such as S2 and S3, launched from pullbacks within ongoing trends, will correspondingly support or resist

FIGURE 3.6   5m chart of DAX futures with higher resolution allowing additional curves following the typical two- to six-hour intraday trend. The black arrows show additional potential launch points for S/R curves.

Source: eSignal and Metastock. www.esignal.com and www.equis.com.

the smaller pullbacks within the ongoing trend. We can see this clearly before the first five-hour trend ends.

The 15m to 60m Trend on the 1m Chart

Research suggests that there is one more consistently identifiable intraday trend below the two to six hour trend that MIDAS day traders should be aware of, namely the 30m to 60m trend, though the duration is quite often less than 30m (15m to 20m) and sometimes slightly longer than 60m. This trend is best identified on the 1m/2m chart. It is illustrated in Figure 3.7 of the same June 2010 DAX contract. This three-and-a-half hour downtrend is ideally suited for the 5m chart, yet its pullbacks—and the resulting displacements—are meaningfully identified on the 1m/2m chart.

Summary of Intraday Trend Timeframes and MIDAS S/R Curves

In summary, the following trend lengths and chart timeframes in Table 3.1 identify themselves as key focal points for the day trader. As such, they're ideal platforms for the launch of MIDAS S/R curves. Knowledge regarding them is essential for understanding the displacement phenomenon and the likely number of signals each curve (related to trend size and chart timeframe) is likely to generate.

FIGURE 3.7 1m chart of the June DAX futures 2010 revealing trend lengths of 20m to just over an hour.

Source: eSignal and Metastock. www.esignal.com and www.equis.com.

TABLE 3.1 Summary of Trend Durations and Chart Timeframes with Approximate Number of Signals

Trend Sizes and Chart Timeframes of Relevance to the Day Trader Using the MIDAS Method

Trend Name/ Description	Trend Size	Chart Timeframe	Purpose	Number of Active Signals for Day Trading
Intermediate-term	six weeks to nine months	Daily chart	Mainly providing broad trend direction	One perhaps two per month (better for swing trading)
Short-term	two to four weeks	120m or 60m	Trend direction and day trading signals	One, occasionally two, signals per day
One-/Two-day trend but sometimes several	One to two days, sometimes several	15m	Day trading signals	Typically three to four each day
Two- to six-hour trend	Two to six hours	5m (possibly 3m or 2m)	Day trading signals	Typically 5 to 10 each day
15m to 60m trend	15m to just over 60m	1m (possibly 2m)	Day trading signals	Roughly 12 to 15 per day

Part One: The MIDAS System as a Standalone Day Trading System

It may appear that the sole purpose of the previous discussion is to identify average trend sizes and recommended chart timeframes in order to increase the number of signals generated by the MIDAS S/R curves. This observation is only partially true because there's an additional purpose associated with the displacement of MIDAS curves that I discuss in the second half of this chapter. However, the observation is true to the extent that such information is important for the creation of a simple standalone MIDAS day trading system in two respects.

First, day traders sensitive to commission costs will vary considerably in terms of the number of trades of interest to them each day. Table 3.1 provides a rough estimate of the number of trades that can be expected per day from the S/R curves depending on the trend of interest and the chart timeframe chosen. Second, day traders would be acutely aware that futures contract sizes (or number of shares traded) and volatility additionally have a bearing on the trend size chosen. Accordingly, the selected chart timeframe that is best suited to these two factors will initially impact money-management considerations and subsequently trade-management strategies in the setting of stop-losses.

Let's explore this second point further for the purpose of creating a simple but robust day trading system I simply describe as "multimarket," which relies on the two to six hour trend on the 5m chart timeframe. In the introduction I spoke about the importance of getting traders to use MIDAS and of traders coming to this book with a range of prior skills and experience. With this in mind, the following system is aimed at newer to intermediate-level traders seeking a straightforward, low-stress day trading or short-term swing trading system. It's aimed too at part-time traders. What follows is a day trading system based on the relationship of the displacement phenomenon to two factors already noted, namely:

1. The size of the move off a given MIDAS curve.
2. The number of trading signals that can be expected from it. Short-term swing traders can adapt the following system according to their needs in relation to these two factors.

The system is illustrated in relation to eight candidate futures contracts, excluding some of the popular U.S. index futures and their e-mini counterparts.[5] Data concerning these contracts are contained in Table 3.2.

For columns five and six, a simple range calculation subtracted the low from the high over seven trading days between May 14 and May 24, 2010, as a guide for intraday volatility.[6] This brief study indicates that intraday volatility has increased substantially since 2007 in the case of the Swiss Market Index futures, the DAX futures, and the Euro futures. By implication, it has also increased for the other contracts listed here.[7]

With Table 3.2 in mind, recall that in Chapter 1 it was argued that MIDAS can be regarded as a genuine standalone trading system in virtue of satisfying eight basic

TABLE 3.2 Contract Specifications for Eight Candidate Markets for the "Multimarket" System

Contract Size and Volatility

Commodity	Contract Size	Minimum Fluctuation	Point Value	Average Weekly Range in Points	Average Weekly Range in %
Australian dollar	100,000 AD	.0001 ($10)	1 pt = $10	212	2.41
Canadian dollar	100,000 CD	.0001 ($10)	1 pt = $10	154	1.55
Euro	125,000 euros	.0001 ($12.50)	1 pt = $12.50	246	1.9
Japanese yen	12.5 million yen	.0001 ($12.50)	1 pt = $12.50	162	1.44
Eurex Xetra DAX	€25 × index	0.5 = €12.50	1 pt = €25	177.5	2.87
Eurex DJ Eurostoxx 50	€10 × index	1.00 = €10.00	1.00 = €10.00	106	3.97
Eurex Swiss Market Index	CHF10 × index	1.00 = 10.00 CHF	1.00 = 10.00 CHF	144	2.17
Eurex German Bund	€100,000	.01 = €10.00	1.00 = €1,000	97	0.7%

criteria. Three of those are relevant here, namely:

1. Consistent setup conditions
2. Logical entry signals
3. Clear and objective stop-losses

I argued that these criteria could be met by combining MIDAS with Japanese candlesticks. Figure 3.8, a close-up 2m chart of the same June 2010 DAX contract, illustrates simply again how the MIDAS S/R curves can meet these three criteria when combined with this style of charting. To recap on Chapter 1, let's briefly apply them here:

1. The setup is the by now familiar condition of price approaching a MIDAS S/R curve. In Figure 3.8 the market is in a downtrend and so the condition applies to a resistance curve.
2. The entry signal is a reversal candlestick on the curve,[8] followed by a break above or below the high or low respectively of that reversal candlestick. Here, since price is in a downtrend, the entry is a break below the low of the two reversal candlesticks highlighted by the arrows.
3. Finally, a stop-loss is set at the high or low of that reversal candlestick. Again since price is presently in a downtrend the stop-loss is placed at the high. The ideal reversal candlestick would be a doji or one of the other smaller candlestick patterns,[9] such as a shooting star, morning/evening star, harami, or hanging man. Large engulfing candlesticks, such as the one highlighted in the rectangle, work less well if at all, since the actual entry often has to be late. This is a factor that also affects the width of the stop-loss, thus making many potential reversal trades untradeable for money-management reasons.

A modest retail trading account of $10,000 using the MIDAS S/R curves in a standalone trading system with 1 percent ($100) of capital risked per trade would be incompatible with the DAX futures on any timeframe higher than the one minute,

FIGURE 3.8 2m chart of the same June DAX contract illustrating the setup, trade entry, and stop-loss. See also Chapter 1 for a further discussion of these topics.

Source: eSignal and Metastock. www.esignal.com and www.equis.com.

even for one contract. When we drop down to a 1m DAX futures chart for trends of roughly 15m to an hour (see again Table 3.1), typical reversal candlestick formations such as dojis, haramis, hanging man patterns, and the various star formations tend to produce ranges of four to five points, which are still fractionally outside of the 1 percent rule but perhaps acceptable to some traders. Figure 3.9 illustrates several such signals with narrow range reversal candlesticks of three to four points. Unfortunately such tight ranges aren't easy to find and there are better alternatives for day traders with smaller accounts who responsibly adhere to trade-management principles.

The Multimarket Day Trading System

A system I'll refer to as "multimarket" can be adapted to different size trading accounts according to the details in Table 3.1 and alternative money-management and trade-management criteria. I've often used a variation of this system.[10] It relies on the 5m chart to highlight the two to six hour trend (see again Table 3.1).

Other intraday liquid markets with similar size contracts could be substituted, including 10-year notes, soybeans, gold, corn and wheat, as well as the popular U.S. stock index futures and their e-mini counterparts.[11] Those traders interested in the cash FX markets will know that a standard lot size has a pip value that's much the same as their futures counterparts, so cash FX markets can also be added to this system. I've discussed how it's possible to use MIDAS in the volumeless cash FX markets in Chapter 10.

FIGURE 3.9 1m chart of DAX June 2010 contract with very narrow range reversal candlesticks of 3–4 points.

Source: eSignal and Metastock. www.esignal.com and www.equis.com.

The system utilizes a multiscreen approach based on a 5m timeframe. Varying the timeframe between observed markets isn't recommended because it confuses due to the sheer number being monitored. Moreover, the 5m timeframe has been calibrated to the average size move identified in Table 3.1 in relation to simple money- and trade-management rules. Excluding the DAX, all of the markets listed above obey the 1 percent rule when the smaller contract size allows stop-losses to be set at a more realistic 8 to 11 points. This range is ideal for the 5m chart format. As regards the setting of price targets, I've here extended the mechanical nature of this system by closing an open position once a price target of a multiple of two times the stop-loss range is reached. Many traders will recommend a risk/reward ratio of 1:3; however, the typical size of moves subsequent to pullbacks to the MIDAS curves on the 5m chart are more realistically of the order of twice the initial stop-loss range. Thus, if a stop-loss range is 8 points we automatically set a price target of 16 points. If price fails to meet this target before reversing we allow the trade to break-even.

In the forthcoming discussion, this system is illustrated on a random trading day, May 28, 2010, on six of the markets listed in Table 3.1, namely:

1. Australian dollar
2. Canadian dollar
3. Euro
4. Japanese yen
5. Swiss Market Index
6. German Bund

According to the rules of the system, the markets are monitored individually on 5m charts on six trading screens, with MIDAS S/R curves launched over the course of the day according to their basic rules of application and subject to three basic provisos:

1. That if price is even mildly porous the setup will be ignored
2. That if the stop-loss range is beyond our 1 percent rule it will be ignored
3. That if a proximate S/R curve is closer to the entry point than the price target of two times the stop-loss range, the setup will be ignored

As it turned out, May 28 wasn't a good random day for the MIDAS method, since there was a lot of congestion and a poor fractal dimension on many of the markets. However, the day was selected randomly in keeping with authentic trading conditions. The other advantage of having to deal with a turbid trading day is that it provides the opportunity to get down to the real trading detail in implementing the MIDAS method. The analysis in the form of a brief running commentary for each market is set out below.

Step-by-Step Commentary and Analysis of the Multi-Market System

May 28, 2010: Australian Dollar Futures

We begin with Figure 3.10, a 5m chart of the June 2010 Australian dollar futures. There's no technical analysis on the chart apart from the ongoing application of the curves from relevant swing highs and lows. Moreover, for the purpose of this

FIGURE 3.10 5m chart of CME Australian dollar futures with half of the MIDAS S/R curves plotted generating signals in candlestick reversal setups (discussed in Chapter 1).

Source: eSignal and Metastock. www.esignal.com and www.equis.com.

analysis I've refrained from projecting curves from the previous day. In real-life trading conditions such projections should be included. I've eliminated them here to contain the discussion as much as possible. The ringed and numbered areas highlight the mechanical nature of the system, with trades taken for the most part[12] if price reacts to a MIDAS S/R curve by creating a familiar candlestick reversal pattern discussed earlier.

The first two setups in Figure 3.10 can't be realistically included from the perspective of trading GMT, since they occur in the overnight Globex Asian-Pacific session (Sydney, Tokyo, Hong Kong, and Singapore). The third ringed area highlights the absence of any setup due to the porosity levels; entries are thus disqualified. The fourth area again emphasizes a disqualified setup, this time because of the proximity of the underlying support curve. The fifth setup is again ignored due to the porosity. The sixth setup is an important alternative to the standard approach of candlestick reversals off the curves, since here we actually have a breakdown through them. For trade-management purposes it is helpful to isolate this move in Figure 3.11 and comment briefly on it. Candlestick (1) is the key bar insofar as it breaks the last support curve. Accordingly, a stop-loss is placed at its high and an entry is triggered if the next candlestick (labeled (2)) breaks its low, which it does in the sixth setup.[13] The stop-loss range on candlestick (1) is eight points and so the trade would be closed out at 16 points.

The seventh reversal highlighted is another disqualified move because the reversal occurred below and not on the curve. The eighth setup is unambiguous, with a stop-loss range of 10 points, which is just permissible on the one percent rule; it easily yields a profit of 20 points. The final setup occurs too close to the overnight Asian-Pacific session, and so again realistically is ignored.

FIGURE 3.11 High resolution chart of the sixth setup in Figure 3.10 with Japanese candlesticks and trade trigger and stop-loss.

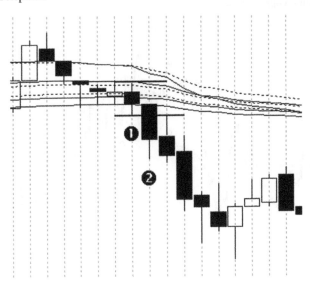

Source: eSignal and Metastock. www.esignal.com and www.equis.com.

Over the course of the day, then, only two satisfactory setups stand out. Both yield a hypothetical tally of 36 points on one contract. The highly conservative nature of this system, highlighted by the limited number of signals on this first market, justifies the need for a market watch list of at least four to five markets throughout a trading day.

May 28, 2010: Canadian Dollar Futures

Figure 3.12 is another 5m chart, this time of the June 2010 contract of the Canadian dollar futures on the same trading day. Let's run through this chart quickly while highlighting its main features. The first setup is again unrealistic due to its being sprung during the overnight Asian-Pacific session in relation to GMT. Setups 2 through to 5 are disqualified because our 1:2 risk/reward ratio is undermined by the proximity of other MIDAS curves. The sixth setup is perfect and again yields 10 points based on the initial stop-loss range of 5 points, even though the move had the potential to make considerably more. The two swing high reversals to the right of this setup occur below the primary resistance curves and are ignored.

Thus, over the course of the trading day only one clear-cut setup emerges that satisfies the criteria, yielding a hypothetical 10 points.

May 28, 2010: Euro FX Futures

Figure 3.13 is another 5m chart of the euro FX June 2010 contract on the same trading day. The first setup is again unrealistic at a little before 3.00 A.M. GMT. The early-bird second setup has a stop-loss range of 12 points and marginally violates the 1 percent rule on our hypothetical startup account. However, if this modest violation

FIGURE 3.12   5m chart of June 2010 CME Canadian dollar futures. The chart highlights why patience for clear-cut trading opportunities is crucial on this system, since only the final setup of the day provided an unambiguous opportunity.

Source: eSignal and Metastock. www.esignal.com and www.equis.com.

FIGURE 3.13 5m chart of the CME's euro FX June 2010 contract. Sooner or later a trader will face difficult decisions when a stop-loss range falls fractionally outside of a trade-management principle such as the 1 percent rule. Here the outcome is significant in terms of the number of potential points to be won had the rule been extended by a point or two.

Source: eSignal and Metastock. www.esignal.com and www.equis.com.

is acceptable the trade hypothetically generates 24 points on our 1:2 risk/ reward ratio. The third setup generates a further 16 points based on an 8 point stop-loss range, even though the euro's rapid displacement means that it's best suited for a topfinder/ bottomfinder curve (see Chapter 4). The fourth setup is ignored because it's mildly porous (frustratingly, if it had been taken it would have yielded 22 points). The fifth setup is a reversal against two resistance curves with a stop-loss range of 11 points; it thus yields another 22 points. The sixth setup also has the same stop-loss range and so also yields the same points tally. The seventh setup is outside of our one percent rule with a stop-loss range of 17 points, along with the eighth setup with a range of 13 points. The ninth setup has a range of 6 points and easily yields 12 points going into the close.

Provided, then, we had been flexible in our trade-management to accept that some of these trades had stop-losses marginally outside of the 1 percent rule, the day generated eight trades with a rough tally of 96 points. If we had rigidly followed the 1 percent rule our tally of points for the day would have been 72 based on five trades.

May 28, 2010: Japanese Yen Futures

Our fourth market, the Japanese yen June 2010 contract on the same trading day, is Figure 3.14. It produces its first setup just after 7.00 A.M. with a stop-loss spread of 6 points; it thus yields 12 points. The second setup closes on a break-even because our target of twice the stop-loss range isn't met. The same thing happens with the third setup. The fourth setup is ignored because the support curves are too near to the price

FIGURE 3.14 The CME's Japanese yen June 2010 futures only yields three successful trades due to several setups being ignored.

Source: eSignal and Metastock. www.esignal.com and www.equis.com.

action. However, price penetrates the curves in what would've been a successful trade and then reverses, pulling back at the fifth setup and then reversing upwards. This time the winning trade target of 12 points is easily met. In the sixth setup, a stop-loss spread of 8 points exactly matches the 1 percent rule and our 16 point price target is easily met. Setup seven has a stop-loss spread of 10 points, so it is ignored. The final setup has a spread of 7 points, but the trade is ignored because of the proximity of an overhead resistance curve. As it happened, price broke through the curve in what would have been a successful trade.

In sum, the day yields five trades, with two breaking even and the remaining three yielding roughly 40 points. Several setups are again ignored due to the application of some fairly tight criteria.

May 28, 2010: EUREX Swiss Market Index Futures

We are omitting the German DAX from Table 3.1 for money-management reasons and are also omitting the Dow Jones Eurostoxx 50 because in terms of contract size and volatility it's similar to the EUREX Swiss Market Index futures. The latter therefore will be our next market in this hypothetical trading day in Figure 3.15.

The first putative setup consists of a series of candlesticks falling against the MIDAS resistance curve launched just before 8.00 A.M. None of these are plausible trading candidates because their stop-loss range is far wider than the 11 points allowed by our 1 percent rule applied to the Swiss market. The second setup benefits from a support curve launched from the last pullback of the previous day. So far I have only launched curves from within the trading day itself. However, in real trading conditions curves should be launched from significant highs and lows in the previous

FIGURE 3.15 EUREX's Swiss Market Index June 2010 futures contract has a similar contract size and intraday volatility range as EUREX's popular Dow Jones Eurostoxx 50 contract. Again cautious attention to factors such as the stop-loss range, price porosity, and the relative proximity of other S/R curves yields a small number of profitable trades.

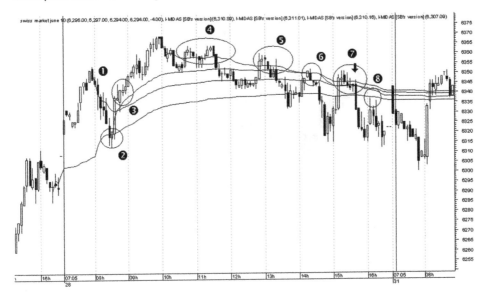

Source: eSignal and Metastock. www.esignal.com and www.equis.com.

day. Nonetheless, despite the range of the stop-loss in the second setup being eight points, the trade isn't taken because the falling overhead support curve is nearer to our entry than the 16 points profit we want to take from this trade.

The third setup is of interest because it's again a variation of how we normally trade the MIDAS S/R curves. The usual procedure is to trade the pullbacks to a curve while taking our entry and stop-loss cues from the candlestick that reverses on that curve. However, we have examined in Figure 3.11 the trade management implications of a breakdown through a curve. The current setup differs slightly from that one insofar as price has already broken through the curve on a long white candlestick whose range is far too wide to set a stop-loss. However, having broken through, price then pulls back to the curve to test resistance becoming support and that's our trade setup. The stop-loss is then placed on the low of the reversal candlestick, and the trade is triggered by a break above its high. Let's create another high-resolution chart of Figure 3.15.

Candlestick (1) is the long white candlestick that broke through the resistance curve. Recall that we didn't enter this trade on the prior candlestick reversing on the lower support curve because of the looming overhead resistance curve. The long white candlestick has too large a stop-loss range for us to utilize the same strategy as in Figure 3.11. However, once price breaks through it then pulls back and tests resistance becoming support in candlestick (2). That's our reversal candlestick, so we set a stop-loss at its low and trigger the trade when price breaks its high on candlestick (3). The stop-loss range of candlestick (2) is 11 points, which is just on our 1 percent boundary. The trade thus yields a 22 point tally.

FIGURE 3.16   High resolution of the third setup in Figure 3.15.

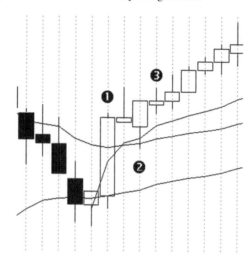

Source: eSignal and Metastock. www.esignal.com and www.equis.com.

The fourth and fifth setups are ignored because of the fairly deep level of porosity. Here the main problem this causes is that reversal candlesticks actually form above the curve, providing no guarantee that they are *de facto* reversal signals. The problem of porosity is tackled independently in a later chapter. The sixth setup is unproblematic with a stop-loss range of 6 points, thus yielding a 12 point profit. The seventh setup is initially another porous response to the same set of curves. However, when price does break back down through the curve it pulls back to retest briefly at the black arrow. This is in fact the bearish equivalent of the bullish setup in Figure 3.16. This very minor pullback is sufficient to create a signal and the stop-loss range is 4, thus yielding an 8 point profit, even though the move is much larger. Finally, the eighth setup produces too large a stop-loss range and so is ignored.

In all, then, the Swiss market yields three plausible trades yielding roughly 42 points.

May 28, 2010: EUREX German Bund Futures

The final market in our watch list in Figure 3.17 is EUREX's popular German Bund futures, the counterpart to CBOT's 10-year note. The first areas to note are the swing low and high identified by the two arrows. MIDAS curves were launched from these two pivots, but almost immediately they conjoined with the prior curve launched from the pivot at the market open. In previous work, I called the phenomenon of two curves joining "curve convergence" and advised deleting one or more of the superfluous curves to cut down on unnecessary processing.[14]

The first setup is unambiguous with a stop-loss range of 7, thus yielding the target of 14 points. The second is another unambiguous pullback with a stop-loss range of 4 points. The problem is that the overhead resistance curve is too close and has also been responsible for this pullback. Thus, an otherwise excellent setup leading

FIGURE 3.17   5m chart of the EUREX Bund June 2010 futures.

Source: eSignal and Metastock. www.esignal.com and www.equis.com.

to a new intraday high is ignored. The third setup is a good pullback onto a curve after price broke through, though it too is ignored because of the proximity of other resistance curves. It too would have yielded a winning trade had it been taken. The fourth setup leads to a losing trade insofar as price rallies back to the resistance curve and then produces a reversal candlestick whose low is quickly violated. However, the resulting move quickly ends, and price reverses back up through the curve. The fifth setup is highly significant insofar as price breaks through the resistance curves and pulls back to a support curve launched from the low prior to the fourth setup. The stop-loss range is 5 points and the trade quickly yields 10 points. The sixth setup is another uncomplicated one with a small stop-loss range of 3; it yields 6 points while price frustratingly continues to mark a new intraday high. The seventh setup is again uncomplicated with a stop-loss range of 5 points, thus yielding 10 points, although the move is considerably larger.

In sum, four successful trades yield 40 points, while several others are ignored, and there is one losing trade.

Observations Regarding the "Multimarket" System

- Although trade setups have been selected conservatively, this six-market watch list has still yielded 18 trades or 21 trades if we had also decided to take the marginal trades in the euro in accordance with the 1 percent rule.
- The 18 trades yield 196 points using a price target of a multiple of 2 times the stop-loss range. The 21 trades yield 264 points.
- Although the Globex currency futures are 24 hours, if we use the 10-hour market session of the Swiss Market Index futures as a typical trading period, a rough estimate of the number of trades per hour in this six-market "watch list" is roughly 1 to 1.8.

- The system is a low-stress, low-risk approach to trading using mechanical procedures and capable of generating a significant profit even on a single futures contract with a relatively small tick size.
- There could be periods of the day when two or more trades are triggered simultaneously, and it would be up to the trader to decide on his comfort zone in such an eventuality. The advantage of this system is the sheer number of low-stress unambiguous trading signals generated, especially on days more conducive than this one to the MIDAS approach. On such days there will be an abundance of signals, and even the most experienced trader could not possibly be expected to trade every signal generated.
- Some traders may feel that a watch list of six markets is excessive. If so, they can be reduced accordingly, though I personally would not use less than four for this system.
- If some traders feel that a system generating 18 or so trades per day is excessive, the system could be run on a 10m, 13m, or 15m timeframe. However, while according to Table 3.1 the number of trades would be less, the larger candlesticks on higher timeframes would create wider stop-loss ranges, which in turn would impact on money- and trade-management considerations. The best option would be to reduce the number of markets in the watch list.
- The system can be adapted with ease for short-term swing trading purposes.
- Traders could experiment with timeframes of less than 5m, but this would obviously generate a far greater number of trade setups, and the risk/reward ratio implications of setting automated price targets would require adjustment.
- Running this system with a watch list of four to six markets with multiple monitors will have a significant impact on computer processing speed. Thus, even while the MIDAS formula can be programmed into a system such as Metastock Pro, processing speed would be less adversely affected if the curves were programmed as external DLLs.
- This system rejects the use of other technical indicators because of the problem of mental overload when watching more than three to four screens simultaneously. However, newer traders should be monitoring economic data releases and certain intermarket relationships on a continuous basis regardless of the technical approach, and there are plenty of introductory studies available for the would-be day trader in the following footnote.[15]
- Some traders might view the absence of additional technical analysis in this system a blessing; others might see it as a disadvantage. This brings us to the second half of this chapter.

Part Two: Using the MIDAS System alongside Other Technical Indicators

In his tenth lecture, Paul Levine was open to the possibility of combining MIDAS S/R curves with other indicators and suggested the MACD, Bollinger Bands, On

Balance Volume, and conventional trendlines. This is all to the good, since many day traders will consider MIDAS not as a standalone trading system but as another tool to enhance other approaches they may already be using.

The following discussion covers a number of familiar and not so familiar technical indicators. As stated in the introduction to this chapter, no trader reading this half of the chapter will have an interest in all of these indicators. Rather, it's expected that readers will pick and choose what's of interest to them based on prior affiliations. The following list has been chosen either because there's evidence that traders are already starting to combine them with the MIDAS approach (Market Profile is a good example) or because I believe there's a particularly good synergy between them and the MIDAS system (moving averages are a prime example). The following indicators are examined:

- Elliott Wave and fractal market analysis
- Fibonacci retracements
- Moving averages
- Day trading pivot point techniques
- Market Profile
- Momentum and volume indicators
- Conventional trend lines

The discussion begins with the Elliott Wave fractal analysis because it's well-placed to help us further explore the displacement phenomenon. As emphasized repeatedly, displacement is critically important when day trading with MIDAS and connects directly to the opening discussion in this chapter concerning trend lengths, chart timeframes, and pivot sizes.

Displacement, Elliott Wave Theory, and Fractal Market Analysis Using MIDAS S/R Curves

Before discussing the standalone system presented earlier, I made an important observation that the discussion of average trend sizes and chart timeframes wasn't merely to increase the number of signals generated by the MIDAS S/R curves for a day trader. In addition, the discussion was motivated by the need to understand more deeply the displacement of MIDAS curves from intraday trends of various lengths. It's now time to return to this topic. We'll look at it first in relation to fractal market analysis and Elliott waves and then in the next section in relation to Fibonacci retracements. There we'll see an important limiting point in displacement to the Fibonacci 38.2 percent level.

A MIDAS curve displaces from price when a new component of the trend accelerates away from it. Because markets are fractal, the displacement phenomenon is taking place continuously at all degrees of trend. Indeed, it's so ubiquitous that it's difficult to keep up with it and many trades are missed as a result of the market reacting to price-volume relationships that are never even identified.

To get a better visual appreciation of this fractal phenomenon, Figure 3.18 is a 5m chart of the June 2010 Canadian dollar futures showing a very clear five-wave Elliot

FIGURE 3.18   5m chart of Canadian dollar June 2010 futures with a five-wave impulse and ABC correction.

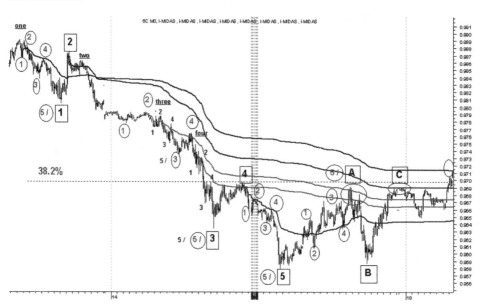

Source: eSignal and Metastock. www.esignal.com and www.equis.com.

impulse plus its corresponding ABC correction spread over three trading days (May 13–16). This is a very busy chart but it's easily broken down as follows:

- The highest fractal level in the pattern is designated by numbers and letters in boxes. I'll call this level, level-W.
- The next-highest level is designated by circled numbers. I'll call this level, level-X.
- The lowest level is signified by unbounded numbers. I'll call this level, level-Z.

With this understanding, let's place several MIDAS resistance curves on this chart and look at their resistance behavior in relation to the three fractal trend levels just identified.

1. Our first MIDAS resistance curve, labeled "one," is launched from the very start of the five wave impulse at level-W. It immediately resists waves at level-X and then displaces from price. It next resists the top of wave C at level-W, two days after it is launched.
2. Our second resistance curve, labeled "two," is also launched from level-W, and it displaces immediately. It doesn't interact with price again until the far side of the chart on May 18, which is also at level-W.
3. The third resistance curve, labeled "three," is launched from level-X and resists waves of level-X and level-Z. It also resists wave A at level-W.

4. The final resistance curve, labeled "four," is launched from level-W and resists waves of level-X, both in the impulse and in wave A.

We can further articulate levels W, X, and Z by going back briefly to Table 3.1. The table reveals that level-W is best analyzed on the 15m chart, since its trend size is typically of one/two days in duration. Level-X is typically represented on the 5m chart, since its size is typically two to six hours, while level-Z is 1m chart material, since its duration is typically 15m to an hour.

Thus, when trading with MIDAS curves intraday it's essential to be aware that a multitude of curves is going to be affecting price at any one time. A curve launched from a swing high two days ago on the 15m chart will by now have displaced from price by as much as 20 percent to 30 percent, meaning that (as Table 3.1 clarified) its signals will be far less numerous than curves launched from smaller portions of the trend on lower timeframe charts. On the other hand, because of the displacement phenomenon the price moves off these displaced curves will be of much greater magnitude, both in price and time. Thus, unless a trader is following a highly mechanical multiple-chart system of the type outlined in the first half of this chapter, he must be aware of the critical role of displacement, both in reducing the number of signals and in creating larger moves off the curves when price does come back to them. In other words, there is a direct relationship between the size of the displacement, the size of the trend it has displaced from, and the resulting size of the move when price comes back to meet it. This relationship can be seen in Figure 3.18 when curves "one" and "two" at level-W have a significant role two days later in halting the ABC correction (also at level-W) after the five-wave impulse has completed. Thus:

> The larger the displacement (though few displacements ever displace more than 38.2% (see next section)), the fewer the signals, but the larger the move off the displaced curve when price eventually comes back to meet it.

A final feature of the chart not commented upon is the Fibonacci retracement level of 38.2 percent, which coincides with wave 4 at level-W. As we see in the next section, MIDAS curves rarely if ever displace more than 38.2 percent, which is why perhaps this Fibonacci level is so potent as a price reversal level.

For Elliott Wave enthusiasts, Table 3.3 provides a rough relationship between wave launch points for curves and the resulting support/resistance roles of curves in relation to subsequent waves. The relationship between Elliott Waves (especially wave 3) and the topfinder/bottomfinder is discussed briefly in Chapter 4. This is a rough guideline at best due not so much to the Fibonacci relationships between waves, which are relatively constant, but due to the degree of acceleration that varies often quite considerably between impulse waves and especially their subwaves.

I close this section by including one more chart of the euro September 2010 futures over one and a half days of trading. Its purpose is to highlight as emphatically as possible the relationship between chart timeframes and trend sizes, which in turn

TABLE 3.3 An Elliott Wave Five-Wave Impulse with Typical MIDAS Support and Resistance Areas. The topfinder/bottomfinder works particularly well in the most accelerated waves, especially wave 3. (See also briefly Chapter 4.)

Elliott Wave Impulse and MIDAS S/R Curves

Launch Point	Typical S/R 1	Typical S/R 2	Typical S/R 3	Typical S/R 4
Start of wave 1	Wave 2 top/ bottom, usually with porosity	Wave 4 top/bottom	End of wave A, provided not more than Fib 38.2%	And/or end of wave C, provided not more than Fib 38.2%
Wave 2 top/bottom	End of subwave 1 of wave 3	Wave 4 top/bottom	End of wave A, provided not more than Fib 38.2%	And/or end of wave C, provided not more than Fib 38.2%
Wave 4 top/bottom	End of subwave 1 of wave 5	End of subwave 3 of wave 5		

governs the displacement phenomenon and thus governs the size of the resulting moves off displaced curves. These associations justify the making of two assertions:

1. Fractal market forecasting with MIDAS curves will be impossibly muddled without the correct appreciation of these relationships.
2. The relationships imply that every fractal level of support and resistance can be captured using MIDAS S/R curves, which adds deeper justification to the assertion that MIDAS can be used as a robust standalone trading system.

Figure 3.19 is a 1m chart of the euro September 2010 futures spanning almost two trading days, June 13 and 15.

1. The thick support curve at the bottom of the chart was launched from a pullback on the short-term trend two days previously. According to Table 3.1, this trend is of two to four weeks in duration and is best analyzed on the 60m chart. It produces roughly a signal a day because the displacement is so large. Because of the large displacement, price moves off the curves are also very large. This can be seen emphatically in Figure 3.19.
2. The dotted support and resistance curves on Figure 3.19 are launched from pull-backs associated with the one to two day trend. According to Table 3.1, this trend is best analyzed on the 15m chart. It produces three to four signals a day. The displacement is still large, and so the corresponding moves off the curves are also similarly proportional in price and time.
3. The trends highlighted in the first two gray rectangles are two to six hours in duration. According to Table 3.1, they're best analyzed on the 5m chart. They're

FIGURE 3.19   1m chart of euro June 2010 futures showing curves from the short-term trend, 1–2 day trend, 2–6 hour trend, and 20m–60m trend.

Source: eSignal and Metastock. www.esignal.com and www.equis.com.

typically associated with five to eight MIDAS signals per day and were the focus of the standalone trading system in the first part of this chapter.

4. The trends highlighted in the last two black rectangles are just over 60 minutes or less. According to Table 3.1, they're best analyzed on the 1m chart. They're typically associated with 12 to 15 signals per day.

Thus, MIDAS provides a day trader with a comprehensive fractal market analysis at all degrees of trend, provided he possesses the prior understanding of the relationship between trend size, chart timeframes, and displacement.

MIDAS S/R Curves and Fibonacci Retracements

In the relationship between MIDAS curves and Fibonacci levels, a critical role is played once again by displacement, which is why displaced S/R curves should never be ignored. However, traders relying on this combination should note that a displaced MIDAS curve rarely if ever displaces more than a Fibonacci 38.2 percent. Only curves launched at the very beginning of trends displace by this much, and no curve launched after midway through the trend (and usually less) is likely to displace more than the Fibonacci 23.6 percent level.

Figure 3.20 is a 5m chart of the British pound June 2010 futures. It will be noted that only the first launched curve displaces by as much as 38.2 percent and that the third curve launched from around a third of the way into the move displaces only

FIGURE 3.20   5m chart of British pound futures illustrating MIDAS displacements to the
23.6 percent and 38.2 percent levels.

Source: eSignal and Metastock. www.esignal.com and www.equis.com.

by 23.6 percent. These are reliable displacement levels for the curves and, as noted,
traders should not expect displacements above these levels and certainly never as deep
as the 61.8 percent level.

This relationship between degrees of displacement and the 23.6 percent and
38.2 percent Fibonacci retracement levels is illustrated again in the next two charts.
Figure 3.21 again shows that the first launched curve doesn't displace more than
38.2 percent and that curves launched later than midway into the trend (usually less)
don't correct more than 23.6 percent. The fact that the earliest MIDAS curves displace
from the trend by these two ratios probably explains why these two Fibonacci levels
are so potent in halting trend corrections.

Figure 3.22 also shows the same relationship between displacements and Fibonacci
levels. The first launched curve again displaces by 38.2 percent and only those curves
launched up to halfway through the trend displace to around the 23.6 percent level.

Combining MIDAS S/R Curves with Moving Averages

In recent years, the use of moving averages for day trading has become extremely
popular. The approach was given an extensive treatment by Bo Yoder in his book
Mastering Futures Trading, and it is also fundamental to the techniques taught by
Greg Capra and Oliver Velez. Several articles on this approach have also appeared
in the trading journals, including *Futures Magazine*. It's also an approach I've long
relied upon.[16]

FIGURE 3.21 5m chart of British pound September 2010 futures with a displacement up to a Fibonacci 38.2 percent from the first launched curve and another two not launched more than midway into the trend associated with the 23.6 percent level.

Source: eSignal and Metastock. www.esignal.com and www.equis.com.

FIGURE 3.22 British pound June 2010 futures showing the same relationship between the degree of displacement in Fibonacci terms.

Source: eSignal and Metastock. www.esignal.com and www.equis.com.

It's beyond the scope of this chapter to provide a detailed introduction to this method. The approach doesn't rely on traditional moving average crossover techniques but works with a more intimate relationship between price and the averages. The number of moving averages used also varies and their lengths and methods vary too, depending on the style of the system advocated. Here I'll illustrate the approach using the parameters I've come to rely on and then discuss how the MIDAS system can be integrated with this approach.

Figure 3.23 is a 2m chart of the DAX June 2010 futures illustrating my variation of this technique. First, while many day traders who use it will rely solely on the 20-period EMA, I always use four moving averages, with the lowest being the 10-period EMA. In Figure 3.23 the need for the 10-period EMA (light gray) is clear from the first setup where, after a gap up, price moves briefly sideways before reversing on to it and then finding support on it for the next three and a half hours. The same thing happens in the pullbacks I've highlighted by the arrows. In general, sharply moving trends pull back to the 10-period EMA and not to its 20-period counterpart. The second setup, on the other hand, finds support on the 20- and 40-period EMAs (see too the gray arrow), my second and third moving averages (dotted and black respectively). My fourth EMA is the 200-period (heavy gray), though it has little influence in the present chart.

The trade-management principles used in this system are identical to those described in the "multimarket" system, namely Japanese candlestick reversals off pullbacks to the moving averages, with similar stop-loss ranges and entry triggers. Price

FIGURE 3.23   2m chart of the June 2010 DAX futures with the 10-, 20-, 40-, and 200-period EMAs (gray, dotted, solid black, and heavy gray respectively).

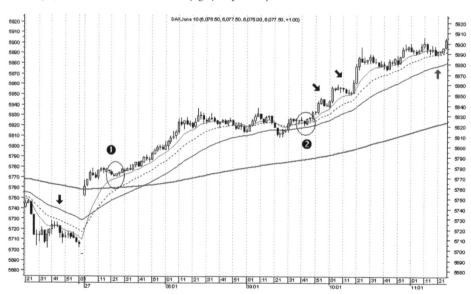

Source: eSignal and Metastock. www.esignal.com and www.equis.com.

targets can also be based on the principle of two times the stop-loss range (as detailed earlier) or they can focus on chart-based criteria. For example, Yoder recommends as a price target the previous swing high in an uptrend prior to the pullback and the previous swing low in a downtrend prior to the pullback.[17] Figure 3.24 illustrates this price target technique at setups (1), (2), and (4). In the case of (1), we have a reversal off the 20-period EMA and a price target of 8.5 points (i.e., the entry of 5948 (= low of the reversal candlestick) minus the swing low (= 5939.5)). In the second setup the price target is 13.5 points and in the fourth it is 10.5 points. This price targeting strategy doesn't always work because price doesn't always pull back to create a swing high or low. For example, in Figure 3.23 there is no significant swing high at setup (2) nor is there much of one at setup (1). Finally, we also see in Figure 3.24 a role for the 200-period EMA: the second setup not only reverses on the 40-period EMA but also on the 200 EMA. Because of the displacement, the 200 EMA interacts with price far less often than the other EMAs. When it does, however, it produces powerful signals and larger moves because it is linked to higher timeframe EMAs that have displaced a greater distance from price. It's beyond the scope of this chapter to discuss these issues, particularly inter-timeframe relationships between moving averages. However, the parallels between displaced moving averages and displaced MIDAS curves should be obvious.

As indicated earlier, trade setups don't involve moving average crossovers on this system. In the first rectangle in Figure 3.24, we see price create a swing high above the moving averages and then break back down through them. This is not necessarily a signal. The first clear-cut setup occurs at point (3) where, after breaking down through the moving averages, price pulls back to create a reversal candlestick on the retest. A

FIGURE 3.24   The same 2m DAX chart illustrating pivot-based price targets and setups.

Source: eSignal and Metastock. www.esignal.com and www.equis.com.

break below the low of this reversal candlestick would be the entry for the trader. The same thing occurs in the second rectangle: after setting a low, price breaks back up through the moving averages and then tests for resistance becoming support on a reversal candlestick on the 20- and 10-period EMAs, albeit with some porosity. However, this isn't an ideal setup. In an ideal setup the moving averages should be logically displaced: in true trending conditions, the proximate relationship to price should be the 10, 20, and 40 EMAs respectively. Ideally, this should also be reflected on a higher timeframe chart, such as the 5m and 15m if one were taking signals off the 1m, 2m, or 3m chart.

There is not the space to discuss this system further. A full treatment would require several chapters and possibly a book-length study, since the system can be created much more substantially by linking moving average relationships across timeframes in a manner similar to the way I mapped out time- and trend-based relationships with MIDAS curves in the first half of this chapter. It's time now to start looking at how MIDAS curves can work alongside a moving average system such as this one.

I want to identify two uses to which standard MIDAS S/R curves can be put in relation to the moving averages system. For convenience I'll call these two uses "supplementary displacement" and "contrarian" respectively.

Supplementary Displacement

The easiest way to grasp this first use is to demonstrate it. Comments can be added afterwards. Figure 3.25 is a 5m chart of the June 2010 CME euro FX futures. Going back to Table 3.1, the downtrend and the gradually rising sideways trend fall firmly into the two- to six-hour trend size typically found on this timeframe.

Our attention is drawn first to the area labeled (1). Here price corrects and marginally breaks through the 10 and 20-period EMAs to find resistance against the 40 EMA (in relation to which it is mildly porous). It also touches the 200 EMA. However, the most dominant curve is R1, the thick black MIDAS resistance curve that was launched from the high labeled "R1" at the arrow. After the setup at (1), price displaces downwards and so another curve, R2, is launched from the high at (1). The setup at (2) is thus a combination of the 20-period EMA plus R2. The setup at (3) is a combination of the 40-period EMA plus the same MIDAS resistance curve.

This first use then is a bolstering of the support/resistance roles of moving averages in trending markets, hence the term "supplementary." The term "displacement" refers to two aspects of this approach. The first is highlighted by setups (1) and (2) insofar as price rapidly displaces from R1 at the first setup and thus requires the immediate launch of another, R2, to keep up with the displacement. The second aspect is captured by setups (4) and (5). By this stage price is drifting in a gradually rising market. However, it's too near to the horizontal for the moving averages to be effective, thus resulting in price whipsawing across them in what would be a hopeless trading situation for moving average users. By contrast, both R1 and R2 have now displaced again from price sufficiently far for them not to be caught up in this whipsawing process. As a result, R2 provides solid resistance in a number of potential setups highlighted by (4),

FIGURE 3.25   5m chart of CME euro FX June 2010 futures with two MIDAS resistance curves and the 10, 20, 40 and 200 EMAs.

Source: eSignal and Metastock. www.esignal.com and www.equis.com.

while R1 resists the end of this sideways drift at setup (5). At setup (5) note that price has even crossed above the three moving averages and is starting to find trend support on the 10-period EMA. This observation brings us to the second use.

Contrarian

Quite often when combining moving averages with MIDAS S/R curves, traders will confront situations where the two sets of curves will oppose one another in terms of their forecasting implications. This is caused by the proximate relationship of the moving averages to price and the displacement phenomenon in MIDAS S/R curves when the latter are now related to larger price movements. We've just seen an instance of this in the fifth setup in Figure 3.25. Another example can be seen in Figure 3.26, a 5m chart of the EURX German Bund June 2010 futures. This is a fairly low resolution chart showing one main trading day, May 17, 2010. As before, the 10, 20, 40, and 200 EMAs are the gray, dotted, solid black, and heavy gray curves respectively. The MIDAS support curve is the heavy black curve, and it was launched two trading days earlier on the morning of May 13, 2010, thus producing a great deal of displacement.

The two black arrows highlight the start of where, according to this moving average system, price is in a firm downtrend insofar as the moving averages are correctly dispersed from price, beginning with the 10-period EMA nearest to it and the 40-period EMA furthest away. There are a number of short trading setups on both downtrends insofar as price pulls back and reverses for several hours against the

FIGURE 3.26 5m chart of EUREX Bund June 2010 contract with moving averages and a two-day-old displaced MIDAS support curve capturing the lows on two adjacent days.

Source: eSignal and Metastock. www.esignal.com and www.equis.com.

10-period EMA or the 40-period EMA. However, on both occasions the downtrends are stopped emphatically by the displaced MIDAS support curve.

For the most part, traders will find that when moving averages and displaced MIDAS curves are lined up against one other in this way there's a tendency for the MIDAS curve to hold sway over the moving averages. The reason again comes back to displacement. As emphasized several times in this chapter, as soon as a MIDAS curve displaces it means that the new phase of the trend has accelerated and that there's a background proportional relationship between the MIDAS curve and this new phase of the trend insofar as when its acceleration completes, its pullback remains intimately connected with the curve. There was a more detailed discussion of displacement earlier in the Elliott Wave and Fibonacci sections, which I won't duplicate here. Suffice it to say that we're always dealing in technical analysis with tendencies, and displaced curves do not always hold price. This obviously raises the question as to the best trading strategy to adopt when price is sandwiched between its moving averages and a MIDAS curve it is approaching, since we are in effect setting up a contrarian play against the moving averages, which is not easy when there are two powerful but opposing forces at work on the chart. Outside of working with Market Profile or oscillators (see below), the best trading advice is to adopt a wait and see policy and let the market tip its hand.

There are two ways of doing of this, one more conservative than the other. Both approaches can be illustrated with a higher-resolution look at the second downtrend in Figure 3.26 ending on May 18. In Figure 3.27 we clearly see the moving averages cross down over one another in the rectangle in the upper left as the first significant

FIGURE 3.27   The same 5m chart showing the second downtrend in higher resolution and highlighting two trading strategies in contrarian MIDAS plays against the moving averages.

Source: eSignal and Metastock. www.esignal.com and www.equis.com.

pullback is held by the moving averages. This is the start of the downtrend in moving average terms. At the point where the 200 EMA crosses price, the latter pulls back more deeply and is held by the combination of the 40 and 200 EMAs. Finally it reaches the underlying MIDAS support curve.

The first and most unambiguous sign that price is going to be held is the doji candlestick on the support curve. Our first entry point is thus a break above the high of this doji with the usual stop placed at its low. However, many traders would be concerned about entering the market at this juncture due to the proximity of the moving averages, especially the 10-period EMA. This is understandable, which brings us to the more conservative approach. Its logic is that if the MIDAS curve is to hold price, the latter must break above all three of the moving averages before they subsequently cross back over one another. In Figure 3.27 this occurs on the small spinning top candlestick prior to the one highlighted by the second arrow. The candlestick highlighted by the arrow pulls back significantly to test the 10 and 20 EMAs before forming a strong white candlestick. This being a pullback candlestick, our stop is placed at its low and the trade is triggered when the next bar breaks above its high.

A final alternative technique is highlighted in Figure 3.28. Sometimes by the time price reaches a displaced MIDAS curve it is severely overbought or oversold. Here overbought and oversold are not being measured by a bounded momentum indicator such as the stochastic, but by how far price has travelled away from the moving averages, especially the 10-period EMA.[18] In cases of overextension, when the moving

FIGURE 3.28 The same 5m chart of the German Bund with a selling climax into a MIDAS support curve launched several days before.

Source: eSignal and Metastock. www.esignal.com and www.equis.com.

averages are spread quite widely and price is far above or below the 10-period EMA, the strategy is to enter on a candlestick reversal on the MIDAS curve with a price target being the 10-period EMA. Figure 3.28 illustrates this strategy when a white harami candlestick forms after the sell-off into another two-day-old MIDAS support curve and when the 10-period EMA is approximately 20 points above the high of the harami. A break above the harami high with a stop on its low (or the low of the penetrating candlestick) triggers the trade back to the moving averages.

Pivot Point Techniques and MIDAS S/R Curves

In this section, I look at the MIDAS S/R curves in relation to two pivot point techniques—traditional floor-traded pivots and pivots based on the Camarilla equation. Readers who use other pivot point techniques, such as Woodie's (Ken Wood) pivot points, Tom DeMark's formula, or Fibonacci pivot levels can take the basic recommendations of this discussion and adapt them to their techniques. I want to focus on a factor common to MIDAS S/R curves and pivot points and demonstrate how, by understanding it, the two can work well together.

Essentially, what all pivot point calculations do is establish by means of yesterday's data key levels where today's market is likely to expand or reverse. As the range associated with each level widens, there's also a greater likelihood that displaced MIDAS S/R curves will have important roles to play in bolstering the various support/resistance roles of the pivot levels, especially those at the further outreaches. By the same token, breakouts will be that much more meaningful if MIDAS S/R curves are also broken in the same process.

Trading Floor Pivots

Traditional trading floor pivots are a popular tool in the cash and futures markets as they have moved off the floor and into computers. For readers not familiar with traditional trading floor pivots, primer articles are plentiful online and two chapter-length discussions can be found in recent books by John L. Person, *A Complete Guide to Technical Trading Tactics*, and John F. Carter, *Mastering The Trade*.[19] The techniques discussed next can also be applied to weekly and monthly pivots (see note 20 for references) for influences on the Short-Term, Intermediate, and Primary trends.

The formula I use in the calculation of trading floor pivots (there are variations) is for three levels either side of the Pivot Point, together with their midpoints, which are additional proven levels to which price responds. Using yesterday's High, Low, and Close the following formula can be programmed into Metastock:

Resistance 3 = High + 2 * (Pivot – Low)

Midpoint = (Resistance 3 + Resistance 2) / 2
Resistance 2 = Pivot + (R1 – S1)

Midpoint = (Resistance 2 + Resistance 1) / 2
Resistance 1 = 2 * Pivot – Low

Midpoint = (Resistance 1 + Pivot Point) / 2
Pivot Point = (High + Close + Low) / 3

Midpoint = (Pivot Point + Support 1) / 2
Support 1 = 2 * Pivot Point – High

Midpoint = (Support 1 + Support 2) / 2
Support 2 = Pivot – (Resistance 1 – Support 1)

Midpoint = (Support 2 + Support 3) / 2
Support 3 = Low – 2 * (High – Pivot Point)

It's often argued that the first role of floor traded pivots is to provide an immediate bias. Depending on whether the market opens above or below the central Pivot Point, the bias will be towards long or short trades respectively. The next role is to establish whether there is a trading range. If there is, the initial range often occurs between the Pivot Point and R1 and S2, though the midpoints can often define this range as well.

Beyond this, floor pivots combined with Japanese candlesticks facilitate two types of trading strategy. Both strategies can be enhanced with MIDAS S/R support curves and give rise to differing implications depending on the extent of the displacement of the S/R curves in question.

Rangebound Strategies with MIDAS S/R Curves

The first is essentially a reversal strategy in rangebound markets defined by the pivots, especially as regards the chart area defined by the R1 and S1 boundaries. Let's take a look at this approach with several MIDAS S/R curves in Figure 3.29, a 5m chart of the EUREX Dow Jones Eurostoxx 50 June 2010 contract over two trading days, May 19 and 20.

The topmost MIDAS resistance curve was launched from a higher swing the previous day, thus demonstrating a fair amount of displacement. The lower one was launched from point (4) as price suddenly displaced downwards. As the trading day of the 19th opens, price falls to S1, rallies up from it, hesitates around the midpoint, and then reverses on the combined Pivot Point and first displaced resistance curve. This produces another downtrend to the S1/S2 midpoint. For the rest of the day price remains within the same range and falls back to the S1 level again, albeit with some porosity. Interestingly, however, the two rally points to (2) and (3) do not stall at any pivot level; instead, they respond to the gradually declining MIDAS resistance curve. A user of the floor pivots on this day would have no explanation for the failure of price to reach the Pivot Point before reversing. MIDAS highlights the reason why.

On the 20th price gaps down and finds support on the Pivot Point/S1 midpoint. It then rallies up to the Pivot Point/R1 midpoint where it reverses at setup (4). Here again the same displaced MIDAS resistance curve is holding the market, just as it did on the three occasions on the previous day. As the fourth setup completes, there is nothing in the trading floor pivots methodology that can predict where price is going

FIGURE 3.29   5m chart of the DJ Eurostoxx 50 June 2010 futures with floor traded pivots and MIDAS S/R curves over two trading days, May 19 and 20, 2010.

Source: eSignal and Metastock. www.esignal.com and www.equis.com.

next. The expectation is that it'll retest the next lower level before either reversing or continuing lower.

However, it has been a basic dictum in this chapter that MIDAS S/R curves should be interpreted in the same way as linear trendlines. Thus, going back to the conventionally labeled trend lengths near the beginning of this chapter, if price breaks an intermediate trendline (i.e., one measuring a trend of between six weeks and nine months in duration), the expectation should be that the subsequent move should be proportionate in price and time. The same assumption as regards the size and duration of curves should be made in the case of MIDAS, including intraday according to Table 3.1.

Applying this principle in Figure 3.29, we see that the upper MIDAS resistance curve was launched from a swing high on the previous day. Referencing Table 3.1, such curves are a staple part of the 15m chart and typically last for one to two days. Thus, a bounce off a curve of this magnitude should produce an equivalent-sized move. This is what we see initially on the 19th, since the displaced MIDAS curve is directly implicated in a sideways pattern that lasts the entire day. Then on the 20th we see the resulting down move after setup (4) lasting most of the day.

The second MIDAS resistance curve launched at point (4) is associated with a move whose duration is typical of the 5m chart. Accordingly, it isn't displacing as much as the first one and is thus capable of helping stop a rally to the S1/S2 midpoint at the fifth setup. The sixth setup is again interesting insofar as there is no direct association between the reversal and a pivot level. The presence of the MIDAS curve again reveals the cause of this reversal.

In rangebound markets, then, a trader who combines trading floor pivots with MIDAS should be looking for an important role to be played by already displaced curves, while adhering to the principle that the size of the expected move off the curves is relative to their displacement. Pivot Points cannot supply this additional information. Indeed, trading floor pivots in themselves provide little if any indication of the size of the move over and above the expectation that price will move to the next proximate pivot level.

Breakout Strategies with MIDAS S/R Curves

The second main use to which trading floor pivots have been put is for breakout strategies. Very often in breakouts, price will break a pivot level and then pull back to it before the breakout continues. This pullback is the sweet spot of the entry for many traders. Price targets are then set in relation to other proximate levels. Figure 3.30 is a 5m chart of the Swiss Market Index June 2010 futures covering two trading days, May 19 and 20.

Beginning on the left of the chart, points (1) and (2) on May 18 highlight that a MIDAS curve launched from the 17th acts as support alongside the Pivot Point/R1 midpoint on two occasions going into the close. On the 19th price gaps down from it and finds support on the S2/S3 midpoint. The displacement on this MIDAS curve is very large, so again a breakdown means that the corresponding move away from this curve will also be proportionately large according to Table 3.1. This is what we do find as the move breaks down over the 19th and 20th.

FIGURE 3.30 5m chart of the Swiss Market Index June 2010 contract showing two trading days, May 19 and 20.

Source: eSignal and Metastock. www.esignal.com and www.equis.com.

A new MIDAS support curve is launched at the first arrow prior to point (3), this time proportionate to a typical 5m move according to Table 3.1. It provides support as price moves above S3. The move ends at S1 and another MIDAS curve is then launched from this swing high. This curve resists price all the way back down to S3 at market close. During this downtrend price breaks the support curve launched at point (3), thus adding significance to the move. On the 20th price breaks back up through this same curve at point (4) and moves up to R1. At points (5) and (6) price bounces around the Pivot Point/R1 midpoint before breaking the two MIDAS curves launched from the 19th. Again the proportionate size of these curves means that the breakdown will be fairly significant, reaching below the most immediate proximate pivot levels.

Breaks of MIDAS S/R curves amidst trading floor pivots, then, provide additional insight into the size of the move expected: the larger the displacement of the curve, the larger the corresponding move involved in the break. Trading floor pivots by themselves provide no indication as to the size of the trend moving between the various pivot levels.

The Camarilla Equation

The Camarilla equation was developed in 1989 by the bond trader Nick Stott. In an interview Stott claimed that his initial interest in Pivot Points derived from Fibonacci levels but that the real basis of the equation stemmed from an important implication of Market Profile of which its practitioners were unaware.[20] Further information about how to trade with the equation can be found at http://www.camarillaequation.com and access to daily data supplied by the algorithm for a fixed monthly fee is available at www.surefirething.com.

The idea behind the equation is one familiar to users of Market Profile, namely that a time series has a tendency to revert to the mean. More specifically, a wide range yesterday tends to drive today's price back towards yesterday's close. As we'll see below, strategies have been developed around this idea in relation to the levels generated by the equation.

The equation comes in two versions, (a) and (b), the latter designed for less-experienced traders. The original version (version (a)) takes yesterday's open, high, low, and close and generates eight levels divided into two groups of four, H4 to H1 and L1 to L4. The most important levels are H4 and H3 and L3 and L4.

The original equation has never been divulged. However, on the basis of Pivot Point data released by users of the equation onto various traders' forums several equations have been back-engineered from the data. One of them produces levels co-extensive with the original Camarilla equation. I've verified this against data purporting to be levels calculated by the original equation. To my knowledge, this equation was developed by a forum user called "sidinuk" and first posted on August 27, 2003 on www.Trade2win.com.[21] The equation is now used fairly extensively across a range of sites whose focus is on short-term trading, including FX sites.[22]

The equation below is the back-engineered version. Unlike the original Camarilla equation, it doesn't use yesterday's open, yet its levels seem to be coextensive with those produced by the original version. It's also worth emphasizing that some sites using this formula add a Pivot Point based on the same floor trader Pivot Point calculation of $(H + L + C)/3$, thus taking the pivot levels to nine. No such reference to a Pivot Point is made in the original Camarilla equation and I'm omitting it here:

$$H4 = (\text{high-low}) * 1.1/2 + \text{close}$$
$$H3 = (\text{high-low}) * 1.1/4 + \text{close}$$
$$H2 = (\text{high-low}) * 1.1/6 + \text{close}$$
$$H1 = (\text{high-low}) * 1.1/12 + \text{close}$$

$$L1 = \text{close-(high-low)} * 1.1/12$$
$$L2 = \text{close-(high-low)} * 1.1/6$$
$$L3 = \text{close-(high-low)} * 1.1/4$$
$$L4 = \text{close-(high-low)} * 1.1/2$$

Later in the same thread on the forum in May 2004 a user called "dc2000" suggested adding to each level a weighting of 0.3 percent in an uptrend and subtracting 0.1 percent to each level in a downtrend. In the charts below I've programmed these equations into Metastock while omitting the weighting. We can now take a look at a couple of charts in relation to the two suggested trading strategies.

As noted earlier, the most important levels are H4 and H3 and L3 and L4 respectively. With these levels in mind, the first trading strategy involves the expectation that the market will reverse if it approaches an H3 or L3 level. This assumption is much more precise than is the case with trading floor pivots insofar as the latter do not emphasize the key importance of certain levels over others. On price approaching H3 or L3, a trader is expected to take a contrary position to the trend direction with a stop-loss fractionally over the other side of the level. This is the same strategy when trading pullbacks to MIDAS S/R curves, albeit the combined candlestick strategy involves considerably more precision.

The second strategy is to view the H4 and L4 levels as breakout levels, this time going with the trend if price breaks above H4 or below L4. This too is a more precise idea than anything to be found in trading floor pivots insofar again as the latter never stresses the importance of some levels in breakouts over others. Thus, in general both types of trading day—rangebound and trending—are covered by the Camarilla approach insofar as rangebound days are related to bounces between narrower levels of volatility and trending days are defined in terms of the outermost levels generated by the equation.

Camarilla-Based Rangebound Days and MIDAS S/R Curves

Figure 3.31 is a 5m chart of the CME's British pound June 2010 futures. It clearly illustrates early rangebound trading before developing into a significant uptrend. The futures open in the Asian-Pacific session and find support at L2 at point (1). A modest

FIGURE 3.31   5m chart of the CME's British pound June 2010 futures with Camarilla levels illustrating both trading strategies.

Source: eSignal and Metastock. www.esignal.com and www.equis.com.

rally then follows before price falls lower and finds support at L3 at the start of the London session at point (2). According to the first strategy, traders should have bought on this move, and they would've been richly rewarded if they had. Subsequent to the start of the rally, price stalls briefly on a virtual touch of H3 (point (3)) and then pulls back to find support on the high of the Asian-Pacific session. It again finds virtual resistance against H3 (point (4)), pulls back to H1 (point (5)), and then breaks above H3 at point (6). The small pullback here is the ideal entry point with a price target of H4. At point (7), H4 resists price before it breaks through and pulls back, creating another ideal entry point at (8). According to the second strategy, a break of H4 is meant to be a signal to go long and traders would again have been rewarded before the uptrend ends well into the U.S. session.

Now let's take a look at a typical rangebound day with MIDAS. Figure 3.32 is the same British pound contract on May 4 and 5, 2010. What we're expecting when MIDAS S/R curves extend into a rangebound day is for the curves to add further credence to any signals associated with the Camarilla levels. The MIDAS curve launched from the low (2) of the 4th bolsters the resistance role of H1 at points (5), (6), and (7) in the Asian-Pacific and London sessions, while the curve launched from the high of the 4th at (1) bolsters the resistance role of H3 at points (8) and (9) and again at (10) with regard to H1. After price touches H3 the second time at point (9) it moves straight to L3, then reverses all the way back to H1. This is a textbook Camarilla range day involving H3 and L3 and one where the signals are strongly boosted by several MIDAS setups.

If there is a weakness in the (a) version of the Camarilla equation, it is that when a market does break out of the H4 and L4 zones the trader is on his own and thus reliant

FIGURE 3.32 Another 5m chart of the CME's British pound futures showing two trading days, June 4 and 5, 2010, with Camarilla pivots and MIDAS.

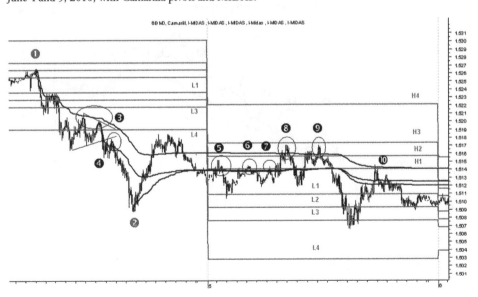

upon other technical tools to inform his decisions. For example, on the 4th price forms a symmetrical triangle on L4 while bouncing down off the MIDAS curve launched at (1) on two occasions. When it breaks down at point (4), it does so in part as a response to the descending MIDAS curve before it displaces sharply downwards. Here we could have launched another MIDAS curve—or more likely a bottomfinder—to keep up with the trend. The curve would then have been used as a price target insofar as any break back above the curve would have ejected us from the short trade. We look at these ideas again in the next section.

Camarilla-Based Trending Days and MIDAS S/R Curves

Figure 3.33 continues our examination of the British pound futures on the 5m chart in relation to Camarilla-style trending days and is a repeat of Figure 3.31, this time with curves added. Starting in the Asian-Pacific session, price finds initial support on L2, produces a lackluster rally, and then falls back to L3 at point (2). This, according to Camarilla trading philosophy, is where traders should be looking for a reversal. Accordingly, when we get a reversal candlestick on L3, we also launch a MIDAS support curve.

Now the rally is supported by the first curve all the way up to H2 at point (3). Price then finds support on the high of the Asian session before breaking all of the other resistance levels all the way up to H4. A key pullback onto H1 at point (5) is supported too by the second support curve, as is a subsequent pullback to H3 at point

FIGURE 3.33　Another 5m chart on the June 9, 2010, of the same British pound futures. A trending day off the L3 low at the start of the London session is expertly analyzed by the five MIDAS support curves alongside the Camarilla levels.

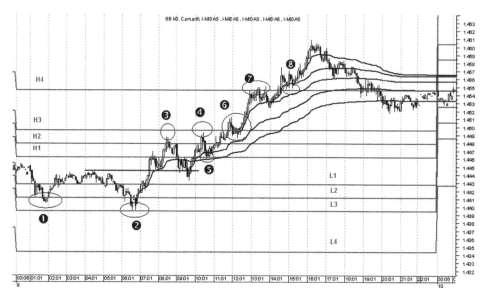

Source: eSignal and Metastock. www.esignal.com and www.equis.com.

(6). At H3 traders might have been fooled initially into thinking that the pullback was actually another reversal, but price continues up to H4 where it is resisted briefly at point (7). Here price is supported by the third MIDAS support curve and thereafter breaks above H4.

As noted in the previous section, once price breaks out of the H4 and L4 levels a trader is on his own unless he uses other technical tools. He isn't alone because a fourth support curve was launched from the low at point (7), which keeps him in the trade until the support curve is broken at 1.4590. MIDAS curves are thus a good tool to rely on once price has trended out of the H4, L4 zones, provided a new MIDAS curve is launched as soon as price displaces and starts accelerating. This is what it does at point (7) in relation to the third support curve, and again at point (8) (just above H4) in relation to the fourth support curve. It's the fifth MIDAS support curve that keeps us in the trade and eventually gets us out at a tight trailing stop at 1.4590. It must be borne in mind too that it was one of Levine's observations that a trend is ready to end once it has been supported by four to five curves.

On the June 9, then, the market trends continually up through all of the Camarilla levels from point (2) at the start of the London session. Throughout this long trend, entry points on the levels are supported by MIDAS support curves. The latter also do an excellent job of keeping us in the trend, provided we keep up with the accelerating portions of the trend by launching new curves from pullbacks.

MIDAS S/R Curves and Market Profile

Since the Camarilla equation allegedly grew out of reflections on Market Profile, it's fitting that a brief discussion of MIDAS and Market Profile should be the next topic. Readers are again warned that it is beyond the scope of this chapter to provide anything more than a cursory introduction to Market Profile before looking at charts. This orientation will not be enough to those new to Market Profile, and they are urged to review some of the reading in the following footnote.[23]

Market Profile was developed by Peter Steidlmayer in the early 1980s and soon afterwards was licensed by the Chicago Board of Trade. The approach uniquely represents price in half-hour segments by letters. For example, if the DAX futures moved between 6,085 and 6,110 in the first half hour of trading and a price increment of five points were chosen, the letter A would be assigned to this period and printed five times. This half-hour assignment continues throughout the day. The resulting letters are known as TPOs (time-price-opportunities). As they're printed, the letters are collapsed as far to the left as possible in order to create the classic side-on, bell-shaped curve unique to Market Profile charts.

Market Profile recognizes two basic forms of market activity: sideways moving equilibrium and periods of trending disequilibrium. The two phases are conjoined in a continuous cycle, during which the market is described as an auction striving to bring about a price range in which buying and selling demand is more or less equal.

During the first phase, the market moves horizontally while seeking balance as it fluctuates between support and resistance. This activity creates the familiar bell-shaped curve turned on its side. The curve is a familiar principle in statistics when measuring standard deviation. The first standard deviation that covers the middle of the curve contains approximately 67 percent of the data; the first two standard deviations cover 95 percent of it. The first standard deviation is known as the "value area" and the peak of this value area is the "point of control" or "mode." It's possible to identify the top and bottom of the value area by means of a simple calculation, which is done automatically in trading platforms. The first two periods of trading (i.e., the first 60 minutes) are known as the "initial balance." Based on various relationships between the initial balance and the value area, Market Profile uniquely identifies several types of trading days:

- Normal days
- Nontrend days
- Normal variations of a normal day
- Trend days
- Neutral days
- Double distribution days

Figure 3.34 is an eSignal Market Profile chart of the euro September 2010 futures for June 16. The volume profile is on the right in gray, and the point of control (PoC) is the longest line of letters with the dashed line. The value area is signified by the vertical gray line just to the right of the letters, while the narrow initial balance and opening price is signified to the left of the letters by the small vertical line and arrow behind it respectively.

FIGURE 3.34   Market Profile on June 16 of the CME's euro FX Globex September 2010 futures.

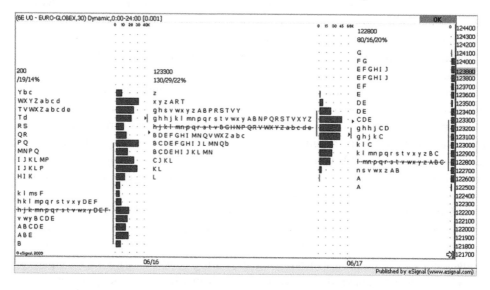

Source: eSignal. www.esignal.com.

During the second disequilibrium phase, markets cease moving horizontally and move vertically. Quite often, the period of disequilibrium (trending market) begins when the bell-shaped curve has completed forming. Sometimes, however, the market skips a beat in what is known as "minus development."[24]

Some experts break this constant cycling down into four phases. The first is the rally that starts the cycle; that is, the move into disequilibrium as prices are auctioned higher or lower. The second phase is signaled by a bar that doesn't set a new high or low in the trending phase. From here the first layers of the standard deviation start to build. The third stage consists of continued building of the bell-shaped curve, often in a characteristic "p" or "b" shape in an uptrend or downtrend respectively. The final stage creates a much broader profile of horizontal development, often filling in the leg of the classic "p" or "b" profile to create a fatter "D" shape. Minus development occurs most often when the fourth step is skipped, resulting in a series of uptrending "p" or downtrending "b" shapes. This is indicative of extreme bullishness or bearishness.

Market Profile identifies two types of trading strategy. The first is a classic range-trading technique of selling the highs and buying the lows. This strategy is valid so long as the equilibrium phase is in force as the market builds its standard deviation profile in phases two, three, and four. Here the high and low of the equilibrium phase are the upper and lower low-volume ends of the value area respectively as the bell-curve is filled in. The second trading strategy is the directional move into disequilibrium as phase four completes. This move typically begins from the high-volume value area, and its start would be signaled by a break of the upper or lower end of the value area. Minus development can make this phase more unpredictable.

So far as combining MIDAS with Market Profile is concerned, it's probably best to see the benefits as mutually supportive. In other words, a regular user of MIDAS will often obtain supportive data from Market Profile and vice versa.

Market Profile Provides Key Prior Directional Bias in Price versus MIDA S/R Curves

Let's begin with an area where information from Market Profile can inform important trading decisions concerning MIDAS. In the section on volume and momentum indicators below, one of their main roles is to provide inside information on whether a given MIDAS curve is likely to hold price. Market Profile can also perform a very similar role.

Figure 3.35 is a 30m chart of the euro September 2010 futures. On June 15 a displaced MIDAS support curve launched from June 10 is rapidly approached by price. This curve had strongly supported price on June 11, so we already know it is active. At the same time, two resistance curves, R1 and R2, had actively resisted price, especially R2, on three key occasions on the 15th as price moved down towards S1.

This is a classic MIDAS squeeze situation. Normally a longer-term, more displaced curve holds sway over its younger counterpart, but this isn't always the case. In the section below on momentum and volume indicators, I examine another way of confronting this problem. Here, however, we turn to Market Profile with the help of Figure 3.36.

FIGURE 3.35   30m chart of euro September 2010 futures with the June 15 being characterized by a squeeze of price between two near-term resistance curves and one longer-term displaced support curve. Market Profile strongly indicates that S1 will hold price.

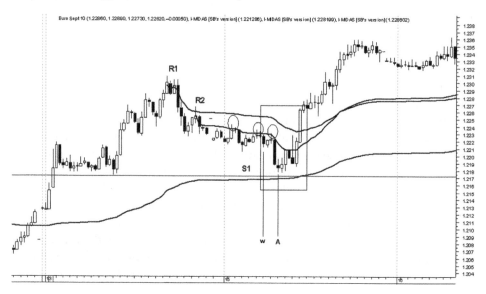

Source: eSignal and Metastock. www.esignal.com and www.equis.com.

FIGURE 3.36   Market Profile for the euro September 2010 futures showing June 15 and the previous day.

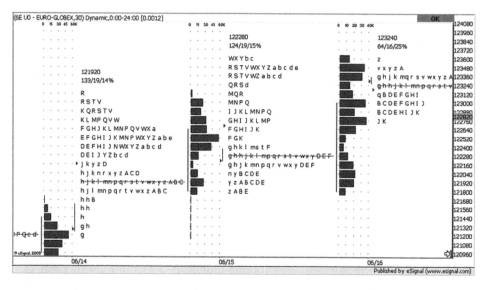

Source: eSignal. www.esignal.com.

Our key concern as to whether S1 will initially support price—and then indeed whether R1 and R2 will fail to resist it—is brought sharply into focus in the rectangular area. Our concerns would probably start at the candlestick I've labeled "w," which corresponds to the lower-case letter in the Market Profile chart.

With the "w" area in mind, one look at the Market Profile chart in Figure 3.36 would have provided a strong indication that S1 would support price and that R1 and R2 would be broken. The first clue comes from the previous day. Here the narrow initial balance in the Asian-Pacific session is characterized by few TPOs and extremely light volume, indicating a rejection of prices at this opening level. The point of control (PoC) is at 1.2192, but this area too is rejected as a second bell curve forms in the upper end of the value area, especially at 1.2252. This type of day Market Profile enthusiasts call a Double Distribution Day (DDD). It's often characterized by a narrow initial balance, which means that the longer-term buyers believe that prices are below value and accordingly push them up. June 15, the day that interests us, also has an extremely narrow initial balance. Moreover by the time bar "w" prints, a significant point of control had been established higher than the previous day's. In all, four observations become relevant to our assumption that S1 will hold price and that R1 and R2 will be broken:

1. Yesterday's rejection of the lower initial balance with low volume in favor of a higher value and volume area.
2. Yesterday being a DDD as longer-term buyers perceived prices to be below value and accordingly created a new value area above the one associated with the PoC.
3. Today's PoC was higher than yesterday's.
4. Today's value area low, resting on yesterday's PoC.

MIDAS S/R Curves Provide Better Trade Entry Timing and Better Trade-Management Options than Market Profile

When a period of trending disequilibrium begins, moves are usually initiated out of the high volume value area. Accordingly a trade is often triggered when price breaks out of the value area high (VAH) or low (VAL). The problem is that a value area is 67 percent of the day's TPOs, and so will often produce a late signal. The added problem is "minus development" when the classic bell profile of the value area might not even have formed fully when the market moves into disequilibrium. Thus, in terms of price and time, Market Profile can often be a blunt trading instrument.

Take a look, for example, at Figure 3.37, a Market Profile chart covering the June 3 and 4, 2010, of the euro September contract. The downtrend begins on June 4 with the letter "I," which signifies the period between 12:00 P.M. and 12:30 P.M. Price initially breaks down from the PoC but soon also breaks down through the VAL at 1.2040 before closing at the end of the U.S. session at 1.1977. The day is in fact another Double Distribution Day, since longer-term sellers perceive price to be above value and begin pushing it down. There is also "minus development" on the day, since the PoC is additionally a part of the initial balance with no build-up of the value area before the move begins. In any case, if a short were entered at the VAL (1.2040) the

FIGURE 3.37　Market Profile of the euro September 2010 futures 3 and 4 June.

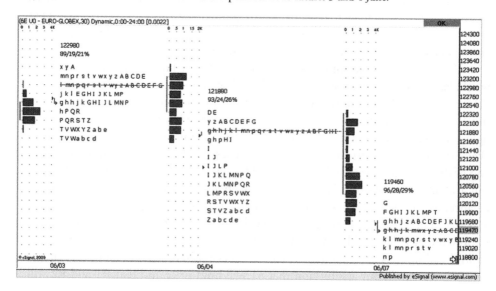

Source: eSignal. www.esignal.com.

trade would be entered extremely late, and the maximum hypothetical profit would be 63 points.

Now contrast the Market Profile chart with Figure 3.38, another 30m MIDAS chart. Here the PoC on the 3rd and 4th is clearly marked, along with the VAL on the 4th of 1.2040.

As price responds to the resistance curve, a sell signal comes on the break of the low of the reversal candlestick at 11:05 A.M. This time period corresponds with the letter "G" on the Market Profile chart. Thus, our sell signal with tight trade-management is actually above the PoC and right against the VAH at 1.2206. Now how we manage the trade hereafter is up to us, but in contrast to the Market Profile strategy, there's a massive hypothetical profit of 229 points. In an article on Market Profile Jayanthi Gopalakrishnan suggests using moving average crossovers as a technique for calibrating entries with profile data.[25] MIDAS S/R curves can work equally well, provided we also input data from Market Profile on the likelihood of an S/R supporting or resisting price.

For example, if we go back to Figure 3.37, what does the Market Profile of June 3 and 4 tell us about the likelihood of the resistance curve holding price in Figure 3.38? It tells us two things straightaway:

1. First, although on June 3 a value area was built around the PoC at 1.2304, price moved down over the course of the day, and a new value area began to build around the 1.2184 area.
2. Second, on June 4 a very narrow initial balance was created in the same area, followed by a PoC, indicating an equilibrium point on yesterday's low. These two factors indicated that the trend was moving down.

FIGURE 3.38   30m chart of euro September 2010 futures with a displaced MIDAS resistance curve resisting price until June 9 and 10.

Source: eSignal and Metastock. www.esignal.com and www.equis.com.

Before leaving this section, let's take a look briefly at the same displaced MIDAS resistance curve resisting price again on June 8. Could Market Profile have predicted that the curve would resist price a second time, bearing in mind that the curve was broken on June 9 and then again emphatically on June 10? The answer is yes. If we look at Figure 3.39, which is the same Market Profile chart moved on a day or two, we see that June 7 was what Market Profile followers call a Nontrend Day.

NTDs are characterized by a narrow initial balance that is barely upset as a flattened bell-shape develops. June 7 typifies this profile, with the PoC being an extension of the initial balance and a clearly established VAH and VAL being created. The profile for June 8 is identical, with a parallel initial balance and PoC. This strongly suggests that the VAH and VAL will continue to be respected.

Finally, what of the temporary break of this MIDAS resistance curve on June 9 and its permanent break on June 10? Looking at the Market Profile chart for June 9 in Figure 3.40, it's difficult to see how Market Profile this time would have predicted a break of the curve. The day is another NTD, with an initial balance and PoC in the same tight vicinity as the two previous days. This continued narrowing of volatility certainly forewarns us of an impending directional move, but nothing in the profile of June 9 provides a clear indication of the impending break of the curve. The profile for June 10 is a different story. Here, although the initial balance yet again duplicates the one of the previous three days, price rapidly breaks the resistance curve and establishes a new PoC at 1.2050 above the curve. This amount of volume establishes a new value area above it and thus establishes a new tier of support. This in turn forewarns that

FIGURE 3.39 Market Profile of the euro moved on a few days and showing two consecutive
Nontrend Days.

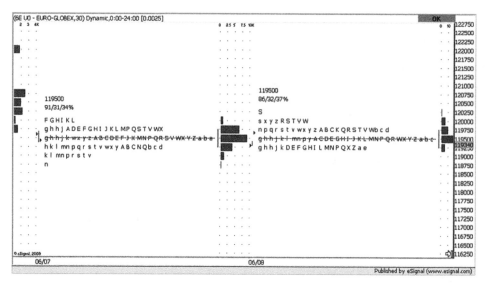

Source: eSignal. www.esignal.com.

FIGURE 3.40 Market Profile of the euro for June 9 and 10 showing a gradually rising value area on
June 10 as price successfully tests the displaced MIDAS curve.

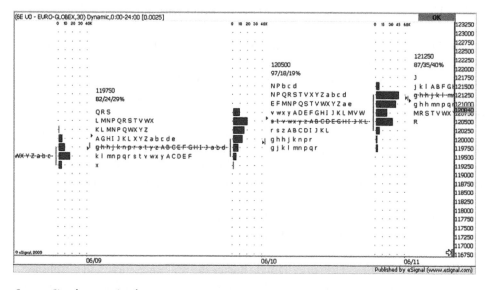

Source: eSignal. www.esignal.com.

the resistance curve will now become a support curve if price touches it. That's exactly what we see on June 10 as price starts breaking away higher.

MIDAS S/R Curves and Volume and Momentum Indicators

Adding indicators alongside MIDAS is a good idea, provided they enhance the analysis and aren't merely chart furniture. Aside from conventional trendlines, which I come to in the next section, I use three indicators with MIDAS for two specific reasons.

First, the indicators in question are George Lane's Stochastic, Granville's On Balance Volume (OBV), and the Elliott Wave (EW) Oscillator, an unbounded MACD-style momentum indicator developed by Tom Joseph and Bill Williams.[26] It should be emphasized that the first half of Chapter 16 discusses how the Stochastic, OBV, and EW Oscillator can be replaced by modifications of OBV. However, for the moment, for readers not familiar with EW Oscillator it's a 34-period simple moving average subtracted from a 5-period simple moving average and displayed as a histogram around a zero line. The indicator produces its highest/lowest momentum reading during the third wave of an Elliott Wave impulse. During the fourth wave it pulls back to its zero line and then produces a negative/positive divergence in relation to the fifth wave, depending on whether it is analyzing an uptrend or a downtrend respectively. To work optimally, the indicator requires a certain number of bars as input. Williams has suggested 100 to 140, and Joseph works to the upper end of this range. If there are more bars on the chart, the indicator is measuring waves of the *n–1*th degree; if there are less, it's measuring waves of an *n+1*th degree higher. I myself don't always use the indicator to such tight parameters or apply it to expertly counted Elliott Wave formations, yet I still find that it gives tighter momentum divergence signals than a standard MACD.

I mentioned the use of these three indicators for two reasons.

1. The first is to help time pullbacks to a MIDAS S/R curve, and for this a stochastic or occasionally Wilder's RSI can be used, though any bound oscillator is in principle viable.
2. The second, more important, reason is to gauge the extent to which an S/R curve is likely to hold price. For this On Balance Volume and the EW Oscillator can be used, though Market Profile can also be applied, as we saw in the previous section. Both indicators are used because sometimes one indicator doesn't diverge while the other does.[27] On Balance Volume works well as an intraday indicator as well as on higher timeframes.[28] Aside from unbounded momentum oscillators such as the EW Oscillator, other trend-strength determining indicators can also be used such as Wilder's Directional Movement or the Fractal Dimension Index discussed in Chapter 1.

To get this section underway, Figure 3.41 is a 5m chart of the Australian dollar June 2010 futures. For the moment, it contains no indicators because we first need to highlight what we'll be analyzing with the indicators. Points A, B, C, and D are

FIGURE 3.41   5m chart of Australian dollar June 2010 futures highlighting pullbacks to, and breaks of, various MIDAS S/R curves.

Source: eSignal and Metastock. www.esignal.com and www.equis.com.

pullbacks to the various MIDAS curves. Points (1), (2) and (3) inside the boxes are areas where curves that have been actively resisting or supporting price have suddenly been broken.

First Use: Timing Pullbacks with the Stochastic

As indicated, areas A, B, C, and D are pullbacks to the various curves. At the lowest area of the pullback, ideally when we're getting one of our Japanese candlesticks reversal patterns on the curve, we want to see the stochastic oversold or perhaps coming out of oversold. Figure 3.42 illustrates this combination. The stochastic is preferred over Wilder's RSI because the latter is a slower indicator than the stochastic, and it isn't always oversold or overbought during pullbacks. This use of the indicators is less important than the second one, which I'll come to next.

Second Use: Anticipating Breaks of the MIDAS S/R Curves by Price

The second use of the indicators is more important than the first one. As indicated, the primary employment of the OBV and EW Oscillator (EWO) is to monitor divergences from the trend, with the expectation that divergences will result in the break of S/R curves.

Figure 3.43 is the same chart, this time with the EW Oscillator displayed in the top pane and OBV in the middle pane. Points W to Z on the indicator panes precede

FIGURE 3.42   Ideal overbought/oversold stochastic locations at the precise time of the pullback.

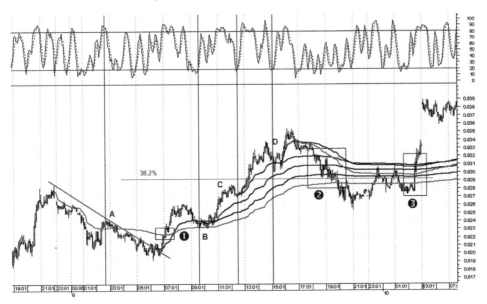

Source: eSignal and Metastock. www.esignal.com and www.equis.com.

FIGURE 3.43   The Elliott Wave Oscillator is in the top pane, and OBV is in the middle pane. Divergences precede breaks of the S/R curves, but we still wait until price confirms these breaks.

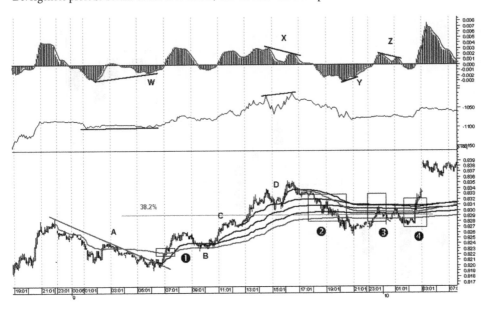

Source: eSignal and Metastock. www.esignal.com and www.equis.com.

points (1) to (4) on the main chart because significant divergences are anticipating price breaking the S/R curves. At W there's a large positive divergence on the EWO, and OBV also diverges moderately. A divergence of this magnitude (over two hours) is a powerful sign that the subsequent move will be large. This is confirmed too by the breaking of a down trendline of five hours duration. At point X only the EWO diverges while OBV actually produces a higher high. No further divergence occurs either in OBV at points Y and Z. It may seem that OBV is inferior to the EWO in exhibiting the signals we're seeking, but there are times when OBV produces a signal and the EWO doesn't.

As for trading breaks of the S/R curves, this topic was covered in Figures 3.11 and 3.16 and the surrounding discussion so I only touch upon the issues again here. In general, when price approaches an S/R curve, no action is taken until price confirms its direction. If price reverses, it does so by creating a classic Japanese candlestick reversal pattern. A stop is then placed on the high/low of the reversal candlestick and the trade is triggered on a break of its low/high respectively. Figure 3.44 is another high resolution example. Price pulls back to a recently launched support curve, and a white harami candlestick forms on the curve. A stop is placed on its low (or in this case the low of the black candlestick) and the trade is triggered when price breaks above the high of the harami.

FIGURE 3.44   A harami candlestick pulls back to a recently launched support curve. A stop is placed on its low, and the trade is entered on a break of its high.

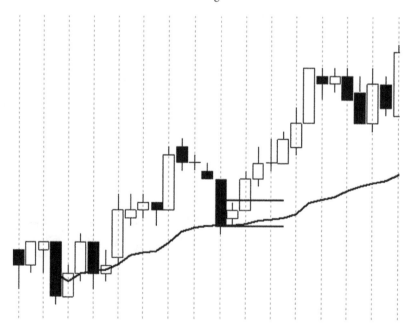

Source: eSignal and Metastock. www.esignal.com and www.equis.com.

FIGURE 3.45 When price breaks the resistance curve, it creates three trade-management scenarios, with the third giving rise to the most conservative trade-management response.

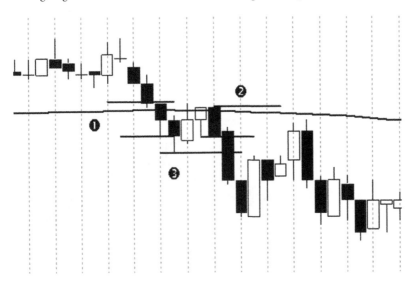

Source: eSignal and Metastock. www.esignal.com and www.equis.com.

If price doesn't create a reversal candlestick on the curve, it is likely to break through in three possible scenarios. Each one has different trade-management implications and they're covered in Figure 3.45.

In the first scenario in Figure 3.45 (labeled (1)), the trade is triggered when the next candlestick breaks the low of the candlestick that penetrated the MIDAS support curve. A stop is then placed on the high of that penetrating candlestick.

In the second scenario (labeled (2)), price breaks down through the resistance curve but then pulls back to it, whereupon it prints a reversal candlestick. The trade is triggered when the next candlestick breaks the low of this reversal candlestick and a stop is placed on its high.

In the third scenario (labeled (3)), instead of the trade being triggered on the break of the reversal candlestick's low, the trade is entered when price breaks the low of the candlestick immediately above (3). In effect, price is testing the previous low rather than the low of the reversal candlestick and this is where the trade is entered. Taking action on this third scenario is the most conservative trade-management approach of the three.

MIDAS S/R Curves on Conventional Trend Lines

I use conventional trendlines with MIDAS S/R curves for two reasons: first, to judge the likelihood of a curve holding price, and thus to supplement the role of centered oscillators such as the EW Oscillator discussed in the previous section; and second, to offer early exits from trades when curves that have produced entry signals have now displaced. Figure 3.46 is a 5m chart of the Canadian dollar June 2010 futures in a solid six-hour uptrend and illustrating both of these roles for conventional trend lines.

FIGURE 3.46 5m chart of the Canadian dollar June 2010 futures showing MIDAS support curves and conventional trend lines. The role of conventional trend lines is both to confirm divergence readings from unbounded oscillators as well as to offer early exit opportunities prior to price reaching displacing MIDAS curves.

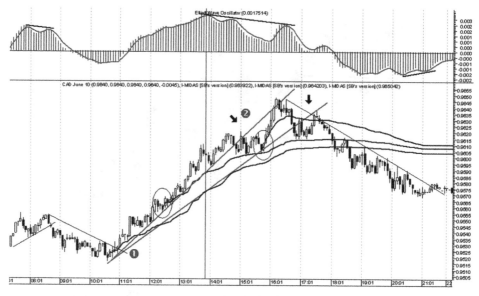

Source: eSignal and Metastock. www.esignal.com and www.equis.com.

When price is rallying in such a solid trend, then regardless of how a long trade was initiated, the aim would be to stay in it for as long as possible. The first MIDAS support curve that was launched from the start of the trend displaces quickly, and a second is launched to keep up with the trend at the first ringed area. This one too quickly displaces but catches the bottom of the pullback at the second ringed area. From here it displaces more heavily and a third curve is launched. It too has displaced slightly by the top of the trend.

The divergence of the EW Oscillator at the vertical line strongly indicates that all three curves will be broken. The role of the trendlines is thus to provide an early confirmation of the oscillator divergence before price does actually break the curves. One such break after the divergence comes at the first arrow. We don't know whether the second MIDAS support curve will support price, but we can exit the trade in anticipation of the test. If the curve holds on a reversal candlestick we can always re-enter, bearing in mind that the trendline will now probably act as resistance. As it happens, price is held by the curve and it rallies again. By this stage, a larger negative divergence has formed on the EWO and price breaks the last of the support curves launched. Soon afterwards it breaks the conventional trendline labeled (1) from the start of the trend. Again the breaking of the second conventional trendline by price gets us out of the trade (had we re-entered) earlier than the displaced curves. Price actually bounces off the two displaced curves to create a lower high, but this is now part of the new downtrend as the second uptrend line becomes resistance, as indeed the first trend line did after point (2).

Thus, the role of conventional trend lines is to confirm divergence readings from unbound oscillators such as the EWO as well as to act as an early mechanism to exit the trade. If price breaks a conventional trend line but reverses on a lower displacing MIDAS curve, a new long trade can still be initiated, albeit with greater associated risk once momentum divergences are in place.

Capturing Today's High and Low with Standard MIDAS S/R Curves

Capturing the high and low of the day using standard MIDAS S/R curves is relatively easy provided a trader understands the displacement phenomenon, as this was outlined in the first half of the chapter in relation to trend sizes and chart timeframes. By definition, the high and low of the day create its widest range, so it stands to reason that they'll only be captured when launching curves from pivots of a similar magnitude; more often than not, these are previous days' highs and lows. Only such pivots ensure that the curves will displace sufficiently to capture subsequent ones of comparable size. If we go back to Table 3.1 where trend sizes and chart timeframes are catalogued, we'll see that the 60m chart produces one to two key signals a day. This is the magnitude we're looking for. This chart timeframe is associated with the short-term trend that normally lasts two to four weeks. The 15m chart, associated with trends of two to several days, is also a candidate timeframe for launching the curves.

Figure 3.47 is a 60m chart of the German Bund December 2010 futures spanning 20 days. The bolded band in the middle is a standard MIDAS support curve, while the two bands above and below it constitute an indicator I call the MIDAS Displacement

FIGURE 3.47 60m chart of German Bund December 2010 futures spanning 20 trading days.

Source: eSignal and Metastock. www.esignal.com and www.equis.com.

Channel, which is the subject of Chapter 14. I'm introducing the indicator here not to explain it but to illustrate the role played in capturing the day's highs and lows by the correct curve launched from the relevant starting pivot on the appropriate chart timeframe.

First, if the reader follows the trajectory of the standard MIDAS curve (bolded), he'll notice that this curve acts as support for the day's low on four occasions over the next 20 days. Next, if he examines the curve fitted to the day's high at point (1) and follows this line, he'll see that it supported the day's low on five occasions while resisting the day's high on two occasions. Chapter 14 will explain in detail how these additional curves are formed. Next, if the reader follows the curve generated from point (2), he'll see that the curve resisted the day's high on seven occasions. Finally, if he follows the plot of the curve generated from point (3), he'll see that it supported the day's low on three subsequent occasions. In all, the combination of these curves either supported the day's low or resisted the day's high on 21 occasions over these 20 trading days. The short-term trend on the 60m chart is important therefore in capturing these swing highs and lows (with the 15m chart as a shorter-term alternative), and it is far better to use the MIDAS Displacement Channel for this task than a solo standard MIDAS S/R curve.

Summary

- The fractal nature of the MIDAS system means that it is capable of being turned into a robust standalone day trading system, provided it is combined with a charting style such as Japanese candlesticks that can generate consistent trade-management principles.
- The development of a straightforward standalone system of the type outlined in this chapter must be a careful product of desired trend length, displacement size, and chart timeframe. All three dictate to the size of moves off the MIDAS S/R curves and associated stop-loss ranges. Table 3.1 summarizes these relationships.
- In addition, the chart timeframe determines fairly precisely the number of trading signals that can be expected each day. Ultimately all of these factors are subordinate to money-management considerations, which in turn impact trade-management strategies.
- The latter should be the first criterion a trader should apply when thinking about a preferred timeframe in relation to his choice of markets, since simple strategies such as the 1 percent rule are directly related to average stop-loss ranges when combining Japanese candlesticks with MIDAS S/R curves.
- Displacement is a critical phenomenon when day trading with MIDAS for a variety of reasons:
  - It determines the number of trades per day in relation to the timeframe chosen.
  - It determines the size of the resulting move when price reacts to a MIDAS S/R curve.
  - When using multiple timeframes simultaneously, it allows us easily to sort larger segments of the trend into smaller ones.

- For these reasons, a day trader is provided with a comprehensive fractal market analysis at all degrees of trend, provided he understands the critical relationship between trend size, chart timeframe, and displacement.
- MIDAS is not merely a standalone system, it works well with—and often complements—other approaches.
  - *Elliott Wave:* It is particularly effective with Elliott Wave theory insofar as the latter is already a detailed fractal system with wave fractal labeling techniques also already in place.
  - *Fibonacci retracements:* Even the largest displaced MIDAS curves seldom, if ever, displace more than 38.2 percent, while smaller displaced curves typically displace to around the 23.6 percent level.
  - *Moving averages:* There is an excellent synergy between moving averages and MIDAS S/R curves, especially in the bolstering role of the S/R curves in pullbacks to the moving averages. However, moving averages on a chosen chart timeframe won't provide much information as to the likely size of the move off them. This is not the case with MIDAS curves. For example, if price reverses off a 20-period moving average on a 5m chart at the same time as reversing off a displaced MIDAS curve associated with the one- to two-day trend (15m), the latter will provide reasonably accurate information as regards the size of the expected move, both in price and time. This level of information cannot be gleaned from the moving averages alone.
  - *Pivot Point techniques:* There is another good working relationship between the two systems, with MIDAS S/R curves again supplying a bolstering role to pivot levels and providing additional information as to the expected size of moves off pivots in relation to the size of the displacement of the S/R curves in question. This role parallels the one in relation to moving averages.
  - *Market Profile:* The role here is very much a complementary one, with MIDAS S/R curves creating a superior trade-timing and trade-management system, and Market Profile providing important background information on the strength of the trend in relation to the S/R curves price is approaching.
  - *Momentum and volume indicators:* Again there is a very good synergy between MIDAS S/R curves, with overbought and oversold conditions on bounded oscillators verifying candlestick reversals on the curves, and unbounded MACD-style oscillators or trend-strength determining tools such as the Fractal Dimension Index providing critical information on the strength of the trend when price has reversed and is approaching MIDAS S/R curves.
  - *Conventional trend lines:* A useful synergy is provided in timing exits from MIDAS-generated trades, especially when trends accelerate away from the displaced curves and a tighter exit signal is immediately required.
- The day's high and low can be captured frequently using MIDAS, especially when applying the MIDAS Displacement Channel, provided the trader uses the 60m (or possibly 15m) chart timeframe and understands that the trend in question is usually the short-term trend.

PART II

The MIDAS Topfinder/Bottomfinder

CHAPTER 4

The MIDAS Topfinder/Bottomfinder on Intraday Charts

Andrew Coles

Little has been said so far in this book about the other major MIDAS indicator, the topfinder/bottomfinder, which for short we refer to as the TB-F indicator. The reason is that this indicator has a far more restricted application than the standard MIDAS S/R curves, and its use also requires more skill in application in addition to an appreciation of what defines a certain type of trend known as an "accelerated trend." Over the next two chapters we look in detail at TB-F curves, beginning with this contribution, which leads the discussion because it contains the necessary step-by-step procedure for launching the curves. Unlike Hawkins, who looks as usual at longer-term charts, the chart illustrations here will be intraday, confirming that like standard MIDAS S/R curves there's no obstacle to applying TB-F curves to other chart timeframes.

An important focus of this chapter is on the practical implementation of TB-F curves, since one of the major weaknesses in Paul Levine's work is that there's no discussion of how the forecasting side of the curves should be incorporated alongside trade-management considerations. This is even more problematic in the case of TB-F curves because of their complexity.

The chapter is in two parts. The first discusses the theoretical aspect of the curves while the second covers factors in their correct application, including tips for accuracy and suggestions for running TB-F curves alongside other trend-exhaustion indicators. The content of this second part of the chapter applies to all timeframes, even though the examples are intraday.

Levine's Two Insights Governing the MIDAS Methodology

Paul Levine believed that the MIDAS approach is governed by two major insights. The first is that the structure of the markets is a hierarchy of support and resistance levels, with each subject to a MIDAS curve launched from a trend reversal point marking a change in market psychology. This idea was discussed in Chapter 1 and it has since been illustrated in the previous two chapters.

The second insight is that there often exists in the markets an underlying structure that dominates, or in Levine's term, "guides" the bull or bear move as it develops from its starting point. This structure is characteristic of a certain type of trend known as an "accelerated trend."

The characteristics of an accelerated trend will be discussed shortly. But it is helpful to understand it simply in terms of the displacement phenomenon discussed in the previous chapter. There were many charts illustrated where price would suddenly accelerate away from a MIDAS S/R curve that had hitherto been supporting it. At the time the recommended strategy was to launch a newer curve with less displacement. However, in circumstances where a trend is accelerating too rapidly, newly launched S/R curves also keep displacing as soon as they're launched. These circumstances are normally ideal for the launch of a TB-F curve.

Part One: The Quantitative Features of the TB-F Algorithm

Paul Levine referred to the quantitative laws that give rise to the standard S/R curves and TB-F curves as the "scientific" component of MIDAS. He called the "engineering" aspect the practical trading rules and techniques based upon the system. In the first part of this chapter I start with the quantitative laws governing the indicator. There is more on this topic in the opening pages of Hawkins' next chapter and Appendix A. Appendix C contains Bob English's TradeStation code for the TB-F.

The TB-F Algorithm in Relation to the Original MIDAS Formula

As discussed in Chapter 1, the basic equation for the MIDAS S/R curves is as follows:

$$\text{MIDAS} = [y(x_i) - y(x_i - d_{ij})]/d_{ij}$$

where

   x_i = cumulative volume on a given bar
   y_i = cumulative average price ((H+L) * 0.5) * volume on bar
   d_{ij} = cumulative volume difference between bars i and j = $x_i - x_j$

In plain English, this equation reads: (cumulative average price)(volume at a given instant) − (cumulative average price)(volume at a period d units of cumulative volume earlier), all divided by d, where d is the cumulative volume displacement measured from the launch point to the given instant.

Here now is the equation for the TB-F indicator:

$$\text{Topfinder/Bottomfinder} = [y(x_i) - y(x_i - e_{ij})]/e_{ij}$$
$$e = d_{ij} * (1 - d_{ij}/D)$$

where again:

x_i = cumulative volume on bar
y_i = cumulative average price ((H+L) $*$ 0.5) $*$ volume on bar
d_{ij} = cumulative volume difference between bars i and j = $x_i - x_j$

It should be pointed out that in the programming of the TB-F algorithm we use the low price when plotting a TB-F support curve and the high price when plotting a TB-F resistance curve. Levine himself used a catch-all average price calculation, but we've found that the former method results in a more accurate curve. This issue is discussed further by Hawkins in Appendix A.

The Critical Role of D in the TB-F Formula

The primary difference between these two equations is the replacement of d with e, where the displacement e is related to the displacement d parabolically through the equation $e = d * (1 - d/\text{D})$. The parabolic aspect of the equation will be explained in a moment. First, let's examine the D component.

D is a critical parameter in e that Levine called the "duration" of the accelerated trend. Sometimes he spoke metaphorically of the start of the accelerated trend as the "launch point" of the move and D as a preprogrammed amount of "fuel," which, in this case, is a fixed amount of cumulative volume. As the accelerated trend develops and its trajectory is followed by the TB-F curve, the fixed amount of cumulative volume in D gradually decreases (or "burns out," to continue the metaphor) as a result of combining D with the parabolic aspect of the TB-F equation. When the fixed amount of cumulative volume in D runs to zero, the TB-F comes to a literal standstill on the chart, thus indicating a point where the trend too is expected to change its cumulative volume signature. This is most obviously manifested in the accelerated trend ending. However, the trend's termination does not mean that the trend will now reverse, since the depletion of the cumulative volume is consistent too with the market entering a resting phase. This resting phase could be for a bar or two, or it could be for a multitude of bars. All the expiration of D means is that some response in the market should be expected. Indeed, whether the trend will enter a resting phase or reverse, the first thing to look for is price moving back to the last most previously active MIDAS curve; that is to say, the one that price had last accelerated away from when the conditions became clear that the launch of a TB-F curve was justified.

Occasionally, as Levine was happy to note, the trend doesn't burn up all of the cumulative volume predicted by D; as a result, it ends prematurely. Hence D is to be regarded as a potentiality and not as a guaranteed outcome. As we see later in the chapter, when the trend does end prematurely before D, it breaks emphatically through the TB-F curve. Consequently, the TB-F algorithm provides a clear indication of a trend's end even when (occasionally) D is not fully consumed.

The D Component and the Correct Launch Procedure of a TB-F Curve

Our next task is to understand how much cumulative volume is to be inputted to D in relation to the correct method of fitting a TB-F curve to an accelerated trend.

Levine's Necessary Requirement for the Correct Launch of a TB-F Curve

With the understanding that D is a fixed amount of cumulative volume set by the user, the reader may wonder how much cumulative volume is required on each occasion of its use. This question can be answered with the help of Figure 4.1.

At point A, marking the accelerated trend starting point, a standard MIDAS support curve (black) is launched. Notice that point B, the end of the first pullback in the trend, doesn't pull all the way back to the support curve because the trend has accelerated away. According to Levine, this is a necessary condition of the application of a TB-F curve. This is what he had to say in Lecture 12:

> Generally speaking, whenever a bounce accelerates to new highs before pulling back fully to the expected (i.e. newly launched) S/R level, one should launch a TOPFINDER, fitting it (provisionally) to the pull-back point. If the move continues to trend strongly without pullback to the S/R level, continue the TOPFINDER, perhaps iteratively readjusting the fitting point as the move matures towards the expected burnout cumulative volume.

Thus, as Figure 4.1 illustrates, when this necessary condition is satisfied, the MIDAS analyst goes back to the point where the standard MIDAS curve was plotted

FIGURE 4.1 According to Levine, a necessary condition of a launch of a TB-F curve is the failure of price to pullback to a MIDAS curve. Here this is illustrated in the failure of price to pullback to a standard (black) MIDAS support curve.

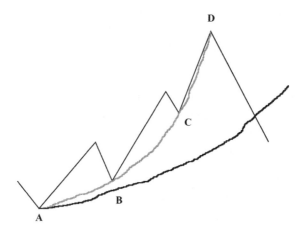

and launches a TB-F curve while fitting it to the first pullback (B) that displaced from the standard MIDAS curve. We leave the original MIDAS curve in place because it's now effectively playing a suspended support role; that is, it's an important near-term price target when the accelerated trend has ended.

This brings us back to a question not answered in the previous two paragraphs, namely how we assess how much cumulative volume—the metaphorical fuel for the move—is required for D. The answer, which we can state in terms of the following condition, is this:

> The amount of cumulative volume required to predict the end of the move is coextensive with the amount required to "fit" the TB-F curve to the first pullback that failed to pull all the way back to the recently launched MIDAS curve.

This is point B in the diagram. As Levine acknowledges, fitting is an iterative process. If too much cumulative volume is inputted, the TB-F curve will underfit the first pullback and plot somewhere near to the standard displaced support curve. If too little is inputted, the TB-F curve will overfit it, meaning that it will plot at an angle somewhere above the price trend and will burn out very quickly, if it hasn't burned out already.

Practically speaking, there are various ways to input D. In the method in StockshareV2 (www.stocksharepublishing.com), for which Hawkins acted as consultant, D is automatically calculated as the user drags the mouse over the pullback. In eSignal and Metastock, we input D manually until a visual fit is obtained between the curve and the pullback. Figure 4.2 illustrates an underfit in the black curve and an overfit in the gray line.

Revised Requirement for the Correct Launch of a TB-F Curve

Readers should be aware of a revised requirement for the launch of a TB-F curve depending crucially on how they input the data into the MIDAS S/R curves and the

FIGURE 4.2   The "fitting" process in D must fit precisely to the low of B in this illustration, otherwise the launch of a TB-F curve is illegitimate.

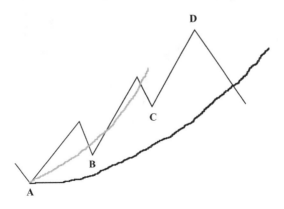

TB-F curves. When using MIDAS, Levine inputted the average price into his standard S/R curves and TB-F curves. This uniformity of data means that Levine's necessary condition for the launch of a TB-F described in the previous section must be adhered to.

However, when it comes to the TB-F curves we've found that the curves are more accurate if the high price is inputted for the bottomfinder and the low price for the topfinder. Hawkins also prefers the same data strategy for the standard S/R curves, with the result that Hawkins must still adhere to Levine's necessary condition described in the previous section due to the uniformity in inputting data.

On the other hand, I still have a preference for the average price in standard S/R curves and so combine the average price with the high and low prices in TB-F curves. In using this combination, what I've consistently found is that Levine's necessary condition can be downgraded to a sufficient condition. I've actually found two reasons for this. The first is that many instances have been encountered where price does pull all the way back to the standard curve and yet the trend is still amenable to a TB-F application. The second is that if Levine's requirement is followed to the letter it can occasionally lead to unsatisfactory results. Let's illustrate both of these points, starting with the first.

Figure 4.3 is a 5m chart of the DAX September 2010 futures with a 30 point downtrend. A standard MIDAS resistance curve (dotted) is launched from the start below the black arrow. It eventually displaces from price in the rectangle, which is just below the second horizontal arrow. According to Levine's recommendation, the TB-F curve should now be launched at a bar proximate to the horizontal

FIGURE 4.3   5m chart of DAX September 2010 futures with a bottomfinder curve launched from the start of the downtrend.

Source: eSignal and Metastock. www.esignal.com and www.equis.com.

arrow. Unfortunately, this is very late into the trend. Moreover, we still get very good results by launching the TB-F from the start of the downtrend despite the lack of the displacement from the standard MIDAS resistance curve plotted with the average price.

Figure 4.4 is the same timeframe chart of the same DAX futures on another trading day and illustrates the same point, this time with a large intraday uptrend of 57 points. First, notice that the standard MIDAS support curve (dotted) doesn't displace until the rectangular area about instead 50 to 60 percent into the move. This means that, according to Levine, a TB-F curve should be launched from the pullback highlighted by the black arrow. The problem is that the only viable pullback for fitting is the one circled right at the top; by then, of course, the move is over. Moreover, despite the fact that the standard support curve doesn't displace until instead 50 to 60 percent into the move, a TB-F curve is launched successfully from the start of the move.

Earlier I mentioned a second reason why Levine's necessary condition should be downgraded to a sufficient condition, namely that if his requirement is followed to the letter it can occasionally lead to unsatisfactory results. Figure 4.5 is the same DAX futures on the same timeframe containing an example of the problem. First, notice that the standard support curve (dotted) displaces at the pullbacks highlighted by the two black arrows. This is again late into the move at around 43 percent. According to Levine, a TB-F curve should now be launched from the pullback prior to this displacement at the gray arrow. The topfinder launched from this pullback is fitted to the two pullbacks from which the standard MIDAS support curve displaced and it does a good job of capturing the remainder of the move. The problem is that this

FIGURE 4.4   The same 5m chart of DAX futures with an uptrend. The standard support curve doesn't displace until 40 percent into the move.

Source: eSignal and Metastock. www.esignal.com and www.equis.com.

FIGURE 4.5   The same 5m chart of DAX September 2010 futures illustrating how following the
letter of Levine's recommendation can often lead to misleading (if still accurate) readings from the TB-F.

Source: eSignal and Metastock. www.esignal.com and www.equis.com.

move is actually a subtrend of the main move. Moreover, the only way of capturing
this main move is to launch the topfinder from the very start of it while fitting it to
the earliest pullbacks that literally come a few points into the move and that haven't
started to displace from the standard curve. Thus, while Figure 4.5 illustrates that
several TB-Fs can be fitted to different subcomponents of the same trend, it primarily
reveals another reason for downgrading Levine's condition to a sufficient one when
combining average prices in standard S/R curves with high/low prices in TB-F curves.

However, if Levine's condition should be downgraded to a sufficient condition
in certain combinations of inputting data, it raises the question of whether there are
alternative criteria a trader should be looking for. I return to this issue in the second part
of this chapter after completing the current phase of the discussion. In the meantime,
one important implication of downgrading Levine's requirement is that there are now
many more chart applications for the TB-F. This is good news for this truly innovative
indicator.

The Relation of D to e in the TB-F Algorithm

Granted that pullbacks still play a critical role in inputting the correct amount of
cumulative volume in D, how is the fitting of the TB-F indicator to a pullback to
be understood mathematically? Readers not interested in this theoretical question can
skip the next two sections and move straight to practical implementations of the
curves. However, for interested traders the answer lies in the relation of D to d in the

e part of the new TB-F formula. Bear in mind that as the move progresses from A to B to C to D the amount of cumulative volume is increasing. This is *d*, the cumulative volume displacement in the standard MIDAS and TB-F curves from the launch point to wherever it is the curve is currently plotting. So if for illustration *d* at point B equals a cumulative volume of 350,000 units, and B represents a third of the entire move, the finite amount of cumulative volume for the entire move; that is, D, is 1,050,000 units. This is the "fuel" required to push the entire move all of the way from point A to its end at point D before the TB-F curve burns out on the chart.

Thus, whereas the standard MIDAS S/R curves represent an average price taken over successively longer intervals as the cumulative volume keeps increasing, the TB-F curve represents an average price taken over successively shorter intervals after the midpoint of the trend as the allotted amount of cumulative volume in D is used up. Levine describes this in terms of the launch point of the TB-F algorithm moving forward in time towards the present, finally catching up when the D units of finite cumulative volume have built up subsequent to its launch.

Illustrating the Parabolic Nature of *e*

Finally, let's turn our attention to the parabolic nature of *e*, the mathematical aspect that gives the TB-F indicator much of its unique properties. This time, instead of looking at an accelerated trend, let's consider one in a tabular format so as to reveal the critical parabolic displacement in the TB-F algorithm. The details are set out in Figure 4.6.

Assume that at point A, the very start of the trend, the cumulative volume is 8 units and that at B, the first pullback, it is 15 units. Therefore at B, $d = 15 - 8 = 7$. Now at B we have assumed that the move is one-third through to completion. Therefore, we fit the TB-F at a cumulative volume of 21 units. Now for the sake of this example, let's assume that from B to the end of the move to D, there are exactly 14 closing prices. Thus, at 14 closes between B and D we have 14 discrete points where we can take a cumulative volume and cumulative price reading. Let's tabulate this, with point B highlighted in gray and the actual start of the move being B-7. To keep things simple, let's also assume that each of these 21 closes (i.e., including the 7 before B) increases the cumulative volume by one unit. Thus, *d* will increase accordingly as on the left hand side, while the corresponding values for *e* are on the righthand side.

In Zone I, which identifies the trend in Figure 4.1 from the launch point A to the first third of the move at B, *e* and *d* are fairly close to each other, with the result that the TB-F curve is not moving that far away from the MIDAS curve. However, bear in mind that it is the failure of price to pull back to the MIDAS curve that justifies the launch of a TB-F curve, since a shorter displacement than *d* is required to "fit" to the price pullback at point B. In Zone II we see that the TB-F curve displacement continues to increase until the halfway point at around B + 4. At this point, price is finding support on the TB-F curve at half of D. In the example in Figure 4.1, D was 1,050,000 units, so price would be hypothetically finding support at around 525,000 units. In Zone III the displacement is now decreasing rapidly. In fact, towards the very

FIGURE 4.6 Tabulated illustration of the critical parabolic nature of the displacement in D of $e = d * (1 - d/D)$ in the TB-F algorithm.

Value for d		Value for e,d *(1 – d/D)	
B – 7 = 0	starting point of trend, A	0*(1 – 0/21) = 0	
B – 6 = +1		1*(1 – 1/21) = 0.9524	
B – 5 = +2		2*(1 – 2/21) = 1.8096	
B – 4 = 3		3*(1 – 3/21) = 2.5716	Zone I
B – 3 = 4		4*(1 – 4/21) = 3.2384	
B – 2 = 5		5*(1 – 5/21) = 3.81	
B – 1 = 6		6*(1 – 6/21) = 4.2858	
B = 7	the first pullback, B	7*(1 – 7/21) = 4.67	
B + 1 = 8		8*(1 – 8/21) = 4.9528	
B + 2 = 9		9*(1 – 9/21) = 5.1426	
B + 3 = 10		10*(1 – 10/21) = 5.239	Zone II
B + 4 = 11		11*(1 – 11/21) = 5.238	
B + 5 = 12		12*(1 – 12/21) = 5.1432	
B + 6 = 13		13*(1 – 13/21) = 4.953	
B + 7 = 14		14*(1 – 14/21) = 4.67	
B + 8 = 15		15*(1 – 15/21) = 4.287	
B + 9 = 16		16*(1 – 16/21) = 3.8096	
B + 10 = 17		17*(1 – 17/21) = 3.2385	
B + 11 = 18		18*(1 – 18/21) = 2.5722	Zone III
B + 12 = 19		19*(1 – 19/21) = 1.8107	
B + 13 = 20		20*(1 – 20/21) = 0.954	
B + 14 = 21	end of trend, D	21*(1 – 21/21) = 0	

end of Zone III, for every new unit traded, the averaging interval shortens virtually by one.

A Theoretical Understanding of an Accelerated Price Trend in Relation to the TB-F Algorithm

It was this dramatic feature of Zone III that, Levine believed, provided the best clue as to what might be going on in accelerated trend.

In short, what Levine concluded can be described in the following terms. Market trends begin when supply is in very little demand. This is the very earliest stage in the accumulation phase when those with the best market intelligence start entering the market. This is Zone I, where we see a rapidly increasing displacement in the TB-F algorithm. The next phase (Zone II) is the active trading phase, the strong trend-following portion of the trend dynamic that Elliott Wave analysts would label a Wave Three. This is where 70 percent-plus of all trading volume takes place. Finally, we have the distribution phase—Zone III—where the number of offers falls off radically and there is a vastly reduced liquidity. Here those with the best market intelligence start selling to unusually late newcomers to the end of the trend. Eventually few buyers are found, and Zone III quickly turns into the start of a new downtrend as the displacement in D has diminished to zero. What we actually see midway through Zone II, however, is that the distribution phase, marked by the start of the diminishing displacement in *e*, begins a lot earlier than most traders have hitherto been aware.

While Levine's account does indeed provide a fascinating backdrop to the displacement phenomenon in *e*, I believe it doesn't go far enough in capturing the remarkable hidden order that exists in accelerated trends. What hasn't received enough emphasis is this: We've already seen that the fixed amount of cumulative volume (the "fuel" for the move) in D is arrived at by "fitting" the TB-F curve to the first appropriate pullback. This means that in cumulative volume terms there's an essential (but entirely hidden) relationship between the displacement in the early part of a trend and the amount of cumulative volume used up over the trend's entire move. If there were not this essential relationship, the TB-F algorithm would have no potency whatsoever in indicating the end of any trend in cumulative volume terms.

Let's probe this point a little further. We know that the period between the start of the move and the first pullback is the accumulation phase of the trend. In fact, the tabulated illustration in Figure 4.6 reveals that the displacement keeps on increasing until halfway through Zone II, which would be the middle of a third wave in Elliott Wave terms. Thus, if we can predict the end of an entire trend in cumulative volume terms from data derived from the accumulation phase of the trend, this means that there must be a much tighter symmetrical relationship between the accumulation phase and the distribution phase than has hitherto been recognized.

This probably means that the deeper the pullback is into the trend, the more accurate D will be, because most of the cumulative volume data from the accumulation phase will be available by that time. Thus, it isn't merely that the displacement phenomenon in D captures so precisely the accumulation/trading-zone/distribution phases of each accelerated trend. Levine is surely correct about this. Rather, the displacement phenomenon in D also shows the remarkable mirror-image symmetry that must exist between the accumulation and distribution phases if the TB-F algorithm is to have any forecasting potency.

Part Two: The Engineering Aspect of TB-F Curves

Now that we've understood the quantitative properties underlying the TB-F algorithm, it's time in the second part of this chapter to look at its application. Hawkins does this extensively on longer-term charts in Chapter 5, so here I want to do two things: first, to offer a number of tips on getting accurate forecasting measurements out of the TB-F algorithm; and second, to integrate its use experimentally with other trend-exhaustion tools.

An Alternative Consideration in the Launching of TB-F Curves

In the first part of this chapter, I discussed Levine's view that it's a necessary condition for the launching of a TB-F curve that price doesn't pull all the way back to a previously launched standard MIDAS S/R curve. This necessary condition was downgraded to a sufficient condition on the basis that a TB-F curve can plot very successfully even when price does pull back all the way to the standard S/R curve.[1] Moreover, there are times when following Levine's necessary condition can lead to undesired consequences, such as TB-F curves measuring smaller subcomponents of trends when they have to be launched later. However, if Levine's condition can be downgraded to a sufficient one, it raises the question of what the most basic criterion is when a trader wishes to launch a TB-F curve.

My own requirement is disarmingly simple, namely that a market must be trending up or down at a minimum of 45 degrees and preferably between 65 and 75 degrees.[2] Thus, I look for the appropriate angle of acceleration rather than a displacement of a pullback from a standard MIDAS S/R curve. As emphasized earlier, the weakening of Levine's original criterion is good news for MIDAS users, since it means that TB-F curves can be applied more frequently to charts. Figure 4.7 illustrates an ideal angle of acceleration with the help of a Gann fan. We'll also see another ideal angle in Figure 4.9.

Identifying the Correct Pullback against Which to Fit D

As emphasized previously, despite the relaxing of Levine's requirement, we still have to fit TB-F curves to pullbacks in order to obtain cumulative volume readings for D.

FIGURE 4.7   60m Eurex Bund September 2010 futures.

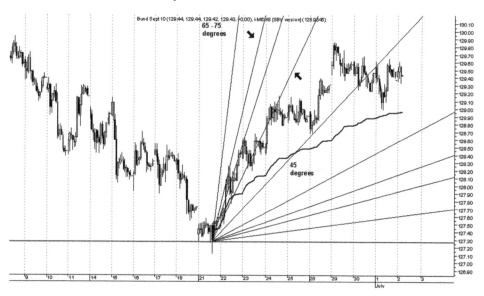

Source: eSignal and Metastock. www.esignal.com and www.equis.com.

From Figure 4.1 it may seem that fitting a TB-F curve to a pullback is a straightforward process. All a trader needs to do, it seems, is to identify a pullback on the trend and fit the curve to it. But this is consistent with very inaccurate readings if the user doesn't know to which pullback he should be fitting the indicator, since there will be many candidate pullbacks as the trend develops. Which is the correct pullback to choose? We can obtain wildly inaccurate results if we don't make the correct choice of pullback.

Figure 4.8 is a 60m chart of the Eurex Bund September 2010 futures showing an accelerated uptrend over seven trading days (June 21 to June 29). A standard MIDAS support curve (gray) is launched from the start of the trend and quickly displaces, ending up at the Fibonacci 38.2 percent level. Given the rapid displacement, we're justified in launching a topfinder curve from the start of the trend, and the most obvious apparent pullback to fit it is P. However, when the topfinder is fitted to P with $D = 8,000,000$ contracts, it predicts a remaining cumulative volume of 1,792,777 and a prediction that there's still another 22.4 percent of this cumulative volume to burn before the trend ends. The problem is that the trend has already ended at the point marked "end of trend." Things have gone seriously wrong here. Why has such an extremely inaccurate reading been produced?

What has happened is that the topfinder has been fitted to too large a pullback in price and time as a result of our hypothetical trader not fully understanding what defines an accelerated trend. Consequently, the amount of cumulative volume required in D to fit the topfinder curve to the very bottom of this large pullback at P means that it is attempting to measure a much larger portion of this trend that isn't actually accelerating (and doesn't even exist). Experience from our web site shows that visitors have expressed considerable confusion over the issue of correctly fitting TB-F curves. It's important therefore to clarify this procedure in order to secure accurate readings. The crux of the matter is defining precisely what is meant by an accelerated trend.

An accelerated trend will be marked by two features (plus an interesting mathematical aspect) that are easy to identify over and above the fact that a standard MIDAS S/R curve has displaced from it.

The Appropriate Angle of Acceleration

First, and most obviously, an accelerated trend will be moving up or down the chart at an angle of at least 45 degrees and usually more acutely (typically between 65 and 75 degrees or higher). This was discussed above in relation to a relaxing of Levine's requirement concerning displacement and it was illustrated in Figure 4.7 with a simple Gann fan. In a moment we also see Figure 4.9 where each Elliott wave at the nth degree is also moving up the chart at a similar angle.

The Absence of a Disproportionate Pullback in Price and Time

An accelerated trend won't possess a noticeably large pullback in price and time, or it can't any longer be regarded as an accelerated trend. Instead, we have to regard the moves on either side of this larger pullback as accelerated. A TB-F curve should ideally

FIGURE 4.8   60m chart of Eurex Bund September 2010 futures with a wildly incorrect cumulative volume reading as a result of fitting the topfinder to an incorrect pullback.

Source: eSignal. www.esignal.com.

FIGURE 4.9   15m chart of Euro FX September 2010 futures with an Elliott five wave impulse with waves of *n*th and *n* – 1th degree.

Source: eSignal and Metastock. www.esignal.com and www.equis.com.

be fitted to a pullback of the $n - 1$th degree in relation to the nth level pivot from which it is launched, unless the nth degree pullback is very small. This may sound abstract, but it is easily illustrated in Figure 4.9 with Elliott Waves that are ideal for highlighting trend sizes and pullbacks. Figure 4.9 contains a standard Elliott Wave five wave impulse, with waves at the nth degree in larger circled numbers and waves at the $n - 1$th degree in smaller noncircled numbers. Notice that the nth-level wave 2 and wave 4 bottoms (highlighted by the arrows) correspond to the same nth degree pullback to which we tried fitting the TB-F in Figure 4.8 when a very inaccurate cumulative volume projection was obtained for the remainder of the trend. By contrast, the ideal pullbacks to which a TB-F curve should be fitted are highlighted by the rectangles.

The Correct Fractal Dimension

As for the mathematical backdrop, Chapter 1 introduced an indicator called the Fractal Dimension Index (FDI) whose function is real-time monitoring of the fractal dimension of a market on any timeframe.[3] Readers will also recall from Chapter 1 Dietmar Saupe's illustration of fractal and nonfractal time series in Figure 1.5. The first two of the five time series are antipersistent (Hurst exponent < 0.5), the third is a random walk (Hurst exponent $= 0.5$), and the last two are persistent (Hurst exponent > 0.5). As the Hurst exponent increases to 0.5 and beyond, the increasing fractal dimension (i.e., 2—the Hurst exponent) becomes more amenable to MIDAS applications, including the TB-F curves when the Hurst exponent is much higher and markets are sharply trending. Figure 4.10 is the same chart as Figure 4.8 but

FIGURE 4.10 Figure 4.8 with the MIDAS curves removed and the FDI in the lower pane indicating antipersistence during the out-of-proportion pullback to which the topfinder is erroneously fitted.

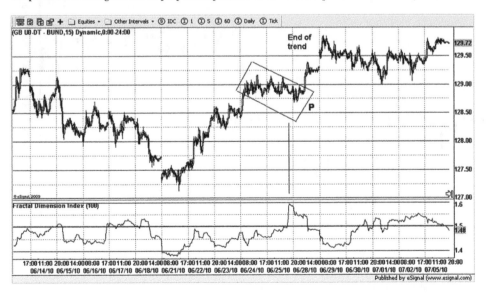

Source: eSignal. www.esignal.com.

with the MIDAS curves removed and the FDI in the lower pane. As the vertical line highlights, the market is not merely random during this oversized pullback but also antipersistent, meaning that price in the pullback is reversing itself more quickly even than in a random price movement. Here the accelerated trend has long ended. What Figure 4.10 is also suggesting is that the market should have a fractal dimension of around 1.4 or lower if a TB-F curve is to function correctly.

With these three observations in mind, let's run the topfinder again, this time in Figure 4.11 on the same euro FX 15m chart with the Elliott wave count removed. Here we're fitting the three topfinders to the correct $n - 1$th degree pullbacks. Notice that all three topfinders behave correctly. Each one is fitted to the first pullback (wave 2 at the n–1th degree in relation to Figure 4.9) and each one terminates precisely at the top of each nth degree wave. Thus, fitting to the $n - 1$th degree pullbacks is always recommended unless the nth level pullbacks are very small.

Elliotticians observe that third waves always have the highest momentum and volume readings and are the most aggressive parts of the trend. Third waves are thus the very best candidates for TB-F curves since they always displace from standard MIDAS S/R curves. They are also usually the longest portions of trends and hence ones where traders will be particularly keen to get an accurate cumulative volume prediction as soon as possible.

In contrast to the correct application in Figure 4.11 and the resulting accuracy in the cumulative volume prediction obtained, take a look briefly at Figure 4.12.

FIGURE 4.11   The same 15m chart of the Euro with the Elliott Wave count removed and the three topfinders fitted to pullbacks at the n–1th degree in relation to Figure 4.9 and terminating precisely at the end of each wave at the nth degree.

Source: eSignal and Metastock. www.esignal.com and www.equis.com.

FIGURE 4.12   When the topfinder is incorrectly fitted to a pullback of the *n*th degree in relation to its launch point, its cumulative volume prediction is wildly incorrect.

Source: eSignal and Metastock. www.esignal.com and www.equis.com.

Figure 4.12 is the same 15m chart of the euro FX futures with the first and third topfinder curve removed and the second one fitted to the *n*th level wave four pullback (see again the wave count in Figure 4.9). Notice that we get the same anomalous reading as in Figure 4.8. On fitting the curve, we learn that the move is only 30 percent done. Indeed, the chart has to be compacted tightly in order to see that the curve actually expired on the chart two trading days later on June 29!

What is actually going on when D has too much cumulative volume is highlighted clearly in Figure 4.13, a 15m chart of the euro FX September 2010 futures. A linear trend line is drawn from the start of the trend at "S" and fixed to the pullback at "P." The trend line is obviously efficacious because it holds price later at the black arrows before the market turns over. A TB-F curve is also launched from "S" and fitted to the same pullback "P." Again "P" is too deep for this topfinder to follow the accelerated portion of the trend up to point "A" and instead it terminates in the circled area at "E." Here the end of the trend marked by the linear trend line and the end of the trend marked by the expiry of D are virtually coextensive. I see this too often on charts for it to be a mere coincidence. A linear trend line projected forward is often therefore a helpful visual yardstick in assessing where roughly a TB-F curve is likely to expire when fitting it to a pullback and thus can help in confirming an accurate input to D. In contrast to the black linear trend line, the accelerated portion of the trend is marked by the gray linear trend line. To get a TB-F expiring here would require a launch from "P" and a much tighter fitting to a pullback such as P*.

Finally, let's return to Figure 4.8, the 60m chart of the Eurex Bund that started our concerns. Figure 4.14 is an update of Figure 4.8, this time with two topfind-

FIGURE 4.13   15m chart of euro FX September 2010 futures with linear trend line analysis and a TB-F fitted to the same pullback at "P."

Source: eSignal and Metastock. www.esignal.com and www.equis.com.

FIGURE 4.14   The same Eurex Bund September 2010 60m chart as Figure 4.8 with two topfinders fitted correctly to pullbacks at the *n*–1th degree and in contrast to the incorrect fitting in Figure 4.8.

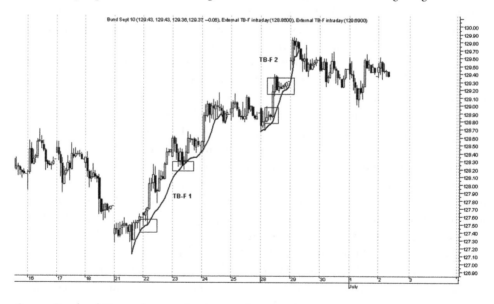

Source: eSignal and Metastock. www.esignal.com and www.equis.com.

ers replacing the incorrectly fitted one. Each topfinder is fitted to pullbacks at the $n - 1$th degree and are measuring the trend components between the nth level pullback to which the pullback in Figure 4.8 was fitted.

Further Ruminations on Fitting D

If we're charting with a very clear price style such as Japanese candlesticks, readers may well wonder about the fine-tuning implications of the fitting of TB-F curves and what in turn the trade-management implications may be. This again is another topic that Paul Levine did not discuss in the level of detail a trader requires. There are in fact two important outcomes a trader should be aware of:

1. A TB-F curve overrunning the trend (= the trend ending before a TB-F terminates)
2. A TB-F curve completing before the end of the trend

Let's look in this section at an example of each of these eventualities and how best to deal with them.

A TB-F Curve Overrunning the Trend

Let's take a look in Figure 4.15 at a 12-hour trend on the British pound September 2010 futures on June 25. A standard MIDAS support curve displaced rapidly from

FIGURE 4.15   15m chart of the British pound September 2010 contract showing a termination of the trend slightly before the expiration of the topfinder.

Source: eSignal and Metastock. www.esignal.com and www.equis.com.

the start of the trend. This was a sufficient condition to launch a TB-F curve (black). It was launched and fitted to the first significant pullback at the $n - 1$th degree. Now the precise fitting was to the very low of the white engulfing candlestick highlighted by the arrow. As a result, the topfinder burned out four candlesticks after the top formed by the white shooting star candlestick (second arrow). If the fitting had been slightly more lax, the topfinder would've taken even longer to burn out. The question, then, is if our fitting isn't a good one, is there a way of getting out of the trade sooner? The answer is yes, provided we're able to use a conventional trend line (gray), as in Figure 4.15, or an alternative such as a linear regression line through price. A break of the trend line (or regression line) sooner than a TB-F curve expires is prima facie evidence that the trend has ended and that a trader should act accordingly. Even if a conventional trend line cannot be fitted to the entirety of the trend (unlike here), it should be possible to fit it to the last component of the trend at the very least.

A TB-F Curve Completing Before the End of the Trend

Figure 4.16 is the same chart as Figure 4.15. This time however while the topfinder (black) is fitted to the same candlestick as before, it is actually fitted to the open of that candlestick rather than to its low. The range between the open and the low is a mere six points, yet the topfinder expires when only 55 percent of the trend is complete. Thus, the resulting variance is exaggerated considerably when only a minor adjustment has

FIGURE 4.16   When the first topfinder expires, a second one is launched just as soon as price breaks above the high of the bar on which the previous topfinder expired. It's then fitted to the first pullback of the n–1th degree as the trend proceeds.

Source: eSignal and Metastock. www.esignal.com and www.equis.com.

been made to the fitting. If a TB-F expires prematurely, how is the scenario to be handled in trade-management terms?

In such a situation I am inclined to do two things:

1. Wait until price breaks above the high of the candlestick on which the topfinder expired. Here in Figure 4.16 we see price doing this on the next candlestick highlighted by the second (horizontal) arrow.
2. Then go back to the last pullback before the first topfinder expired and launch a new topfinder (gray curve) from this candlestick. In Figure 4.16 this point is also highlighted by the same horizontal arrow. This new topfinder is then fitted to the first $n - 1$th degree pullback as the trend resumes. Here this is highlighted in the circle. This second topfinder also runs over the end of the trend by several bars. To counteract this, we can again create a conventional trend line as recommended earlier.

Advice on Fine-Tuning the Fitting of D

To prevent either of these two scenarios occurring, the fine-tuning aspect of the fitting is obviously the most critical aspect of using the TB-F indicator along with the correct choice of pullback, since as highlighted in Figures 4.15 and 4.16 a mere variation of 6 points in the futures can mean a TB-F expiring as early as 55 percent into the trend or predicting as much as 55 percent of the trend still to run when it's about to complete. Either way this is a huge margin to contend with. This is another topic not discussed by Levine and it's not an easy problem to solve. That being said, here are few rules of thumb I personally follow in applying the TB-F (the following applies to uptrends and should be reversed for downtrends):

1. In pullbacks where there's a wide range between the low and the open, as in Figure 4.17, I'll fit the TB-F to a point midway in this range and try and look for small contiguous pullbacks for fine-tuning the fit. The fine-tuning aspect to the smaller pullbacks is especially important when the range is particularly wide.
2. In pullbacks where the range between the low and the open is much narrower, I'll sometimes fit to the low, as in Figure 4.18, but to err on the side of caution I'll still fit the curve to as close to the midpoint as I can. Again I'll also look for small contiguous pullbacks for the fine-tuning.

Forecasting Implications of Working with TB-F Curves

A number of readers of our blog on the MIDAS Market Analysis web site have raised queries concerning the forecasting implications after a TB-F terminates on the chart. My answer has always been that all MIDAS curves, whether TB-Fs or standard S/R curves, are nonlinear trend lines. It is helpful therefore to go back to the discussion in Chapter 3 to understand the forecasting implications. For higher timeframe charts,

FIGURE 4.17   When there's a wide range between the low and the open, the recommendation is to fit a TB-F curve to the midpoint of this range while also looking for small contiguous pullbacks for fine-tuning.

Source: eSignal and Metastock. www.esignal.com and www.equis.com.

FIGURE 4.18   When the range between the low and the open is narrow, I usually fit to the low of the candlestick that defines the low. Again, I look for small contiguous pullbacks as a part of the fine-tuning.

Source: eSignal and Metastock. www.esignal.com and www.equis.com.

Chapter 3 began with conventionally labeled longer-term trend lengths as they're defined in standard technical analysis textbooks:

- Secular-term trend = constructed from a number of primary-term trends and normally lasting between 10 years to as long as 25 years.
- Primary-term trend = nine months to two years, reflecting investors' attitudes to unfolding market fundamentals and closely associated with the three to four year business cycle.
- Intermediate-term trend = roughly six weeks to as long as nine months, though sometimes longer but rarely shorter.
- Short-term trend = two to four weeks, though it can be slightly shorter or slightly longer.

Following this, a new set of data for relationships between chart timeframes and intraday trend lengths was summarized in Chapter 3 in Table 3.1. Here we can distill this table:

- One-/Two-day trend = ideally analyzed on the 15m chart and generating three to four MIDAS signals each day.
- Two- to six-hour trend = ideally analyzed on the 5m chart and producing 5 to 10 MIDAS signals each day.
- 15m- to 60m-trend = ideally analyzed on the 1m chart and creating roughly 12 to 15 MIDAS signals each day.

With this information, let's take a look at two examples of the termination of a TB-F curve and its forecasting implications, the first on a higher timeframe chart and the second on an intraday chart, starting with the higher timeframe example.

Figure 4.19 is a chart I discussed on the site blog on November 16, 2009, warning that the end of the downtrend in the U.S. dollar index was imminent based on the information that two bottomfinders were 96.3 percent done and 97.7 percent done respectively. BF-1 had been launched from April 20, 2009, while BF-2 had been launched from June 15, 2009. If possible, it's always a good idea to launch a second TB-F from another segment of the trend because coextensive signals from different durations (the D component) are more convincing and can also help remove some of the concerns raised earlier regarding mildly inaccurate fittings leading to large variances in the cumulative volume predictions. In Figure 4.19, BF-1 and BF-2 were both measuring the intermediate trend. The implication therefore was for a countermove of between a minimum of six weeks to nine months. This meant that the two proximate displaced resistance curves, R1 and R2, would not be expected to hold price after the acceleration had completed.

Figure 4.20 brings us up to date at the time of this chapter in early July 2010. As we can see, the result has been a six-and-a-half-month uptrend, as marked by the solid gray linear trend line. Three support curves, S1 to S3, have been launched during this uptrend and the three rectangles highlight areas where the price move was

FIGURE 4.19   U.S. dollar index continuous futures with two bottomfinders and two resistance curves, as discussed in a blog on the web site on November 16, 2009.

Source: eSignal. www.esignal.com.

FIGURE 4.20   The same daily chart of U.S. dollar index moved on by several months after the November 2009 bottom.

Source: eSignal and Metastock. www.esignal.com and www.equis.com.

an accelerated displacement ideal for a topfinder. When S3 displaced during the last portion of the uptrend, a topfinder (solid black curve) was launched, and it expired at the top of the trend. This topfinder was again measuring the intermediate trend (eight weeks), so the minimum we could now expect is a proportionate move with S2 and S1 possibly playing an important support role at a 38 percent displacement. As I've updated the chart in the past few days, the six-and-one-half months linear trend line has also now been broken, so we could see an even larger intermediate term countermove, in which case S2 and S1 would not be expected to hold price.

Let's give one more example, this time intraday. Figure 4.21 is a 5m chart of the Canadian dollar September 2010 futures on June 28, 29, and 30. The downtrend starts on June 29 at the break of support at the black arrow. A second MIDAS resistance curve, R2, is launched from the start of this downtrend and it displaces from the pullback at the gray arrow. Accordingly, a bottomfinder is launched from it. The bottomfinder terminates at the very bottom of the trend after being fitted to some minor pullbacks circled. The pullbacks highlighted by the rectangle are deep and so the fractal dimension of the trend begins to decrease. This is a cause of initial concern because we don't want to input too much into D for fear of getting an inaccurate forecast for the bottomfinder. In any case, once the bottomfinder terminates, price then breaks the linear downtrend line. The downtrend is 18 hours in duration—with the actual length of the bottomfinder being 13 hours—and probably better analyzed on the 15m chart. Consequently we can expect a countermove of comparable size. What we get is a countertrend that retraces a fraction of 38.2 percent and lasts 13 hours.

FIGURE 4.21   5m chart of Canadian dollar September 2010 futures showing an 18-hour downtrend and a 13-hour bottomfinder.

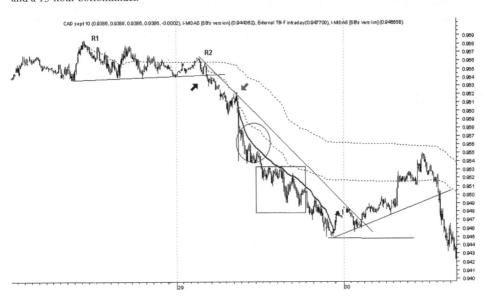

How to Trade with TB-F Curves

As we've seen in previous chapters, the primary role of standard MIDAS S/R curves is to time contrarian plays in relation to pullbacks in the larger trend. However, insofar as the wider purpose is to participate in the ongoing trend standard S/R curves are also trend-following.

TB-F curves can be used in trend-following trading techniques as well as contrarian trading techniques. Each involves different approaches. In the next section we'll look at how TB-Fs would be traded when attempting to follow the immediate trend. Later we'll look at contrarian plays.

How to Get into the Trend When Using a TB-F Curve

The issue of how to get into the trend when using a TB-F curve is another major one for traders and yet it's never addressed by Levine. Consequently, it's another issue that urges the application of trade-management rules. In this section I want to address it by offering a quick step-by-step guide to how I am inclined to use this indicator in real-time trading.

Step One

The first step is simply observational, as illustrated in Figure 4.22, when we notice that a price movement off a pivot appears to be starting to move up or down rapidly at the appropriate angle (as discussed earlier). Sooner or later, as in Figure 4.23 of the same developing trend, price must pull back for our fitting procedure; before this, there is no option to apply a TB-F curve. Figures 4.22 and 4.23 are all we're likely to see in the start of a putative new move and pullback.. If in Step (1) we were getting into the trade later when the trend was well under way, Step (1) and the subsequent steps described here wouldn't be as complex.

FIGURE 4.22   A 5m chart of the DAX September 2010 futures.

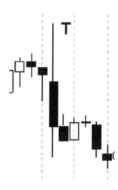

Source: eSignal and Metastock. www.esignal.com and www.equis.com.

FIGURE 4.23   Fit a TB-F curve to a pullback that looks to have finished forming. This will be trial-and-error insofar as the pullback identified may not be a pullback at all or price may not even be starting a new downtrend.

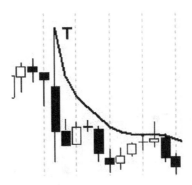

Source: eSignal and Metastock. www.esignal.com and www.equis.com.

Step Two

Once a pullback has taken place and price starts moving down again from it, a TB-F is fitted to the pullback using the methodology discussed earlier. This will be trial-and-error insofar as a pullback we think has completed may not have finished. Alternatively, the market may not actually be starting a new downtrend at all. However, assuming that we've identified an appropriate pullback we're still not trading this trend, but now that we have a cumulative volume prediction we're immediately trying to identify an entry point.

Step Three

The only logical way of entering the trend is to wait until price breaks below the low that was created prior to the pullback to which the TB-F was fitted. In Figure 4.24 that point is highlighted by the thick horizontal line. The trade is triggered on the next candlestick that breaks the low of the candlestick that broke the pullback low, with a stop-loss placed at the high of that candlestick.[4] The two arrows highlight these points. Alternatively, more aggressive traders could enter the trade as soon as the pullback low is broken.

Step Four

Set a price target: the simplest way of doing this is to put one's faith in the running down of D. Earlier discussions of what to do if the TB-F expires before price or keeps running on after the trend has ended should be borne in mind. As it happens in our example, the downtrend moves another 70 DAX index points after the entry point before the trend runs into its first significant congestion (highlighted by the rectangle in Figure 4.25). This would probably have been an exit point, even though the bottomfinder would still be predicting a little more cumulative volume left to run.

FIGURE 4.24   The trade is triggered when price breaks the low of the pullback to which the TB-F is fitted.

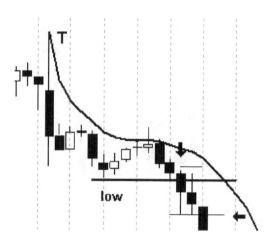

Source: eSignal and Metastock. www.esignal.com and www.equis.com.

FIGURE 4.25   A completed downtrend in the DAX futures with the heavy congestion being an ideal exit point, even though the TB-F ultimately contained this congestion and terminated at the end of the trend.

Source: eSignal and Metastock. www.esignal.com and www.equis.com.

How to Trade with the TB-F in Contrarian Trading

In contrarian trading with the TB-F curves, a trader will have already plotted a TB-F curve and will be awaiting the completion of the cumulative volume in D and the termination of his curve on the chart. If possible on much larger trends, he will also have launched a second, or even a third, curve from smaller components of the trend to support the D reading in his primary curve.

Confirmation of the trend ending is vital when using the TB-F in contrarian trading, since as we've seen, the change in the volume signature associated with the termination of D is compatible with a period of lengthy congestion, a short pause in the trend, or its termination. In my experience, the termination of the trend follows the expiry of D much more often than not, but this cannot be taken for granted. Accordingly, there has to be a price-based confirmation of the trend ending, such as price emphatically breaking down through the TB-F curve or breaking a standard linear trendline. Alternatively, a contrarian trader can work with the additional indicators discussed below, the role of which is to add credence to the assumption that the trend is ending.

For more aggressive traders, a termination of D followed by a reversal Japanese candlestick might be sufficient. As discussed in Chapter 3, a stop would be placed on the reversal candlestick's high and the trade would be triggered on the break of its low. When timing the end of downtrends, the procedure would be reversed.

In the following sections, I discuss several supporting tools that can be used alongside TB-F curves when applying it in contrarian trading conditions.

The Supporting Role of Other Volume and Momentum Tools

In the second part of the previous chapter, I drew attention to On Balance Volume and the Elliott Wave momentum oscillator in their roles as divergence indicators when assessing whether a given MIDAS S/R is likely to hold. A similar role can be played by these indicators in relation to examining what is likely to happen when a TB-F curve terminates on the chart. Indeed, one of the biggest objections to divergence signals is that it's extremely hard to time them, since they often seem to go on and on. The TB-F is an excellent tool for precision-timing divergence signals in accelerated trends.

However, as indicated earlier, one can't assume that a trend change will follow a TB-F termination. All we can know for sure is that the cumulative volume signature will change. However, this is compatible with a short resting phase, a much longer sideways interval, or indeed a trend change. A strong divergence pattern in one of these indicators would support a trend reversal or at least a very significant sideways interval. Often too, the length of time of the divergence is proportional to the duration (in time) of the subsequent move, so this again is additional information that can be factored into the analysis. As noted, divergences are a blunt tool insofar as a trader never knows how many divergences there are going to be before the trend ends.

FIGURE 4.26   The same 5m chart of Canadian dollar futures with the Elliott Wave Oscillator added in the upper pane.

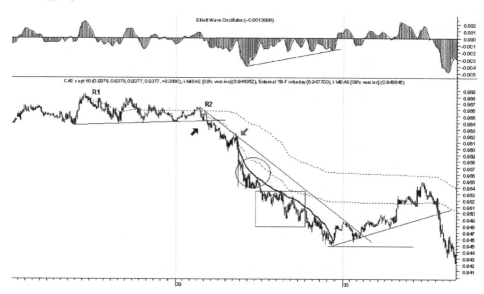

Source: eSignal and Metastock. www.esignal.com and www.equis.com.

Help is at hand if we drop down to consecutively lower timeframes and wait for a uniform pattern of divergences. Alternatively we can use a TB-F curve to provide accurate information, provided the trend is accelerating. Figure 4.26 is the same chart as Figure 4.21, this time with the Elliott Wave (EW) Oscillator in the upper pane. Its divergence (of 11.5 hours) is plain to see.

As mentioned in the previous chapter, I use the EW Oscillator because I believe it produces sharper signals than the standard MACD. Readers interested in this indicator can note the simple formula to program it in Metastock:

$$Mov(C, 5, S) - Mov(C, 35, S)$$

On Balance Volume produces similar divergence signals. I use both indicators because sometimes one of them will provide signals that the other has missed.

More Precise Methods for End-of-Trend Analysis

As mentioned, end-of-trend divergence signals can be blunt insofar as divergence indicators can continue diverging for some time before the trend ends. One solution is to drop down to consecutively lower timeframes, as suggested above. Alternatively one can choose a more precise indicator such as Tom DeMark's TD Sequential or a Fibonacci technique.

MIDAS and DeMark's TD Sequential

Before proceeding, I make the usual proviso about there being insufficient space to provide a detailed introduction to this indicator. TD Sequential is one among several variations of bar counting techniques that Tom DeMark developed in the mid-1970s that can be applied (like MIDAS) to most markets and timeframes. In an article entitled "Applying TD Sequential to Intraday Charts," DeMark describes TD Sequential as having three stages: Setup, Intersection, and Countdown.[5] The Setup phase is described in the same article as follows:

> This phase consists of at least 9 consecutive closes less than the close four bars earlier for a buy setup, and at least 9 consecutive closes greater than the close four bars earlier for a sell setup. Setup clarifies whether a trader should be expecting to buy or sell the market.

This phase can be coded into Metastock as follows:

```
{BuySetup}
Sum(C<Ref(C,-4),9)=9;
{SellSetup}
Sum(C>Ref(C,-4),9)=9
```

Coding the Intersection and Countdown phases of TD Sequential is beyond the scope of this chapter. However, as Jason Perl recently pointed out, while the implications of a TD Setup are often ignored, how the market responds to a Setup determines whether it is rangebound or in trend mode insofar as the subsequent TD Countdown component is associated with a directional trend.[6] Each time price completes a TD Setup, the price extremes are identified by a TD support and resistance line known as the Setup Trend (TDST). If price fails to break through the TDST, there's an opportunity to take a contrary position insofar as the market doesn't have the momentum to start the TD Countdown phase; that is, to break through the TDST. Let's illustrate this briefly in Figure 4.27, a 15m chart of the Euro September 2010 futures.

The TD Setup starts from point (1) and completes at point (2) when Metastock fires off the first gray spike. No further bar beyond the TD Setup phase has the momentum to break below the TDST support line into the TD Countdown phase, so there is an opportunity to take a contrary long position on the appropriate candlestick reversal. At point (3) another TD Setup starts because price fails to break above the TDST resistance line from point (1). At the same low Metastock fires off another gray spike, indicating that a second TD Setup phase has completed. Again price has no further momentum to break below the TDST support line, and so another contrary long position can be considered in relation to the appropriate candlestick reversal signal. At the gray points (5) and (6) price breaks above the TDST resistance line, suggesting the risk of a developing bull trend, though as we can see, this doesn't happen on either occasion.

FIGURE 4.27 15m chart of Euro FX September 2010 futures with completed TD Setup phases and corresponding TDST support and resistance lines.

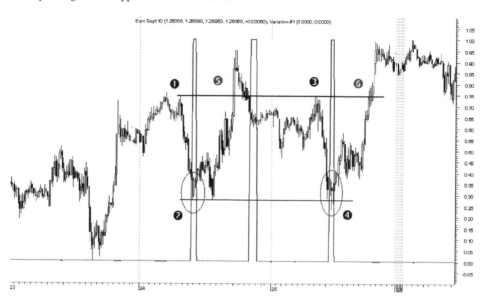

Source: eSignal and Metastock. www.esignal.com and www.equis.com.

Now let's take a look at Figure 4.27 again in Figure 4.28 when MIDAS is added. First, the TD Setup phases between (1) and (2) and (3) and (4) are very amenable to TB-F analysis insofar as their momentum components nearly always develop as an accelerated trend. As regards the breakouts above the TDST resistance line in points (5) and (6), while the actual breakouts are warnings that a developing bull trend might be in the offing, the cumulative volume prediction in the two topfinders launched from the TDST support line add a clear cumulative volume target above the TDST resistance line. As it happens, both predictions accurately foretell of a trend reversal, with the top marked (A) being a useful point from which to launch a standard MIDAS resistance curve (dotted), which (with some porosity) also resists price at point (3) alongside the TDST resistance line.

When using MIDAS curves, especially TB-Fs, I will frequently have indicators such as TD Sequential and TD Combo running in the background. An automated firing off of one of these indicators in relation to the end of an accelerated trend as indicated by an expired TB-F curve, or price pulling back to a standard MIDAS S/R curve, is a very powerful contrarian combination and shouldn't be ignored.

MIDAS and Bar-Counting on the Fibonacci Number Sequence

There are a number of sophisticated applications of Fibonacci to time relationships in the financial markets, including the Lucas series, Christopher Carolan's Spiral Calendar, and William Erman's Ermanometry. One of the simpler, more well-established

FIGURE 4.28 Combining the TD Setup component of TD Sequential with TB-F curves.

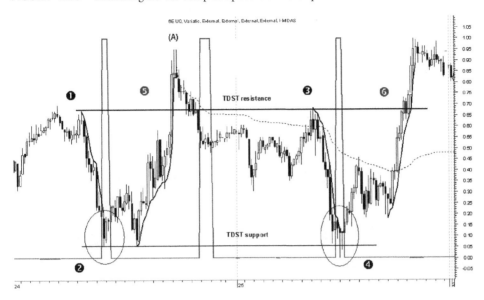

Source: eSignal and Metastock. www.esignal.com and www.equis.com.

methods is the application of the Fibonacci number sequence. In his book *Technical Analysis of the Financial Markets*, John Murphy describes this technique as follows:

> Fibonacci time targets are found by counting forward from significant tops and bottoms. On a daily chart, the analyst counts forward the number of trading days from an important turning point with the expectation that future tops or bottoms will occur on Fibonacci days—that is, on the 13th, 21st, 34th, 55th, or 89th trading day in the future. The same technique can be used on weekly, monthly, or even yearly charts.[7]

A little experimentation reveals that this technique can also be applied intraday to hours or even minutes with often impressive accuracy. For the purpose of this book I have written a small program that can be applied intraday (or daily) to run alongside MIDAS curves.

Figure 4.29 is a 5m chart of the September 2010 British pound futures on July 6 and 7 with the Fibonacci number sequence running as follows: 5, 8, 13, 21, 34, 55, 89, 144, 233, 377, 610, 987, 1597, 2584, 4181, and 6765. Readers will notice Metastock firing off a gray spike similar to the TD Sequential signal when a minute is reached corresponding to a number in the Fibonacci series.

There are two launch points for the indicator in Figure 4.29, point (1) at 1:16 A.M. GMT and point (2) at 8:31A.M. GMT. Most of the major pivots (highs and lows) are caught, and there are several instances where there are overlapping signals, which obviously adds to the conviction that a genuine turning point is at hand.

Figure 4.30 is a 5m chart of the Eurex Bund September 2010 futures and is another illustration, this time with MIDAS curves added. From the "start" point, we see pivots

FIGURE 4.29 5m chart of British pound September 2010 futures showing two Fibonacci sequences catching many of the intraday highs and lows, in some instances as a result of overlapping counts.

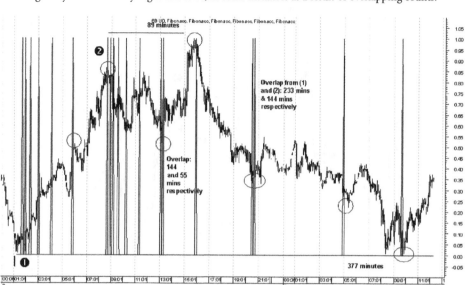

Source: eSignal and Metastock. www.esignal.com and www.equis.com.

FIGURE 4.30 5m chart of Eurex Bund September 2010 futures with another Fibonacci number sequence highlighted by the vertical pointers.

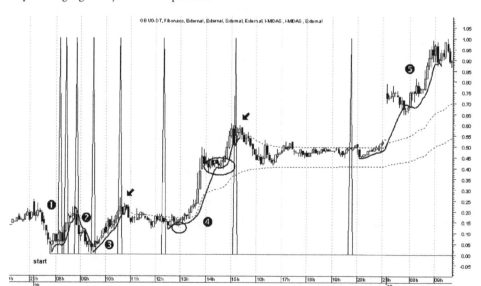

Source: eSignal and Metastock. www.esignal.com and www.equis.com.

caught on 13, 21, 34, 55, 89, and 144 minutes. Five TB-F curves are launched on this chart, as numbered in sequence from left to right. The fourth TB-F is fitted to the first ringed pullback and not to the second one in view of what was discussed earlier regarding the danger of fitting to larger pullbacks. Here it's a mere coincidence that it also fits to the second pullback. Two standard MIDAS resistance curves (dotted) are also launched from pivots highlighted by the arrows.

The technique here would again be to have this simple Fibonacci bar-counting technique programmed into Metastock so that the latter can fire off signals automatically in much the same way as the DeMark indicator. Indeed, the two techniques can be run alongside one another. The Fibonacci technique can be used alongside standard MIDAS S/R curves when price is pulling back to them or when TB-F curves are terminating. Again the confluence of signals in price and time is powerful and should not be ignored.

Thus, more precise end-of-trend indicators such as DeMark's TD Sequential or the Fibonacci sequence applied to price bars are ideal companions to the TB-F curves as well to standard MIDAS S/R curves. It is much too laborious to try calculating indicators like these by hand on intraday charts, but if they can be programmed they produce powerful automated systems. For the price dimension, I am a strong advocate of using MIDAS curves with standard moving averages, as I discussed fairly thoroughly in the second part of the previous chapter.

Summary

- In his lectures Paul Levine suggested that a necessary condition for the launch of a TB-F is that a price correction doesn't pull all the way back to a standard MIDAS S/R curve. He established this in relation to the average price being used in standard S/R curves as well as in the TB-F curves. However, with regard to the TB-F curves, we prefer using the high price in relation to the bottomfinder and the low price in relation to the topfinder. Hawkins also prefers the low price for standard support curves and the high price for standard resistance curves. Hawkins thus retains Levine's uniformity, even though he no longer uses the average price. While, however, Coles also prefers the high/low option for the TB-F curves, he prefers the average price for the standard S/R curves. As a result, he can downgrade Levine's original necessary condition for the launching of curves to a sufficient condition. By downgrading in this way the TB-F curves can be used more frequently, and it also prevents certain unwanted trend analyses from occurring.
- Care must be taken in the fitting of the TB-F in two respects. First, in relation to launching TB-F curves from pullbacks at the nth degree, pullbacks at the $n-1$th degree are prime candidates for fitting unless the nth degree pullbacks are very small. For the mathematically minded who use indicators such as the Fractal Dimension Index, trends should have a fractal dimension below 1.5 (= Hurst 0.5). Finally, trends should ideally be trending at the 65 to 75 degree angle.

- Care must be taken over the actual point of fit, since as illustrated in the chapter a difference of a mere 6 points can generate a variance in a TB-F's prediction by as much as 50 percent.
- In using TB-F curves a trader has to worry about two issues. First, will the trend end before the TB-F curve? Second, will the TB-F curve run beyond the trend of the trend? Care over fitting to the pullback can alleviate these problems. However, if they do occur, a linear trend line fitted to all or (more usually) the last segment of the trend can help in the case of the first problem (a linear regression line on the price trend can also help). In the case of the second issue, we can launch a second curve subject to the conditions of its launch discussed in the main body of the chapter.
- Other end-of-trend signals, such as divergences, are ideal companions to TB-F curves, since we can never be sure what is going to happen once a TB-F completes. It may be that the market will hesitate for a few bars, or it might become rangebound for a considerable time. Alternatively the trend may reverse. Divergences can help assess the size of the likely response after the termination of the TB-F curve.
- By programming time-based indicators into a platform such as Metastock we can have an automated system comprising DeMark indicators and/or simple Fibonacci techniques that can run alongside the MIDAS curves.

CHAPTER 5

Applying the Topfinder/Bottomfinder to the Investor Timeframes

David G. Hawkins

In this chapter I show the topfinder/bottomfinder (TB-F) on the timeframes used by position traders and investors—daily, weekly, monthly, and even quarterly bars charts.

Because the TB-F is such an unusual indicator, before delving into the specifics of this chapter, we spend the first six sections on a broad, conceptual overview of the TB-F, including its likely origin.

A Most Unusual Indicator

The topfinder/bottomfinder (TB-F) is so completely different from anything else in Technical Analysis (TA), both in its structure, use, and interpretation that it's worth taking some time here to understand its uniqueness. One of the basic concepts behind the TB-F is also behind the works of Richard W. Arms Jr. and Steve Woods (discussed in more detail in Chapter 7). However, the entirety of how the TB-F works is truly unlike anything else. For example, there are many indicators in TA that plot curves on a chart. Typically, the indicator has some kind of formula that yields the values of the curve, which the charting software then plots, and then the user goes on to draw conclusions based on how the curve interacts with other elements on the chart as the curve evolves over time. Indeed, that's how the MIDAS S/R curves work. At first glance, those who are familiar with the rest of TA may assume that this is how the TB-F works, since there is a formula, and we do plot a TB-F curve on the chart. However, with the TB-F, the sequence of events is the reverse of all other indicators. The TB-F's curve cannot be independently plotted by any software. There is a specific procedure for generating the curve, one that requires active user involvement, and it's the successful completion of the curve-generating procedure that produces the primary result of the TB-F, the curve itself being of secondary importance. Once the curve is first plotted, you already have the main result without having to wait for it to evolve over time; thereafter, there are some additional insights to be gained as time and the curve go on, but the primary result is already in hand. No other indicator works this way.

The Basic Program of the TB-F

Paul Levine[1] developed the TB-F in order to characterize an accelerated price move while it is in progress. He recognized that a price trend that is sufficiently rapid—accelerated—is a powerful, almost explosive event. Such events do not meander on endlessly; they have uniquely recognizable beginnings, middles, and ends as in Figure 4.6 of Chapter 4. Each accelerated trend has a specific amount of cumulative trading volume that it consumes during its run, and once that is expended, the move is over. The purpose of the TB-F, when applied to an accelerated trend that is in progress, is to identify, from the behavior that the trend has already displayed, what the total cumulative volume of the trend will have been once it ends. Having such information is, of course, very valuable to the trader, because then the trader can identify the end of the trend when it arrives, without having to wait for subsequent price action to reveal that the end has already passed.

Chapter 2 demonstrated how the hierarchy of MIDAS S/R curves can signal the end of a trend, and this works well compared to non-MIDAS methods. However, in that methodology, one must wait, beyond the end of the trend, for price to pull back and penetrate the latest curve in the hierarchy. For accelerated trends, the benefit of using the TB-F is that the trader knows when the end arrives, without having to wait for a pullback.

Every accelerated trend has a specific amount of cumulative volume that fuels its run, that characterizes its behavior, and that must be consumed before it ends. Levine figured out how to use MIDAS methods to discover what this total amount of "fuel" is, long before the trend ends.

What Is an Accelerated Trend?

Let's see how an accelerated trend is different from a nonaccelerated trend, how it begins, develops and ends, and how the MIDAS S/R curves behave during its run. First, though, let's examine a typical nonaccelerated trend. Look at Figure 2.11 in Chapter 2. This is a downtrend with four significant pullbacks, tracked by that fivefold hierarchy of resistance curves. Notice that each pullback comes right up to the previous R curve. There isn't much of anything that's different about this downtrend as it progresses. It just keeps going along until, for some unapparent reason, it ends with the penetration of R5. At any point before the end, there's nothing about this downtrend that would tell you whether you're at the early, middle, or later stages of it. This is the characteristic nature of nonaccelerated trends: specifically, that the pullbacks all come to (or close to) their previous curves in the hierarchy.

Now look at Figure 2.10 in Chapter 2. Here, the first major pullback, which occurs in mid-May, is very far above S1. This is the principal defining characteristic of an accelerated trend, that the first significant price pullback is far from the S/R curve launched from the beginning of the trend. If you were sitting in late May looking at this curve, you would know that you were dealing with a strongly accelerated trend.

As an accelerated trend progresses, and as you launch successive curves in the hierarchy, there is a tendency for the pullbacks to get closer to the curves that were launched before them. In Figure 2.10 of Chapter 2, you see that the start point for S3 is much closer to S2 than the start of S2 was to S1; and at the next pullback, price came right down to S3. Although this does not always happen as neatly as in Figure 2.10, it is a typical behavior of an accelerated trend.

Discovering the Topfinder/Bottomfinder

What follows is a plausible scenario for the process that Levine[2] went through to discover the topfinder. This may not be the actual path he took, but it could have been, given the things he wrote about it. In going through this, you can gain an appreciation for what the topfinder is, how it works, and how it is related to the standard MIDAS S/R curves.

Figure 5.1 is a monthly bars chart of Johnson & Johnson, JNJ, from 1993 to 2000. The first pullback, in 1996, is far above S1, so this certainly is an accelerated trend. There are three pullbacks in this trend, the second one being much more prominent and significant than the other two. (This example was chosen for its simplicity, having only one major pullback to deal with.) We have the fourfold hierarchy of S curves following this trend, S1 through S4. The problem facing Levine was, if you were in early 1998 and saw that two pullbacks had already developed, how could you discover how much further the trend had to go? Let's use hindsight to help answer this question. We see how the whole trend actually did develop. There was one more pullback, in 1998, and then in late 1999 it ended, having consumed 68.03 million shares of cumulative volume.

S5 and S6, the dotted curves, are included even though the pullbacks there are minor and would not normally be identified, in order to illustrate the fact that, as the starting point of an S curve gets closer and closer to the end of the trend, that curve gets correspondingly closer to the price bars. And, in the extreme limit, if you launched the S curve from the very last bar of the trend, then of course that ending price bar would sit exactly on the curve. This is analogous to the situation at the beginning of the trend, where the first bar sits right on S1. Now look in the vicinity around the middle of this trend. The S2 curve happens to be close to the major pullback where S3 is launched. I have launched a new curve, S21, choosing its starting point so that it exactly captures the major pullback.

FIGURE 5.1   JNJ monthly bars, an accelerated uptrend.

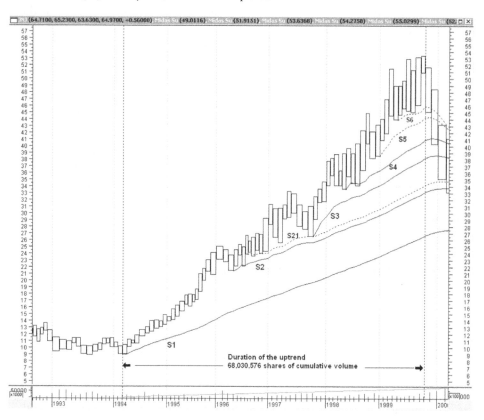

Data Source: Reuters DataLink.

All the above could well have led to Levine's "Aha!" moment, his great idea for the solution to this problem. He may have realized that he could generate a new, special MIDAS curve that would touch both the beginning and the end of the trend and also touch the pullback in the middle, *if he allowed the starting point for the calculation of the points on the curve to move forward as the curve developed*. At the beginning, the curve would start where S1 starts; when the curve got to the major pullback around the middle of the trend, the starting point for the calculation of the curve would have moved up to the point where I've started S21, thus capturing the pullback. Thereafter, the starting point would move forward fast enough so that it finally catches up to the present moment right on the last bar of the trend.

To make this scheme work, he had to devise a way to control how fast the starting point for the calculation of this special curve moves forward. At first, it would hardly move at all, the curve being very similar to S1. But then it would start to move faster, so that, when the curve is at the big pullback near the middle, its calculation starting point is where I've made S21 start. Then it accelerates more, and finally catches up to the present moment right at the end of the trend.

He called this special curve the topfinder/bottomfinder (TB-F). It is a MIDAS curve, the only difference from the standard MIDAS S or R curve being that the starting point for the calculation of the points on the curve does not remain fixed at the beginning of the trend, but rather moves forward, accelerating in just the right way so that the curve captures the pullback(s), and the starting point for the calculation lands on the end of the trend when the curve gets there.

Instead of talking about the starting point accelerating, let's think about it in an equivalent way. Consider the distance between the present moment, meaning wherever you are along the TB-F curve, and the starting point for the calculation of the point for the present moment. At the beginning of the TB-F curve, that distance is zero, and gradually increases during the first half of the trend. Then, during the second half of the trend, that distance shrinks back down to exactly zero at the end of the trend. As illustrated in Figure 5.1, when you're calculating the TB-F curve at the location of the major pullback, which is just a bit beyond halfway in the trend, the distance back to the starting point for the calculation is the distance back to where curve S21 starts.

Levine[3] called this distance "e," this separation between the present moment and the starting point of the calculation, and gave a formula for it, as shown in the previous chapter. The way the formula works is that at the exact middle of the trend, the distance is one-quarter of the whole distance to the end, and that's the largest it gets. In Figure 5.1, the major pullback is a bit beyond halfway, and you can see that the distance back to the start of S21 is a bit less than one-quarter of the total distance to the end of the trend.

Using the TB-F

Now, back to our original problem, as illustrated in Figure 5.1. Let's assume we can't see this whole chart; and it is early 1998; that's where the hard right edge of the chart is. We know there have been two pullbacks, a minor one and a major one, but we don't know what comes next. Generating the proper TB-F curve, the one that fits the major pullback and ends in the future at the end of the trend, requires knowing in advance what the total duration of the trend will be. ("Duration" refers to cumulative volume, not time.) So, how can we proceed? The answer is to discover what that total duration is by trying a number of different guesses as to what that duration could be, and seeing what kind of TB-F curve each guess generates. We want a TB-F curve that captures the major pullback, so we *keep iterating our choice of the duration until we get a TB-F curve that* does *capture the pullback. And that duration is the answer.* It allows you to locate and mark the projected end of the trend, a point in the future, on the horizontal axis of your Equivolume chart.

In March 1998, the total cumulative volume traded since the beginning of the trend was about 48 million shares. We know that when the trend ends, the cumulative volume will be something more than that. We could try a guess for the duration of, say, 60 million, or 70 million or something else. If your guess is too large, the TB-F curve will be below the major pullback, and if it's too small, the curve will be above

FIGURE 5.2   The TB-F applied to Figure 5.1.

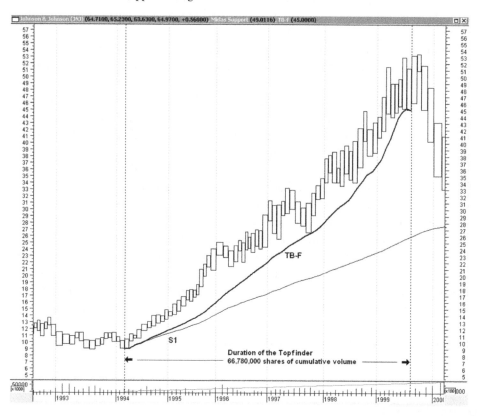

Data Source: Reuters DataLink.

it. The TB-F curve in Figure 5.2 was generated after trying several guesses for the duration, and finally finding that a value of 66.78 million shares produced the TB-F curve shown, which exactly captures the major pullback. I did not use hindsight to find this number. I simply found, by successive iterations, what value of the duration would generate a curve that captures the major pullback. It was not necessary to look beyond early 1998.

In this example, the value for the duration that generated this fitted curve was 66.78 million shares. The actual duration of the trend turned out to be 68.03 million. The TB-F curve ended just two price bars short of the real top, a very close call.

An Interesting Mathematical Observation

As we've observed here and in the previous chapter, when fitting a topfinder to an accelerated uptrend, a smaller value of D raises the curve, while a larger value lowers it. (The converse applies to bottomfinders fitting to accelerated downtrends.) It's interesting to examine how far down the TF curve can be driven by increasing D.

Look at the formula for e in the previous chapter. In the limit when D becomes infinitely large, the denominator of the formula becomes 1, and e becomes d. This means the TF curve becomes S1 (assuming, of course, you start both curves from the same point with the same price data). So, the lowest you can push the TF curve is to make it coincident with S1; it can never be any lower. (Similarly, the highest you can push a bottomfinder curve is to make it coincident with R1; it can never be any higher.)

One way to think of this is that the S1 curve is actually the TF curve with infinitely large D. And the fitting process can be thought of as starting with infinite D (the S1 curve), then bringing D down from infinity, thus raising the curve, until the curve touches the fit point.

A related question is, how far above the S1 curve must the fit point be in order to obtain a useful topfinder, a question that Coles has dealt with at length in the previous chapter. Here I just observe that if the value of D for the fit turns out to be very much greater than the value of d at the fit point, then the usefulness of the fit is questionable. Coles's application of Gann methodology that he showed in the previous chapter can be helpful here.

This completes the conceptual overview of the TB-F. Now, it's on to how to apply it to the markets used by position traders and longer-term investors. I will show this through a large number of examples, which collectively will motivate the summary of a list of specific rules for fitting the TB-F, given at the end of this chapter.

Fitting the TB-F Curve in Chart Views Other than Equivolume

Figure 5.3 shows the weekly bars chart of Bruker Corp. (BRKR), during its accelerated uptrend in 2009, to which the topfinder has been fit to the pullback marked Fit Point—the week ending September 25.

As of this writing, the topfinder is 90 percent complete, with the horizontal position of the end projected to be at the dotted vertical line. This is a weekly bars Equivolume chart in MetaStock. This example was chosen because the price box at the fit point is so much larger than all the other ones that it clearly illustrates the problem of using the Candlevolume display when fitting a TB-F curve.

The TB-F curve is actually a broken line graph, with each point on the curve defined at the horizontal location of the right edge of each box. In MetaStock, using the TB-F plug-in we've produced, if you move your cursor to touch the TB-F curve at a point directly beneath that fit point box, a little text box pops up saying:

TB-F
Date: 9/25/2009
Value: 9.17039

And if you double-click on the TB-F curve, the parameters entry box for the TB-F pops up for entering the start date of the curve and your choice of the duration, D.

FIGURE 5.3   BRKR weekly bar in Equivolume Chart.

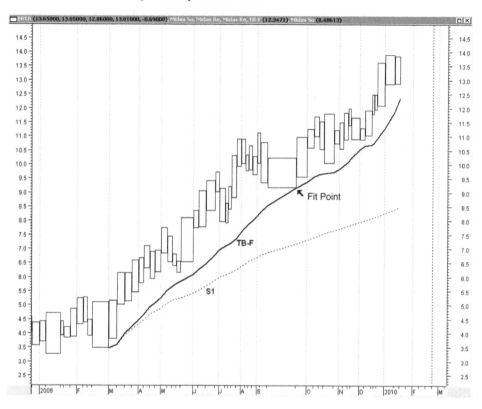

Data Source: Reuters DataLink.

After several iterations, I found that when I used D = 1.651 million, that value is
what produces the curve shown here, whose height at September 25 is 9.17039, which
matches the price box's low of 9.170 to four significant figures. The main point here is
that, when a topfinder curve is fit to a price bar, it must coincide with lower right-hand
corner of the box, and similarly for a bottomfinder, the curve must touch the upper
right hand corner.

The curve is properly fit in Figure 5.3. Now, in Figure 5.4, the only difference
from Figure 5.3 is that I've changed the display from Equivolume to Candlevolume,
without changing anything else. The same price and volume data is plotted in
these two figures, and the two TB-F curves are identical. In Figure 5.4, the TB-F
curve is still properly fitted to the price data; it just *looks* as though it isn't fitted
correctly because it doesn't appear to be touching the price candle. But if you draw
a box around that large candle, you'll see that it is the same box that's in Figure
5.3, and the lower right corner exactly touches the curve at the place still labeled
"Fit Point."

If your chart starts out in Candlevolume display and you attempt to fit a TB-F
curve to a pullback candle, you must *not* try to fit it to the bottom (or top) of the

FIGURE 5.4   Same as Figure 5.3 but with Candlevolume display.

Data Source: Reuters DataLink.

candle's central whisker; you still have to fit it to the corner that would be visible if you were using Equivolume display. So, this is why I advise that you start out in Equivolume display when doing a fit, then after properly fitting it, you may want to change to Candlevolume display to gain the extra insight that candlesticks can give.

Now, look at Figure 5.5. Here, I've changed the display to Candlesticks, in other words, a time-based chart. The only other change I made was to move the arrow and the words "Fit Point" slightly to the left so that they refer to the bottom of that candle's central whisker. In this form of display, there is no significance to the horizontal width of the candle; the candle is only displaying price data. So, if you start out with this form of display, then you should fit to the end of the candle's whisker. The same would be true of a simple price bars display.

The TB-F and the S1 curves in Figure 5.5 look quite different from the way they do in the previous two figures. However, they are the same, in the sense that the height of each point on each curve is exactly the same on all three charts. Because these curves are volume-weighted in their construction, they look smooth on Equivolume and Candlevolume displays, and rather lumpy on time-based charts.

FIGURE 5.5   Same as Figures 5.3 and 5.4 but on time-based candlestick display.

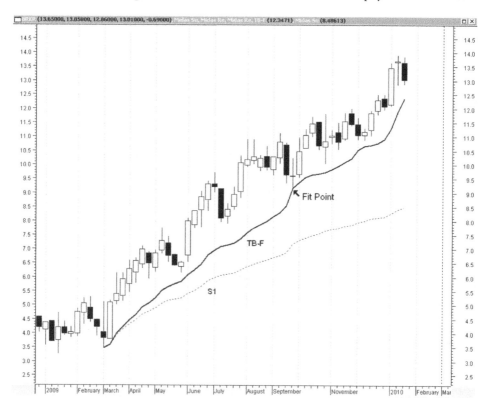

Data Source: Reuters DataLink.

Fitting to More than One Pullback

Most accelerated trends display more than one significant pullback, some showing three, four, or five. So, to which pullback should one fit the TB-F curve? More specifically, what procedure should one use when encountering more than one pullback as the move progresses? Let's start with several examples to motivate the final, full answer to this question.

Let's place ourselves early in the trend shown in Figure 5.3, a few weeks after the first pullback appears, and let's pretend that we have no idea what's coming later. Figure 5.6 shows this, where the hard right edge of the chart is at June 26, 2009. A month earlier a distinct pullback occurred, which is far above S1, so we launch S2 from there, and we do a TB-F fit to that pullback. A value of 975,000 for D fits the curve nicely. The low of the fit point bar is 6.15, and the height of the TB-F curve there is 6.1507. The cumulative volume from the starting bar of March 6, 2009 to June 26, 2009 inclusive is 597,745 so the percent complete is 597,745/975,000 = 61.3 percent.

FIGURE 5.6 Fitting to the first pullback.

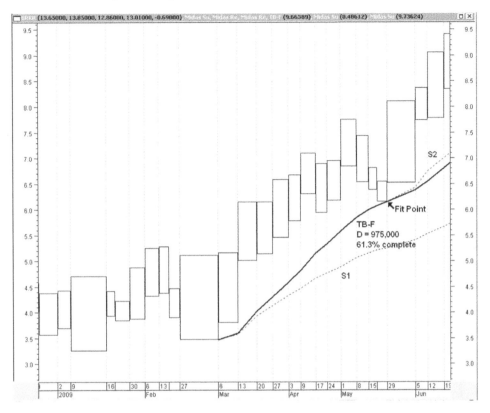

Data Source: Reuters DataLink.

Now see how the trend progresses as the weeks go by. Figure 5.7 is as of August 7. We see that the July 17 bar was another pullback, but it did not come down to the TB-F curve. What should be done at this point? Notice that the second pullback is relatively close to the TB-F curve, so let's experiment with a different value of D to see if we can generate a curve that comes reasonably close to fitting both pullbacks. The low of the first pullback is at $6.15, and the second is at $7.90. I tried several reduced values of D, attempting to get a curve that splits the difference between the two fit points, being as much above the first one as below the second. After several iterations, I found that D = 946,000 produced the curve shown in Figure 5.8, a curve that is only two cents above the first fit point and two cents below the second one.

Looking at Figure 5.7, you wouldn't think that such a nice fit as shown in Figure 5.8 could be achieved. In Figure 5.7, which is fit to the first pullback of $6.15 to within four significant figures, at the second pullback the curve is down at $7.79, 11 cents below the low of that pullback at $7.90. You might think that by splitting the difference, you'd end up with a curve that is five cents or six cents away from each fit point. The reason it worked out so differently is that the TB-F curve is a highly

FIGURE 5.7 The progress of the trend as of August 7, 2009.

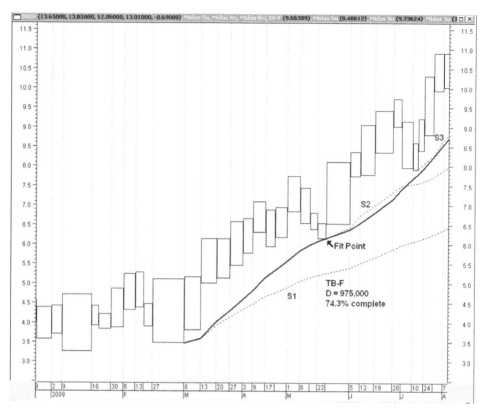

Data Source: Reuters DataLink.

nonlinear function of D, changing its height by quite different amounts in different sections of the curve. It's almost as if, given the chance, the curve *wants* to fit to the pullbacks! The lesson here is whenever you encounter a situation like Figure 5.7, you should not be discouraged from trying to find a fit that comes reasonably close to both of them. Very often, you will find such a fit, and that's a curve that should be kept going forward.

Now we move several weeks forward, to October 16, a bit beyond the end of this topfinder, as shown in Figure 5.9.

We see that the TB-F curve ended at the September 18 box, one box before that large square box of September 25. Now, with the benefit of hindsight, compare this with Figure 5.3, a very different picture. By walking forward from the starting bar of March 6th, we have generated this TB-F in Figure 5.9, which ended on September 18, but Figure 5.3 shows a TB-F of a much longer duration. Does this invalidate Figure 5.9? No, not at all. The behavior of price after the curve ended is distinctly different from before. This well-fit topfinder follows an accelerated uptrend that exhibits a distinctive behavior, and after it ends, things are really very different. The answer to

FIGURE 5.8   TB-F curve fitted to two pullbacks.

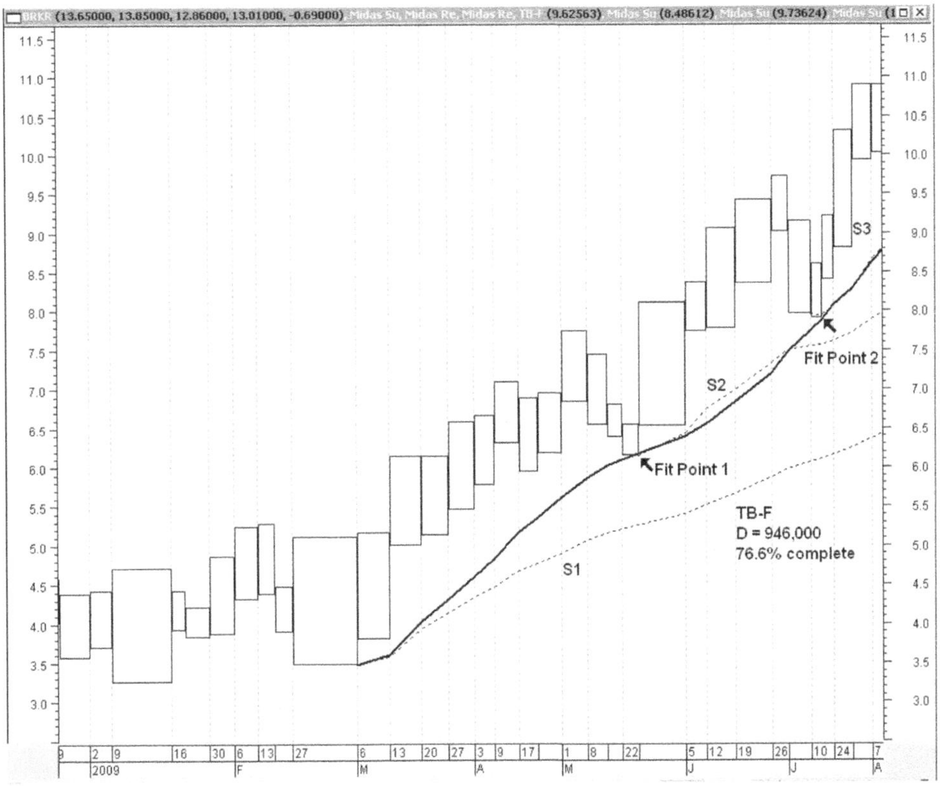

Data Source: Reuters DataLink.

the question, "What happens after a TB-F ends?" is much like that classic quote from Monty Python's Flying Circus: "And now for something completely different."

The Figure 5.9 curve ended just one bar after the highest point at that time, and then with the next bar, that large square box, price consolidated down to S3, which was started from fit point 2 and which was the closest-in support curve, and turned up from there. This is consistent with how we understand the behavior of TB-F curves, which is that, once such a curve ends, price will consolidate, and if it does not break below the closest-in support curve, then it's likely to be starting a new uptrend. The fact that the old uptrend ended does not predict what comes next. All we can expect after the end of a TB-F is at least a brief consolidation before price decides what it will do next.

Figure 5.9 shows an accelerated uptrend that started on March 6, had two price pullbacks, and ended at the high on September 11. The TB-F curve, which was carefully fit to the two pullbacks, ended one price bar later. (Actually, the TB-F's duration extended a bit into the large square box, but this software ends the curve at the latest complete box.) Now, with hindsight, we can see that it probably would have

FIGURE 5.9   Beyond the end of this topfinder.

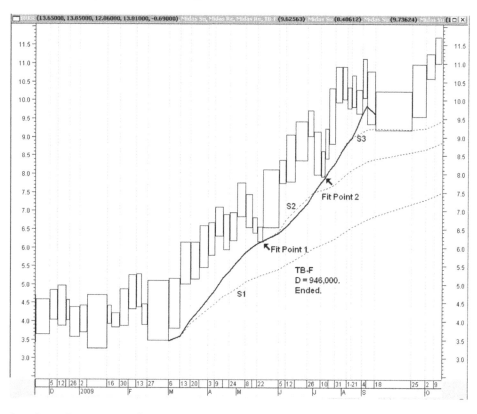

Data Source: Reuters DataLink.

been better to fit exactly to point 2, as that would have brought the end of the curve in a bit, making for a more accurate capture of the top of this trend. As we're beginning to see, fitting to the latest pullback is often the best choice.

Let's continue with our walking-forward exercise. In Figure 5.9, we're sitting at October 6, and we see that huge pullback of the square box of September 25. There's no way that the old TB-F curve could be adjusted to reasonably cover all three of these pullbacks, nor should one even consider doing that, since the old curve has ended and we're now into some kind of different behavior. Therefore, the thing to do is launch a new TB-F curve that is fitted to the September 25 pullback, and that's what we did in Figure 5.3. So, looking at both Figures 5.9 and 5.3, we've identified a shorter TB-F within a longer one: an example of the fractal nature of the market.

In Figure 5.3, we see that, after the September 25 pullback, there was another one, five bars later, on October 30. Should we apply the same procedure to this as we did with the earlier TB-F, trying to adjust the curve to fit to both pullbacks? I tried that, and could not get a curve anywhere near to both pullbacks simultaneously. So, in Figure 5.10, I've fit a new TB-F curve to the October 30 pullback, and find that it ended two weeks ago.

FIGURE 5.10   Fitting a TB-F curve to the October 30 pullback.

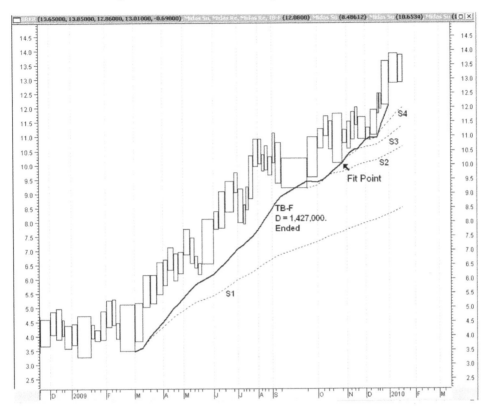

Data Source: Reuters DataLink.

Figure 5.11 collects in one chart all three of the TB-F curves we've found. The two that have ended are the thin curves and the one that's still running is in bold, with its projected end at the dotted vertical line. So, sitting here today, as of this writing (January 25, 2010), I don't know the complete outcome, although I would tend to lean toward the one that has finished, since it is fit to the latest pullback. What should a trader do at this point? If I already owned this stock and was looking for an exit point to profit from this huge uptrend, looking at the two longer TB-Fs here, I'd conclude that this uptrend is either over or very near its end, and I would be looking for an exit trigger. The topfinder that's still running is 90 percent complete, and I know that price is often volatile during the last 10 percent of a TB-F curve. Following Elder's Triple Screen system[4] as described in Chapter 2, I would drop down to the chart of the next shorter timeframe, daily bars, and watch for price to break below the closest-in support curve on that chart, which would be my sell trigger.

If I did not own this stock, and if I had some reason from fundamentals or from overall market conditions to think this stock is a good shorting candidate, I would not use the above-mentioned trigger for going short, because the end of a topfinder

FIGURE 5.11   All three topfinders on one chart.

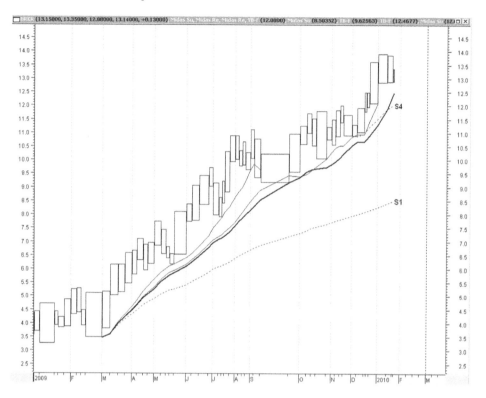

Data Source: Reuters DataLink.

does not necessarily mean it's going to go down, as you can see from the end of the shortest TB-F curve on Figure 5.11. For initiating a short position, you need to know that the uptrend is over *and* that a new downtrend has started. So, I would watch to see if price breaks below S4 on this weekly bars chart, as that would be the definition of the start of a new downtrend. You readers have the benefit of hindsight to see what actually did happen!

Here's one more example of fitting to multiple pullbacks. Figure 5.12 is the monthly bars chart of that Internet darling, Cisco, ticker CSCO, covering its incredible 10-year extremely accelerated uptrend to the peak of the dot.com bubble. It went from a (split-adjusted) low of 6.86 cents in 1990 to its all-time high of $82 in March of 2000, a 119,434 percent increase! The chart is log scale on price to accommodate this huge range.

This uptrend had four pullbacks. Imagine that you did a walk-forward exercise to fit the TB-F as we did in the previous example. First you'd fit to the first pullback, then adjust the fit as the second and third ones appeared. At the fourth pullback, marked with the arrow, it turns out that fitting exactly to that one not only also captures the first one, but nicely splits the difference in error between the second and third pullbacks, so this is the best fit for this uptrend. The duration for this TB-F is 1.9407

FIGURE 5.12　Cisco's long-term rise to its dot.com peak.

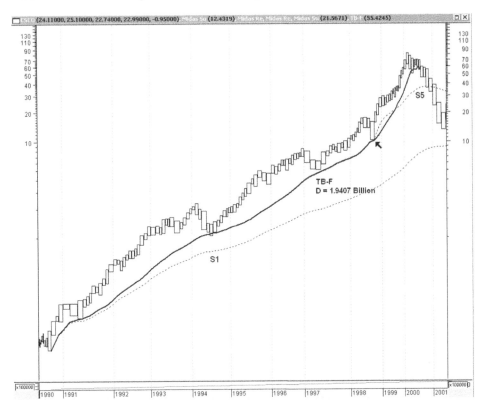

Data Source: Reuters DataLink.

billion, which overshoots the top of the trend. The actual duration of the uptrend was 1.8653 billion, so the TB-F overshot it by 4 percent. At the price peak, the TB-F was 96 percent complete. This again points out that, once a TB-F is more than 90 percent complete, price can get quite volatile, and the TB-F may loose its accuracy in that final 10 percent region.

Once you're within the final 10 percent of a TB-F, you could look at the next-lower timeframe chart to get a better fix on the end of the accelerated trend, and that's what is shown in Figure 5.13, the weekly bars chart from late 1998 to mid 2000.

There were multiple, although not prominent, pullbacks during the more shallow first half of this uptrend, and one very distinct pullback in the later half (at the arrow). It is best to fit to that late one both because the move is so accelerated there and because, as we're beginning to see in these examples, in general a fit to a later pullback gives a better result. This TB-F ended at the next to the last bar in the uptrend. The actual duration of the uptrend was 200 million, so the TB-F undershot it by less than 1 percent quite a remarkable performance during extremely volatile times.

I was using the TB-F methodology during the peak of the dot.com bubble, saw that the top of the market had come, and exited all of my equity positions during the first few months of 2000, thus avoiding a loss from the bursting of that bubble.

FIGURE 5.13   Cisco on weekly bars as it comes to the dot.com top.

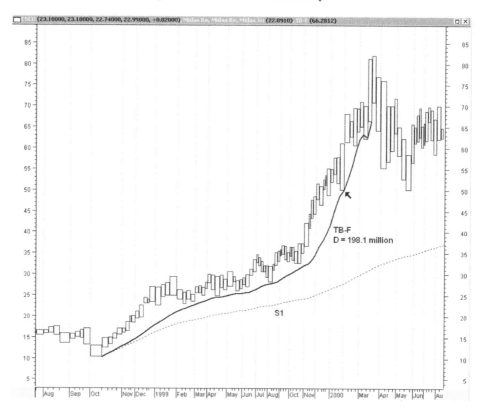

Data Source: Reuters DataLink.

All of the examples so far have been of topfinders. To see a beautiful example of a bottomfinder, go to Figure 5.16. There, a bottomfinder perfectly captured the crash of 2008.

Nested TB-Fs: The Fractal Nature of the Market

Working through the BRKR example here in Figures 5.3 through 5.11, we saw one example of the fractal nature of the market and how TB-F curves display this characteristic. By walking forward from the starting bar, we arrived at Figure 5.11. Early in the move, after one short TB-F curve ended, within a few further bars we were running a longer-term TB-F, both curves coming from the same starting bar. We had one TB-F curve nested within a longer one. The portion of the price move covered by the shorter TB-F was all of a kind, a steeply accelerated uptrend with a unique appearance. After the shorter one ended, a different-looking behavior became evident, which was tracked by the longer TB-F. This nesting of one TB-F within a longer one is very common.

It's not at all uncommon to have what I call "triple nesting," where there is a short TB-F within a longer TB-F, which itself is within a much longer one. This is what is shown in Figure 5.14, the daily bars chart of Oracle, ticker ORCL, from late 1998 into early 1999.

Imagine you start the walking-forward exercise at the starting bar in early October. By late October you see that pullback at mid-month, which is far above S1, so you fit T1, the first TB-F curve, to it, and sit back and watch the situation evolve. In early November, the curve ends in the middle of a cluster of four bars at nearly the same price level. That cluster may be considered to have been a brief consolidation. T1 covered a period of a steep, almost linear uptrend, of uniform appearance.

Then suddenly, there was a gap up on large volume, starting more of an uptrend. From mid-November through late December, there were several pullbacks, and you may have tried fitting a TF to the early ones in that time range. But, by late December, it would have been obvious that the T2 curve I've put on here is the best one, since it fits to three different places. T2 ended at a price bar, which at that time was the high for the move, and a few bars later, at the first price bar in 1999, there was a significant pullback. That pullback came down to and supported at the closest-in S curve (not shown here), and price moved up from there, indicating that the move beyond T2 was going to be more of a longer duration.

FIGURE 5.14   ORCL with a triple nesting of TB-F curves.

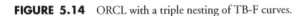
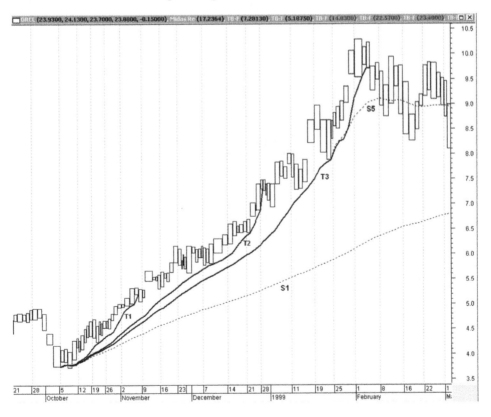

Data Source: Reuters DataLink.

As 1999 progressed, you can see that volatility increased, and the general appearance of the price behavior was distinctly different from what it had been during T2. By late January, it would have been apparent that the best way to fit T3 was as shown in Figure 5.14. T3 ended two bars after the top. The value of D for T3 was 45.2 million, whereas the actual duration of the whole uptrend was 43.85 million, so T3 overshot the top by only 3 percent, a very good performance in locating the top of this uptrend. S5 is the closest-in support curve, launched from the latest pullback in T3's range. Three bars after T3 ended, price broke down through S3, indicating that further price action was far more likely to be a downtrend, and that certainly is what happened.

TB-F Curves on Different Timeframes

In Chapter 2, I showed that S/R curves launched from the same date on different timeframe charts are different curves, which need to be considered separately. So it should come as no surprise that TB-F curves are also different on different timeframes. Figure 5.15 shows the S&P 500 index, ticker, GSPC, on weekly bars from January

FIGURE 5.15   S&P 500, weekly bars, with two fitted topfinders.

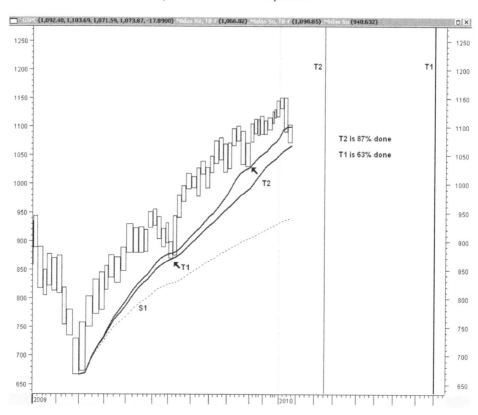

Data Source: Reuters DataLink.

2008 through the end of January 2010, the date of this writing. The great market crash of 2008 to 2009 came to a sharp V bottom in the first week of March of 2009, and then the market launched into a robust uptrend, rising sufficiently above its S1 to allow for TB-F fits. There was a major pullback in July, marked by the first arrow, so a topfinder, T1, is fit there, which is currently 63 percent of the way to completion, and the horizontal location of its projected end is the thick vertical line at the right edge of this chart. Continuing with a walking-forward exercise, the next pullback was in November, at the second arrow, and fitting a topfinder, T2, to that, we find that it is 87 percent complete, with its projected end at the horizontal location of the thin black vertical line. If average weekly trading volume continues as it has been recently, T2 will end in about a month and a half, but T1 not until about seven months from now.

Now let's compare the two topfinder curves in Figure 5.15 with one launched from the same date on a monthly bars chart, Figure 5.16, which takes a much longer view of the situation, from 2003 to the present. (Notice how beautifully that bottomfinder launched in May of 2008 captured the crash.) Now we have a topfinder curve running, launched from the March 2009 bar, and fit to the July bar, at the arrow. It is currently

FIGURE 5.16   S&P 500 topfinder on monthly bars chart.

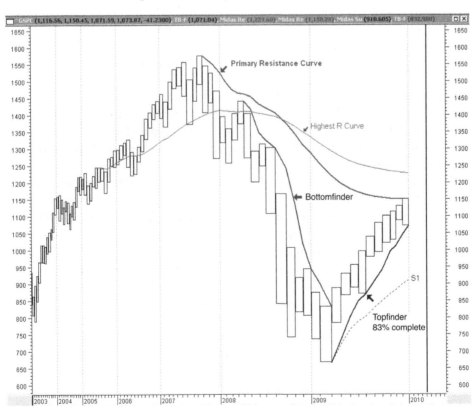

Data Source: Reuters DataLink.

83 percent complete, with projected completion location at the thick vertical line on the right side of the chart. If monthly trading volume continues as it has been recently, the end of the topfinder will come in about three months, which is neither the month and a half nor the seven months that are projected by the two running topfinders on the weekly bars chart. So, clearly, TB-F curves launched from the same date on two different timeframe charts are very different.

Which one of these three quite different projections for the end of this powerful retracement rally is correct? I don't know. Of course, you, the reader, by the time you see this, will know. And I am not going to update this section in the final edit of this book before it goes to press several months from now because I want to use this illustration to show how TB-Fs are used before they end, without the benefit of hindsight. Going forward from now, I will watch as each of these ends, and consider other indicators along with the endings of the TB-Fs to decide if the uptrend is truly at an end. I am constantly monitoring Figures 5.15 and 5.16, and I periodically update and comment on them in our blog at http://midasmarketanalysis.com/blog-2/, which I encourage you to follow. In fact, as I am writing this section, I am making three important posts to the blog, which expand upon Figures 5.15 and 5.16 in more detail. There, I give some reasons to believe that the uptrend may have already ended, at least as far as its maximum price goes. By going to this blog at the time you're reading this chapter, you'll learn about how this uptrend actually did end, and how well these TB-F curves fared. I'm really looking forward to seeing how this develops!

In the previous example, Figures 5.15 and 5.16, the topfinders are well fit and reasonably well behaved on both timeframes. Quite often, though, it is very difficult to get a good fit on one timeframe, but easy on another. Figure 5.17 shows such an example, with the daily bars chart of IBM from mid 1992 through March of 1993. This is an awfully busy chart with lots of details, all of which have to be there. I've put the price on a log scale so that the bottom half of the chart is expanded for better visibility. Let's see what difficulties we encounter as we try to walk through this accelerated downtrend.

The first significant pullback comes in early September, at the point marked 1. We fit our first bottomfinder to this point and watch it progress; it's the lowest of the four curves on this chart, between points marked 1 and 2. In early November there's a second pullback, marked 2, which breaks above the first TB-F curve, so we fit a second curve to that point. At mid-November, the first curve ends, but price makes no response to the ending whatsoever. Price just keeps on drifting down, the same way it was doing since the point marked 2. Therefore, we must declare that the first curve is a failure since it wasn't followed by any kind of a consolidation or change in the character of the price trend.

At the end of November there's another even stronger pullback that rises above the second curve; we start a third curve fit to that point, marked 3.

About a week later, the second curve ends, but what follows is also certainly not a consolidation, rather, it is two sharp down-gap days. So we also have to declare the second TB-F curve a failure, since it too was not followed by any kind of a consolidation. (By this point, you may be getting rather discouraged with this methodology!)

FIGURE 5.17   IBM, daily bars, with attempted bottomfinder fits.

Data Source: Reuters DataLink.

In late December, at the pair of places marked 4, there are two small pull-backs; however, being so small and relatively inconsequential looking, would you have thought to fit a TB-F curve to them? Perhaps not. I've put it in with hindsight, but let's assume that at first you didn't do that. Starting in mid-January, several new, quite large pullbacks occur, not only piercing curve 3, but turning curve 3 into an upwards trending curve. Bottomfinders don't do that, they're supposed to go *down*! By mid-February you see that price is showing higher lows as well as higher highs, so we're clearly now in a new uptrend; hindsight shows that the end of the downtrend was in early January, and you completely missed it. Curve 3 goes on to end ignominiously in the latter half of February, totally useless since it overshot the end of the trend by a month-and-a-half in time, and by 30 percent in cumulative volume.

If you had the foresight to put in curve 4, that would have worked acceptably well, overshooting the bottom by only five days and 7 percent in cumulative volume. But look at what you could have learned by just following the procedure I outlined in Chapter 2 for detecting the end of a trend with a hierarchy of S/R curves. The penetration of R5 occurred the very next day after TB-F curve 4 ended, so no real advantage was gained by using the TB-F methodology, even if you had inserted curve 4.

Newcomers to the TB-F will often run into difficulties similar to this when they try to fit a TB-F to a trend that is not accelerated, where they did not test first by putting the S1 or R1 curve on the chart to see if the first price pullback was far from that curve. But in this case, you can see in Figure 5.17 that points 1, 2, and 3 are all well below R1, and yet there still were excessive difficulties.

Now look at Figure 5.18, which covers the same time period as Figure 5.17 but expressed in weekly bars. There's only one significant pullback, and the TB-F curve that fit to it did very well, overshooting by only 2 bars, putting the end on a price bar that was a repeat of the end bar. What a thing of beauty! Fitting this curve was effortless and successful, whereas the attempts on the daily bars chart were an exercise in utter frustration. In Figure 5.16, the bottomfinder worked so perfectly tracking the crash of 2008 on monthly bars, but when I attempted to fit a BF curve to the same launch date on a weekly bars chart, I ran into difficulties similar to those shown in Figure 5.17.

FIGURE 5.18   The weekly bars version of Figure 5.17.

Data Source: Reuters DataLink.

Bottomfinders Are Sometimes Problematic

The previous section is a good segue to this one. In Figure 5.17 we saw that trying to fit a TB-F to that curve was fraught with problems, even though the downtrend was sufficiently accelerated. I've found that this happens much more often with bottomfinders than topfinders, and the many times that it does happen, you do not get a better result by shifting to a longer timeframe.

Let's go back to the example shown in Figure 5.14, and extend the chart into the future to see what happened. This is shown in Figure 5.19. After T3 ended, there commenced a big, sloppy downward sloping consolidation that finally broke into an accelerated downtrend starting in early March of 1999. Fitting a bottomfinder to this was easy, since there were only two pullbacks, marked by the arrows, and one curve nicely captured both of them. But the result was a failure, the curve overshooting the bottom by 39 percent in cumulative volume.

This is another case where the simple hierarchy of resistance curves would've done a much better job of identifying the bottom. Curve R3, dotted, is launched from the

FIGURE 5.19   Figure 5.14 extended three more months, and a bottomfinder added.

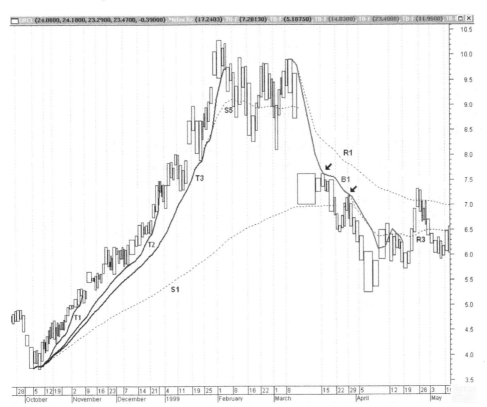

Data Source: Reuters DataLink.

second pullback, at the lower arrow, and it was penetrated just two price bars after the bottom, a far more timely signal than the end of the bottomfinder. I tried switching to a weekly bars chart, but there were too few bars on it in this time period with which to fit a bottomfinder. This simply is an accelerated downtrend for which the TB-F methodology does not work.

Figure 5.19 is quite a study in contrasts. The left side is a perfect example of a triply nested hierarchy of topfinders, nicely fit, and identifying the final top with great accuracy. But on the right, on the down side, everything seems to fall apart. Even the general visual appearance of the downtrend is messy. This is the same stock on both sides, with probably many of the same traders active during both the uptrend and the downtrend. Why does the TB-F methodology work so well on one side, but not the other?

It's not that bottomfinders never work; often they do, just as well as topfinders. I haven't done a thorough statistical study of the frequency of failures of bottomfinders, but I have seen a distinctly noticeable difference between them and topfinders. Very approximately, it seems to me that bottomfinders fail to work on at least one third of the accelerated downtrends to which I've attempted to fit them. But, topfinders work well on the very large majority of accelerated uptrends. Some of the failed bottomfinders do work if shifted to a longer timeframe chart, but others don't.

Technicians have long recognized that, in general, there's a difference between a descent into a bottom and a rise into a top. In April of 2007, Carl Swenlin, President of DecisionPoint, in a blog entry on Stockcharts.com, said: ". . . tops tend to be rounded trend changes, and bottoms tend to be formed by sharp changes in direction accompanied by internal up thrusts."[5] Indeed, it's those up thrusts upon approaching a bottom that often throw off a bottomfinder fit. In his 1994 book, *Volume Cycles in the Stock Market*,[6] Arms recognized and made good use of a distinct difference in the behavior of bottoms as opposed to tops, something that I'll delve into in more detail in Chapter 7.

Why should this be? We know that uptrends are driven by greed and downtrends by fear. But psychologists have shown that people in general are much more averse to suffering financial losses than they are to missing out on gains. So, there is a real dichotomy between downtrends and uptrends. We might even say that, in addition to fear driving a downtrend, there often is outright panic. I think that when panic is present, it can disrupt the pattern of an accelerated downtrend to the point that a bottomfinder can no longer be reliably fit to it.

My co-author reports that he does not notice any difference in applicability of the TB-F methodology between top- and bottomfinders in the markets and timeframes that he works with. But his markets are dominated by professional traders who trade as often by short selling as they do by purchasing a security, so on average one would expect that there would be more symmetry between uptrends and downtrends. Also, these traders are highly disciplined, and thus are less likely to fall victim to panic. But in the markets and timeframes that I inhabit, position trading and investing in equities, many of the participants, even at large institutions, consider themselves "investors," and disdain the discipline of trading. So, those folks can be susceptible to panic, often exacerbated by the panic of their clients.

What Comes after a TB-F Ends?

The short answer to this question is, "something different." The most distinguishing feature of a TB-F is that it identifies a region of price movement, which is an accelerated trend *with a uniquely distinctive price pattern*, one that is easy to recognize visually on a chart. After a TB-F ends, the pattern of price movement will be noticeably different. I've made references to these situations in a few places earlier in this chapter, but here I want to show an example, which, to the novice who may be unclear about what a TB-F really does and does not do, might look like a failure of the methodology.

Look at Figure 5.20, and for the moment, ignore the ellipse I've drawn in there. This is a weekly bars chart of IBM from February 1982 to October 1983. The solid curve is the TB-F that was fit to the first pullback, marked by the lowest small arrow. By the time the curve ends, you see that it also fits very well to the major pullback at the large arrow, and then goes on to fit at four other bars, marked with the small arrows, which would imply that this must be a very valid and significant topfinder. Yet, look at what happens immediately after the last bar—price pops above the last bar and doesn't come down again. To the novice user of the TB-F method, this looks

FIGURE 5.20 The Overhead Consolidation. IBM, weekly bars.

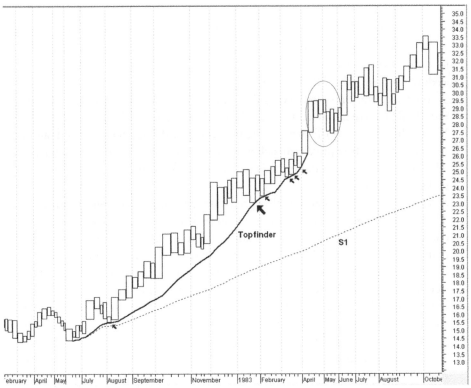

Data Source: Reuters DataLink.

like a failure of the methodology since not only does there seem to have been no consolidation, but price just kept going on up; the novice expects that a topfinder will end at the top.

But this is not a failure. Look at the price behavior from the beginning to the end of the TB-F curve; it is all of a uniquely distinctive pattern, a pattern that ends with the last bar of the curve, after which the pattern is quite different. What about the requirement that the end of a TB-F be followed by a consolidation? The region enclosed by the ellipse *is* a consolidation—a group of bars that go sideways. This group happens to reside immediately above the last bar of the TB-F curve, so I like to call this kind of consolidation an Overhead Consolidation. A well-fit TB-F curve that is followed by an Overhead Consolidation and by further price behavior of a different pattern is a perfectly valid example of a TB-F. This kind of consolidation, the Overhead variety, actually occurs fairly frequently.

Figure 5.20 is an excellent example of what a TB-F does and does not do. It does identify an accelerated trend with a unique price pattern, followed by a consolidation which may be of the overhead variety. But, despite the catchy name that Paul Levine gave it, it does not necessarily find the top.

Summary

- The process of fitting a TB-F curve to an accelerated trend that is in progress reveals what the total cumulative volume will have been at the end of the accelerated trend. It does not predict the date or price at the end, only the cumulative volume.
- Procedure for fitting the TB-F Curve
  1. Test for acceleration by observing if the first price pullback is far above (below) the S1 (R1) curve launched from the beginning of the trend.
  2. If it is, then start a TB-F curve at the beginning of the accelerated trend, and fit the curve to the first price pullback by iterating the value of D in the algorithm. The value of D that fits the curve is the projected total cumulative volume at the end of the trend.
  3. As the trend progresses and further price pullbacks appear, attempt to make one TB-F curve fit as many pullbacks as possible. If it cannot, then start new TB-F curves at the beginning of the trend and fitted to the new pullbacks. More often than not, the curve that fits to the latest pullback is the most accurate.
  4. If a curve ends with no price response—no consolidation and no change in the trending behavior of price—then discard this curve as invalid.
  5. If great difficulties arise in fitting, move up to a chart of the next higher timeframe and do the fitting there. And if that also doesn't work, go back to tracking the trend with a hierarchy of MIDAS S/R curves.
  6. When the TB-F curve gets to within about 10 percent of its end, expect price volatility to increase, and start using other TA tools to test for and verify the end of the trend.

- After a TB-F curve ends, there will be at least a short consolidation, followed by price behavior of a different pattern than there was during the just-ended trend. Beyond this, the ending of the curve does not predict price movement, which may be in either direction.

- The best use of a TB-F is as an exit strategy, the end being the exit point. For entrances, if a TB-F is running in the opposite direction from your intended trade, then the end of that TB-F is a necessary but not sufficient condition for your entry. If the TB-F is running in the same direction as your intended trade, and if it still has a good ways to go, then this is supportive of your trade; but if the TB-F is near its end, you should withhold your entry until seeing what happens after the TB-F ends.

PART III

The Longer-Term Horizon, Other Volume Indicators, and Broader Perspectives

CHAPTER 6

Applying MIDAS to Market Averages, ETFs, and Very Long-Term Timeframes

David G. Hawkins

In this chapter, I address applying the MIDAS techniques to market averages and exchange-traded funds, instead of just individual securities. The concern immediately encountered is that, for many of the popular averages, the index publisher does not provide volume data with the average. A few do, such as for the Dow Jones Industrial Average, the New York Stock Exchange Index, and the NASDAQ Composite Index, but most don't.

So, what does it mean to try to use the MIDAS mechanisms, which are intimately tied to volume data, on something for which there are no volume data? To illustrate the approach I use, let's first, before going over to market averages, examine an example of MIDAS support curves on the daily chart of a stock, Hewlett Packard Co., ticker HPQ. Figure 6.1 shows time-based, daily bars, from February through October 2009, with the volume data shown in the histogram in the lower pane, which is zero-based. The two solid curves are standard MIDAS support curves launched from the lows of March 9 and July 14.

Now let's ask ourselves, if the volume data were missing, how could MIDAS curves be drawn? The key is recognizing that lack of volume data does not mean there was no volume; after all, trades were reported. What it does mean is we just don't know how the volume *changes* from bar to bar. So, not knowing how the volume changes, the best that can be done is to assume that all bars have the *same* volume. And that's the assumption that's made in calculating the dotted curves in Figure 6.1; the algorithm for the support curve has a statement in it that says that every volume datum is one.

Look at the upper pair of curves, launched July 14. The two curves, solid and dotted, are virtually coincident. Now look at the volume under these curves. It has some day-to-day variations, but the straight line fit to the volume data is essentially

FIGURE 6.1   Standard MIDAS curves (solid) and curves calculated without volume data (dotted).

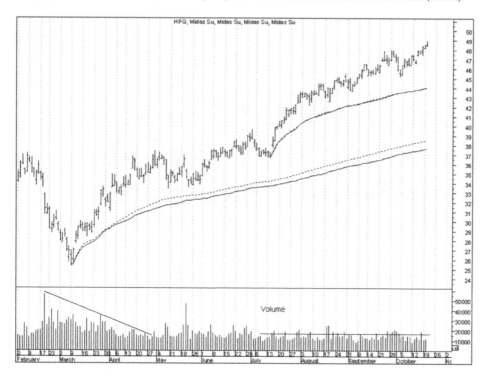

Data Source: Reuters Datalink.

flat. So, that situation allows us to calculate a MIDAS support curve in the absence of volume data by assuming that every volume datum is one.

Now look at the lower pair of curves, launched March 9. They begin at the same point, but then they move apart up to the end of April, after which they are essentially parallel. You can see the trend line fit to the volume data from mid-February to late April, and it's steeply declining. From this, an obvious conclusion is that a significant trend in volume will drive the two curves apart. The ratio of the volume on the start date to the volume in late April is about 2.5:1, so it takes this amount of volume change to make the curves noticeably different.

Let's do one more example of a stock, this time one that has very large, systematic trends in volume. Figure 6.2 is the time-based weekly bars chart of U.S. Steel, ticker X, from May 2007 through mid-October 2009. Again, the solid curve is the standard MIDAS curve, while the dotted one is calculated by setting every volume datum to one.

For the first year on this chart, the volume data are quite flat, but, starting near the peak in June of 2008, volume began the first of four large trends, as marked by the trend lines. You can see how perfectly the standard curve captured the high in September 2009, while the no-volume curve is far away. The ratio of the highest volume, at the beginning of May 2009, to the volume on the curves' launch day is

FIGURE 6.2 U. S. Steel, weekly bars, with standard MIDAS curve (solid) and a no volume curve (dashed).

Data Source: Reuters Datalink.

about 5:1. On the one hand, this shows how important it is to include volume in the calculation; otherwise, the resistance of the September 2009 high would have been missed. On the other hand, it shows how strongly the volume must be trending in order for it to make a significant difference.

Using MIDAS with the Indices—The S/R Curves

Now, let's directly apply the MIDAS S/R curves to the market indices. Start by looking at an index for which accurate daily trading volume data are available, such as the New York Stock Exchange Index, a cap-weighted index of all of the common stocks trading on the New York Stock Exchange. Figure 6.3 is its weekly bars chart from before the all-time market peak in 2007, through the crash of 2008, and well into the subsequent retracement in 2009.

The volume data that are used here are those reported for this stock exchange every day in the *Wall Street Journal*, and which are collected and made available by Reuters DataLink under their symbol, KNYSV.

This chart supports a typical hierarchy of four MIDAS resistance curves, starting from the all-time market high in late 2007. You can see all of the usual features of

FIGURE 6.3 The New York Stock Exchange Index, weekly bars from 2007 to 2009, with hierarchy of resistance curves.

Data Source: Reuters DataLink.

such a hierarchy with which, by now, you should be familiar. R1 resists the first two pullbacks in price. Price thereafter stays far below R1. R3 is launched from the high just before the crash, and during the retracement in early June 2009, R3 nicely captures that local high. R4, launched from the peak in early 2009, gets strongly breached by the nascent retracement, after which R4 changes to support, and perfectly captures the price pullback in early July 2009.

Figure 6.3 is a classic, "textbook" illustration of a hierarchy of MIDAS curves, as I've shown many times on individual stocks. So, obviously, the MIDAS curves work perfectly well on a market index for which we have valid volume data.

Now, let's look at the differences when the curves are calculated without volume, which is accomplished by setting each volume datum to one. This is shown in Figure 6.4.

You can see that the MIDAS curves on these two charts are very similar. The only differences are that R3 doesn't quite capture the high in June of 2009, and R4 is ever so slightly penetrated by the low of July 2009. These differences are small, and most users of Figure 6.4 would probably say these curves are good enough. The volume variations going into the crash and early retracement are almost a factor of two, so this trend of volume produced those small displacements of R3 and R4, but resulted in curves that were still pretty good.

FIGURE 6.4   The same as Figure 6.3, but the MIDAS curves calculated with no volume.

Data Source: Reuters DataLink.

At this point, a working conclusion from these observations would be that if your volume data have trends that are less than about 2:1, calculating the MIDAS curves "without volume" will, for the most part, be adequate.

Figures 6.3 and 6.4 encompassed the volume changes that occurred around the crash of 2008. Let's look now at the only other event in the last 100 years that is comparable to 2008, the great crash of 1929. The New York Stock Exchange Index wasn't published back then, but I do have daily data for the Dow Jones Industrial Average. Figure 6.5 is the time-based weekly bars chart of the Dow for that period.

Notice that the standard MIDAS curve (solid) perfectly captures the top of the retracement from the crash, a very significant achievement. Indeed, traders back then could certainly have benefited from this insight! The no-volume curve (dotted) only approximately works here, and would have left some doubt in the minds of traders.

The time period from the curves' launch to the retracement top has three significant volume trends in it, with volume ratios of 4.7:1, 2.3:1, and 2.6:1, much greater than in the 2008 crash. With this much greater volume variability, the no-volume curve is modestly off the mark. This supports our working conclusion.

FIGURE 6.5   Dow Jones Industrial average, weekly bars, December 1928 through June 1930.

This chart was created in MetaStock which, because of Y2K concerns, doesn't allow charting for the 1930s, so I had to add 50 years to the time data to get them to plot. Despite what the horizontal axis says, this chart really does cover from December of 1928 through June of 1930.
Data Source: Yahoo Finance.

The Validity of Volume Data

Later in this chapter, I will extend our analyses to much longer timeframes, going back many decades. The price series of the New York Stock Exchange (NYSE) Index, in its present form, only goes back to 2003. But the S&P 500 Index has daily data available back to 1950, and it has been reverse-engineered to extend monthly data all the way back to 1871. Both of these indexes are broad-based, mostly large cap, and as such, their price movements over the last seven years have tracked each other reasonably closely. So from here on, I use the S&P 500. However, Standard & Poor's, the owner of the index, does not provide trading volume data with it. For many years, I constructed a faux volume for the S&P 500 by adding together the NYSE and the NASDQ volumes, and that seemed to work reasonably well.

Recently, the financial web site, Yahoo Finance, started showing the daily trading volume for both the NYSE and the S&P 500 indexes, as well as for some others, and it allows free downloads of the historical data on these indexes going back many years. This is, of course, enormously convenient and cost-effective for traders, analysts, and authors. So, let's take a close look at the volume data they're providing. Looking at the NYSE Index, the daily volume shown on Yahoo Finance is very much larger than that reported by the *Wall Street Journal* and Reuters. For example, on July 16, 2010, the *Wall Street Journal* reported that the total share volume of the NYSE was 1,491,572,667 shares; but Yahoo Finance reported it was 5,297,353,000. The key to understanding this huge difference comes by going to the NYSE's own web site, nyse.com, where, for this date, it reported the NYSE listed volume was exactly the same as what Yahoo Finance is reporting. Then, in a linked note, it states: "The NYSE Listed Volume number on nyse.com represents shares traded in all markets for all NYSE-listed issues. ..." So, this larger number is a composite of all trades done on all exchanges for the stocks listed on the NYSE, undoubtedly including the new all-electronic trading platforms. The numbers reported by the *Wall Street Journal* and Reuters are just the trades done through the NYSE itself.

Now, when we look at the daily trading volume that Yahoo Finance quotes for the S&P 500, we get quite a surprise—the numbers are exactly the same as they report for the NYSE index, all 10 digits of them, going back as far as their historical data are shown. This of course cannot be correct, since there are several thousand stocks in the NYSE index, and only 500 in the S&P 500. Yahoo Finance's site does not provide any explanation of this, and they have not responded to my inquiries. They are simply using the NYSE composite trading volume as the volume of the S&P 500 index.

Figure 6.6 shows how these two sets of volume data compare since 2004, the upper pane being the volume that's traded only directly on the NYSE, and the lower

FIGURE 6.6 NYSE volume and NYSE composite volume, weekly bars.

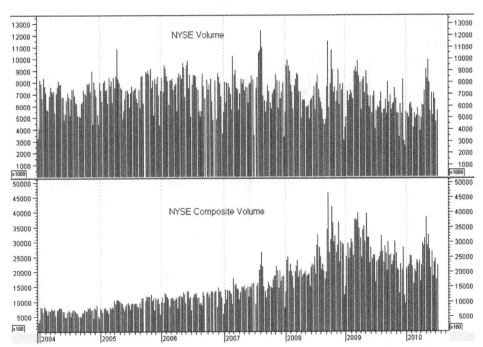

Data Sources: Reuters DataLink and Yahoo Finance.

one being the composite volume of the NYSE stocks that are traded on all exchanges and platforms.

In 2004, the composite volume was only 25 percent greater than the NYSE volume, but by September 2009, it had grown to about three times greater. Thereafter, the two sets of volume data seem to be running in parallel. This shows that during the period from 2004 to 2009, the stocks listed on the NYSE transitioned from being traded mainly on the NYSE to being traded mainly elsewhere. And since nowadays any small price differences that may arise between exchanges are rapidly arbitraged away, it's just as if these stocks are being traded on one huge exchange, a virtual exchange that is the superset of all the exchanges and platforms that these stocks actually trade on. Therefore, one could argue that it now makes more sense to use the composite volume with the NYSE index. That certainly would be true during the transitional years of 2004 to 2009, but now that the two sets of volume data are tracking each other, it won't make any difference which set is used. Indeed, I have reconstructed Figure 6.3 using the composite volume, and it looks exactly the same.

We have one more issue to elucidate before moving on—whether it's useful and proper to use the NYSE composite volume as the volume of the S&P 500 index. Figure 6.7 shows the S&P 500 index, weekly bars, using the NYSE composite volume, on

FIGURE 6.7 The S&P 500 index using NYSE composite volume. Compare with Figures 6.3 and 6.4.

Data Source: Yahoo Finance.

the same timeframe as Figure 6.3. The curves are calculated with volume. Compare this chart with Figure 6.3 for the NYSE index, and you see that these R curves behave in the same way on this chart as they do on Figure 6.3.

This very close correspondence between Figure 6.7 and Figure 6.3 shows that using the NYSE composite volume as the volume for the S&P 500 index is a valid choice, and this is the choice I'm using from here on.

Using MIDAS with the Indices—The TB-F

Now let's apply the TB-F to market indices. Since the MIDAS S/R curves work well on indices, there's every expectation that the TB-F will also. In Figure 6.8 are three

FIGURE 6.8   S&P 500 Index, daily bars, with three completed topfinders.

Data Source: Yahoo Finance.

completed topfinders fit to daily data of the S&P 500 (using the NYSE composite volume). The points they are fit to are quite late in the moves; about a week after each fit point, the topfinder ends, and price enters a consolidation. Notice that the TB-F is working just as it does on individual stocks. There are further examples of TB-F fits to market indexes later in this chapter.

Using Exchange-Traded Funds Instead of Market Indices

The development of exchange-traded funds (ETF) in recent years has been a boon to traders and investors alike, allowing one to trade the ETF that's tracking a market index as if it were an individual stock. So, let's look at the application of MIDAS techniques to ETFs, as compared to the underlying indices. Since these ETFs trade exactly like stocks, with valid volume data for them readily available, all of the MIDAS techniques apply.

By design, the sponsor of the ETF keeps its price as close as it can to that of the underlying index (or, at a fixed ratio to the index, such as one-tenth the value). For a large, liquid ETF with robust trading volume, its price chart will be virtually indistinguishable from that of the underlying index. But, its trading volume is not directly linked to that of the index. Sometimes, large volume on the ETF will indirectly filter through to the index, but the association will be a loose one. If there were significant differences in volume between the two, one might suspect that some MIDAS curves and TB-Fs will look different on the ETF than on the index.

The ETF commonly known as the Spider, ticker SPY, tracks the S&P 500 index. It is the oldest ETF, having started trading on April 23, 1993. It is very heavily traded every day, with trading volume being among the largest, if not the largest, of any ETF. Figure 6.9 is the same as Figure 6.7, except that SPY is plotted instead of GSPC which is the ticker for the S&P 500.

You can see that the solid curves, the MIDAS R curves calculated with volume, are identical in these two figures. (The dotted curves, the no-volume R curves, are somewhat different.) So, SPY, at least on the short to intermediate-term, is an excellent proxy for GSPX, and the results of applying MIDAS methods (with volume) are the same on both.

Other ETFs don't have as much trading liquidity as SPY. The less liquidity there is, then the more often it is that both the volume and the price data differ from that of the underlying. So, the behavior of the MIDAS S/R curves and the TB-Fs will be correspondingly different.

Let's now extend further back in time, on monthly bars. Figure 6.10 is the S&P 500 on monthly bars from late 1999 through October 2009, a Candlevolume chart. The R curve is launched from the peak in 2000, and nicely captures the peak in early 2004 and the one-bar pullback in late 2005. The S curve that's launched from the low in mid-2006 perfectly captures the sharp one-bar pullback in mid 2007.

But now, let's shift from the index to its ETF, SPY on the same timeframe and same MIDAS curves. This is shown in Figure 6.11. Here you see that the S curve is

FIGURE 6.9   Spider ETF (SPY). Compare to Figure 6.7.

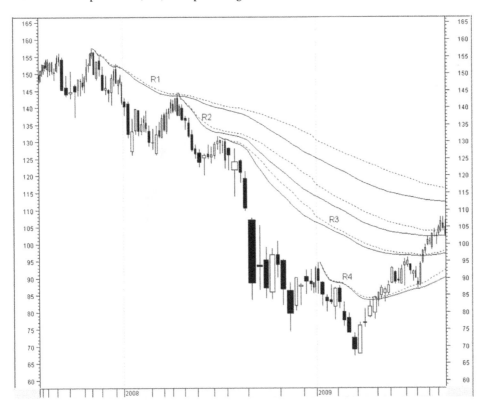

Data Source: Reuters DataLink.

essentially the same. But the R curve is very different, completely missing the 2004 peak. The dotted curve is a no-volume R curve launched from the same date, and it is closer to matching the R curve of Figure 6.10.

To understand what's going on here, notice the extreme variation in volume (bar widths) on this chart, compared to Figure 6.10. SPY's volume started out very low in its early life and has exploded over time, increasing much more rapidly than the increase in the volume of the underlying index. So, as we saw in some examples early in this chapter, a steep trend in volume is displacing the MIDAS R curve.

All of the other ETFs are much younger than SPY, many only a few years old, and new ones are being created all the time. The steep trends in volume on these are often more severe than on SPY. One should be careful about applying MIDAS techniques to any ETF unless you are in a recent region of trading where the volume is not rapidly trending. Putting MIDAS curves and TB-Fs on ETFs that have steep volume trends will give indications that are very different from what one would get using the underlying index.

What should one do when analyzing an index that has no volume data with it, even from Yahoo Finance, but does have a tracking ETF? If you're working in a date

FIGURE 6.10 The S&P 500 from 1999 to 2009, with two MIDAS curves.

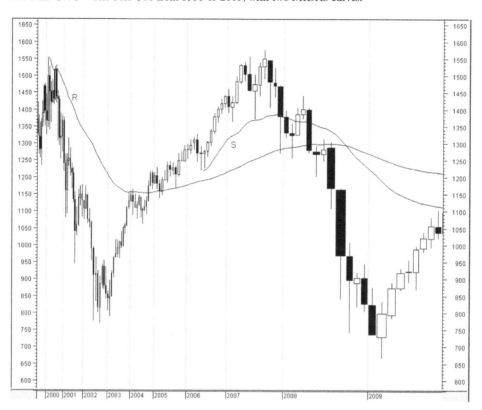

Data Source: Reuters DataLink.

range that is near the beginning of the ETF, then your only choice is to use no-volume MIDAS curves and TB-Fs applied to the underlying index.

The conclusion drawn in the preceding paragraph may seem to conflict with the lesson learned early in this chapter. There, in the examples shown in Figures 6.2 and 6.5, you see that if a MIDAS curve is applied to a date range containing one or more volume trends that have peak to valley ratios greater than 2:1, using the standard MIDAS curve gives a better result than calculating the curve with no volume. But, in this section of this chapter, with ETFs, I seem to be saying the opposite—that if the MIDAS curve is on an ETF's region of very steeply trending volume, you should use the no-volume curves. But there really is no conflict. The steep volume trends that occur in the early life of an ETF are grossly different from the volume data in the underlying index, even though the price data are essentially the same. The ETF's big volume changes are the result of the new ETF finding a market for itself and traders starting to pile in. But, because of the unique way that ETFs are structured, its price is locked to that of the underlying index, and, unlike an ordinary stock, a big surge in trading volume will *not* move the price. So, an ETF is a strange creature whose price is essentially unrelated to its volume. The success of the MIDAS techniques is based on the natural way that price and volume interact on a freely traded security, such as

FIGURE 6.11 Same as Figure 6.10 except that this is the ETF SPY, and a dotted no-volume R curve.

Data Source: Reuters DataLink.

a stock. But when that natural interaction can't happen, MIDAS curves won't work correctly. Then, a better alternative is to use the no-volume MIDAS curves.

When an ETF matures, its trading volume tends to correlate more closely with that of the underlying index, even though there are some differences on a bar-to-bar basis. So, one gets excellent results with the standard MIDAS techniques applied to those ETFs.

In the case of an index that has no published trading volume, even on Yahoo Finance, if it has a tracking ETF, one old enough to be mature, then it's likely that its trading volume is approximately paralleling the unknown volume of the underlying index. So, in that case, it is preferable to apply the standard MIDAS techniques to the ETF, instead of using the no-volume curves on the underlying index.

MIDAS Applied to Long- and Very Long-Term Timeframes

The strategies I have explained so far in this chapter help to prepare us for the peculiarities of applying MIDAS to long- and especially very long-term timeframes—charts of monthly, quarterly, and yearly bars. Just as there were unique problems dealing with

ETFs, the very long-term timeframe presents even different problems about whether and when it's better to use no-volume MIDAS curves than standard ones. As a first indication that things are different in this realm, consider the situation shown in Figure 6.12. This is a time-based monthly bars chart of the S&P 500 for the few years before and after the crash of 1987. The solid curve is a standard MIDAS support curve, and the dotted one is the no-volume version. They are launched from July 1984, the beginning of the steep uptrend that preceded the crash. This crash was a very violent, compact event that occurred entirely within the month of October 1987. Going from the high to the low of that month was a 34 percent loss, greater than what happened in any month during 1929.

The ratio of the volume of October 1987 to the volume of July 1984, the start month of the curves, is 3.7:1, so, according to what was demonstrated early in this chapter, the standard MIDAS curve should work better than the no-volume one. And yet, the opposite is true here. The low of October 1987 lands right on the no-volume curve. (To be exact to five significant figures, the low of October 1987 was 216.46, and the level of the no-volume curve there was 216.07, an utterly insignificant difference.) The standard curve is far from it.

Next is an even more striking example. Figure 6.13 is the time-based quarterly bars chart of the S&P 500 from the mid 1970s to late 2009. The two MIDAS curves,

FIGURE 6.12   Analyzing the crash of 1987.

Data Source: Reuters Datalink.

FIGURE 6.13   The quarterly bars chart of the S&P 500 from 1976 through 2009.

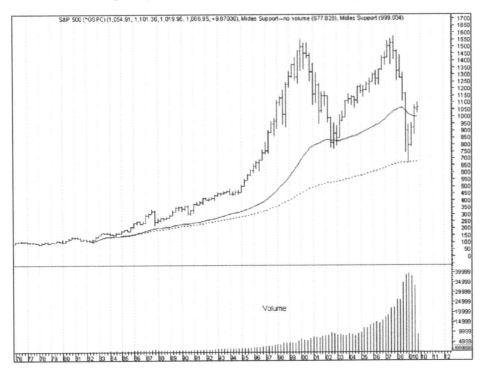

Data Source: Reuters Datalink.

standard (solid) and no-volume (dotted), are launched from the third quarter of 1982, since that was when the huge "Baby Boomer Generation" very long-term bull market started in a breakout from the malaise of the 1970s. The low after the crash of 2008 landed right smack dab on the no-volume curve! The standard curve is meandering insignificantly, very far above. The ratio of the crash low's volume to the launch date's volume is about 90:1.

As discussed earlier, one of the greatest strengths of the MIDAS curves is their uncanny ability to capture a huge, panic spike low in price, revealing a hitherto hidden order in a situation that, at the time, seems to be out of control. As I've said before, one of the reasons that a MIDAS curve does this capturing is that the large volume on the spike low bar "draws" the curve up to the end of that bar. But now, in the very long-term timeframe, panic spike lows are being captured by curves that are calculated *without* volume.

What's going on here? Why are things seemingly reversed? What's different about the scenarios in the very long-term timeframe compared to things on the weekly and daily bars charts? The one obvious big difference is a relentless, enormous, monotonic uptrend in volume, as you can see in the lower pane of Figure 6.13. To get a better view of this situation, Figure 6.14 shows the entire set of data for the S&P 500, back to 1950, with both price and volume shown on log scales.

FIGURE 6.14   S&P 500 quarterly bars, log scale, from 1950 to 2009.

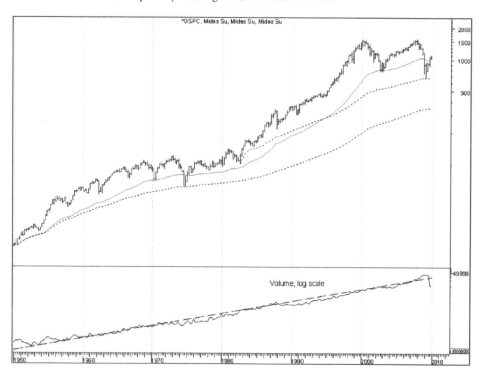

Data Source: Yahoo Finance.

The volume goes from a low of 69 million shares in the third quarter of 1952 to 398 *billion* shares in the first quarter of 2009. The dashed line in the lower pane is a fitted semilog trend line to the volume data. Although there are some fluctuations of the volume around this trend line, the volume trace stays quite close to the trend line, much more so than the price would to a trend line fitted to price. It's obvious that this relentless uptrend completely dominates the behavior of the volume over time, rendering the fluctuations to insignificance. This is what is so different about the very long term timeframe. On all shorter timeframes, it's the *fluctuations* in volume that dominate, instead of an overall trend. It should not be surprising that the behavior of MIDAS curves would be quite different on this timeframe.

In the price pane of Figure 6.14, the upper dotted curve is the same one that's in Figure 6.13. It's launched from the beginning of the generational bull market that ran from 1982 to 2007. The one prior to that, the "Bob Hope Generation" bull market, began in late 1949 and ran until the early 1970s. The price data in Figure 6.14 start at just about the beginning of that bull market, so I've started a no-volume MIDAS support curve there (the lower dotted curve), and sure enough, it perfectly captures the spike low of 1974 that came after the end of that bull market! This is the same thing that happened with the upper dotted curve with respect to the Baby Boomer Generation bull market. These behaviors are too exact to be coincidental. This must be something of major significance.

Does this mean that the standard MIDAS curves have no place on this timeframe? Maybe not. The solid curve on Figure 6.13 is a standard MIDAS support curve, calculated with volume, launched from the beginning of 1950, and it exhibits an amazing behavior; it perfectly captures the lows that come before the major spike lows at the end of the two bull markets. It captured the low in early 1970, during the short recession that was going on then, just before the final rise of that generational bull market. Subsequently, it goes on and does the same thing late in the next generational bull market, capturing the late 2002 low during that short recession, just before the rise to the crash of 2008. This behavior also seems too precise to be coincidental.

Back to 1871

Good data on the U.S. equities market have been recorded since 1871. Professor Robert Shiller of Yale University has collected these data and formed the S&P 500 index back to 1871. He updates and publishes these data every month on his web site, www.irrationalexuberance.com, publicly available for downloading. These are monthly data only, and without volume, but he also includes data on dividends and the cost-of-living inflator.

Figure 6.15 shows these S&P 500 data back to 1871 on yearly bars, log scale on price. It shows an overall modest uptrend from 1871 to 1942, after which an enormous, highly accelerated, very long-term uptrend starts.

The dotted curves are MIDAS S/R curves, calculated with no volume, of course, since there are no volume data available. The solid curves are three topfinders, the smaller two having been fit by the method of adjusting D so that the curve fits two or more of the pullbacks, splitting the differences on the closeness of the curve to the pullbacks. The one covering the 1950s and 1960s reasonably well identified the top of that uptrend. The one launched in 1974 ended rather early, however. The longest one, which is still running, is fit only to the 1974 pullback because, as of this writing, I do not know if the 2009 bar is a low, so I'm leaving the curve running through it.

Inflation Adjustment

Now, let's use the price data that Professor Shiller provides and that have been adjusted for inflation (see Figure 6.16). This is a *very* different picture, indeed! First, there is no enormous very long-term uptrend starting in 1942; that year is just another low. Probably the biggest feature difference in this chart is the appearance of those four huge bulges in price, marked 1, 2, 3 and 4, separated by the lows of 1877, 1920, 1949, and 1974, marked by the arrows. On this scale, it appears that the current bulge, the fourth one, may not have completed going down. Notice also that these bulges alternate in their appearance; the first and third ones are smoothly rounded, but the second and fourth are jagged, with lots of volatility.

There is an excellent explanation for these huge price bulges, and for their alternating appearances, provided by Harry Dent Jr.[1] He uses a demographic analysis, based

FIGURE 6.15 S&P 500 back to 1871 on yearly bars, unadjusted.

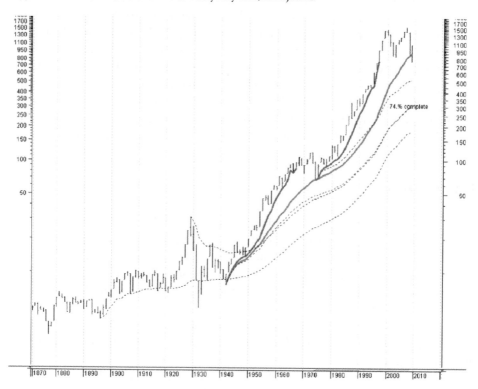

Data Source: Prof. Robert Shiller, Yale University.

on birth rates and immigration data, to identify generational bulges in our population that work their way through the economy and drive the markets. He says the second bulge is due to what he calls the Henry Ford Generation, the third one to the Bob Hope Generation, and the fourth, of course, to the Baby Boomer Generation. (He gives no name for the first one, so I'm calling it the Edwardian Generation.)

Since it takes several decades after people are born for their productive efforts to have any effect on the economy and the markets, he's able to project market behavior way into the future. He foresees that the current decline in the market, from the peak in 2007, will continue for many more years, not finally coming to an end until around 2020, after which the next bulge will begin, the fifth one, brought on by the group he calls the Millennial Generation.

He analyzes the alternating nature of these bulges, calling the second and fourth ones here Growth Booms, and the first, third, and fifth ones Maturity Booms. Growth Booms are characterized by extremely energetic innovations in our economy, whereas each Maturity Boom serves to consolidate the gains of the preceding Growth Boom. I will adopt his terminology and conclusions here while examining this very long-term timeframe.

FIGURE 6.16 S&P 500 on yearly bars since 1871, inflation-adjusted.

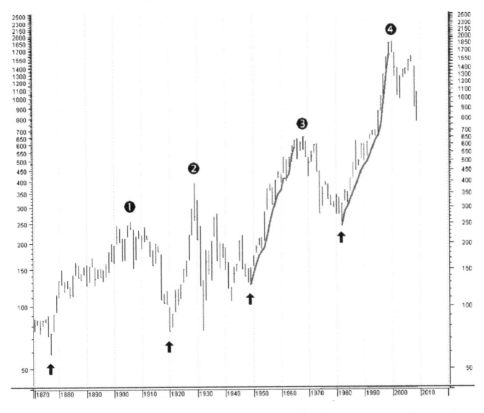

Data Source: Prof. Robert Shiller, Yale University.

In Figure 6.16, the beginnings of those two topfinders have been reset from 1942 and 1974, to 1949 and 1982, since those latter years now appear as the clear beginnings of the major new uptrends. Notice that these TB-Fs fit much better than they did on the unadjusted price data, both clearly identifying the ends of their uptrends. A take-away from this is that, in this very long-term timeframe, the TB-Fs appear to work better, not only on no volume, but especially on inflation-adjusted data.

A Closer Look at the Very Long-Term

Figure 6.16 gives us a broad overview of this timeframe, but, in order to see the finer details in the behavior, let's shift from a yearly bars display to quarterly bars, shown in Figure 6.17.

On this chart are four very significant MIDAS S/R curves (S1, S2, S3, and R1), along with three horizontal support levels (H1, H2, and H3). Each of the S curves is launched from the beginning of a generational bulge. S1 is launched from the sharp low in the second quarter of 1877, the beginning of the Edwardian Generation's

FIGURE 6.17   S&P 500 on quarterly bars since 1871, inflation-adjusted.

Data Source: Prof. Robert Shiller, Yale University.

bulge, and goes on to support all four price pullbacks during that long bulge. That's quite a remarkable performance for an analytical technique that wasn't known until the late twentieth century! S2 is launched from the fourth quarter of 1920, the beginning of the Henry Ford Generation's bulge. It passes all the way through that bulge with no price reactions to it; then, in the fourth quarter of 1974, 54 years after it was launched, it provides the perfect support for the sharp bottom of that recession—quite a remarkable achievement! S3 starts from the beginning of the next bulge, that of the Bob Hope Generation, in the middle of 1949. After price broke down through it in the early 1970s, it became resistance, and in the third quarter of 1976, it nicely resisted price, which then rolled on down to the 1982 low. Right now, S3 appears to be coalescing with H3, so, going forward, this S3/H3 combination can be expected to be important support. In the same vein notice that in a few years, S1 will coalesce with H2, identifying another very significant support level on the chart.

This chart does not show what would be S4, launched from the beginning of the Baby Boomer's bulge in mid-1982, because so far it hasn't done anything of significance. But, compared to the other older curves, S4 would still be very young. Maybe some decades from now, it too will perform an amazing capture of an important spike low.

The resistance curve R1 is launched from the top of the Bob Hope Generation's bulge, in the fourth quarter of 1968. Price has blown through it, so it's now a support curve. Notice how well it captured the sharp low in the first quarter of 2009.

It does show that, on very long-term *inflation adjusted* price data, the no-volume MIDAS S/R curves, launched from major generational turning points, are highly significant, many decades later. Like good homemade pea soup, they just seem to get better with age!

The Very Long-Term Horizontal S/R Levels

Figure 6.18 shows a closer view of the region of Figure 6.17 where the three horizontal levels cross the prices, 1900 through 1990.

The first level, H1, is positioned halfway between the peaks of 1901 and 1906. About eight decades later, in 1982, price came down sharply, at the end of the Bob Hope Generation's bulge, and turned around essentially at that level. H2, defined at the peak of 1929, resisted the price peak in 1956 and then supported the drop in 1960, these events being 27 to 31 years after the level was established. H2 again acted

FIGURE 6.18   S&P 500 on quarterly bars, 1900–1990, inflation-adjusted.

Data Source: Prof. Robert Shiller, Yale University.

as resistance in 1976. H3, established in the mid-1960s, served as resistance in 1987, and support in 1992.

The Bavarian Deer Herd

If you stripped off the horizontal time axes from Figures 6.17 and 6.18, so that the length of time they cover is not displayed, and if you showed these charts to any technical analyst, he or she would simply observe that these curves and horizontal levels are behaving just as one would expect support/resistance indicators to work. But let's examine this further. Support/resistance theory was developed on charts of much shorter timeframes. The theory says that traders' memories of price extrema at the beginnings of these indicators are what drive their behaviors when price later comes back to those levels. But now, S/R behavior is appearing 27 to 80 years after the initial peaks and troughs! Most if not all of the market participants who were active when these curves and levels were established are no longer around when the subsequent S/R reactions occur. So, the theory can't possibly be right. Yet, these tools work, just as well as they do on shorter timeframes. How can we understand this? Certainly, it's not individual traders' memories that are at work here.

It seems as if there is some kind of group dynamic or group memory that transcends the individuals and lasts for many generations. Individuals are not consciously aware of it. Look at R1 on Figure 6.17. I was a young adult in the late 1960s when this curve is launched, only just beginning to be interested in the markets. My interest and involvements have continued to grow since then. But I can assure you, that when the market made that sharp V low in March 2009, the inflation-adjusted price level of the market in 1968 never once entered my mind. Similarly, when the market made its major generational bottom in 1982, not only had none of the participants been active in the markets in the early 1900s, where H1 is launched, but it's unlikely that any of them, in 1982, were contemplating what the inflation-adjusted S&P 500 was in the early 1900s.

On November 4, 2009, Cecilie Rohwedder,[2] in an article in the *Wall Street Journal*, described a similar situation in the field of nonhuman animal behavior. During the Cold War, the border between Czechoslovakia and the Bavarian section of Germany was heavily fortified with barbed wire, electric fences, and gun-toting guards. This split a herd of deer that used to freely roam the forest on both sides of the border into two herds that could no longer cross the border. Many years later, in 1989, the Berlin wall came down, the Cold War ended, and the border fortifications were removed. According to the author, now there's a small walking path there. Examining this border area using Google Earth, one can see that the forest has completely grown back, with no traces of the old fortifications, but no obvious walking path. The forests on both sides of the border are now in national parks, which are run as wildlife preserves. There is no longer any impediment to the movement of animals across the border. Yet, recent studies by German scientists, using GPS-equipped collars on the deer, have shown that the herd on the Bavarian side refuses to cross the border. The animals come up to the border, turn around, and walk away. Similar studies of the herd on the Czech side show the same behavior.

The natural lifespan of these deer is only a few years, so none of these animals was around when the fortifications existed. For that matter, neither were their parents nor grandparents. These animals certainly do not have any memory of the fortifications. And yet, they turn around and walk away from the border, as if there is some kind of group memory that transcends the individuals and the generations. This is the same behavior that's obvious now with S/R tools on very long-term price charts. The simplistic theory behind technical S/R tools cannot explain the real behavior of traders over very long-term timeframes.

Here is another example of a situation where the theory doesn't account for the practice. The ancient practice of acupuncture is based on an elaborate, fanciful theory of human anatomy that posits special organs and pathways connecting various parts of the surface of the body. The only problem is, as any anatomist knows, none of these organs or pathways actually exist. So, the theory behind acupuncture is totally bogus; and yet the practice works.

The success of acupuncture presents medical science with a challenge to come up with a scientifically valid explanation, which, so far, it hasn't. The Bavarian deer challenge zoologists to explain their behavior. And similarly, the success of S/R tools on very long-term price charts calls on the new field of Behavioral Economics to come up with an explanation. But, the lack of scientific explanation should not make us avoid using these tools. The deer still turn at the German-Czech border, acupuncture still works, and so do our S/R tools.

What Can Be Said about the Very Long-Term Future?

Technical Analysis cannot predict the dates and values of future prices. But, it can anticipate significant events, and identify them once they appear on the charts. Furthermore, it can combine very synergistically with some fundamental analyses, such as Harry Dent Jr.'s demographic work.

Figure 6.19 is an illustration from a presentation that I gave to a group from the Boston Chapter of the American Association of Individual Investors in November of 2008.

The gray background curve is Harry Dent Jr.'s[3] Spending Wave (Dent, 1993) that he constructed from demographic work to illustrate the effects of population bulges on the economy and the markets. The solid curve is the inflation-adjusted S&P 500 index, on a linear scale, which I sized vertically and horizontally so that it matches the 1929 peak and the 1932 low of the Spending Wave. No other adjustments to that curve were made.

The extent to which the inflation-adjusted S&P 500 tracks the Spending Wave in Figure 6.19 is quite remarkable. Yes, the peak in 2000 is far above the Spending Wave,

FIGURE 6.19   The inflation-adjusted S&P 500 Index, overlaid on Harry Dent Jr.'s Spending Wave.

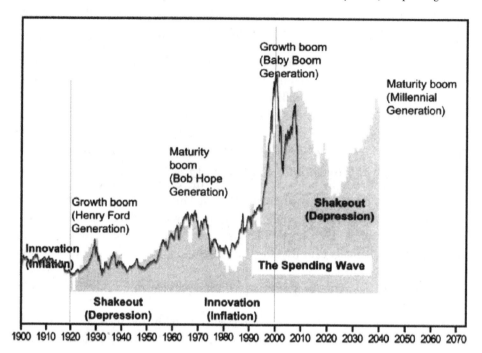

Data Sources: Prof. Robert Shiller and Harry Dent Jr.

but that peak was due to the excessive euphoria of the tech bubble; the Spending Wave is not constructed in a way that can model such shorter-term manias. The Spending Wave should still be a good guide to the expected very long-term behavior of the market. And that guide tells us to expect that the current shakeout in the market will continue to a deep low sometime around 2020.

Now, let's see how what's been learned earlier in this chapter can be used to help us identify the coming shakeout low when it arrives. Look again at Figure 6.17. The first and third price bulges, the Edwardian and the Bob Hope ones, are both Maturity booms. When the Bob Hope boom dissipated, it fell from its high in 1968 to its sharp V bottom in 1982, right at H1, the level of the top of the Edwardian boom. A very nice symmetry is there, where the end of one Maturity boom goes down to the level of the top of the previous Maturity boom.

Now the market is descending from the top of the fourth bulge, the Baby Boomer one, which is a Growth boom. So, if the same symmetry were to hold here as it did with the fall from the Bob Hope boom, one would expect this fall to end at the level of the top of the previous Growth boom, the Henry Ford one, in other words right at H2, the level of the top of the market in 1929. And let's remember, in the future, H2 will have been strongly reinforced by its merger with S1, giving us more confidence in this expected support at the bottom of our current decline.

In Figure 6.17, the level of H2 is 391.23, therefore, is that the price level that the S&P 500 is expected to get down to at the coming bottom? No. All that can be said is that the expected level will be the *inflation adjusted* high of the S&P 500 in 1929, which happened to be 391.23 at the time of this writing (November, 2009). The way that Professor Shiller updates this database is that, every month, he lists the latest value of the S&P 500 index as reported by Standard & Poors. Then, he takes the latest cost of living inflator, and applies it to *all* of the *previous* values of the S&P 500, all the way back to 1871. This raises all of the previous numbers, while holding the latest one constant. This means that, going forward, all of the data points on these charts will continually rise with inflation, month after month. And if actual deflation happens, as some observers are now saying might come about, then the data points will fall. One doesn't know what the level of the H2/S1 combination will be when the bottom of the market arrives. But one can anticipate that it will be the same as the high of 1929, a number that will be different from 391.23; how much different we simply cannot know in advance because we don't know what inflation/deflation will do between now and then. We'll know it when we get there.

It is quite possible that the current decline will not behave with such nice symmetry compared to the previous decline by going down to H2/S1. For instance, the decline may end at H3/S3, or at some other significant support level. Indeed, in Figure 6.19, the level of the Spending Wave at the bottom of the coming shakeout suggests that price may not go further down than the H3/S3 level. If the decline is highly accelerated in its late phase, then one will be able to fit a bottomfinder to the data, and thus be able to identify the bottom when that TB-F ends.

I'm adding this last paragraph in proof, just before this book goes to press, writing this on December 21, 2010. I wrote the rest of this chapter over a year ago. Since then, I've had time to understand the significance of the Federal Reserves' first round of quantitative easing (QE1), $1.6 trillion of new money injected into the monetary system at the beginning of the financial crisis. Now, the Fed has started QE2, another $0.9 trillion more of new treasury purchases. (The actual amount of QE2 will end up being substantially more since the Fed is also rolling over those Treasuries in their portfolio that mature.) And some observers are expecting there will be a QE3 and QE4 to follow. These levels of quantitative easing are without precedence in our history. The Fed didn't do anything similar to this in the 1930s or in the 1970s, time periods when the market reached washout bottoms. These amounts of new money are so huge that they most likely will have a significant effect on the long-term stock market in the upward direction. It is possible that the effect will be strong enough to keep the market from going through the final washout phase that I was anticipating in the previous paragraphs. The market may not get down to the H2/S1 level or even the H3/S3 one. Since this situation is historically unprecedented, we can't expect long-term history to repeat itself. We are entering truly uncharted territory. But what we can and always should do is keep updating our charts with significant S/R curves, and watch for either turns at or penetrations of them.

Summary

- *Short- and intermediate-term timeframes.* If the volume trends on your chart encompass changes in volume that are less than 2:1, the no-volume MIDAS curves will be very close to the standard curves.
- *Exchange-traded funds.* In the mature portion of an ETF's chart, the standard MIDAS curves work just as well as if they were applied to the underlying index that includes volume data. But, in the immature regions that have very steep volume trends, one should only use the no-volume curves.
- *Long-term timeframes—years.* If the volume data are totally dominated by a strong, pervasive trend, the no-volume MIDAS curves generally work better. But there may be some special instances where the standard curves can give some unique insights.
- *Very long-term timeframes—many decades.* The MIDAS S/R curves and TB-Fs work very well as long as they are calculated on inflation-adjusted prices and without volume.
- *Projections for the long-term future.* The MIDAS methods work nicely in combination with Harry Dent Jr.'s demographic projections.

CHAPTER 7

EquiVolume, Midas and Float Analysis

David G. Hawkins

In this chapter, I explore the commonalities between the EquiVolume system of analysis of Richard W. Arms Jr.,[1] the Midas TB-F Method of Paul Levine,[2] and the Float Analysis of Steve Woods.[3] Although these three authors have never acknowledged each other in their publications, their three methodologies are founded on a basic principle first enunciated by Arms in 1971.[4] Because of this, these three techniques work together in very complimentary ways.

The Basic Principle—"Volume Leads to Volume"

In his 1971 book, Richard W. Arms Jr. presented a very basic principle. He said:

> The cornerstone of price projection in EquiVolume charting is: *volume leads to volume*. The volume that is generated in the building of a base is almost exactly the volume dissipated in the ensuing advance. Similarly, the volume occurring in a top formation is very close to the same as the volume involved in the subsequent decline.[5]

This is quite an assertion! Could things really be that elegantly simple? Can it be that if you measure the total volume traded as a stock goes across a base or a top, that this will be the same volume that's traded in the trend that comes next? Indeed, that is exactly what he meant.

Before examining why this could be true, let's look at two examples. First, go back and look at Figure 5.9 in Chapter 5. Here we see a topfinder fit to that uptrend. In that chapter, I mentioned that this TB-F curve actually extends a ways into the next bar, that large square-shaped box of September 25. In fact, it extends 70 percent of the way, so this TB-F really did overshoot the top by an uncomfortable amount. You can see on the left side of this chart that there is a low, flat area of price that precedes the start of the uptrend. Let's expand this view to better see that area, as shown in Figure 7.1.

We see that a well-defined base did precede the uptrend. In making this chart, I first placed the two dashed vertical lines at the places that are obviously the beginning and end of the base. Next I calculated the volume going across the base. Then I placed the third dashed vertical line to the right of the second one as closely as possible at the same distance from the second one as the first two are spaced. (The charting software, MetaStock, does not allow one to place a vertical line within a price box, only between two.) And sure enough, that third line turns out to be located right at the place where the steep slope of the uptrend ends and the consolidation begins. The number of shares traded going across the base, 621,078, is almost exactly equal to the number going up to the top of that trend, 621,398.

The method shown here of placing the dashed vertical lines is the one that Arms[6] described, which he calls "price projection." Notice that this means that the second vertical line is at a somewhat different location from the start of the topfinder curve. The volume extent, that is, the horizontal width, of the topfinder begins at the left side

FIGURE 7.1   Expanded view of Figure 5.9 from Chapter 5.

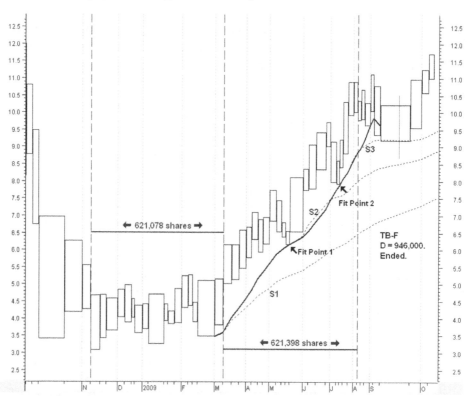

Data Source: Reuters DataLink.

FIGURE 7.2 Price projection of ORCL, applied to Figure 5.19 of Chapter 5.

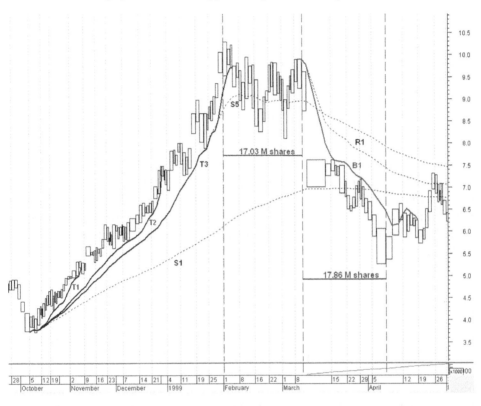

Data Source: Reuters DataLink.

of the box it starts at, because the calculation of the TB-F must include the volume of the starting bar. Measuring from that left side to the right by 946,000 shares lands at that little vertical line segment that I've hand-drawn in on the large square box on September 25. In this particular example, Arms's price projection method produced a much better result than the topfinder, but that's not always the case.

Let's do one more example, this time a flat top leading to a downtrend. Look at Figure 5.19 in Chapter 5, where we had that very problematic bottomfinder. Now see, in Figure 7.2 in this chapter, what an Arms price projection shows. The top is 17.03 million shares wide. Measuring to the right of the second vertical dashed line by that amount places you right at the middle of the bottom price bar of that downtrend. Thus, price projection called the bottom exactly.

Why Does Price Projection Work?

The basic program of any part of Technical Analysis is to generate mathematical, graphical models of the psychological behavior of market participants. Here we have a model, Arms's price projection, which often works. So, what behavior of traders is it capturing when it works? Let's consider a flat bottom, a base, on a chart. It occurs after a downtrend. During that base, the new buyers, attracted by what they see as bargain prices, are snapping up the shares being dumped by discouraged holders who have owned the stock since it was much higher in price and are finally giving up on it. The downward pressure from the discouraged holders balances the upward pressure from the new bargain investors all the way across the base.

Once all the discouraged holders have finally sold out, the only pressure on the stock is upward from new bargain buyers, so the stock breaks out of the bottom and starts a new uptrend. At that point, most of those holding the stock are the value investors who bought in during the bottom in expectation of higher prices, so these folks in general will want to keep holding the stock as the uptrend gets underway. The only way to get trades to happen is for the buyers to bid up the stock sufficiently to entice holders to sell. At first, they will get traders with a short trading timeframe who are willing to sell at prices only modestly above the base, but after those folks exit, prices have to be bid up higher and higher to get holders who have longer and longer trading timeframes to be willing to sell. Eventually, the uptrend will get high enough to flush out all of the holders who bought in during the base. *This means that the total volume traded during that uptrend will have been equal to what was traded going across the bottom.*

What energized the uptrend was the reluctance of holders who bought in at bargain levels during the base to sell until each one of them finally saw a high enough price to motivate them to take their profits. So, we can consider the total volume traded across the bottom to be a bolus of fuel that drives the uptrend.

Once that fuel has been expended, we have a different dynamic. At that point, virtually all of the holders of the stock have bought in at various price points during the uptrend; therefore, they are all momentum players, as opposed to the value investors who bought in during the bottom. Value investors are relatively content to sit by and wait for price to go up, thus constricting the supply of stock available for trading, which drives prices higher. But momentum players hop on during an uptrend, and have one finger on the exit trigger, ready to bail out at any sign that the trend is over. So, the price behavior after this point will be different, since the supportive presence of the value investors is gone, often bringing the trend to a halt and starting a new downtrend. But even if price does progress higher from this point, its behavior will be different. On a chart, this change of price behavior is usually very clearly visible as a distinct change in the pattern of price movement from one of a steady, robust uptrend to something less bullish, or even bearish.

Now, consider the complementary opposite situation, a downtrend following a flat top. If the top has been sufficiently long, then most of the holders of the stock will have sold out to new buyers, all having come in at nearly the same price. The new owners of the stock bought in because they were expecting higher prices. But if, for whatever fundamental or market reasons, a small breakdown in price starts below the range of prices across the top, then some stop-loss orders start to be hit, which pushes the price even lower, and a cascade of selling pressure ensues: prices going lower and lower, until the pain of the paper losses finally gets great enough to flush out even the most determined holders who bought in at the top. Once all of those have sold out, the selling pressure is relieved, and the downtrend stops. Therefore, *the total volume traded in the downtrend will equal the volume traded across the preceding top.*

Although Arms[7] didn't mention it when he first stated the price projection principle, it does also apply to consolidations that turn out to be neither tops nor bottoms. Consider the situation at the very beginning of the last paragraph, a significant flat area after an uptrend. But this time, let's say that, for whatever fundamental or market reasons, there is a small breakout of price above the range of the flat top. Right away, all those who bought in across the flat region will sit on their hands, because a new uptrend is what they've been waiting for; it's why they bought in. Now we're in the same kind of situation as described in the first part of this section. A new uptrend will commence, and continue until it has flushed out all those who bought in across the previous flat area, so the uptrend will consume the same trading volume as happened across the flat. This is an example of a consolidation within an overall uptrend, which will last at least until all of the "fuel" stored up during the consolidation has been spent. Thereafter, there might be further upward motion of the price, but its pattern will be different, and usually less robust.

And finally, the fourth variation of this theme is the consolidation that happens during an overall downtrend, after which the downtrend continues until the fuel stored during the consolidation is consumed. At this point, it should be obvious how the argument goes about this situation.

In summary, whenever there is a flat area of a chart that goes on for sufficiently long enough to have substantially changed the ownership of the stock, the subsequent trend will consume a cumulative volume about equal to that which was traded going across the flat area. This is true whether we have an uptrend after a base, a downtrend after a flat top, or a trend resumption after a consolidation. *The trading across a flat area provides the fuel for the subsequent trend.*

This explanation of price projection is, of course, a simplification of what happens in real trading environments. There are very long-term holders of the stock who won't trade at all in the timeframes of these flats and trends, and on the other hand there are swing traders and day traders who go in and out of the stock many times during any one of these patterns. These two groups, very approximately, will tend to cancel each other out, making the description here work on a large number of occasions.

The Connection between Price Projection and the Topfinder/Bottomfinder

In the previous section we saw that an identified bolus of volume provides the fuel for a trend. Here is what Paul Levine said of the topfinder/bottomfinder in his twelfth article:

> Since technical analysis is often referred to these days as "rocket science," we can employ this metaphor by likening a move in a stock to a rocket launch. Already we have referred to a trend reversal as the "launch point"; now we imagine that—as with a

rocket—the move's duration is pre-programmed by loading a given amount of "fuel," which in our case is a fixed amount of cumulative volume. During the powered phase of the launch, the rocket's control mechanisms act to follow the nominal trajectory defined by the TOPFINDER curve. When the fuel is completely burnt, the rocket returns to the Earth's surface represented by the S/R level.[8]

The common principle between price projection and the TB-F is Volume Leads to Volume: One can identify a fixed amount of cumulative volume, the "fuel," which drives a trend, such that when this amount of volume is expended, the trend ends. Later, I'll show that this is also behind Steve Woods' Float Analysis.[9]

With price projection, the fuel is identified ahead of the trend as the cumulative volume across the preceding flat area, whereas with the TB-F, the fuel gets identified partway through the trend by the process of fitting the TB-F curve to pullback(s) from the trend. Price projection applies to any trend, whereas the TB-F only works with properly identified accelerated trends. Price projection is inapplicable if there is no flat before the trend, whereas the TB-F works no matter what precedes an accelerated trend. These two methodologies overlap considerably in their applicabilities, but neither one can completely replace the other, so we need to keep both in our tool kit.

Price projection shows us one way of identifying the bolus of fuel for a trend, but, there are many TB-Fs that work very well, having not been preceded by a flat. So, what is it that pulls together the fuel for such TB-Fs? I do not know of an answer to that question based purely on chart analysis. One probable source could be that some fundamental event, such as an earnings surprise, sufficiently energizes some group of the investing public to participate in the stock in such a way that an accelerated trend unfolds, one that can be tracked by a TB-F. In general, some exogenous event provides the energy to fuel the trend, the strength of that event determining the size of the bolus of fuel so imparted to the stock.

Using Price Projection

I have been using price projection for many years, and thereby have learned some peculiarities of its behavior that Arms[10] has not described. Two of these are summarized in the examples that follow.

The first situation is where the flat area is far from flat, having quite a bit of price variation across it, and where the trend clearly starts well before the flat area ends. The challenge in these circumstances is how to identify the width of the flat, and where to identify the beginning of the trend. I've chosen an example that is rather extreme in these concerns in order to clearly demonstrate how to handle it. This is shown in Figure 7.3, the daily bars chart of IBM from June 1993 through early February 1994.

The first problem is how to identify the width of the base. From what Arms[11] has written, one would probably choose the dashed horizontal line segment, which measures between the sharp lows across the base. But I have found that, in general, it is better to measure it between the points where price first descends into the base

FIGURE 7.3 IBM with both price and TB-F projections from a base.

Data Source: Reuters DataLink.

region and where it later breaks out above it, and in this example, this is shown where it is labeled, "Base Width 6.06 Million Shares."

The second problem is where to identify the beginning of the trend. Arms's[12] examples always have the trend start at the point where the base ends. But I have found that when the trend clearly starts from a point deep within the base, that's the point from which to start measuring forward by the width of the base, even though this makes for considerable overlap between the base and the trend. I started measuring the uptrend at the low in late September, and extended to the right to a bar that brings the cumulative volume as close as possible to 6.06 million shares. The closest was 6.03 million. Doing it this way, price projection identifies the end of the trend exactly in this example. In general, this method works very well for most examples of this type.

It's interesting to compare the result of price projection with TB-F curves. First of all, one shouldn't launch a TB-F from that low in late September, because an S curve launched from there turns out to be an "S foothill" curve, as shown here. So, the TB-Fs are started from the point from which the real S1 for this accelerated uptrend starts. T1, the first TB-F, is fit to the pullback at about the halfway point as marked by the lower arrow, and it ended just one bar short of the real end of the accelerated uptrend, undershooting it by only 5 percent, which is very good. T2, the second TB-F is fit to the latest pullback, at the second arrow, and it went far beyond the end of the accelerated trend, overshooting it by 18 percent. But, it turns out that the bar at which T2 ended is actually the real high. So, overall, I'd say that both price projection and the two TB-Fs all worked very well in this example.

The second situation illustrated here is of a consolidation. See Figure 7.4, a daily bars chart of Sirius XM Radio (SIRI), from June through December of 2004.

The first two dashed vertical lines locate the consolidation, which is measured from *between* the big bar that came up into the consolidation and the one that broke out above the consolidation, *not* inclusive. This method of identifying the consolidation's width is the same as what I used in the previous example for the base width, and is the one that usually gives the best results.

The consolidation's width is 17.37 million shares and, measuring to the right from the point where the following uptrend starts by as close as possible to that width, places the third dashed vertical line as shown: 17.65 million shares from the beginning of the trend, at a high price of about 7. Now, you might object that the trend actually went on by about that much again, all the way up to a top at a high price of about 9.4, so did the price projection method fail here? No, it didn't, because the region between the latter two dashed vertical lines is a far steeper, more highly accelerated uptrend than

FIGURE 7.4   SIRI with consolidation, price projection and topfinder.

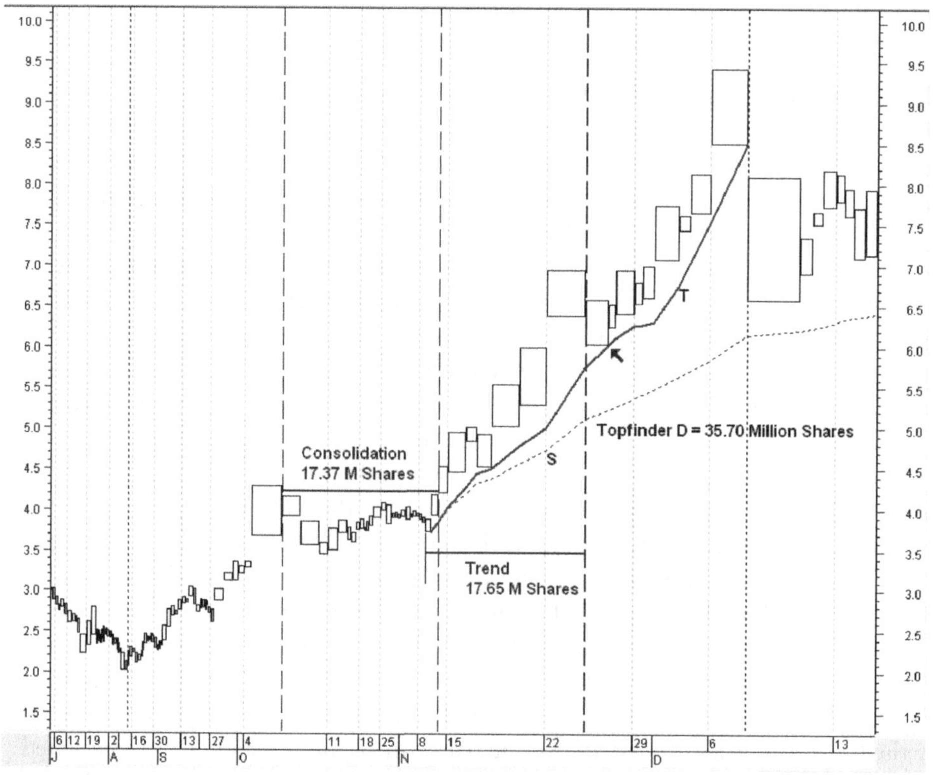

Data Source: Reuters DataLink.

what came after it. So, this region that price projection captured is a self-contained accelerated uptrend, which ended right where price projection said it would. After that ended, price responded by dropping down, at the arrow, then it resumed the larger, longer timeframe uptrend that had started in April. The consolidation stored up fuel that it unleashed, producing a more accelerated portion of the longer-term trend until that fuel burned out.

I tried fitting a topfinder to this highly accelerated region, but there aren't enough price bars there. Most likely, if I had hourly price data, dropping down to that timeframe would give me enough bars for a fit. So, on this daily bars chart, I did the fit to the pullback marked by the arrow, and it ran right up to the top.

There are two more interesting features in this example. I placed the first of those two dotted vertical lines to the left of the consolidation's start by the same distance as the width of the consolidation, and the second one at a similar equal distance after the third dashed line. These four vertical lines divide the long-term uptrend into four equally spaced parts, each line being at a dividing point between distinctly different behaviors on the chart. Apparently, there is some kind of periodicity going on in cumulative volume, and I'll have a lot more to say about such things later in this chapter. And finally, the width of the consolidation happens to be very nearly equal to one-half of the float for this security, which means that the first half of this longer trend, from the April low to the end of the consolidation, is about one float. Notice how very different the second half of this long trend looks from the first. Apparently, a cumulative volume of one float has some significance, and that's a good segue to the next section.

Steve Woods's Float Analysis

In Steve Woods's two books published in 2000 and 2002,[13] he introduced a system called Float Analysis, which actually is a special case of Arms's price projection methodology. It is based on a stock's float, that fraction of the outstanding shares that are available for trading by virtue of there being no restrictions on the owners to keep them from trading the stock. Whenever the trading goes through a period where the cumulative volume traded is equal to the float, it's approximately correct to say that the stock has all new ownership of the shares that are available for trading at the end of that period, so that will affect the dynamics of the trading going forward. Go back now and reread the section earlier in this chapter called, "Why Does Price Projection Work?" and in each instance where I referred to the volume traded going across a flat area, assume that that volume is at least equal to the float, and you have a pretty good idea for the basis of Woods's system.

Woods[14] recognized that whenever a stock breaks out from the range of prices that occurred during one float turnover, there is a strong likelihood that a new trend will ensue in the direction of the breakout. The trader could use such a breakout as an entry signal, or the trader could wait until price pulled back to support/resistance and then resumed movement in the direction of the new trend. He further identified that support/resistance often comes at something he calls the half-float level.

Woods[15] developed a unique charting indicator called float channel lines that, when placed on a chart, clearly show every time a float breakout occurs, and where the support/resistance from the half-float level is. StockShare LLC has developed a very nice plug-in for their charting program that puts the float channel lines and boxes on the chart and gives a very convenient way of moving them around; that's what I'm using for the figures in this section. There is also a plug-in available for MetaStock, but I have not tried it. This charting method has usefulness in tracking other examples of Arms's price projection that involve volume turnovers that are not necessarily of one float, and I'll show those in Chapter 8.

Figure 7.5 shows how this charting system works. This is the daily bars chart, CandleVolume, of SeaChange International, ticker SEAC, from June 2005 through March 2006. The large gray rectangle is called the float turnover box. It is referenced to the date of its right side, which is November 23, 2005, in this illustration, and the structure of the box is backward-looking. The horizontal width of the box is set to be one float. The level of the top of the box is that of the highest price before the reference date, and the bottom of the box is at the lowest price before the reference. Imagine grabbing onto the box at the dot on the middle of the right side and dragging

FIGURE 7.5   SEAC with float channel lines and boxes.

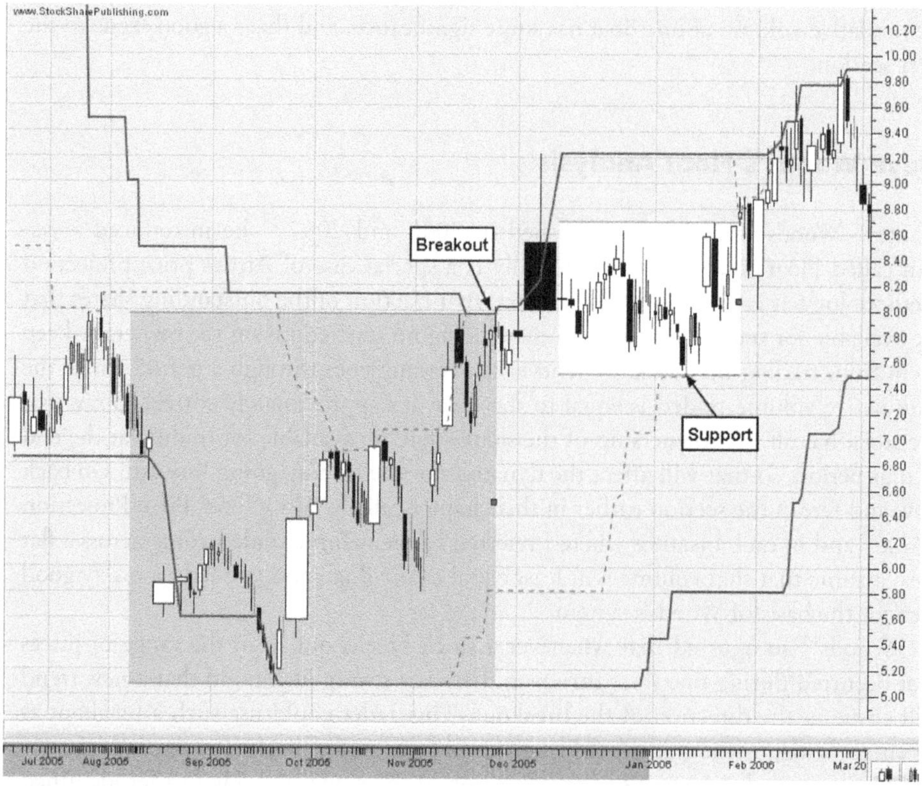

Data Source: Yahoo Finance.

this box backwards and forwards along the chart, which the software does allow you to do. The box's height automatically rescales to the maximum price range within it as you drag it. The upper right and lower right corners of the box are crucially important. Imagine that there are pencils stuck into those two corners, upper and lower right, and that the pencils draw two thick lines on the chart as you drag the box back and forth. Those two so-drawn lines are the thick lines shown on this chart, and they form what is called the float channel.

The smaller rectangle, the bright white one, is called the half-float turnover box since its width is set to one-half of the float, but otherwise it behaves the same way as the full float does. If one drags that half-float box around, it will generate the dotted lines shown here, which often serve as support or resistance to price movement.

You can see where a price breakout occurred, right where I've located the float box. Price moved up from there and later consolidated back down, and found support at the half-float line, lifting off from there. That liftoff place would have been a good entry point.

Figure 7.6 shows this form of charting applied to Figure 5.9 of Chapter 5, BRKR on weekly bars. I placed the float turnover box in the base, right at the point of

FIGURE 7.6   BRKR weekly bars on a float channels chart.

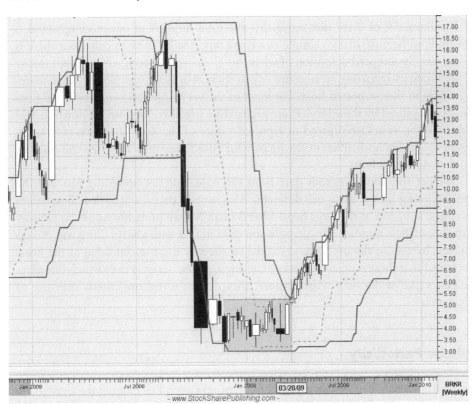

Data Source: Yahoo Finance and Reuters.

the breakout. This box fits very nicely in the base, so we have a good example of a one-float turnover base formation. The size of one-float, as reported by Reuters, is 64.85 million shares.

I've extended the view of this chart back another half-year to show you the approach to and descent from the previous top. Back there you can see some of the problems and limitations of this methodology. The large black down bar early in that top does break down through the half-float line, which give a signal that the trend is over. That one is a pretty good signal. But look what happens just before the end of the top—a float breakout to the upside signal, which would seem to be saying that this was a consolidation and not a top, tempting one to go long this stock. But, very shortly thereafter, price crashes down, breaking down through both the half-float line and the full-float channel in one bar, a rather late sell signal. On the right side of the chart, look at the uptrend, which may already have ended, yet the half-float line is far below the price, meaning you'd have to give up a lot of profit before getting a sell signal from it. In general, the problem is a paucity of timely signals with this methodology. A good way to remedy this would be to combine Midas S/R curves with this method.

Another problem with this method is that float data can be wildly inaccurate. In this example with BRKR, Reuters reports that the float is 64.85 million shares, but three other very highly respected financial data web sites give very different values. Yahoo Finance reports 49.33 million, Bloomberg says 56.06 million, and MSN gives 85.5 million. All of these sites agree that the total number of outstanding shares is 164 million, because that's a simple fact that's reported by the company. But there is no universally accepted definition of what the "float" is, and companies do not report it. So, financial reporting services are left to their own devices to decide what shares to include in their reported float. For most of the very large cap companies, the float numbers reported by these services are pretty close together, but moving down to mid and small cap issues, the spread in reported values of the float often gets very large. Figure 7.7 shows how different the picture for BRKR becomes if we use the smallest number, 49.33 million.

We get the same breakout date from the base, but the preceding top and the uptrend going into it are quite different. Also, notice that the half-float line comes up to and supports at the large September 25 bar. So, we probably would be happier with the smallest number. But the solution does not lie with always using, say, Yahoo Finance, because it doesn't always give the smallest or most useful value of the float. I've found that there is no consistency at all among these services as to which one gives the best value of the float. Furthermore, they do not reveal the criteria they use to calculate it.

Volume Periodicity

There's another part of Arms's work that's often very useful in judging the trends of a security, what he calls Volume Periodicity, described in his book, *Volume Cycles in the*

FIGURE 7.7   BRKR weekly with the smallest reported float.

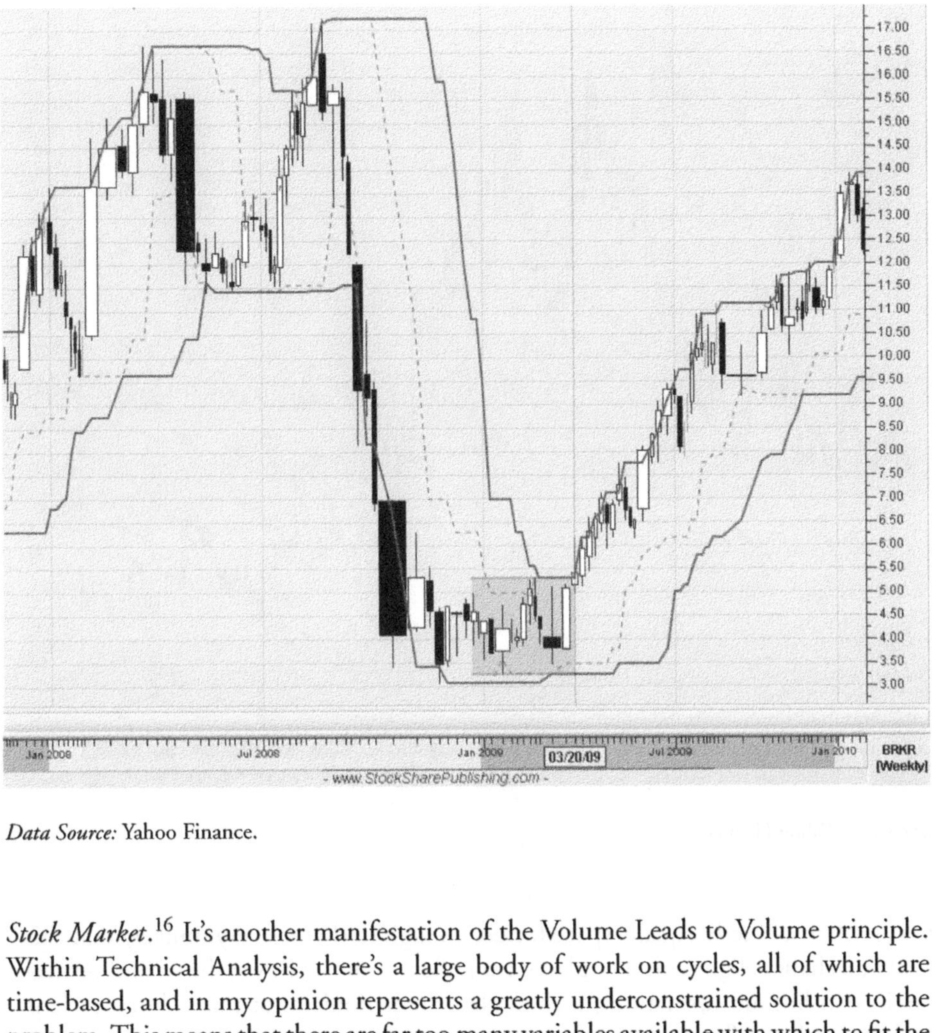

Data Source: Yahoo Finance.

Stock Market.[16] It's another manifestation of the Volume Leads to Volume principle. Within Technical Analysis, there's a large body of work on cycles, all of which are time-based, and in my opinion represents a greatly underconstrained solution to the problem. This means that there are far too many variables available with which to fit the data. There are an infinite number of time periods, amplitudes, and phase relationships that the analyst may choose from, making it possible to find a combination of time cycles that will fit any data. Hindsight works perfectly with time cycle analysis, but it usually fails upon walking forward with the fit that one has achieved.

Arms's[17] Volume Periodicity is a much simpler, more direct observation of cycles that naturally appear in a security's price movement as a function of cumulative volume instead of time. Let's start first with a traditional time-based chart, Figure 7.8, the monthly bars chart of Eastman Kodak, EK, from 1996 through 2005. The dotted vertical lines are placed at major lows, which are obviously not evenly spaced, so there is no regular periodicity in time.

Now, look at Figure 7.9, which is the same as Figure 7.8 except that the display has been switched to CandleVolume. In this chart, the lows marked by the dotted vertical

FIGURE 7.8   EK monthly bars, time-based chart.

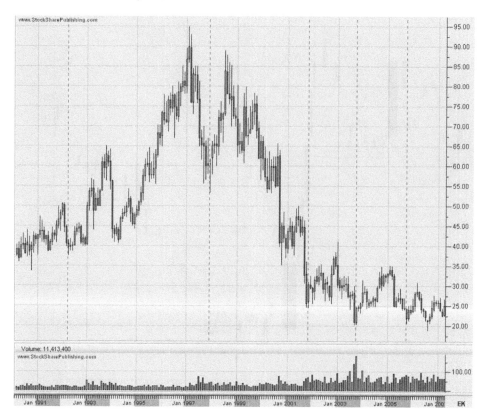

Data Source: Yahoo Finance.

lines are almost exactly equally spaced, close enough so that it's very unlikely that this could be a chance alignment. I've placed a one-float turnover box at the second vertical line, in that bottom formation, to show that the periodicity of this volume cycle is much larger than a float, which is true of most stocks on monthly bar charts.

Kodak is a large cap stock, so next let's look at a more modest-sized example, Pitney Bowes, ticker PBI, monthly bars from 1993 to the present, in Figure 7.10. Again, the small gray box is a one-float wide turnover box, and it's placed at that top in 2007.

There are four vertical lines, each at a significant low. Additionally, I've placed a fifth line off into the future at the same spacing. This shows that at the time of this writing, PBI is about halfway in cumulative volume to the next projected major low, if the volume periodicity continues for another cycle. The way to use this information is to watch this chart as it develops going forward, and if, when price arrives at that fifth line it forms a low and starts to rise, then this could be the place for buying the stock, a buy signal that would come much sooner than waiting for subsequent price action to confirm that a new uptrend is underway.

FIGURE 7.9   Same as Figure 7.8 but on CandleVolume display.

Data Source: Yahoo Finance.

Notice that the lows are regularly spaced in cumulative volume, but the highs are not. This is a common characteristic of volume periodicity, indicative that lows and highs are indeed two quite different phenomena. The positions of the highs move around from cycle to cycle, while the lows remain nailed to a fixed periodicity. If the security is in a general uptrend that extends for more than a cycle, then there is a tendency for the highs to shift to the right, and conversely to the left during overall down motion. You can see some of that behavior in this example. During the second cycle and a ways into the third one, there's a general uptrend, and you see that the peak of the second cycle, in early 2005, is located far to the right side of that cycle. But then abruptly the trend changes in the third cycle, and its peak, where the float box is, is on the far left side of that cycle. The stronger the overall trend, then the greater the shift of the peak within a cycle. All this shifting takes place while the lows stay firmly anchored in their regular volume periodicity.

In Figure 7.11, Cisco Systems, CSCO, monthly bars since 1996, we see a well-established volume periodicity, except there is that apparently anomalous behavior

FIGURE 7.10　PBI on monthly bars, CandleVolume display.

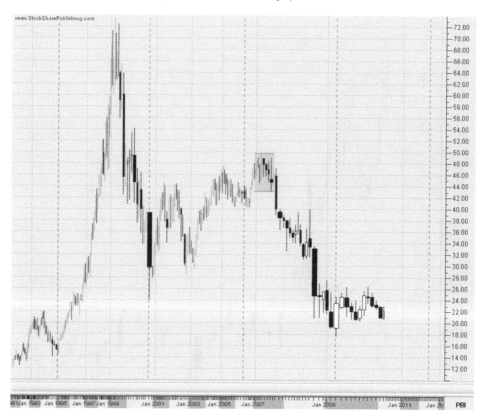

Data Source: Yahoo Finance.

where the peak at the top of the dot.com bubble in 2000 comes exactly where a low would be expected to have been, given the subsequent periodic behavior.

What really happened here is that the ascent to that peak was so strong that the shifting of the peak to the right side of that channel shifted it all the way to the right edge, onto the spot that would normally mark a low. When this happens, this is usually a major high for that stock.

Volume periodicity is not a constant throughout a stock's trading. It comes in, lasts for a few cycles, then dissipates. Figure 7.12 shows a monthly bars chart for JP Morgan Chase from the late 1980s into early 2008. We see that a volume periodicity started in late 1990, lasted for three cycles, then, at the position of the dotted vertical line where the next low would have been expected, there is no low. A few months ahead of that point, the financial crisis of 2007–2009 had started, which completely changed the nature of the trading in this stock, obliterating the volume periodicity.

Volume periodicity typically doesn't last for more than about five cycles. One of the longest I've seen is shown in Figure 7.13, taken from a presentation I made in 2006 to a section of the Boston chapter of the American Association of Individual Investors.

FIGURE 7.11 CSCO's huge peak where a low would be expected.

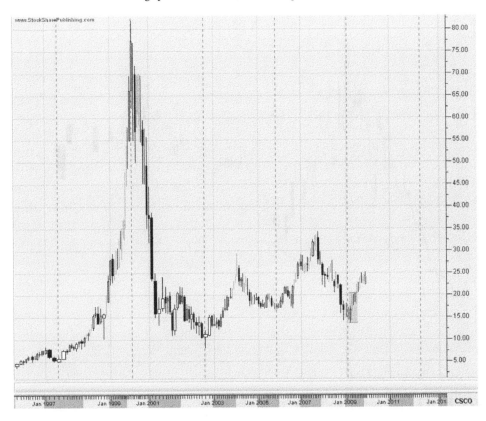

Data Source: Yahoo Finance.

It shows monthly bars of Scientific Atlanta, ticker SFA, from 1993 to 2006. This is also another example of a manic peak in price that right-shifted within its cycle so far that it landed on the projected position of the next low. We see six complete cycles, and part of a seventh; trading ended at that point when Cisco bought Scientific Atlanta. We'll never know how many more cycles it would have run but for that acquisition.

Although all of the foregoing examples have been on monthly bars charts, volume periodicity happens on all timeframes. Figure 7.14 is the daily bars chart that covers the base in Bruker Corp., BRKR, that occurred in 2009 and during the first several months of the following accelerated uptrend. The base consists of three cycles of volume periodicity, and as the subsequent very strong uptrend got underway, we see not one but two maximally right-shifted peaks landing on the next two projected low locations. The periodicity dissipated after that.

In his book, Arms[18] explored further aspects of volume periodicity, including a unique method for graphically displaying the fractal nature of a security's trading, which is very interesting in and of itself, but not germane to our work here, so I'll leave that for you to read on your own.

FIGURE 7.12 JPM monthly bars, showing volume periodicity that dissipated.

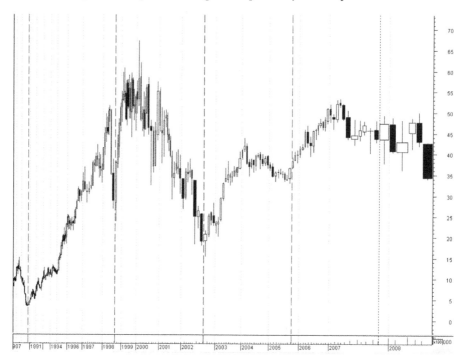

Data Source: Reuters DataLink.

FIGURE 7.13 Six volume periodic cycles of Scientific Atlanta.

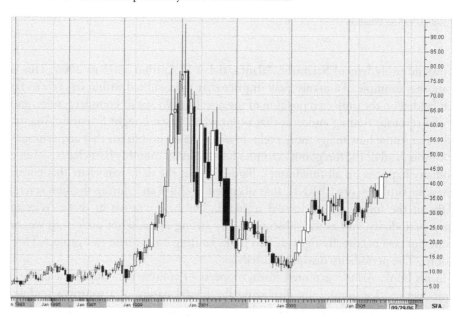

Data Source: Yahoo Finance.

FIGURE 7.14 BRKR daily bars, with volume periodicity.

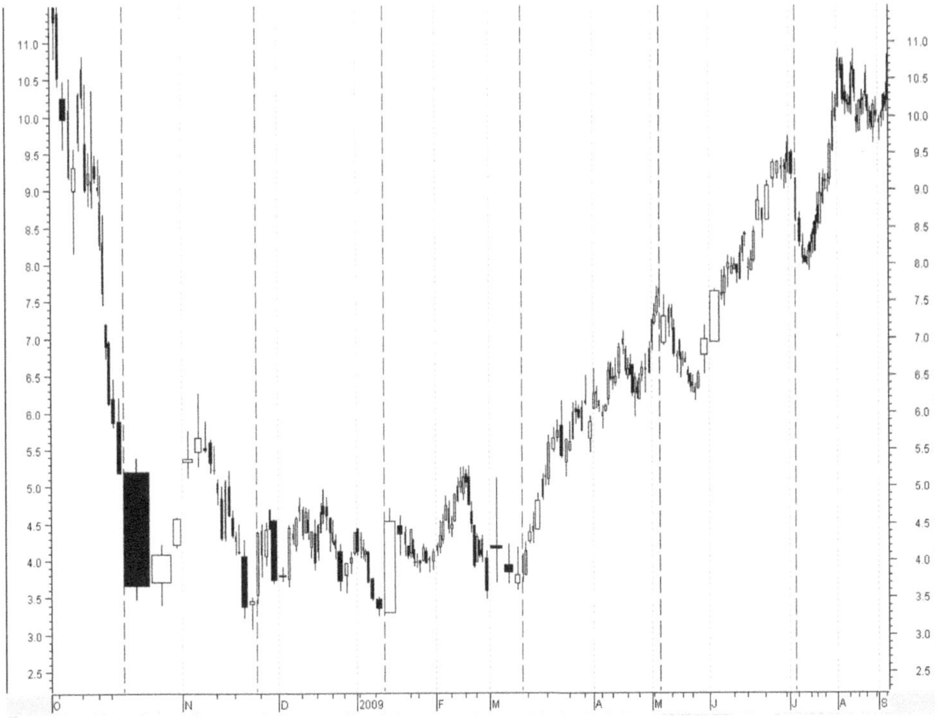

Data Source: Reuters DataLink.

Summary

- Arms's fundamental principle, Volume Leads to Volume, is the basis for his price projection method,[19] Levine's topfinder/bottomfinder,[20] Woods's[21] Float Analysis, and Arms's[22] Volume Periodicity.
- Because of this common basic principle, these techniques work together in a very complementary manner when combined into a systematic method of trading.
- Although the ordinary Midas S/R curves are not based on this principle, using them also in such a combined trading system adds greatly to the effectiveness of the system, which I will demonstrate in another chapter.

CHAPTER 8

Putting It All Together

David G. Hawkins

In this chapter I pull together the techniques I have presented in earlier chapters, and show how they can be used profitably in trading. There are various styles of trading that go by names such as trend following (also known as momentum trading), trading base breakouts (and the complementary opposite, top breakdowns), and picking tops or bottoms. The MIDAS S/R curves and TB-Fs, along with the supportive techniques I have presented already—the works of Elder,[1] Arms,[2] and Woods[3]—can be used in combination very beneficially in all of these trading styles. In this chapter, I'll show examples of these.

Trend Following

In February 2006, I gave a presentation to the Computerized Investing Group of the Boston chapter of the American Association of Individual Investors on the topic of how to use the MIDAS methods and their supportive techniques in the trend following style of trading. I summarized it with 13 bulleted points, specific directions, on how to do this kind of trading. Looking at that now, I see it has held up quite well over these years. So, here are the 13 steps, with only minor edits to bring them fully into line with my earlier chapters of this book. These directions were written for trading on the long side—purchasing a stock—rather than short selling, but it should be obvious how to recast it for trading on the short side.

Trend Following Trading with MIDAS and Its Supportive Methodologies
1. On your long-term chart, identify the trend. If it is an uptrend, then proceed. Put the major MIDAS curves on this chart. Look for volume periodicity and price projections, mark them into the future, and identify a price target.
2. On your intermediate- (or short-) term chart, put on float channels and see if the last float breakout was up or down. If it was a breakout to the upside,

then proceed. If not, then monitor the stock until an upside float breakout occurs.

3. On your intermediate-term chart, put in the significant MIDAS support curves under the current price, and carry over and mark the levels of the ones from the long-term chart. Put in the level of the 50 percent float turnover curve. Together, these form a ladder of support levels below the current price.

4. Switch to your short-term chart. Copy over the ladder of support levels from the intermediate-term chart, and add any significant support curves that originate on the short-term chart, including any close-in resistance curve above the current price.

5. Monitor your short-term and intermediate-term charts as they develop going forward. Watch for price to retrace down through the ladder of support levels until it stops at one and just starts to turn up.

6. On your short-term chart, enter when price breaks above either an important close-in resistance level or above the high of the bar that bounced up off the support.

7. Place your stop just below the support off which price just bounced, and above the next-lower support level.

8. If you get stopped out, enter again when price turns up at a lower support level. It may take you several such entry attempts to get one that holds.

9. Once in, monitor the stock, and trail the stop up, keeping it just under the support curve above which you entered.

10. On your intermediate-term chart, launch a new MIDAS support curve from the point where price bounced up. As time goes on, if price comes down to and bounces up off this new curve, launch a new S curve from this spot, and move your stop up to trail under this new curve.

11. Identify all significant resistance levels up to your target, using MIDAS resistance curves from all three timeframe charts.

12. Consider selling at least some of your position if price stalls out at, and just starts to turn down from, a significant resistance level that's below your target.

13. Exit when price reaches your target, or if a well-fit TB-F ends roughly in the vicinity of your target.

I'm going to show one example of using these steps, one that won't necessarily exercise all of the provisions in these 13 steps, but will give you a flavor for how to apply these. Let's say that in early 2005 you became interested in Hewlett Packard, ticker HPQ. I'm assuming that your investing timeframe is anywhere from several months up to a year or so, so that your intermediate-term chart, your primary chart, is of the weekly bars.

Step 1

You start by watching the long-term chart, monthly bars, and by the end of June, this chart is as shown in Figure 8.1. Shortly after that low in August 2004 was established, the volume periodicity became obvious, as marked by the dashed vertical lines, so you would be thinking that HPQ is likely in a new uptrend. You launched a resistance

FIGURE 8.1   HPQ long-term chart at mid-2005, monthly bars.

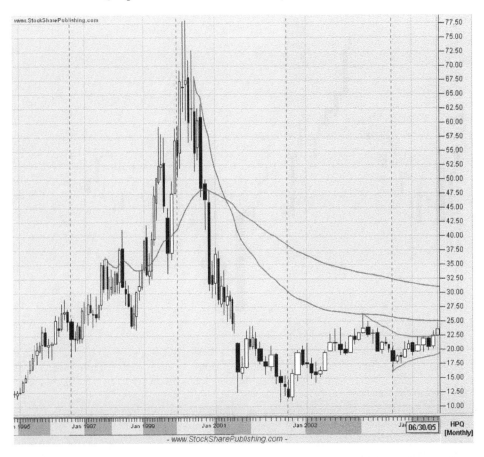

Data Source: Reuters DataLink.

curve from the highest price in 2000, but then adjusted its start to capture the high at the beginning of 2004, a calibrated curve. Then, you put in the highest resistance curve, whose start you find is in mid-1997. Finally, you put in the resistance curve launched from January 2004. By June 2005, price has broken above that January 2004 resistance curve while remaining above the support curve launched from the August 2004 low, thus confirming that HPQ is in a long-term uptrend.

As for a price target, you could anticipate that the current long-term uptrend, which started in August 2004, will have as much upward extension as the previous one, which started in late 2002, a move of 15.36. Adding this onto the low at August 2004 ends up at 31.34, so that's your target.

Steps 2 and 3

Next, you set up your intermediate-term chart, Figure 8.2, weekly bars. The three horizontal line segments on the right are drawn in from the levels of those two

FIGURE 8.2   The intermediate-term chart for HPQ, with float channels.

- www.StockSharePublishing.com -

Data Source: Yahoo Finance.

resistance and one support curves from the monthly bars chart. You put in the R curve from the January 2004 high and the S curve from the August 2004 low. You also start a new S curve from the local low of April 29, 2005.

The values of the float for HPQ from the four major financial web sites vary from 2.26 billion shares to 2.36 billion, with three of them clustering around 2.35 billion, so here 2.35 billion is used. You see that the tall white candle of late May has broken above the top of the float channel, so HPQ is now in float breakup mode.

Step 4

Next you set up your short-term chart, daily bars, Figure 8.3. The six horizontal line segments along the right side are the levels you've marked from the S/R curves from the monthly and weekly bars charts. The lowest curve, an S curve, you launched from the August 13 low. The next curve up you launched from the May 12 low, and the

FIGURE 8.3   The short-term, daily bars chart, with S/R levels transcribed from the monthly and weekly bars charts.

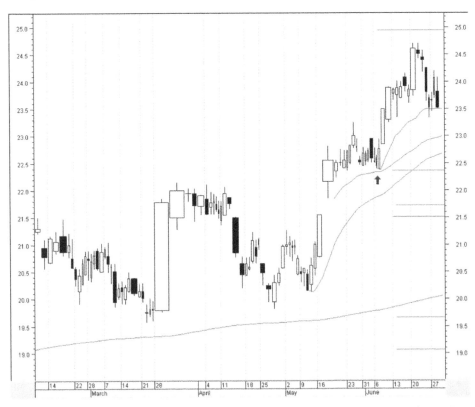

Data Source: Reuters DataLink.

third S curve is a calibrated curve to fit to the early June low, at the arrow. Finally, you launched the S curve from that low at the arrow.

Steps 5 through 7

Now, you sit back and monitor the daily (and weekly) bars charts, and watch for price to retrace down, stop at one of the support levels, and bounce up from it. You don't have to wait long! In Figure 8.4, you see that price did exactly that on that tall white candle of July 5, which broke down through the highest S curve, came sufficiently close to the next S curve, and bounced strongly up, closing far above the highest S curve. That's your entry signal, so you enter on the open of the next day, the bar marked with the arrow, getting you in at 23.80. Next, you put your stop-loss order in at the dashed horizontal line segment, which is halfway between the second and third S curves, at 22.84. So, the stop is 15 cents below the S curve above which you entered. As you trail your stop up, going forward, you should keep it 15 cents or further below that curve.

FIGURE 8.4   Your entry at the open of the arrowed bar, and stop-loss at the dashed line.

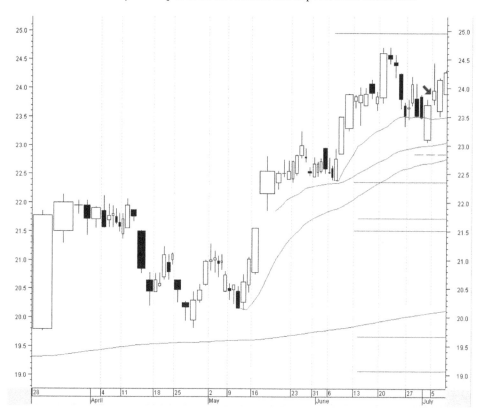

Data Source: Reuters DataLink.

Steps 8, 9, and 10

These steps have to do with trailing your stop up. At first, you trail it under the curve that the price bounced up off of on the day before you entered. That curve is the one shown in Figure 8.4, which was launched from mid-May. Let's see how this goes over the next month or so after you entered. Figure 8.5 is Figure 8.4 extended through August 17, where I've removed some of the curves and lines, which are no longer needed at this point, to keep the chart from getting too cluttered. In early August, price came down close to the S curve above which you entered, and then gapped up strongly from there. At that point, your stop has been trailed up, always 15 cents below that curve, and is marked there by the dashed horizontal line.

Next I'm showing here in Figure 8.6 the application of Step 10, the weekly bars chart, which I've extended forward in time into early November. An S curve is launched from the entry bar, and, in accordance with Step 10, a new one is started from where price bounced up in early August, and then the stop is trailed up under that new one, the upper curve in Figure 8.6.

FIGURE 8.5 Daily chart through mid-August, with trailing stop.

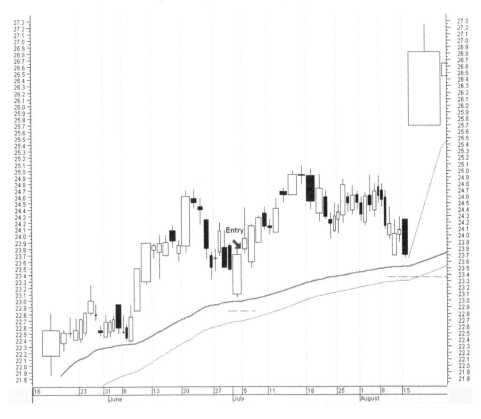

Data Source: Reuters DataLink.

During the week of October 28, the price spiked down, hitting the stop, the dashed horizontal line segment, and taking you out at a price of 26.28. So, your profit from the trade was 2.48, a 10.4 percent gain (not including commissions and any slippage in getting your entry and exit executed).

Analysis

You the reader may think that with all this hindsight available to me, I might have picked a more advantageous example with which to showcase my 13 trading rules. But, this example is more realistic. Trading isn't easy, and it isn't always hugely profitable. And sometimes, trading is very frustrating. In this example, we see that no sooner were you stopped out, then the price went down and bounced strongly up off the next lower S curve. If you were a disciplined trader, in accordance with Step 8, you would have turned right around and entered again, and continued following these same trading rules.

Figure 8.7 shows the weekly bars chart extended out to a longer timeframe, with the full fivefold hierarchy of S curves that this long uptrend ultimately spawned. Here

FIGURE 8.6   Weekly bars, showing where the stop was hit.

Data Source: Reuters DataLink.

we can see more clearly what happened. Your entry was in early July, and exit in late October. The gray box is a float turnover box, which I've placed on the chart to outline a consolidation. I sized the box to fit the consolidation, which happens to be two-thirds of one float. Then, I placed that second box, the bright white one of the same width, where the uptrend started, and it ended right where you got stopped out. This is very similar to the situation illustrated in Figure 7.4 of Chapter 7—a consolidation within an uptrend, where price temporarily dropped down when the fuel from the consolidation ran out, but then the longer-term uptrend resumed. It was that sudden price drop that stopped you out. But if you had been paying attention to the price projection from that consolidation, as illustrated in Figure 8.7, this drop would not have been unexpected. Then, seeing the strong bounce off the next-lowest S curve would have encouraged you to get back in, following these trading rules, which would have guided you up to the top, finally taking you out at the last bar on this chart, probably at a price of about 31.5, which is quite close to your target of 31.34. So you would have captured a good portion of this whole uptrend, and in all, it would have been a successful two round-trip trade exercise.

FIGURE 8.7 Weekly bars on an extended timeframe.

Data Source: Yahoo Finance.

In addition to seeing the price projection, Figure 8.7 shows that the first price pullbacks of this uptrend were far above the first support curve, which would have encouraged you to apply the topfinder.

Figure 8.8 shows a topfinder, T1, the thin curve, fitted to the pullback marked by the lowest arrow, the week of August 19. Assuming you got back into the stock after having been stopped out in late October, as time progressed, and you saw those later pullbacks marked by the upper two arrows, you would have fit a new topfinder to them, T2, since in general a TB-F curve fit to the latest pullback(s) is the most accurate one. In April 2006, as price started penetrating T2, that TB-F curve would have been well over 90 percent done. Furthermore, this uptrend was already sporting a fivefold hierarchy of S curves, so these two situations, plus the fact that price had already hit your target, would have strongly encouraged you to exit. This would have gotten you out probably a dollar higher than if you had waited for S5 to be broken.

FIGURE 8.8   Two topfinders applied to HPQ weekly bars.

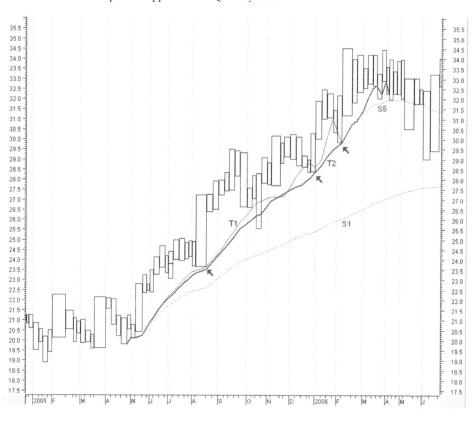

Data Source: Reuters DataLink.

Finally, another critique of my 13 steps is that, after a float breakout occurs, it calls for waiting until a pullback to and turn up from support before entering. This is a very conservative requirement, which is meant to keep you from losing in case the breakout is only what Wyckoff's followers call an "upthrust," a momentary breakout that quickly reverses back into the previous consolidation. Yes, sometimes upthrusts do happen, but just as often, the opposite also happens, which is that the breakout turns out to be so strong that a significant pullback doesn't happen for a long time, so you'd end up losing a substantial portion of the new trend. An example of this latter situation is shown in Figure 2.9 of Chapter 2, where the breakout above the S foothill curve occurred at about 12, but there was essentially no pullback until price had run all the way up to about 22. So, we have three possible scenarios upon a breakout: first is the upthrust, second is a nice pullback allowing you a good entry, and the third is the breakout followed by a long uptrend with no tradeable pullback. What many traders do is to put half of their position on at the breakout, and hold back the other half for a pullback entry.

Calling Bottoms

It's obvious from the preceding section that adhering to the 13 steps of trend following inevitably leads to a delayed entry on a developing trend, for two reasons. One is that the long-term chart must clearly show that an uptrend is in progress, and the second is the requirement from float analysis that the status must be float breakout. If the new uptrend starts from a V bottom, these two requirements, especially the float one, will usually cause the trader to miss a good portion of the trend. This section shows how a trader, who is more aggressive than one who strictly follows the 13 steps, may use the techniques I've written about here for entering after a V bottom.

Let's go back to the example of the previous section. As mentioned there regarding Figure 8.1, "shortly after that low in August 2004 was established, the volume periodicity became obvious, as marked by the dashed vertical lines, so you would be thinking that HPQ is likely in a new uptrend." But this time, instead of waiting for a float breakout to occur, let's see how much closer we can get to not only identify the bottom, but get an entry after the bottom that has a reasonable chance of working. To have identified the volume periodicity low, we must be sitting two or three price bars after it, placing the present moment at, say, early November.

The key to this new technique is to drop down to your intermediate-term chart, weekly bars, as shown here in Figure 8.9. The dotted vertical line identifies the volume periodic low, which was at that huge black bar of the week of August 13. R4 is the fourth curve in the four-fold hierarchy of resistance curves from the preceding downtrend. You launch S1 from the bottom of the August 13 bar. As the weeks go by from then until the present, November 5, we see that price rose up, perforated R4 somewhat, then declined back down, but didn't even get all the way down to S1. Instead, in our present week, price has strongly broken above R4. So, we have *price breaking resistance while simultaneously holding support.* This is the classic MIDAS definition of an uptrend, and it's occurring on this weekly bar chart's timeframe. I would have entered at the close of this week, getting me in at 19.69, and placing the stop a modest distance below S1, as shown here at about 17.30. Thereafter, you should manage the trade pretty much as the rest of the thirteen trend following steps show.

To summarize this "calling the bottom" technique, use volume periodicity on your long-term chart to identify a probable bottom. But then, switch to your intermediate-term chart, and enter if and only if price breaks resistance while holding support on this timeframe, putting your stop below the first support curve.

Now, I'm going to stick my neck out and give an example that is not from hindsight, but is current, an entry I recently made using this "calling the bottom" method. This is another case where, by the time you are reading this, you'll be able to see how this is progressing, if indeed I haven't been already stopped out! In addition to being current, it's also a small cap (almost micro-cap) stock, compared to previous examples of rather large companies. The company is the Providence & Worcester Railroad, ticker PWX, a regional freight railroad company operating in southern New England, a sentimental favorite of mine. I've owned this stock for many years, and just now have used the "calling the bottom" strategy to add to my position.

FIGURE 8.9   HPQ weekly bars just after the August 2004 low.

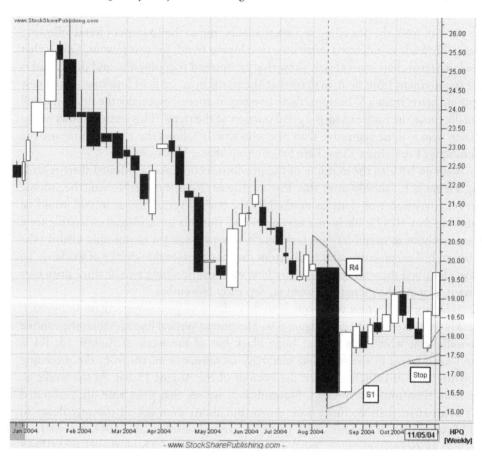

Data Source: Yahoo Finance.

I have a many-years-long horizon for PWX, so my long-term chart is the quarterly bars chart, the intermediate is the monthly bars, and the short-term is the weekly. (It's so thinly traded that the daily bars chart is not useful.) The stock, in its current form, has been publicly traded since 1988, and Figure 8.10 is the quarterly bars chart, CandleVolume, for its whole trading history.

The low at the end of the first quarter of 2009, which corresponded with the overall market low after the crash, made clear a reasonable designation of volume periodicity for PWX as shown by the dashed vertical lines. The sloping trend line shown here further supports the identification of the March 2009 low as the major, multiyear low.

One might object, based on Arms's[4] price projection principle, that the large, broad top that extended over 2006 and 2007 has certainly not spent all its downward force on the stock since the end of 2007. I agree, that is a concern, but the drop from the 2007 high has been so large, and the volume periodicity and trend line

FIGURE 8.10 PWX, quarterly bars, since its 1988 IPO.

Data Source: Reuters DataLink.

indications so compelling, that I'm willing to overlook the price projection negativity. It will probably cast a depressing influence over the stock for a while more, until that bolus of negative fuel is fully dissipated, but it probably won't push the price below the 2009 low.

Figure 8.11 is my intermediate-term chart, monthly bars, and shows my "calling the bottom" entry. One day in January 2010, PWX popped strongly above both R3 and R2 while holding above S1, so I entered there, which turned out to be the high for the month. Since then, as of this writing (February 17, 2010), things seem to be moving in the right direction.

Base Breakouts

Traders who are watching a base formation in progress, and intending to buy the stock if and when it breaks out, often would like to buy it while it's still in the base, if they can have some assurance that the breakout is imminent. There is a technique using a MIDAS resistance curve that can identify such situations, giving the trader an entry

FIGURE 8.11   PWX on monthly bars, showing a "calling the bottom" entry.

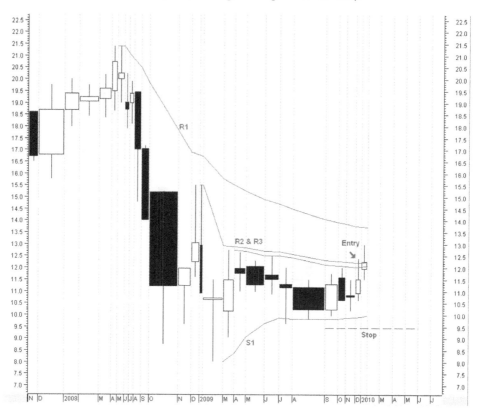

Data Source: Reuters DataLink.

that is lower than the breakout price. The prerequisite is that the base needs to be at least a half float long. Then, one looks for a high price bar within the base, somewhere around the middle. Next, you find the starting point for an R curve, back in the downtrend that preceded the base, which fits to that high price bar in the middle of the base. When price breaks above this R curve, it usually is in a run-up to the base breakout, and can be traded at that point.

The example here is a small cap biotech stock, Clinical Data, Inc., ticker CLDA. Like PWX in the previous section, CLDA is lightly traded, and it takes several years to trade one float, so the chart here is of monthly bars. However, this technique is not specific to small cap stocks or long timeframe charts. It works just as well on a large cap with a daily bars chart, provided that the base is at least a half float long.

Figure 8.12 shows CLDA from late 1995 up to 2002. Let's say you're observing this in late 2000, and see the S foothills curve giving good support, which encourages you to believe that a breakout may be on its way. By this point, you see that the cumulative volume traded since it dropped into this base is approximately one half float (depending on whose float numbers you believe!). So, by trial and error, you find

FIGURE 8.12   CLDA monthly bars, base breakout pattern.

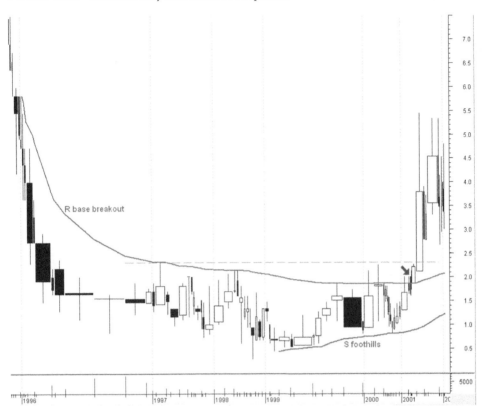

Data Source: Reuters DataLink.

a place back in the preceding downtrend, February 1996, which produces the R curve shown here that so nicely captures those first three highs within the base. Three later price bars do puncture the R curve but don't close above it. Finally, at the arrow, the price bar of May 2001 closes above the R curve at a price of 2. That should be your entry.

The dashed horizontal line defines the top of the base formation at 2.30. Absent this R curve method, you'd have to wait until that level was broken. It may not seem like much of an advantage to get in at the arrow instead of at the subsequent breakout above 2.30, but often such base breakouts are very strong, almost explosive up moves, so that it may be very difficult to get an entry that's close to the breakout point. But with this R curve method, you can get in during a more orderly trading regime, probably in this example getting an entry very close to 2.

This is an aggressive entry method. There's no guarantee that price won't fall far back after your entry and before the eventual base breakout. This is why it's good to have some additional supporting evidence, such as that S foothills curve, or perhaps evidence of accumulation going on, which often precedes a breakout.

Summary

This chapter showed how to apply the techniques of earlier chapters to different trading scenarios, specifically

- Trend following
- Calling the bottom
- Base breakouts

PART IV

New Departures

CHAPTER 9

Standard and Calibrated Curves

David G. Hawkins

"Standard" is the name I'm giving to the MIDAS S/R curves as defined by Paul Levine. Specifically, a Standard Curve is launched from a significant price turning point. After working with these curves over many years since Levine[1] introduced them, I have noticed that often, subsequent turning points are not captured by the Standard Curves. Sometimes, the failure to capture is only a minor porosity, but often turning points after the launch point are either significantly above or below the curve. In Chapter 2 I addressed this situation by looking at the curve launched from the same date but on the next-higher timeframe (or sometimes even the next-lower one). Often, that does give insight, producing a curve that captures the pullback in question. But it doesn't always work. In this chapter I'll describe a new technique, the Calibrated Curve, which discovers a significant capturing curve every time. I'm going to motivate this calibration methodology with a series of examples, then summarize it at the end of this chapter with a list of specific directions for implementing it.

Discovering the Calibrated Curves

Figure 9.1, a daily bars chart of the NASDAQ Composite Index, shows the first three standard resistance curves in the hierarchy of resistance curves that starts from the high on August 15, 2008. The topmost curve, number 1, behaves beautifully, capturing both the close-in price retracements, plus the first major high after the launch. However, the second curve floats far above the next high after its launch point, while the third curve dives way below the two succeeding major highs.

Let's try launching a new curve somewhere after the start of number 2 at a place such that this new curve does catch the third high, the high from which number 3 is launched, a place I'm calling the Calibration Point. Figure 9.2 shows the result.

FIGURE 9.1 A hierarchy of three standard resistance curves.

Data Source: Reuters Datalink.

The fact that the new curve captures the Calibration Point is trivial; its starting point was chosen to make it capture that point. But what is very far from trivial, what is in fact hugely significant, is that this new curve goes on to perfectly capture subsequent highs, points that were not captured by any of the standard curves. I didn't expect this would happen when I first tried this, so it came as a major surprise.

Examples

Could this just be a fluke, a peculiarity of this one example? Let's try it on several other charts, different tickers and different timeframes. In the following charts, the standard curves are dotted, and the new Calibrated Curves are solid.

FIGURE 9.2 A Calibrated Curve, inserted between two primary curves.

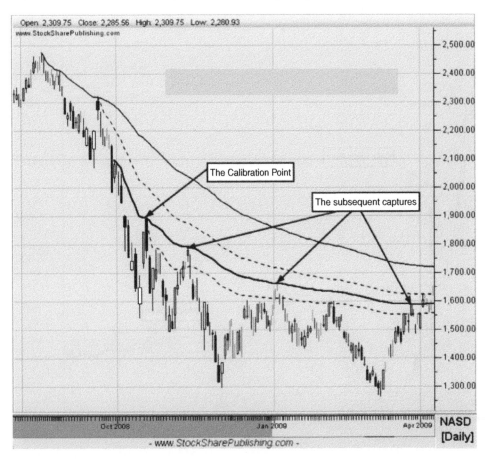

Data Source: Reuters Datalink.

Figure 9.3 is the weekly bars chart of AT&T, ticker T, from 2001 through mid-2006.

That huge price drop in late November 2002 was due to a major divestiture and reorganization, after which it really became a completely different company, so you might expect that technical analysis (TA) tools like MIDAS curves would not hold their significance across such a discontinuity. And yet, the Calibrated Curve that is defined by the high just before the divestiture perfectly captures the retracement in 2006.

Figure 9.4 is the weekly bars chart of IBM from 1992 through 2009. The standard curve launched from the 1993 low nicely captures the sharp low of 2002. Now look at the curve calibrated to the low in early 1996. It captures the late 1996 low, but even more dramatically, 12 years later, it perfectly catches the spike low of 2008.

FIGURE 9.3 Another Calibrated Curve between two primary curves.

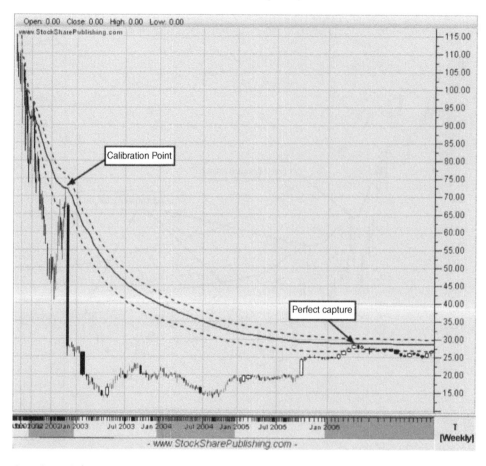

Data Source: Yahoo Finance.

Figure 9.5 is the monthly bars chart of Southern Company, ticker SO, from 1987 to 2009. The curve calibrated to the 1990 low perfectly captures the very sharp spike low of early 2009, 19 years after the Calibration Point, which is quite a testament to the power of this methodology.

And finally, Figure 9.6 is an example from the small cap world, Bruker Corp., ticker BRKR, weekly bars chart. The Calibrated Curve captures those three lows in mid-2008, which the Standard Curves completely missed.

I see many of these examples on a regular basis, so much so that this must be an important category of curves.

Curves that Are Both Standard and Calibrated

A common occurrence, as shown in many examples in this book, is that a Standard S or R curve goes on to support or resist a subsequent pullback in price. Curve number 1

FIGURE 9.4   IBM Standard Curve (dotted) and Calibrated Curve (solid).

Data Source: Reuters Datalink.

in Figure 9.1 is a good example. After that point, that curve should now be considered to be both a Standard Curve and a Calibrated Curve. This recognizes that it has added significance going forward. If you have such a curve on your chart, you should keep it there, watching for further captures of price pullbacks, even a long time later.

Figure 9.7 is the monthly bars chart of the American conglomerate General Electric, ticker GE, beginning in 1989. The lowest of these four curves here is a support curve launched from the low in the recession of 1990. The curve perfectly captures the price pullback in November 1991. Upon seeing that happen, you should keep this curve on the chart, because, as you see, 11 years later, in late 2002, it caught the low after the bursting of the tech bubble.

Not all curves turn out to be useful. The second-from-the-bottom curve in Figure 9.7 was launched from the price turning point in 1992, and went on to perfectly support the price pullbacks in 1994. But after that, it has not, as yet, proved to be useful.

The third from the bottom curve in Figure 9.7 was launched in March 1995 in order to capture the sharp downthrust in price that occurred in September 2001,

FIGURE 9.5   A Calibrated Curve can be valid over a very long timeframe.

Data Source: Reuters Datalink.

right after the 9/11 terrorist attacks. So, strictly speaking, this is only a Calibrated Curve. This launch point is very close to the price turning point in late 1994, so this curve is just slightly off being a Standard Curve. So far, since 2001, this curve hasn't been useful.

The highest curve in Figure 9.7 is a very good example of one that is both Standard and Calibrated. It is launched from the price turning point in early 1997, very nearly caught the downspike in late 1997, and perfectly captured the deep low during the Asian currency crisis of 1998. Notice that, nine years later in 2006, it caught that shallow pullback in price that started in 2005.

Curves that Show Just Minor Porosity

Sometimes a Standard Curve comes quite close to capturing a pullback in price, showing just minor porosity. But now, with the calibration process in mind, let's see what can happen when one adjusts the starting point to put the capture exactly on.

FIGURE 9.6 Calibrated Curve captures three lows missed by Standard Curves.

Data Source: Yahoo Finance.

Figure 9.8 shows the daily bars chart of Corning, Inc., ticker GLW, from late 2008 through early 2009.

There is a major pullback in price in mid-October 2008, which somewhat pierces the primary resistance curve, shown dotted here. Should it be left that way, as good enough? Notice what happens if you move the starting point back just a few bars, until the solid curve here exactly captures the pullback. Later, it's obvious that this Calibrated Curve goes on to exactly capture the major upsurge of price in early January 2009, an upsurge that significantly penetrated the original Standard Curve. So, it's often, in fact usually, worth adjusting the starting point of a Standard Curve a little to get a perfect capture on the first price pullback. Whether you consider the adjusted curve still to be a Standard Curve, or now just a Calibrated Curve, is only a matter of semantics. The important fact is that the curve now works much better going forward.

FIGURE 9.7   Some curves are both Standard and Calibrated.

Data Source: Reuters Datalink.

Looking again at Figure 9.7, the third curve from the bottom is an example of a primary curve that was slightly shifted to catch a major price pullback.

Let's look at one more example, because it so beautifully illustrates the unique power of the MIDAS method. Figure 9.9 is the weekly bars chart of the NASDAQ Composite Index from 1994 through 1998.

There was a significant low on December 9, 1994, so a primary support curve, dotted, is launched from there. From mid-1995 through mid-1996, the market suffered a sharp correction, going from 1250 down to 1000. The bottom of that correction was marked by that tall doji candle on July 19, 1996.

The dotted curve in Figure 9.9 comes close to that candle, but doesn't quite touch it, so let's move the starting point to January 3, 1995, to get a Calibrated Curve, the solid curve, which does exactly touch it. As time goes on, these two curves move closer together, virtually merging, due to the fact that the average trading volume is increasing significantly. The next major event was the Asian currency crisis of 1998, a very scary time to be in the market. Prices dove deeply, recovered somewhat, and then fell even more sharply. In the final washout week of October 9, 1998, price ranged from a high of 1615 to a sharp, spike low of 1344. Had you been in the market at that time, watching this crisis unfold, would you have suspected that 1344 was the bottom? The *only* way you could have known it was if you had these MIDAS curves

FIGURE 9.8   A primary resistance curve (dotted) and the adjusted Calibrated Curve (solid).

Data Source: Yahoo Finance.

on your chart. No other methodology in Technical Analysis could have so securely identified this bottom.

A few words on trading strategy are in order with regard to this example in Figure 9.9. Hindsight is, of course, always 20-20. Suppose you were in the market in October 1998, closely watching as the final large candle formed during the week of October 9. And suppose you already had these MIDAS support curves on your chart, so you saw price come down and touch these curves. At the moment they touched, you do *not* know that price will turn up from there; but what you do know is that the curves mark a fight-or-flight point, where prices will either robustly turn up, or definitely move further down. In other words, there will be a noticeable price response to the curves. By the end of that week, you would have seen that price had recovered sharply to close up at 1492. At that point, you know that the curves are holding, that price has been supported there, and you can then make your moves in the market accordingly.

Had those curves not been there, you would have just as well expected the following week's bar to be lower as higher. Some people say that the long spike low whisker of that October 9th week's candle indicates a washout, a bottom, and you don't need a MIDAS curve there to tell you that. But, look at the candle five weeks earlier, and

FIGURE 9.9   NASDAQ Composite Index, weekly bars, 1994–1998.

Data Source: Yahoo Finance.

the one in late 1997. They also had long lower whiskers, but they did not mark the final lows of the trends they were in. And, there were not any well-identified MIDAS curves at the bottoms of those two candles.

Analogies to Horizontal Lines and Trend Lines

A standard MIDAS curve is determined by one point, its starting point, which is at a significant price turning point. In this sense, it is analogous to traditional horizontal support and resistance lines, since they also are defined by the one price at a turning point. But Calibrated MIDAS Curves need two points for definition: first, the price turning point that is used as the Calibration Point, and, second, the starting point that generates a MIDAS curve that captures the Calibration Point. So, in this sense, the Calibrated Curves are analogous to straight trend lines, since a trend line is also defined by two points.

Prior to the MIDAS method, technicians drew sets of horizontal S/R lines on a chart. Then, perhaps on a separate chart for clarity, they drew sets of trend lines. The same can now be said for MIDAS S/R curves. One can generate a set of Standard Curves, then, perhaps on a separate chart, a set of Calibrated Curves. Together, these provide a very rich, deep identification of likely support and resistance areas on a chart.

Summary

- First, launch standard MIDAS S/R curves from the major price turning points. These curves are called Standard MIDAS Curves.
- If a significant turning point after an S/R curve launch point is far from being captured by the S/R curve, try launching a new S/R curve from several different starting points until the new curve exactly captures the subsequent turning point. The subsequent turning point is called the Calibration Point, and the new curve is called a Calibrated Curve.
- Keep both the original S/R curve and the new Calibrated Curve on your chart.
- If a significant turning point after an S/R curve launch point only slightly misses being captured by the curve, shift the starting point of the curve a few bars to either side until the curve exactly captures the subsequent turning point. Thereafter, keep this curve, instead of the original one, on your chart.

CHAPTER 10

Applying the MIDAS Method to Price Charts without Volume

A Study in the Cash Foreign Exchange Markets

Andrew Coles

At the end of his lectures, Paul Levine began to investigate whether the MIDAS method could be applied to price series other than U.S. stocks. He looked at a variety of daily charts of U.S. and foreign stock indices, and his research suggested that MIDAS worked well enough on these new data sets. In this chapter I'll develop this program more extensively by applying the MIDAS method to the volumeless cash foreign exchange markets. Given the vital role that volume plays in the MIDAS method, this may seem like an eccentric and even mildly contradictory undertaking. However, readers can be assured that there's a method in the apparent madness and that the outcome of this chapter will be a robust application of the MIDAS method to the cash FX markets.

MIDAS and Cash Foreign Exchange Markets

It will be helpful to begin by obtaining clarity on the question of what we as traders actually mean by market volume data. In his book *Trading for a Living* Alexander Elder[1] distinguished three ways in which volume is reported in the financial markets.

1. The least controversial is in terms of the actual number of shares or contracts traded. This method is often viewed as the most objective. Back in 1991 Elder cites the New York Stock Exchange as reporting stock data in this way.

2. Another is in terms of the number of trades that took place. This approach is criticized for being less objective than the first because it does not distinguish between, say, a small three-unit trade and a significant 1,000-unit trade. Writing in 1991 Elder cites the London Stock Exchange as reporting volume by this method.
3. The third approach is in terms of the number of price changes (or ticks) during a particular time period. Back in 1991 Elder noted that most U.S. futures exchanges reported volume in this way. This is no longer true of all futures markets today since the inception of electronic futures contracts, though it is still true of the cash foreign exchange markets.

As noted, volume data as defined in the first two methods of reporting are absent in the cash foreign exchange markets, both for traders who work through Electronic Network Communications (ECNs) and market makers. This is because over 90 percent of currency trades are OTC (over-the-counter), meaning that trading parties deal directly with each other. A consequence of this is that the currency market is a decentralized global network of buyers and sellers: no centralized exchange/clearinghouse exists where orders are matched and where volume is recorded at each price level. In March 2007 the Chicago Mercantile Exchange (CME) and Reuters launched a central clearinghouse called FXMarket Space. This trading platform was aimed at the institutional market with plans to extend it more widely, but it was closed in October 2008 due to insufficient liquidity. Thus, at the time of this writing, the OTC structure of the FX market remains as the only viable means of trading the cash markets.

Volume data as defined in Elder's third method of reporting are available in the cash FX markets, but only intraday, and even here the actual relevance of these data is controversial among cash FX traders, since the preferred definitions of meaningful volume are taken to be those provided in one and two and ultimately in definition one.

Despite the controversy surrounding the value of tick data as a proxy to true volume, I'll look below at tick data when applying MIDAS intraday to the cash FX markets. The results will be compared with those in the FX futures with actual volume data. Of course, whatever these results reveal, cash FX traders face the additional problem of the complete absence of volume data on higher-timeframe charts. We'll deal with this problem later.

A Comparison of the MIDAS S/R Curves Using Cash FX Intraday Tick Data and Intraday Futures Volume Data

The test is conducted on a five-minute chart of EUR/USD and its counterpart in the futures markets, the CME Globex Euro FX futures December 2009 contract.

For the purpose of the test, cash FX data from eSignal have been used, which are in turn sourced from GTIS FOREX. The feed from the latter is derived from 150-plus contributors, so it is representative of a fairly broad base of trading. This will still not satisfy many cash FX traders because, returning to Elder's distinctions, three objections are frequently leveled against tick data. The first is that tick volume can imply that a large number of price fluctuations equates with big volume; however, this need not be the case if the market is thinner than normal and only a relatively small order flow is needed to move the market. Second, a significant amount of tick volume related to, say, a cross such as GBP/JPY is as likely to be coming from GBP/USD and USD/JPY as it is from the actual cross whose tick volume is being reported. As a result, the specific volume dynamics of a given currency pair are genuinely unknown. Third, even though a feed such as GTIS FOREX is significant in terms of the number of contributors from which it is sourced, it still represents only a sample of the total trading being done; as such, critics argue, it's akin to taking a representative survey rather than accessing truly global foreign exchange trading data.

Nonetheless, we'll now test the MIDAS system on cash FX tick data in EUR/USD and compare it with the Globex euro FX December 2009 futures contract. Figure 10.1 is a 5m chart of EUR/USD covering one 24-hour trading period on November 3, 2009, adjusted to GMT. On the main price pane there are three MIDAS resistance curves (R1, R2, R3) following the downtrend, while from the final low of a triple bottom there is one MIDAS support curve (S1). In the lower pane, a 5m tick volume histogram is plotted with a 10-period moving average. The volume distribution is a reflection of the global shift in trading emphasis between the three centers in the cash foreign exchange markets. The Asian session (Tokyo, Hong Kong, and Singapore) runs from 11:00 P.M. to 9:00 A.M. GMT, the European (London) session from 7:00 A.M. to 5:00 P.M. GMT, and the U.S. (New York) session from midday to 10:00 P.M. GMT. Overlapping hours between Asia and Europe are between 7:00 A.M. to 9:00 A.M.

FIGURE 10.1   24-hour session of EUR/USD with five-minute tick volume data in the lower pane covering the Asian, European, and U.S. trading sessions GMT.

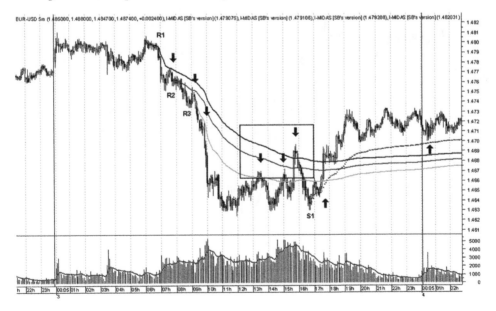

Source: eSignal and Metastock. www.eSignal.com and www.equis.com.

GMT, and Europe and the United States between midday to 5:00 P.M. GMT. Heaviest trading volume in EUR/USD can be seen during the Asia-Europe overlap and the European-United States overlap GMT.

When we look at the main price pane, we see that all three MIDAS resistance curves (R1, R2, R3) plot satisfactorily before further resisting price in a series of porous price penetrations within the boxed area. S1, the support curve, also plotted within normal MIDAS parameters, supports the arching upward price move on two occasions.

We can contrast Figure 10.1 with Figure 10.2 on the same day and trading timeframe, this time with the 24-hour Globex euro FX December 2009 futures. Since we're comparing the effect of volume characteristics between the cash and futures markets, it's relevant to point out that a modern quote vendor such as eSignal will have two options for volume, Electronic and Total Volume. The former is only for electronic futures contracts such as the e-minis, Globex contracts, or contracts traded through modern electronic exchanges such as EUREX. The latter is for anything that still trades in open outcry sessions or in the pit, such as the full S&P 500 and crude oil contracts. Any intraday trading volume associated with the latter is, in fact, tick volume data, the same type of data we are currently assessing with regard to the cash FX markets. Intraday trading volume associated with electronic futures contracts is the actual contract volume being traded, that is, definition one by Elder's criteria.

The first thing to notice on Figure 10.2 in comparison with Figure 10.1 is the inevitably flatter volume characteristics, especially during the Asian session and the

FIGURE 10.2   24-hour Globex session of the CME Euro FX December 2009 futures.

Source: eSignal and Metastock. www.eSignal.com and www.equis.com.

latter part of the U.S. session. On the chart pane there's an acceptable uniformity between the two curve sets here and in Figure 10.1. However, one noticeable difference is that the curves on the futures charts are more closely bunched together. Because of this, the gray circle within the black box highlights the extent to which price penetrates the curves (particularly R1) before reversing to test the low. With this degree of penetration, price goes beyond an acceptable level of porosity, whereas the more marginal penetration in Figure 10.1 can acceptably be described as a porous price move.

These subtle differences in the plotting of the two curves, which are largely the result of the variation in volume characteristics between the two markets, is so important as to justify a separate chapter to follow this one. In the next chapter, price-volume characteristics and how they affect the plotting of MIDAS curves will be thoroughly analyzed, and rules will be suggested to overcome these and other subtle differences.

In the meantime, when comparing the behavior of the two sets of curves in relation to the remaining chart areas, we find cases where the cash (tick) volume versions hit the reversals marginally better than the futures and vice versa. It would not be appropriate to go a stage further and perform a correlation analysis of the two curves because aside from the obvious volume differences, there are as well marginal differences in the price levels reached in the two markets. Instead, requiring further discussion in the next chapter are several key price-volume relationships and their effect on MIDAS curves. It will be shown why the displacement of a MIDAS curve can be heavily dependent upon volume fluctuations and what can be done about it. In the current context, volume fluctuations are underlined emphatically over a 24-hour period as the trading sessions shift from one center to another, with volume disproportionally larger in the cash markets and futures during the trading overlap periods mentioned above; that is, the middle of the 24-hour trading period GMT. During these periods, volume tends to trend up and down far more, as can be seen by the 10-period moving average on the volume histograms in Figures 10.1 and 10.2. During periods of sustained volume trends, the lesson of the next chapter will be that MIDAS curves plotted without volume often have an equally important role to play as standard volume-based curves. The importance of volume-free S/R curves in the FX market is ironic given the concerns that launched this chapter, and I shall discuss below volume-free MIDAS S/R curves and TB-F curves in much greater detail.

A Comparison of the MIDAS Topfinder/Bottomfinder Curves Using Cash FX Intraday Tick Data and Intraday Futures Volume Data

Turning to the topfinder/bottomfinder (TB-F) indicator, Figure 10.3 covers half of the 24-hour trading session of November 2, 2009, in the cash markets in the same 5m chart format. Between 2:00 P.M. and 7:00 P.M. GMT the market rose parabolically

FIGURE 10.3 A sudden parabolic uptrend in the cash market followed by price swiftly returning to a similar level.

Source: eSignal. www.eSignal.com.

for an hour before falling back swiftly to the same proximate level in a similar price move. This acceleration of the trend both up and down is a textbook application of the TB-F to both sides of the trend.

The duration (cumulative tick volume) of the topfinder is 70,000 while the duration (cumulative tick volume) of the bottomfinder is 60,000. Both perform extremely well, with the topfinder fitted very early into the trend at the minor pullback at 1.4750 and terminating on the Doji candlestick which completed the trend. The bottomfinder curve is fitted to a more noticeable pullback ending at the 1.4780 level and terminates on a penultimate bar prior to another Doji candlestick, thus embodying another successful application.

Figure 10.4 covers the same trading timeframe, this time again in the 24-hour Globex session of the CME Euro FX December 2009 futures. On the left, the topfinder curve is fitted to the same minor pullback at 1.4752 with a duration (cumulative futures volume) of 70,000. This is an identical figure to the cash market terminating on the very same bar (this time a Dark Cloud Cover candlestick)! On the right, the bottomfinder is fitted to the same pullback at 1.4775 with a smaller duration (cumulative futures volume) of 54,000. This bottomfinder also terminates on the same penultimate bar prior to a Piercing Pattern reversal candlestick formation.

What these two brief comparisons reveal is that there's absolutely no obstacle to applying the MIDAS curves to the cash foreign exchange markets with intraday tick

FIGURE 10.4 Two TB-F curves fitted to the same parabolic pattern in the CME Globex Euro FX December 2009 futures.

Source: eSignal and Metastock. www.eSignal.com and www.equis.com.

volume. Indeed, the durations required to fit the TB-F indicators in both markets reveal that the volume dynamics in both markets are actually pretty similar despite their apparent differences.

Options in the Cash Foreign Exchange Markets for Higher Timeframe Charts

Intraday trading in the cash foreign exchange markets is unfortunately only a part of the picture so far as MIDAS is concerned. There's also the problem of higher-timeframe charts where all three variations of volume data, as defined by Elder, are absent. For higher timeframe charts such as the daily and weekly timeframes, a cash foreign exchange trader has four options:

1. Apply MIDAS purely to the futures market equivalent of the underlying cash market and work with the corresponding volume.[2]
2. Apply MIDAS with futures open interest data.
3. Apply MIDAS with volume related to currency Exchange Traded Funds (ETFs)/Exchange Traded Notes (ETNs).[3]
4. Apply MIDAS without volume.

Options One and Three—Replacing Cash Forex Markets with Futures Markets or Currency ETFs/ETNs

The first and third options are solutions of a sort but they are only a partial help in so far as a number of currency crosses in the cash foreign exchange markets do not have liquid equivalents in the futures markets or the currency ETFs/ETNs. As a result, a trader resorting to these counterpart markets for volume is obtaining data that may be very unrepresentative of the actual cash volume equivalent. The significance of this will again be addressed in the next chapter.

For example, as can be seen in Table 10.1, as of September 2009 fewer than 40 ETFs/ETNs were available for trading in the United States, and of those available the daily volume averages were low.

As we see in the next chapter, this is significant because more volume often equates with more curve displacement, so if a cash FX trader were relying on price levels derived from MIDAS S/R curves with thinly traded volume data, the result would be a significant deviation from the cash markets. In such circumstances, a trader may be better off ironically to rely on volume-free S/R curves, which is an option I come to below. Of course, there isn't the same problem for cash foreign exchange traders seeking

TABLE 10.1   Top 20 Most Active Currency ETFs/ETNs (date as of September 1, 2009)

Name	Symb	Leverage	Inverse	60 day avg vol
PowerShares DB U.S. Dollar Bull	UUP			833,572
CurrencyShares Euro Trust	FXE			305,439
PowerShares DB U.S. Dollar Bear	UDN		yes	293,596
CurrencyShares Australian Dollar	FXA			187,778
CurrencyShares Canadian Dollar	FXC			186,604
CurrencyShares Japanese Yen	FXY			166,462
PowerShares DB G10 Currency Harvest	DBV			105,027
ProShares UltraShort Euro	EUO	2×	yes	102,342
CurrencyShares British Pound	FXB			90,197
CurrencyShares Swiss Franc	FXF			72,158
ProShares UltraShort Yen	YCS	2×	yes	66,743
WisdomTree Dreyfus Brazilian	BZF			65,926
WisdomTree Dreyfus Chinese Yuan	CYB			53,590
WisdomTree Dreyfus Emerging Currency	CEW			24,170
Market Vectors Double Short Euro	DRR	2×	yes	22,595
WisdomTree Dreyfus New Zealand	BNZ			17,008
ProShares Ultra Yen	YCL	2×		12,048
ProShares Ultra Euro	ULE	2×		8,737
CurrencyShares Mexican Peso	FXM			7,744
iPath Optimized Currency Carry ETN	ICI			7,310

Currency-based ETFs have been only moderately successful compared to other exchange-traded products.

Source: TradeStation and *Active Trader* 10, no. 11 (November 2009).

volume in highly liquid futures market equivalents, but few currency futures have this degree of liquidity in comparison with the cash equivalents. While therefore this first option is a partial solution, it should be supplemented with an investigation into options two and four. We look at the fourth option in the remainder of this chapter before turning to MIDAS with open interest data. The latter possibility is a large and important topic in its own right, quite apart from the motivation to come to it when cash FX volume data are absent. I've therefore treated it separately in Chapter 12.

Using MIDAS S/R Curves in Markets without Volume: The Daily and Weekly Cash FX Charts

Technical analysts describe the intermediate trend as lasting between six weeks and nine months and the primary trend as between nine months and two years. The ideal chart timeframe for looking at the former is the daily chart, while for the latter the weekly timeframe is best. To remind ourselves again, on neither of these two chart timeframes does the cash FX trader have volume data.

Taking the MIDAS S/R curves first, we have found that a solution to the problem of the absence of volume involves the insertion into the MIDAS formula of a nominal "1" unit of trading volume in lieu of an empty cumulative volume field.

This solution may seem counterintuitive and surprising to many readers, given the explicit volume component in the VWAP math upon which the MIDAS system is based. My first task therefore is to reassure readers that the resulting formula can generate accurate and meaningful support and resistance curves on the daily and weekly cash FX charts. To begin this process, let's take a look at the weekly timeframe in Figure 10.5 at several primary trends in GBP/USD constituting the larger secular trend between 2001 and 2007.[4]

Moving from left to right, a resistance curve, R1, resists two swing highs in the primary downtrend between 2000 and 2002 before the main secular uptrend begins. S1 supports this secular trend on two key occasions, while another support curve, S2, supports a primary segment of this trend twice in 2004. We can look in more detail at the second primary segment of this secular trend between 2006 and 2008 in Figure 10.6.

In Figure 10.6 I have dropped down to a daily chart in order to reapply the MIDAS support and resistance curves with a nominal "1" in the algorithm instead of the absent cumulative volume. Moving from left to right, we see that R1 captures two swing highs in the downtrend with a large porous swing high in the middle. S1, the main support curve supporting the primary trend, does an excellent job of capturing the swing lows, while S2 and S3 also capture all of the significant swing lows as the intermediate trend continues to higher levels. On the far right, beyond the end of the trend in mid-November 2007, S3 becomes a resistance curve with some price porosity to a new intermediate downtrend.

Hopefully these two charts will demonstrate to skeptical readers that MIDAS support and resistance curves can be plotted to considerable effect on higher-timeframe

FIGURE 10.5 A Secular seven-year uptrend in GBP/USD between 2001 and 2007 with two primary uptrends between 2002 and 2004 and 2006 and 2007.

Source: eSignal and Metastock. www.eSignal.com and www.equis.com.

FIGURE 10.6 A primary segment of the secular trend between 2006 and 2008 on a daily chart of GBP/USD.

Source: eSignal and Metastock. www.eSignal.com and www.equis.com.

cash FX charts without volume, provided the MIDAS S/R algorithm is plotted with a nominal "1" instead of an actual cumulative volume feed from the market.

However, while this methodology resolves the problem of using the MIDAS S/R curves when volume is absent, some readers may query whether the role of volume is redundant in the MIDAS method, and whether its VWAP background isn't a misleading conceit. For it may be argued that volume-weighting seems to account for very little in the accurate functioning of MIDAS S/R curves. This issue will be examined thoroughly in the next chapter. It will be shown that volume-weighting does have a crucial role to play in the creation of MIDAS curves, but that nominal curves do, too. As we'll see, everything depends on the volume characteristics accompanying trends and, in some cases, the absence of volume.

However, to alleviate concerns here I can set up a fairly simple experiment. For it we can take a daily chart of the GBP continuous futures with a standard MIDAS S/R curve and a second nominal curve. As well as comparing the two curves visually, a simple correlation analysis of the two curves is plotted. Let's take a look at these results in Figure 10.7.

In Figure 10.7 there are four MIDAS support curves launched from two anchor points: February 27, 2006 and October 16, 2006. The solid lines are standard MIDAS support curves while the dotted lines are nominal curves. The upper pane is a correlation analysis, measuring the relationship between the two curves launched from February 27, 2006. A correlation coefficient ranges between +1.0 and −1.0. The former is a perfect positive correlation while the latter is a perfect negative correlation

FIGURE 10.7   Daily chart of CME Globex euro FX continuous futures.

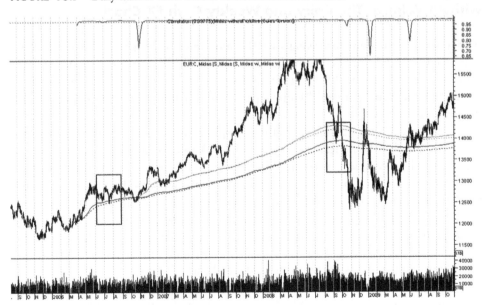

Source: eSignal and Metastock. www.eSignal.com and www.equis.com.

(a low correlation, say 0.10, means that there is no significant relationship between the two variables); 90 percent to 95 percent of the time the correlation coefficient between the two curves is between +1.0 and +0.985, with occasional dips to +0.74, +0.94, +0.655, and +0.79 respectively. Thus, for the majority of the time the two curves are close enough not to raise concerns about their creation. In practice, what the occasional variability means is that one curve or the other will experience slightly more price porosity than the other. For example, in the black rectangle on the left the swing low is porous in relation to the solid (volume-based) curve but coincident with the nominal curve. In the rectangle on the right the opposite is the case. Hence, Figure 10.7 reveals what we suspected in Figures 10.5 and 10.6, namely that the divergence between the two curves is not that significant and certainly not significant enough for anyone using the nominal curves to worry that they're being misled by their signals.

In the next chapter I'll bring out the subtleties involved in working with standard and nominal curves and draw attention to how volume trends dictate which of the two curves should be used. For now, however, the results of this simple correlation analysis do not contradict the more complex issues raised in the next chapter. Without anticipating its concerns, sharply trending volume trends (plus their direction) are the key to understanding MIDAS curves more analytically. However, if the reader looks at the volume histogram in Figure 10.7 covering the secular trend in the continuous futures of the euro, he'll notice that there's no persistent volume trend as there is in the stock market indices or in individual stocks. In fact, the volume profiles in the currency futures are often more like they are in the cyclical commodity futures markets.

Using MIDAS Topfinder/Bottomfinder Curves in Markets without Volume: The Daily and Weekly Cash FX Charts

It may seem even more surprising that the more complex topfinder/bottomfinder (TB-F) curves can be applied to higher timeframe cash FX markets without volume data. In fact however the TB-F algorithm, like the standard S/R curves, requires no more than the same nominal "1" to replace actual cumulative volume data from the markets.

To see that this is so, a simple parabolic displacement can be created that mimics the more complex theoretical example given in Chapter 4. Readers will recall that the volume displacement d is replaced by the more complex e in the TB-F formula, so that e is related to d parabolically through the equation $e = d * (1 - d/D)$. D is the variable in this equation, the "duration" of the move that's inputted by the user according to a "fit" between the TB-F curve and the first pullback in a trend. The whole point of creating the parabolic conditions in e, of course, is that e goes to zero when d approaches D. The result is the TB-F's ability to terminate on the chart when the volume characteristics of the accelerated trend end.

With this recap, here's an illustration of how adding "1" to the TB-F formula results in the same parabolic profile. We start with the formula $e = d * (1 - d/D)$, bearing in mind that the cumulative volume at the start is subtracted from that on the current bar. Let's also assume that D is a mere five units, otherwise the illustration will be too long. Thus we have:

$$(1-1)*(1-(1-1)/5) = 0$$
$$(2-1)*(1-(2-1)/5) = 0.8$$
$$(3-1)*(1-(3-1)/5) = 1.2$$
$$(4-1)*(1-(4-1)/5) = 1.2$$
$$(5-1)*(1-(5-1)/5) = 0.8$$
$$(6-1)*(1-(6-1)/5) = 0$$

Now let's apply this nominal TB-F to a market without volume to see what we get. In Figure 10.8 we return to the primary trend between 2006 and 2008 of GBP/USD of Figure 10.6, this time focusing on the downtrend between July 2008 and January 2009 and the uptrend between March 2009 and June 2009. There were two accelerated portions of the downtrend suitable for the launch of a bottomfinder and one accelerated portion of the uptrend. The first bottomfinder was launched on July 15, 2008 and fitted to the gradual curvature of the downtrend before the acceleration increased (this fitting was confirmed lower down by a minor pullback). The duration was 40 units. The second bottomfinder was launched on September 25, 2008, to the pullback highlighted by the black arrow; here the duration was 87 units.

FIGURE 10.8   Three TB-Fs launched in accelerated portions of a downtrend and uptrend on a daily chart of GBP/USD without actual cumulative volume data.

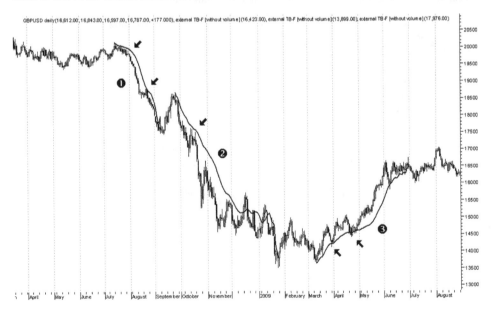

Source: eSignal and Metastock. www.eSignal.com and www.equis.com.

Finally, the topfinder was launched from March 11, 2009, and fitted to two pullbacks highlighted by the two arrows; this time the duration was 80. All three nominal TB-Fs performed admirably, capturing the ends of all three trends with ease, despite the absence of actual cumulative volume data.

If we compare the fitting of these TB-Fs with the fitting of actual TB-Fs with cumulative volume from the corresponding chart of the CME Globex GBP continuous futures, we see in Figure 10.9 that the trajectory of the curves is virtually identical.

Unlike the standard MIDAS S/R curves, there are, as indicated in earlier chapters, two functions to the TB-F curves and not just one. The first function, which TB-F curves have in common with standard S/R curves, is a support/resistance role on the accelerated portion of trends to which it is fitted. The second is its parabolic termination on the chart, which, when it occurs, signals that at the very least a different volume signature will now ensue, if not the start of a new trend or a significant period of market resting.

So far, as the second of these functions (the parabolic termination) is concerned, Figure 10.8 demonstrates that this function can be duplicated in cash charts without volume. The duration that produces this parabolic termination in the cash market is roughly of the order of 0.0001 percent to 0.00016 percent in relation to the more massive duration required in the continuous futures in Figure 10.9. There the duration for the first bottomfinder was 370,000, for the second bottomfinder it was 520,000, and for the topfinder it was 620,000.

FIGURE 10.9   The same accelerated portions of the intermediate trend as in Figure 10.8, this time with cumulative volume from the CME Globex GBP continuous futures.

Source: eSignal and Metastock. www.eSignal.com and www.equis.com

FIGURE 10.10 Here the nominal TB-F curves are plotted as dotted lines alongside the TB-F curves with cumulative volume

Source: eSignal and Metastock. www.eSignal.com and www.equis.com.

So far as the first function is concerned (the role of TB-F curves as standard accelerated S/R curves), if we look at Figures 10.8 and 10.9 and compare the three curves, we see that there is very little to choose between them.

In Figure 10.10, the final chart of this chapter, I've used the same continuous futures as in Figure 10.9, with the same standard curves plotted. However, I've also plotted the nominal curves for a more direct comparison.

If the reader looks hard, he can just about see the nominal TB-F curves running alongside as the dotted black curves. The only significant divergence in the S/R role comes at the gray arrow, where the nominal version in the second bottomfinder experiences some volatility momentarily before realigning with the cumulative volume version. The result is that the cumulative version does a slightly better job at resisting this final swing high before the trend terminates.

Summary

- Despite the concerns raised by cash FX traders regarding the reliability of tick data as a substitute for volume data, the MIDAS system performs more than adequately when using intraday tick volume in comparison to intraday near-month futures volume data.
- Because of the shift in trading centers globally in the 24 cash FX markets, certain times of the day, particularly during trading session overlaps, will often result in

sustained volume trends, or at least in sharp volume fluctuations. Ironically in the former case, it's important to consider using volume-free MIDAS S/R curves and TB-F curves to confirm price swings as much as standard curves, especially when the volume-based MIDAS curves are likely to be subject to porous price moves. I shall explain in more detail in the next chapter why this is important.

- TB-F curves, like standard MIDAS S/R curves, perform more than adequately in the cash volume-free FX markets. This is true for TB-F curves both in their function as standard S/R curves in accelerated trends and in their function as parabolic terminators.

- Over the longer term, MIDAS S/R curves perform very adequately when volume data are missing, and probably better than they do in the stock markets, because volume data often do not trend so much as they do in the stock markets. As a result, the volume profile is much flatter, which the next chapter will reveal to be an important consideration when looking at the displacement between MIDAS S/R curves plotted with cumulative volume from the market and without it.

CHAPTER 11

Four Relationships between Price and Volume and Their Impact on the Plotting of MIDAS Curves

Andrew Coles

The previous chapter voiced the need to analyze more thoroughly the changing relationship between volume, price, and MIDAS curves. In this chapter these relationships will be analyzed with a view to establishing guidelines for the implementation of standard curves plotted with cumulative volume versus nominal curves plotted with a nominal "1" in lieu of a market volume feed.

The first occasion when the price-volume relationship was referred to in Chapter 10 was amidst the comparison of the 24-hour intraday volume dynamics of the FX cash market versus the FX Globex futures shown in Figures 10.1 and 10.2. There it was pointed out that periods of more heavily trending volume (particularly during trading center overlaps between Asia and Europe and Europe and the United States) can affect the chart position of MIDAS curves. An example was that the curves in the Globex euro futures were significantly flatter than their counterparts in the cash market during the same session due to the larger volume trends occurring in the cash market. Here we'll explore why this should be so.

In Chapter 10 it was also suggested that it may be better not to use volume at all in so-called nominal MIDAS curves. As illustrated there, actual cumulative volume can be replaced by a nominal "1" unit of cumulative volume in algorithms in volumeless markets. The deeper analysis in this chapter explains why volume-free MIDAS curves have such an important role to play in certain market environments.

Finally, after reading Chapter 10 a reader might have raised the question whether the volume component in the VWAP calculation is actually needed at all. This chapter conclusively shows that volume *is* needed, albeit within the context of a deeper understanding of how the MIDAS system functions in relation to fluctuating volume characteristics.

Relationships between Price and Volume Trends and the Four Rules Affecting the Plotting of MIDAS Curves

Let's make a start by providing four possible relationships between a price and volume trend:

1. Rising price trend + increasing volume
2. Rising price trend + decreasing volume
3. Falling price trend + decreasing volume
4. Falling price trend + increasing volume

When applied to the MIDAS curves, these four relationships can be transformed into four simple rules:

Rule #1: Rising price trend + increasing volume = MIDAS support curves are pulled up towards the rising price trend.

Rule #2: Rising price trend + decreasing volume = MIDAS support curves are pulled down from the rising price trend.

Rule #3: Falling price trend + decreasing volume = MIDAS resistance curves are pulled up from the falling price trend.

Rule #4: Falling price trend + increasing volume = MIDAS resistance curves are pulled down towards the falling price trend.

Let's illustrate these rules with a volume trend highlighted by a four-period simple moving average.

Figure 11.1 illustrates **Rule #1**. Figure 11.1 is a 1m chart of the Xetra DAX December 2009 futures with the rising price trend highlighted between the two vertical gray lines. The increasing volume trend is emphasized by the four-period moving average. The black arrows highlight a mini-blowoff top in the volume followed by a negative divergence in the volume trend as price goes on to make a new high. Notice that the displacement between the standard MIDAS support curve (solid) and the nominal curve (dotted) is widest at the point of the blowoff in volume, thus illustrating the first rule that increasing volume will pull the support curve up towards a rising price trend.

One more chart will be used to illustrate **Rule #1**, this time a 5m chart of the CME Group December 2009 gold futures. The uptrend of approximately four hours in Figure 11.2 is highlighted between the vertical gray lines. Volume is fairly flat to begin with so both curves are in close proximity. However, as the volume increases the standard (solid) support curve also begins to rise towards price, displacing upwards from the nominal support curve.

FIGURE 11.1   1m chart of Xetra DAX December 2009 futures.

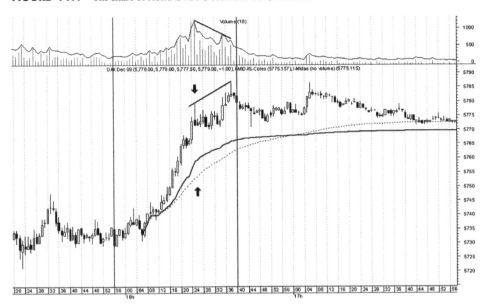

Source: eSignal and Metastock. www.eSignal.com and www.equis.com.

FIGURE 11.2   5m chart of CME Group gold December 2009 futures.

Source: eSignal and Metastock. www.eSignal.com and www.equis.com.

FIGURE 11.3   CME Globex 5m chart of Australian dollar December 2009 futures.

Source: eSignal and Metastock. www.eSignal.com and www.equis.com.

Let's turn to **Rule #2**, that a rising price trend plus decreasing volume results in a standard MIDAS support curve being pulled down from the rising price trend. Figure 11.3 is a 5m chart of the Globex Australian dollar December 2009 futures. The uptrend lasts for approximately nine hours from November 27 to 30. Notice first that as the trend begins volume is increasing. According to **Rule #1**, this should pull a standard support curve up towards price. This is what we see before the middle vertical black line when the standard (solid) support curve is above the nominal (dotted) curve. After the black line, volume starts to decrease, and this is when we see the standard support curve displace across the nominal curve and then further displace from it and the price as the volume continues to decline.

Figure 11.4 is another illustration of **Rule #2** in the same 5m chart of the Australian dollar futures, this time with an eight-and-a-half-hour uptrend late into November 25. Apart from a volume spike, volume decreases consistently as the price rises, resulting in the standard (solid) support curve being significantly below price and the nominal (dotted) support curve.

Next, we can illustrate **Rule #3**, that a falling price trend plus decreasing volume results in a standard MIDAS resistance curve being pulled up from the falling price trend. Figure 11.5 is a 5m chart of the EUREX Bund December 2009 futures. A two-and-a-half-hour downtrend with falling volume highlighted by the four-period moving average reveals that the nominal (dotted) curve does a better job of capturing the swing high at the black arrow because of this rule, since the standard (solid black) curve is displaced upwards.

FIGURE 11.4 5m chart of CME Globex Australian dollar December 2009 futures.

Source: eSignal and Metastock. www.eSignal.com and www.equis.com.

FIGURE 11.5 5m chart of EUREX Bund December 2009 futures.

Source: eSignal and Metastock. www.eSignal.com and www.equis.com.

FIGURE 11.6   5m chart of EUREX Bund December 2009 futures.

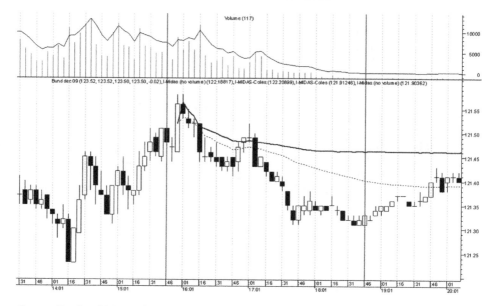

Source: eSignal and Metastock. www.eSignal.com and www.equis.com.

Figure 11.6 is another 5m chart of the EUREX Bund December 2009 futures illustrating the same phenomenon. Here there is a three-hour downtrend with declining volume highlighted by the same four-period moving average. Here again the standard (solid) MIDAS resistance curve is displaced upwards with falling volume in relation to the nominal (dotted) curve below it.

Finally let's illustrate **Rule #4**, that a downtrend plus increasing volume should result in a standard MIDAS curve being pulled down towards price. Figure 11.7 is another 5m chart of the German Bund December 2009 futures. The trend between the two gray vertical lines lasts approximately five hours. Notice that volume increases between the start of the trend and the middle vertical black line before then starting to decrease in the manner we've seen in the previous two charts. Notice how as the increasing volume reaches a climax just before the vertical black line that the standard (solid) MIDAS resistance curve is closest to price. Thereafter, as the volume declines rather than increases, the standard resistance curve begins to displace upwards in the manner we've just seen in the previous two charts.

Applying the Rules to Applications of Standard and Nominal MIDAS S/R Curves

Now that these four rules have been illustrated, let's utilize them to obtain a better understanding of the circumstances under which it's more appropriate to use nominal curves in place of standard curves. While all chart timeframes are relevant to this

FIGURE 11.7   5m chart of EUREX Bund December 2009 futures.

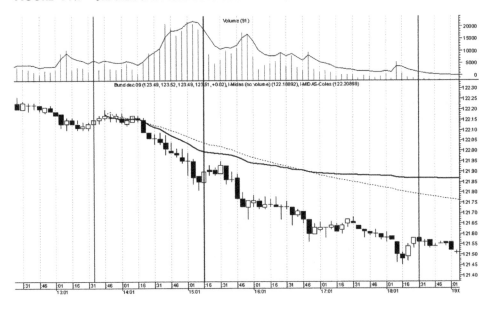

Source: eSignal and Metastock. www.eSignal.com and www.equis.com.

analysis, some of the more spectacular examples of the displacement phenomenon due to volume trends occur on the longer-term charts, especially when the trends have been in existence for many months or years. Thus, it's vital to consider using nominal curves over the primary and secular term trends.

Figure 11.8 is a daily semi-log chart of the NYMEX Platinum continuous futures. The first vertical gray line marks the start of a large 10-year secular bull trend beginning in 1998 and lasting into 2008. Between the first vertical line and the second one marked E1, the price trend rose, but volume declined, as highlighted by the 100-period moving average of volume. After this second vertical bar, volume increased with price all the way up to the 2008 high (E2) before it began to decline along with it. Although there is still some price porosity, the standard (solid) support curve did a better job of capturing the price swing low at E1 highlighted in the first gray oval than the nominal (dotted) support curve because of **Rule #2**. However, in the second gray oval—again with some price porosity—the nominal support curve more accurately captured the enormous price swing low than its standard counterpart. Again this would be explained in virtue of **Rule #1**. The same phenomenon would also be explained by **Rule #3**, that a downtrend plus decreasing volume results in a MIDAS support curve being pulled up from the falling price. Thus, we have two rules that are predicting price should be heavily porous with respect to the standard support curve at the second oval, and this is precisely what we see.

Again we need to keep a close eye on volume in relation to the price trend when assessing whether to use a standard or a nominal MIDAS S/R curve, especially in relation to longer-term price moves with persistent volume trends. For example, in the

FIGURE 11.8 NYMEX continuous platinum futures in a long-term secular uptrend between 1998 and 2008.

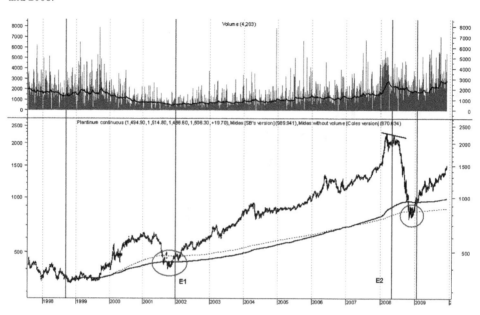

Source: eSignal and Metastock. www.eSignal.com and www.equis.com.

case of the secular trend in platinum futures, the first support curve (which has a key role in supporting major pullbacks at the end of trends) is very likely to be displaced upwards due to a persistent upward trend in volume. In such circumstances, there is no question that a nominal support curve will produce a more accurate zone of support than a standard support curve.

Let's look at another example, this time a six-year secular uptrend in NYMEX Palladium futures from 1996 to 2001 with a dramatic displacement. Figure 11.9 highlights the start of the uptrend with the first vertical gray line, from where a standard (solid) support curve is launched alongside a nominal (dotted) curve. In contrast to the previous platinum chart, there is in Figure 11.9 a persistent volume downtrend throughout the price uptrend and even in the price downtrend after 2001. **Rule #2** states that a price uptrend plus a volume downtrend results in price being pulled down from the rising price trend. This is what we see dramatically almost from the outset, when the standard curve rapidly displaces downwards below the nominal curve. The end result is that when Palladium futures correct back to the 300 level the nominal curve is far above price, while the standard curve captures the swing low at the 300 level accurately. Here a trader would most definitely select a standard curve over a nominal one.

Finally, there are some circumstances where, like applying Fibonacci corrections, we'd want to apply standard and nominal curves depending on the depth of the correction under analysis. Figure 11.10 is a monthly chart of the Dow Jones Industrial

FIGURE 11.9 NYMEX continuous palladium futures in a secular uptrend.

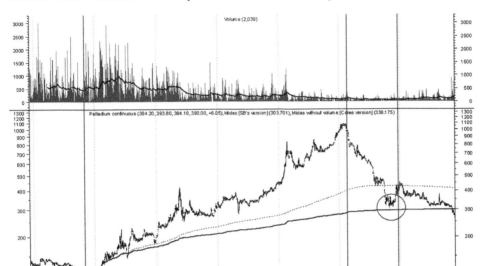

Source: eSignal and Metastock. www.eSignal.com and www.equis.com.

FIGURE 11.10 Monthly long-term chart of the Dow Jones Industrial Average with volume in the lower pane. The power of displacement in this chart is remarkable in providing support for two of the most significant bottoms in recent stock market history.

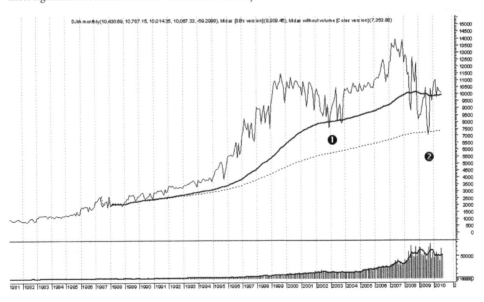

Source: Metastock. www.equis.com.

Average with volume in the lower pane. A standard support curve (solid) is launched from the bottom of the 1987 stock market crash and creates a powerful support level for the 2003 market bottom. The height of this curve is explained by **Rule #1**, that rising price and volume uptrends result in a MIDAS curve being pulled up towards the price trend. After the 2007 high the subsequent 2008–2009 crash broke this curve and provoked the launch from the same 1987 bottom of a nominal curve, the rationale being that the persistent uptrend in volume would create a significant displacement of a nominal curve with the potential to influence the 2009 bottom. That's indeed what we find in this remarkable chart of the power of displacement in affecting two of the most important bottoms in recent stock market history.

Using Relative Strength or Ratio Analysis

Whether we decide to use a standard curve or a nominal curve in the analysis depends on clear access to a volume histogram plotted with a simple trend line (or as here a moving average) in order to detect the volume trend. Sometimes, however, the volume trend is not so easy to detect, as in the left side of Figure 11.11. In such cases it's possible to use relative strength or ratio analysis. Ratio analysis is where one data set is divided by another so as to compare the relative strength of the two.

In Figure 11.11, for example, we see a standard volume pane (top) with a 50-period moving average. The lower price pane contains weekly data of the EUR/CHF

FIGURE 11.11   CME EUR/CHF weekly continuous futures cross.

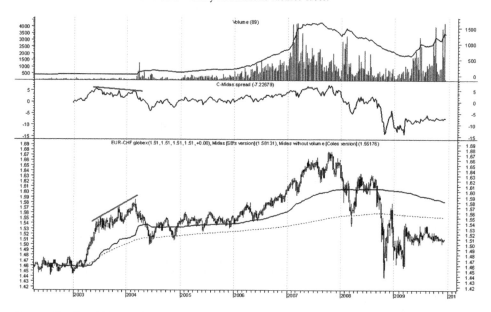

Source: eSignal and Metastock. www.eSignal.com and www.equis.com.

continuous futures cross, with a standard (solid) curve and nominal (dotted) curve. Notice in the mid-2003 to mid-2004 period that while the EUR/CHF futures are rising, there's a negative divergence on an indicator in the middle pane. This indicator is a ratio of the futures closing prices divided by the standard MIDAS curve. When the ratio line is rising, it means that the price component is outperforming the MIDAS curve, which means in turn that the price component is outperforming the volume component. Thus, the negative divergence between mid-2003 to mid-2004 means that the MIDAS curve is outperforming the price component, which in turn means that volume is outperforming the price. This information cannot be derived from the volume histogram/moving average alone because the data are flat. Nonetheless, because price is rising between mid-2003 and mid-2004 while the volume component is also rising in virtue of the negative divergence in the ratio, this means (according to **Rule #1**) that a standard MIDAS curve will be pulled up towards price. Consequently, any significant correction is likely to penetrate the upwardly displaced standard curve and find support on the nominal curve. This is what we see in Figure 11.11 twice in 2004.

The final illustration of this chapter is Figure 11.12, a 5m chart of the CME Globex Euro FX December 2009 futures. In the central pane we see an eight-and-a-half hour downtrend lasting from 11:00 to 17:30. The first two-thirds of the downtrend have rising volume, while the last third has falling volume. This is when the ratio analysis in the top pane diverges sharply upwards against the price downtrend. This positive divergence means that prices are outperforming the MIDAS resistance curve, which

FIGURE 11.12   5m chart of CME Globex Euro FX December 2009 futures.

Source: eSignal and Metastock. www.eSignal.com and www.equis.com.

means in turn that prices are outperforming the volume component, and thus that prices are falling more heavily than the volume trend. This would not be detectable by looking at the volume histogram alone. By **Rule #4** (a falling price trend plus increasing volume), a standard resistance curve should be pulled down towards price, which is what we see in Figure 11.12.

Summary

- When examining the intraday cash forex markets with their futures markets equivalents in Figure 10.1 and 10.2 in Chapter 10, attention was drawn to the flatter curves in the futures. In virtue of this chapter we can now see why, according to volume characteristics, there would be variation in the curves as a result of fluctuations in volume data between the two markets.
- Likewise when Chapter 10 warned that using illiquid futures or ETNs of counterpart cash FX markets could result in inaccurate support and resistance predictions in the latter, this chapter again explains why this kind of extrapolation could be a danger.
- When Chapter 10 raised the question of whether an actual cumulative volume feed from the market is redundant in light of the results obtained from using nominal curves, the present chapter shows emphatically that there is a crucial role for both types of curve depending often on the length of the price trend being examined and its relation to the underlying volume trend. In particular, upwardly and downwardly displaced standard curves are unlikely to catch the ends of significant pullbacks. Here it is far better to use nominal curves.
- In sum, this chapter establishes through its rule-based analysis when standard curves are more likely to be effective and when nominal ones are. The identification of underlying volume characteristics in relation to price trends is key to the effective application of this rule-based analysis.

CHAPTER 12

MIDAS and the CFTC Commitments of Traders Report

Using MIDAS with Open Interest Data

Andrew Coles

In Chapter 10 one of the possibilities considered for longer-term FX traders was to use the MIDAS method with open interest. At the time, this option wasn't considered further because it was suggested that it should be a significant area of investigation in its own right. Accordingly, the remainder of the chapter explored so-called nominal curves in the FX markets. One motivation for this chapter would therefore be to explore "open interest curves" (Open Interest Weighted Average Price (OIWAP) instead of VWAP) in the FX markets as an alternative to "nominal curves." Yet open interest is regarded as a quite distinct form of market information and any investigation of MIDAS with open interest should therefore give rise to a new and potentially interesting avenue of inquiry in its own right, quite apart from aiding analysis in the foreign exchange markets. Some studies view open interest as a form of sentiment data alongside other well-known sentiment indicators, such as the put/call ratio, option volatilities, and the VIX.[1] Other detailed studies, especially of the Commitments of Traders (COT) report, regard it as a type of fundamental information alongside other widely used fundamental indicators.[2] However, regardless of how open interest is viewed, it is widely seen as providing an extra dimension to market analysis beyond purely technical information. There is therefore a compelling reason to investigate open interest alongside the MIDAS method, quite apart from the concerns raised in Chapter 10.

There's also a further motivation for this chapter that didn't become apparent until it was being written. It has to do with the large ongoing gap in the average futures trader's knowledge concerning open interest that I hope this chapter will address. Surprisingly, this gap still has to be filled despite the excellent work that has been published on the Commitments of Traders (COT) report over the past decade. While writing, I have found it necessary to rely on this material on a number of occasions. As a result, I hope readers will agree with me that this chapter also gains value from its educational input, especially where it summarizes (and even charts) key COT report indicators developed over the past decade. Discussion of MIDAS isn't lost in this overview of course. But hopefully this chapter gains value as a summary of every recent major study on the COT report over the past decade in addition to its exploration of MIDAS applications.

There's a lot to get through in this chapter, and with new traders in mind there follows a brief introduction to open interest before discussing the Commitments of Traders (COT) report. Thereafter it'll be possible to move on to more advanced areas of the discussion.

An Overview of Open Interest and Open Interest Data Options

For traders new to futures, open interest is the actual number of outstanding futures contracts held by traders in a given market at the end of each trading day. However, because the futures markets are a zero-sum game—meaning that for every long contract purchased there must also be a contract sold and vice versa—open interest is merely the total number of longs or the total number of shorts, but not both. A modern data supplier such as eSignal will have two primary options for charting daily open interest. The first will show the open interest value specific to the contract being charted, while the second will be the total open interest for all active contracts.[3] Normally a trader would be interested in the latter and not the former. This is because open interest fluctuates considerably for each contract, due to the open interest significantly increasing and decreasing at the beginning and end of its life. This fluctuation has nothing to do with overall market interest. It's merely a function of the natural lifespan of an individual futures contract. Thus, to gain insight into the actual level of market interest on a continuous basis, attention should focus more on the total open interest for all active contracts. Open interest (along with futures volume) is reported a day late, so a trader must also be content with a 24-hour lag in data reporting.

The means by which open interest figures change on a day-to-day basis is often the source of confusion to those new to futures trading. It is helpful therefore to spend a paragraph explaining how these changes occur. Table 12.1 is based on John Murphy's presentation in Chapter 7 of his book *Technical Analysis of the Financial Markets*[4] and is as good a primer as any on this topic, though we'll see below that more recent research on open interest by Larry Williams and other contemporary authors does challenge a great deal of what has been taken to be orthodoxy in evaluating volume and open interest.[5]

TABLE 12.1 Illustration of How Open Interest Changes in the Simple Transaction of a Futures Contract

Buyer of futures	Seller of futures	Change in open interest
1 Purchases one new long	Sells one new short	Increase by one contract
2. Purchases one new long	Sells the first long contract	No change in the data
3. Purchases former short	Sells new short	No change in the data
4. Purchases former short	Sells former long	Decrease by one contract

Let's spend a few moments on the four scenarios outlined in Table 12.1 and how they affect changes in open interest.

1. In the first scenario assume that two traders (a buyer and a seller) are initiating a new position. Because the futures market is a zero-sum game, this means that one contract offsets the other and the open interest increases by one contract.
2. Next, let's assume that later in trading the first trader goes long another contract but that another trader from whom he buys is merely liquidating an old long position of his own. The result is no change in the open interest data.
3. The third scenario reverses the previous one. The trader who was merely liquidating a long decides to initiate a new short by one contract. As it happens, he sells to a trader who has decided to cover his short. Hence, there is no change in the open interest.
4. In the final scenario both traders are closing out former positions, so the open interest decreases by one contract.

The Orthodox Interpretation of Changes in Open Interest

Next, it will be helpful to summarize the orthodox interpretation of open interest. This knowledge will be helpful when we see below how newer COT indicators have been developed that challenge much of this orthodoxy.

According to the orthodox view, an uptrend is healthy if it is supported by rising volume and open interest, since fresh money is assumed to be entering the market. Where they're falling, the trend is said to be weak and at risk of ending, since the uptrend is assumed to be caused by disillusioned short covering. Here money is leaving the market and the trend would be assumed to end once the short-covering has completed. Downtrends are said to be healthy if the volume and open interest are also continually rising, since new money is entering the market in increasingly new short selling. However, a downtrend is assumed to be in jeopardy if volume and open interest start to decline, since the price decline is assumed to be caused by the longs being forced to close their positions. The downtrend would be assumed to end once the discouraged longs have completed their selling.

A First Look at Standard MIDAS Support/Resistance Curves with Open Interest

This introduction to open interest is sufficient to move us on to what would be a first reason for using the MIDAS approach with open interest instead of volume.

Figure 12.1 is a weekly chart of continuous CBOT soybean futures. The lower pane is weekly volume with a 50-period moving average, the upper pane is weekly open interest data, and the middle pane between the two vertical bars is an aggressive 20-month primary price uptrend from June 2006 to February 2008. Because the chart is somewhat compressed, it's difficult to appreciate just how sharply the volume moving average is trending downwards in the lower pane. Thus, what is interesting about this chart is that we have a situation that the orthodox view of the relationship between volume and open interest doesn't countenance, namely sharply declining volume throughout the uptrend and steadily rising open interest. Declining volume in an uptrend is meant to be bearish, whereas increasing open interest is meant to be bullish. However, regardless of interpretations we now have fairly extensive experience of these price-volume relationships in virtue of studying Chapter 11. There it was emphasized that four rules can be applied to these relationships that govern the choice of which type of curve should be applied in certain types of circumstance. Sometimes actual cumulative volume is justified resulting in a standard MIDAS curve, whereas at others so-called nominal curves are better that use one unit of cumulative volume artificially inputted.

FIGURE 12.1   Weekly chart of CBOT continuous soybean futures.

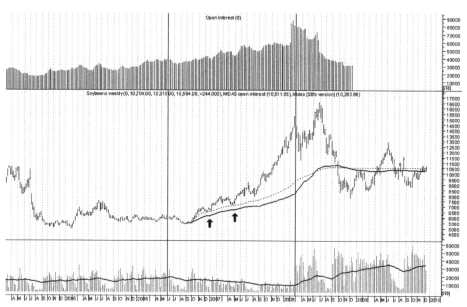

Source: eSignal, Metastock and COT Collector. www.esignal.com, www.equis.com, www.cotcollector .com.

In Figure 12.1 we have another instance where these rules should be applied insofar as a rising price trend plus declining volume evokes **Rule #2** of the previous chapter, namely that a rising price trend plus decreasing volume entails that standard MIDAS support curves are pulled down from the rising price trend. Thus, because a downwardly displaced standard support curve is going to be less effective in catching ongoing pullbacks in the trend, we can replace volume in the algorithm with the open interest, which is actually rising alongside the price uptrend. Notice in Figure 12.1 the two arrows showing that whereas the standard (solid) support curve was indeed displaced below price, the open interest (dotted) curve perfectly captured the swing lows of December 2006 and May 2007 in virtue of the rising open interest. Thus, here lies a first justification for preferring open interest in some cases to volume. It is worth solidifying this justification in the following rule.

Rule for open interest. If in an uptrend volume is declining but open interest is rising, open interest will produce more accurate support curves for ongoing pullbacks in the trend than volume (see again **Rules #1** and **#2**). Moreover, if in a downtrend volume is decreasing while open interest is rising, then open interest will produce more accurate resistance curves for ongoing pullbacks than volume (see again **Rules #3** and **#4**).

Briefly, it's possible to demonstrate **Rules #3** and **#4** as applied to open interest in Figure 12.2, a weekly chart of NYMEX Platinum continuous futures. In the lower

FIGURE 12.2　Weekly chart of NYMEX Platinum continuous futures. This time Rules #3 and #4 are exemplified when price is in a sharp downtrend.

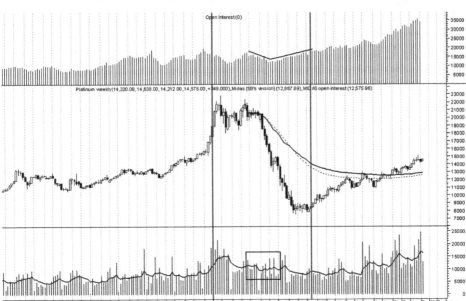

Source: eSignal, Metastock and COT Collector. www.esignal.com, www.equis.com, www.cotcollector .com.

pane, the moving average highlights that volume is in an intermediate downtrend between 2008 and 2009 as prices also descend parabolically. However, the open interest profile in the top pane is a little more complex, first declining and then a third of the way through starting to increase. Initially, the standard (solid) resistance curve is below the open interest (dotted) resistance curve, because **Rule #4** states that in a falling trend plus increasing volume, MIDAS resistance curves are pulled down towards the price. We see this initially because while open interest is falling, volume (highlighted in the box) is leveling off and actually increasing slightly. Thereafter, the open interest (dotted) curve crosses below the standard curve because of **Rule #3**, which states that in a falling price trend plus decreasing volume MIDAS resistance curves are pulled up from the falling price trend (while according to **Rule #4** they should be pulled down if volume (or in this case open interest) is increasing).

Again, therefore, we find a legitimate role for open interest in MIDAS S/R analysis if there is a relevant divergence between volume and open interest relative to the direction of a price trend under scrutiny.

Pursuing MIDAS and Open Interest More Deeply

So far in this chapter I've briefly explored a role for open interest in MIDAS studies parallel to the one discussed in Chapter 11. However, my main goal in this chapter is to examine open interest data more thoroughly alongside MIDAS to arrive at a new and genuinely helpful set of market timing tools.

To do this, we must have a reasonable understanding of how open interest is broken down in the weekly Commitments of Traders (COT) report published by the Commodity Futures Trading Commission (CFTC). Thus, the next section will again be expository in nature as we gain sufficient information on the COT report to be able to investigate in the remainder of the chapter two primary questions:

1. Which category of open interest data from the COT report is best suited to the application of the MIDAS indicators?
2. What type of signal can we expect from the MIDAS tools in relation to the trading setups identified by experienced users of COT report data?

Concise Overview of the Commitment of Traders (COT) Report

Let's make a start by establishing a little background on the COT report and then identifying the key components of it.

The Commitments of Traders (COT) report is prepared by the Commodity Futures Trading Commission (CFTC). The CFTC's Large Trader Reporting Program, which is of interest to us here, collects market data and positional information from U.S. exchanges, clearing members, futures commission merchants, foreign brokers, as well as individual traders. These reports are filed daily with the CFTC and aggregate data of reported positions are published by the CFTC in its weekly COT report.

This report is compiled every Tuesday and published every Friday at 3:30 P.M. EST. To quote the CFTC, it "provide[s] a breakdown of each Tuesday's open interest for markets in which 20 or more traders hold positions equal to or above the reporting levels established by the CFTC."[6] The report is available in four formats: futures only and a futures-and-options combined report, plus a long and short version of each report. The short version of the futures only report, which attracts the interest of most traders, breaks the open interest down into reportable and nonreportable positions. For the former, data are provided for commercial and noncommercial positions, spreading, changes in open interest from the previous report, percents of open interest by category, and numbers of traders. As we see below, most traders tend to focus on the general open interest numbers plus the commercial and noncommercial positions. The long report contains all of the information in the short report plus a grouping of the data by crop year and the positions held by the largest four and eight traders. There are also several additional reports that reveal aggregate futures and option positions of noncommercial, commercial, and index traders in 12 selected agricultural commodities.

In September 2008 there was a recommendation for even more transparency in the CFTC's *Staff Report on Commodity Swap Dealers & Index Traders*. As a result, on September 4, 2009, the CFTC began publishing a Disaggregated Commitments of Traders report covering 22 commodity markets, with remaining commodity markets added on December 4, 2009. The older report, which the CFTC now refers to as the Legacy Report, only separated reportable traders into the two well-known commercial and noncommercial categories (plus nonreportables). The new disaggregated COT report creates four categories: (1) producer/merchant/processor/user; (2) swap dealers; (3) money managers; and (4) other reportables.[7] In all other respects, the new disaggregated COT report is compiled in the same way as the Legacy Report.

At the time of writing in late 2009, the Disaggregated Report and Legacy Report are being published together through to the end of 2009. Meanwhile, the CFTC is requesting feedback on the new report and will review whether to continue publishing the Legacy Report alongside the Disaggregated Report or to replace it with the Disaggregated Report.

Understanding the Main Players in the Legacy Report

Setting aside the new Disaggregated Report pending the decision of the CFTC, it was noted above that experienced COT traders have traditionally tended to focus on the short format, futures only version of the Legacy Report. This report can be found on the CFTC's web site in relation to the 10 main futures exchanges in the United States. For example, Table 12.2 is the weekly December 18, 2009, Legacy Report compiled from the Chicago Mercantile Exchange of the Euro FX futures.

In this report we can easily identify the three categories of traders from left to right: noncommercials (hedge funds, commodity pools, and CTAs), commercials (producer

TABLE 12.2 Legacy Cot Report Compiled from the CME of the Euro FX Futures and Released on
December 18, 2009

EURO FX-CHICAGO MERCANTILE EXCHANGE FUTURES ONLY POSITIONS AS OF 12/15/09					Code-099741			
NON-COMMERCIAL			COMMERCIAL		TOTAL		NONREPORTABLE POSITIONS	
LONG	SHORT	SPREADS	LONG	SHORT	LONG	SHORT	LONG	SHORT
(CONTRACTS OF EUR 125,000)					OPEN INTEREST: **132,017**			
COMMITMENTS								
42,987	**59,435**	**671**	**39,669**	**40,728**	**83,327**	**100,834**	**48,690**	**31,183**
CHANGES FROM 12/08/09 (CHANGE IN OPEN INTEREST: -47,277)								
-9,048	6,889	-5,357	-36,348	51,587	-50,753	-50,055	3,476	2,778
PERCENT OF OPEN INTEREST FOR EACH CATEGORY OF TRADERS								
32.6	45.0	0.5	30.0	30.9	63.1	76.4	36.9	23.6
NUMBER OF TRADERS IN EACH CATEGORY (TOTAL TRADERS: 126)								
32	49	10	28	23	65	77		

and consumer hedgers), and nonreportable positions (small speculators and small hedgers).

So far as the numbers are concerned, interpreters of the COT report will tend to focus on the net figure of each group. This figure is calculated from the numbers in the first row (here in bold print) after the total open interest figure (here also in bold print standing at 132,017). We've already been introduced to this total open interest figure—it's the total number of longs or shorts, not the combination of the two. The net figure of each group is conventionally calculated by subtracting the short position from the long position, though readers interested in looking more deeply at this topic can consult Appendix A of Stephen Briese's book *The Commitments of Traders Bible* where alternative net position formulas are discussed.[8]

According to the Table 12.2, the commercials are net short –1,059 (39,669 – 40,728), the noncommercials are also net short –16,448, while the nonreportables are net long 17,507. Some readers have probably seen in online and printed reports the net position charts derived from these numbers. Figure 12.3, a continuous weekly chart of CBOT rough rice futures, shows in the lower pane the net positioning of each group over the past decade.

A good introduction to net positioning charts, and particularly to the basic types of commercial and noncommercial net positioning patterns a trader should be alert to in relation to price behavior at market extremes, can be found in Chapter 5 of Briese (2008).

Identifying the Key Players in the COT Report

Besides the numbers, it was emphasized earlier that the Legacy COT Report identifies three key trader groups: noncommercials, commercials, and nonreportables. Sufficient

FIGURE 12.3 Continuous weekly chart of CBOT rough rice futures with the lower pane revealing the net positioning of each group over the past decade.

Source: www.timingcharts.com.

information on these groups will be provided here to enable us to explore the two remaining points of inquiry in this chapter, though readers requiring more detail should consult the books by Briese (2008) as well as the important book-length studies of the COT report by Williams and Upperman.[9]

Nonreportables (Small Speculators and Small Hedgers)

This group tends to be the least respected of the three and is often regarded as the "dumb money." The advice, as recommended by Williams (2005), is usually to take an opposite position to them whenever possible.[10] Other commentators, such as Briese (2008), are more cautious about advocating this policy, arguing that when the group is charted, there is often insufficient movement in its positions in relation to the various tools and trading strategies relied on to make it worthwhile (though compare again Williams (2005)).[11] Briese also argues that this group not only consists of small speculators but also a diverse group of small commercial hedgers, consequently it's a group whose trading tendencies are often difficult to generalize.[12]

Due to space limitations I'll omit the nonreportables from further consideration, though, as mentioned, this group is treated by Williams.

Commercials (Producer and Consumer Hedgers)

In many shorter chapter-length discussions of the COT report, the commercials are often referred to collectively and their characteristic activities are lumped together in terms of either *en masse* buying or selling. However, longer expert-length studies such as those by Upperman (2006) and Briese (2008) carefully distinguish the producer side of the commercials from the consumer side, even though they share the same goal of alleviating their risk in the cash markets.

The commercials are negative-feedback traders, meaning that they buy (average down) all the way down a declining market and sell (average up) all the way up a rising one. The key therefore in timing market extremes is to buy the moment the commercials stop buying and to cover or sell short the moment the commercials stop selling.[13] Negative feedback trading is possible for the commercials, first, because they control the large financial resources necessary to meet margin calls, and second, because they have offsetting cash positions boosting inventory gains. If they wish, the commercial hedgers could make delivery against their short positions and take delivery to settle long positions, though this rarely happens, since only a small percentage of open interest actually goes to delivery.[14]

We obtain a better understanding of the commercials if we follow the lead of the experts and separate them into the commercial producers and commercial consumers. A commercial producer sells forward production in the futures markets with the aim of locking in currently quoted selling prices. He would be an oat or soybean farmer in the agricultural sector, an oil producer in the energy sector, or a Japanese car manufacturer exporting cars to Europe in the foreign exchange sector (the manufacturer would be "producing" euros as a result of his sales to Europe). Commercial producers must always hedge by going short, since they are protecting themselves against falling commodity prices.

Commercial consumers are of course the group obtaining the raw product wholesale from the producers and buy forward consumption in the futures markets in order to fix future inventory costs.[15] Examples include large food manufactures purchasing agricultural produce wholesale such as oats and soybeans, companies in the airline industry purchasing fuel, house builders purchasing lumber and other raw materials, and European car importers from Japan who would need to hedge ("consume") long yen in the foreign exchange markets.

Once this distinction between the commercial hedgers is made, it becomes easier to understand the fundamental dynamic between supply and demand when commercial hedging reaches extremes at the long and short end of the market.

Noncommercials (Large Speculators such as Hedge Funds, Commodity Pools, and CTAs)

Excluding spreading,[16] this group controls roughly 15 percent of the open interest on each side of the market. Experts such as Briese[17] regard the spreading numbers as meaningless for directional bias so far as most markets are concerned, so they won't be of concern to us here. Because the noncommercials are by definition speculative traders they assume the risk from the commercial hedgers with speculative profit as the end goal. Unlike the commercials, the funds buy into uptrends and sell into downtrends. Their strategy is purely trend-following and, as a result, is always at the wrong side of the market at extremes.

Choosing the Appropriate Category of Open Interest

This breakdown of the COT report reprises the first of the two questions raised earlier, namely which category of open interest we should consider using along-side the MIDAS tools. Since we're excluding the nonreportables, we have three options:

1. The net positioning of the noncommercials
2. The net positioning of the commercials
3. The total open interest data (which, as noted earlier, is 132,017 in Table 12.2)

For a trader new to open interest data, trying to decide between these three key options, the situation is confusing. In the book-length studies of the COT report by Upperman (2006) and Briese (2008) the focus is on net commercial data with total open interest sidelined. However, in an online study entitled "Forecast the FX Market with the COT Report"[18] Kathy Lien does suggest looking at total open interest for one type of trade setup but argues that the net noncommercial data are the most important. The same view on net noncommercial data is taken by Grace Cheng[19] in her recent book *7 Winning Strategies for Trading Forex*, while total open interest data are ignored. In another recent book, *Sentiment in the Forex Market*, Jamie Saet-tele[20] argues that there's no real advantage to following total open interest if one is already studying the combined net positioning of the commercials and noncommer-cials. Finally, in his 2005 book *Trading Stocks & Commodities with the Insiders* Larry Williams predominantly advocates looking at net commercial data but also thinks there is an important role for total open interest as well as for net noncommercial data.

However, despite the confusing first appearances, there is actually more clarity on these options when we dig a little deeper. We'll need to spend the next two sections uncovering it. Let's make a start with total open interest, even though it is largely ignored in Upperman (2006), Briese (2008), Cheng (2007), and Saettele (2008). The conclusion of the next section will be that total open interest can have a very important, and sometimes even essential, role to play with the MIDAS tools (though less so for other indicators), even if it is largely excluded from the studies of some experts. This view is bolstered by the discussion earlier of the useful role total open interest can often play in relation to various types of volume trend identified in Chapter 11.

MIDAS and Total Open Interest

Total open interest is used in one type of COT report trading setup by Lien, it's the focus of an entire chapter in Williams (2005), and it's very guardedly recommended in Saettele (2008). As noted, the latter argues that there's no advantage to following total open interest if one is already studying the net positioning of the commercials and noncommercials.[21] He points out that for those who do look at total open interest the orthodox interpretation is fairly compelling, since increasing open interest in both uptrends and downtrends is key to confidence that they'll continue. However, he objects that this is backward looking; it only tells us what has happened and not what is likely to happen. He concludes with the following observation.

> Also … open interest is extremely volatile in its fluctuations. In fact, tops in open interest occur on a three-month cycle. This is because the contract months for currency futures are March, June, September, and December. … The result is a short-term top in open interest every three months, usually during the second or third week of the contract month.
>
> [This] … makes it difficult to extract meaningful information, at least during the middle of the trend. However, major tops and bottoms do tend to occur when open interest is at its highest within a specific period. In this sense, open interest is valuable at the same time as the Composite COT [the indicator that results from his combining of commercial and noncommercial net positioning data (see text following)]. (p91)[22]

Thus, he extends an olive branch to those following total open interest insofar as major market turning points do usually occur when the data are at their highest over an appropriate lookback period.

The only persistent advocate of total open interest in recent discussions is Larry Williams (2005). However, contrary to orthodoxy Williams argues that the data must be interpreted on the basis that high levels of total open interest are associated with market tops and bottoms rather than being confirmers of the trend.[23] Recall that this is the opposite of what was being advocated in the introductory discussion of open interest.

From this unorthodox observation, he develops a market timing tool based on a 12-month stochastic of total open interest he calls the COT Index. This indicator has become better known in recent years due to its use by a growing number of web sites that chart Commitments of Traders data.[24] The formula for the COT Index (either with a one- or a three-year lookback period) is this:

((Current week's value − Lowest value of lookback period)/

(Highest high of lookback period − Lowest value of lookback period)) ∗ 100

This formula can be programmed into Metastock as follows:

$(Sum(OI - LLV(OI, 52), 3)/Sum(HHV(OI, 52) - LLV(OI, 52), 3)) * 100$

Figure 12.4 is Williams' weekly chart of soybeans with the same stochastic signals highlighted by the four vertical gray lines. The two outermost vertical black lines highlight the period covered in Williams' chart.

As a filter for trade entry Williams recommends drawing trend lines over the stochastic. One example on the chart is in 2000–2001. However, the problem with this filter is that it can be lagging, and it can't always be drawn effectively when the stochastic movements between the 80/20 levels are close to the vertical in orientation, which they often are.

An alternative is given in Figure 12.5, which is the same chart except that I've created a 3-period moving average %D line from the original %K line in Figure 12.4. The %K line is the quicker line in the stochastic, so the original line in Figure 12.4 becomes the faster dotted line. Here the filter is the crossing of the %K line over the %D line in the standard 80/20 overbought/oversold zones. The result avoids the two drawbacks highlighted, though a trader might still prefer to see the stochastic crossing back over the 80/20 lines before taking action as well as a significant confirmatory signal in the price action.

FIGURE 12.4 Weekly chart of soybean futures with the COT Index highlighting high and low readings in total open interest data at temporary market tops and bottoms.

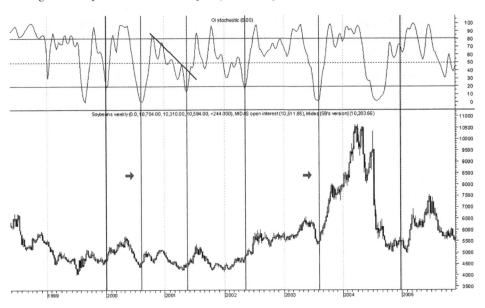

Source: eSignal, Metastock and COT Collector. www.esignal.com, www.equis.com, www.cotcollector .com.

FIGURE 12.5 The stochastic of total open interest this time has added to it a faster %K line which resembles the familiar stochastic oscillator.

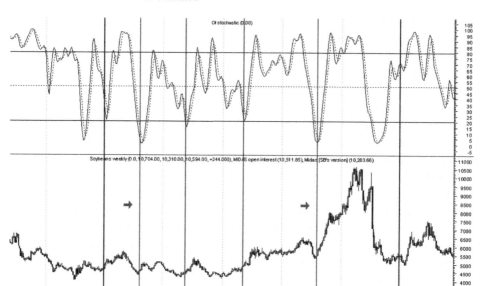

Source: eSignal, Metastock and COT Collector. www.esignal.com, www.equis.com, www.cotcollector .com.

In sum, then, in both Figures 12.4 and 12.5 high stochastic readings are associated with high total OI readings at market tops and vice versa at market bottoms. Actually, astute readers will notice that this market timing tool combines the orthodox and unorthodox views. The incorrect orthodox view is that uptrends don't top out on high open interest readings (but they do, as Williams' unorthodox observations show), while the correct orthodox view is that downtrends should find their bottoms on declining or very low levels of open interest. Examples of the latter are highlighted by the vertical gray lines next to the two arrows. Indeed, insofar as low levels of total OI are evidently associated with market bottoms, Williams seems to overstate the case in linking market bottoms with high levels of total OI.

Williams indirectly addresses Saettele's point that misleading tops in total open interest data occur on a regular three-monthly cycle by observing that this phenomenon actually only occurs in stock index futures and currency futures markets such as the British pound. Commodity markets such as soybeans, silver, wheat, gold and others don't exhibit it. Williams sums up as follows:

> The lesson is that [total] OI can be very helpful to us. Think of it as the masses, the crowd. Markets by their very nature cannot have everyone buying the lows and selling the highs. However, the opposite, buying the highs and selling the lows, is true. So look for times when there is no OI if you want to find a market that is going to get really interesting.[25]

Hence, on the surface we have a powerful reason for using total open interest based on a contrarian reinterpretation of how open interest should be read at market extremes.

However, this section wouldn't be complete without making two further observations. The first is that despite the usefulness of the COT Index it is far from being immune to the usual problem of timing market tops and bottoms. Where they can be applied, the TB-F curves do a much better job at capturing these market extremes. The second observation is that in some market conditions total open interest is the *only* form of data available for the MIDAS tools, since net commercial and net non-commercial data often can't be used when they generate persistent negative numbers that can't be processed in the MIDAS curves.

As far as the first observation is concerned, Figure 12.6 is a weekly chart of continuous soybean futures. It illustrates that even with filters on the COT Index such as trend line breaks or moving average crossovers, familiar timing issues persist. Note in the stochastic period between 2006 and early 2008 (highlighted in the gray box), it becomes overbought extremely early and remains there while whipsawing back and forth, producing many false sell signals during a parabolic uptrend.

The topfinder applied to total open interest cuts through this ambiguity. To see this, ignore the whipsawing COT Index and look at the strategy of applying the four TB-Fs. The topfinder labeled (1) (black curve) was launched from the pullback after the break of the 2005 high when resistance became support. It was fitted to the next pullback at the second arrow. The second topfinder labeled (2) (gray curve) was

FIGURE 12.6 The same chart of soybean futures moved on a few years.

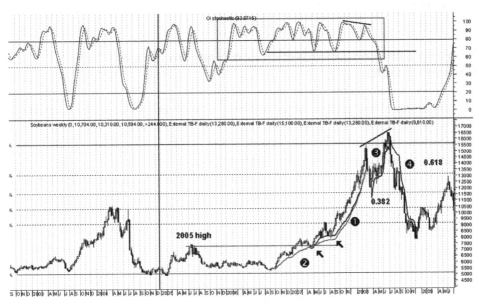

Source: eSignal, Metastock and COT Collector. www.esignal.com, www.equis.com, www.cotcollector .com.

subsequently launched earlier from the start of the move and fitted to the pullback from which the first topfinder was launched (first arrow). Topfinders fractally launched produce powerfully accurate convergent signals, as indeed they do here. The third topfinder was launched from the pullback to the Fibonacci 38.2 percent level and caught the top when the COT Index had finally stopped whipsawing and had broken its support at around the 70 level. The bottomfinder (4) was launched from the point where the third topfinder had completed and was fitted to the pullback at the Fibonacci 61.8 percent level. By the time of this fitting the COT Index was already oversold and remained there even when the bottomfinder had terminated. By contrast, the COT Index didn't break back above the 20 level until the 2009 trend was halfway complete. In this brief illustration, then, the TB-F curves are sharper, more accurate, and produce more timely signals.

As for the second observation, we've already seen critics of total open interest argue that the extremes identified by it can also be identified by the net positioning data, thus making the former redundant. We'll come to the net positioning data soon. In the meantime, it's essential to point out that there are occasions when the net data can't be used with MIDAS if there are persistent negative numbers produced as a result of creating them, since they cannot be processed in the MIDAS formulae. A good case in point is the following weekly chart of continuous soybean futures in Figure 12.7. In this chart, we see net positioning of the noncommercials and commercials repeatedly move into negative territory before the noncommercials (large traders) start trending positively from around 2007 onwards. By contrast, the open interest has been steadily trending upwards since mid-2004. The open interest numbers will always be positive and therefore can always be used with the MIDAS curves. I'll return to this observation later.

Choosing between Commercial and Noncommercial Positioning Data

The conclusion of the previous discussion was that although many experts on the COT report downplay the significance of total open interest data, there are often occasions when it is essential to use them with the MIDAS tools. When the data are used, they create excellent curves with timely and accurate signals.

Of course, this conclusion doesn't exclude using net positioning data with MIDAS. It thus leaves open the question of how we use these data as well as which among them we should choose to use. The latter part of the question can be a particular source of confusion, as we saw earlier when looking at the often conflicting views of the experts.

I want, in this section, to get clear on the question of whether current expertise has a preference for noncommercial or commercial net positioning data in the COT report, and then to see what kind of indicators it builds from them. Finally, we'll be in a position to see how MIDAS performs alongside them.

At times it will seem as though I'm veering away from discussing MIDAS. But as I've said on several occasions I want this chapter to offer a concise summary of

FIGURE 12.7 Weekly chart of continuous soybeans with total open interest in the bottom pane and the net positioning of the commercials, noncommercials, and nonreportables in the middle pane.

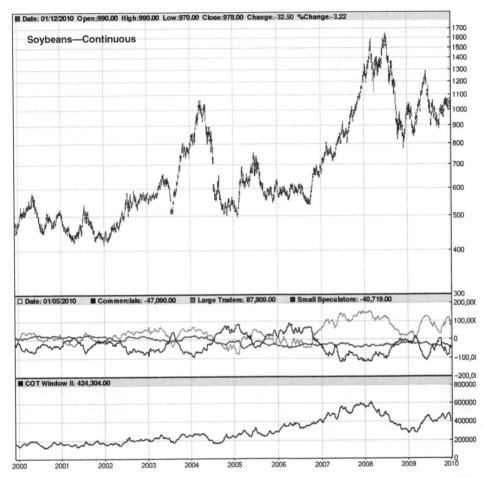

Source: www.timingcharts.com.

contemporary expert thinking on the COT report as well as a discussion of the role that the MIDAS system can play in analyzing the data. As stated in the introduction, I hope the reader will agree that the undertaking is justified when it results in a single chapter summarizing the last decade's vital research on open interest data and the COT report.

The first question to address is which among the net positioning data—the commercials or the noncommercials—we should follow. Then we can look at what current expertise thinks we should be doing with the data when we have them. Finally, we can examine how best to integrate the MIDAS system alongside expert thinking on these two primary issues.

In her online article referred to earlier, Kathy Lien states that we should always be following the noncommercials (funds) and not the commercials (hedgers). Her reason, focusing on the currency futures, is that the largest percentage of commercial currency trading is done in the cash markets. Consequently commercial positioning data are unlikely to give a true reflection of actual market positioning. Cheng (2007) also holds the same view, arguing more generally that the noncommercials are trading purely for speculative profit and will close losing positions, while the commercials are hedgers who are happy to retain losing positions.[26] The point presumably is that you can't rely on the latter group for market direction, because it is largely impervious to it and will diligently retain its hedging stance regardless of the ongoing trend.

However, these recommendations to follow the noncommercials (funds) are not made in the three book-length studies of the COT report by Williams (2005), Upperman (2006), and Briese (2008). All three advise that commercial net positioning should be prioritized, although all three also admit to maintaining their indicators on the noncommercial and even in some cases nonreportable data. However—and this point is vital—all three studies also emphasize that it is the net positioning of the commercials *at market extremes* that's of critical importance. I'll return to this proviso on numerous occasions in the remainder of this chapter.

In stressing the importance of commercial net activity, Williams (2005) argues that buying and selling in the cash market is the very business of the commercials. It stands to reason therefore that these people will know the markets better than the outsiders.[27] This is not to say that he doesn't look at the noncommercial or indeed the nonreportables. In separate chapters he even applies the same COT Index, advocating taking an opposite position at market extremes identified by the COT Index.

Upperman (2006) also argues that the commercials must be regarded as the most knowledgeable participants in each market because their livelihood depends on their determination of futures prices. This point is made more clearly when the commercials are broken down into the commercial producers and consumers. This distinction was introduced earlier. Commercial producers have unsurpassed knowledge of the manufacturing and production side of their market. As Upperman notes:

> They [namely, commercial producers] understand the fundamentals of production very well; they know how much it costs to produce a commodity, and probably know how much money they can get for it too. They also know what their supply is, and they know what market demand is.[28]

This is true too of the commercial consumers, exemplified by the large corporations and businesses who trade directly with the producers and who must always be net long when hedging to prevent rising commodity prices. Like the former group, they are also deeply in tune with the fundamentals affecting the supply side of their operations.

Stephen Briese (2008) also argues that the commercials, as well as controlling 75 percent of total open interest in the COT report, must be expected to hold an informational advantage over other market participants. He points out:

> These [commercial] firms have long-standing relationships within, and an understanding of their industry, bred of decades or centuries of dealing in the cash business. They maintain their own networks of correspondents up and down the supply chain. Much of what passes as fundamental news originates with commercial houses. Even granting the possibility that fundamental developments are accurately and completely conveyed to the public, you would assume that commercials have already acted on the information before disseminating it. While we may not be able to overcome this informational edge, the *Commitments* report does serve to level the playing field, if you know what to look for (and how to interpret it).[29]

The deepest level of expertise on the COT report, then, is overwhelmingly of the opinion that it is the commercials who should be watched the closest and not the noncommercials.

But if this is so, the next question is what current expertise does with the data. What sort of indicator is created from the commercials' net positioning, and how is it used?

Measuring the Market with Commercial Net Positioning Data

Let's make a start on this brief survey with the contributions of Williams (2005). We'll then see how the MIDAS tools can slot in alongside them.

The COT Report Indicators of Larry Williams

While discussing Williams's views on total open interest earlier, we saw that one of his indicators is the COT Index, based on George Lane's stochastic with a lookback period of either one or three years. Williams also applies it to the net positioning data. The key to this indicator is the normalized market extremes it produces at the 80/20 levels. Because the commercials are negative-feedback traders, the extreme stochastic readings must be interpreted inversely to how they're normally read, that is, an "oversold" extreme is a sell signal and an "overbought" extreme is a buy signal.

Later in his book, when he examines more deeply the relationship between the commercials and total open interest, Williams justifies the development of two more indicators. The rationale behind the first is to get clear on how changes in total open interest are related to the net positioning data of the commercials. For example, a good thing to know in an uptrend in total OI is if it is being caused by the noncommercials and nonreportables adding longs while the commercials are decreasing their longs, or whether the opposite is occurring. An indicator to establish this information takes the commercials' net position as a percentage of total open interest (i.e., the commercial long position divided by the total open interest, or the commercial short position divided by the total open interest).[30] This indicator is charted in the next section when comparing its results with those of the MIDAS topfinder/bottomfinder.

The next indicator addresses which aspect of the commercial net positioning we analyze—the long or the short side. To solve the problem, Williams takes the net long data of the commercials and subtracts from them the net short data. The result is then divided by the total open interest, as in the previous indicator. This indicator will also be charted in the next section when comparing it with the TB-F curves. Finally, he puts the resulting dataset into the same stochastic formula, this time using a 26-week lookback period. He calls the index WILLCO, short for Williams' Commercial Index. When it rises, traders should look for opportunities to go long and vice versa. We can understand this rationale if we go back to the now-familiar distinction between the commercial producers and consumers. The former always need to be net short whereas the latter always need to be net long. Accordingly, any imbalance that exists between these two subgroups is connected to supply and demand. If the short hedging of the commercial producers is at an extreme, it means that there's an excess on the supply side and prices are likely to fall. If the long hedging of the commercial consumers is at an extreme, it means that there's a supply side deficit and prices are likely to rise.

What all of Williams's indicators have in common is their aim of identifying market extremes. Emphasized earlier, it's not merely that commercial net positioning data assume an importance over other COT data—it's that they do so when signaling a market extreme; that is, a supply/demand imbalance.

The COT Report Indicators of Stephen Briese

The main indicator Briese discusses in his book is the COT Index, the same indicator we've been introduced to. Like Williams, Briese also applies the COT Index to the other two groups that make up the COT report, though again it's the commercial net positioning data that are of greatest significance. Briese selects a three-year lookback period for the indicator, though he justifies this by nothing more than happenstance: Curtis Arnold, the Index's originator, only had historical data that extended back three years! Briese acknowledges that this probably isn't optimal and advises analyzing the time cycles of different futures markets to locate it. The trading timeframe should also be taken into account—shorter-term market traders should reduce the lookback period accordingly (thirteen weeks is one such period considered).[31]

Briese also introduces a second indicator derived from the COT Index he calls the COT Movement Index. This indicator is based on the popular rate of change (ROC) formula and is simply the difference between the current reading of the COT Index and its reading over a newly selected six-week lookback period.[32] A +40 /−40 point surge on the Movement Index frequently marks the end of a countertrend price reaction in an ongoing trend. A chart of this indicator will be provided in the next section, when it will be compared alongside the standard MIDAS support/resistance curves, since the primary purpose of these curves is to identify support and resistance areas within ongoing trends. I'll look at how they fare when volume is replaced by net positioning data.

Finally, Chapter 11 of Briese's book contains another study of relevance insofar as he surveys several other well-known indicators applied to COT data to see if they can improve over the COT and Movement Indexes. These indicators include the COT MACD-Histogram, the COT-RSI, and COT-Bollinger Bands. All three indicators get an approval rating, especially the first two.

The COT Report Indicators of Floyd Upperman

It's difficult to summarize Upperman's statistical COT indicators because a lot of what he uses remains proprietary. He emphasizes monitoring the positioning of the commercial producers and consumers separately while looking for statistical anomalies. If the commercial longs are at a statistical extreme while the shorts are within normal statistical boundaries, we have ground for assuming that the commercial consumers are behind this one-sided extremity, indicating a bullish outlook.[33] He identifies extreme net commercial positions by two boundaries he calls the "upper commercial limit" (UCL) and "lower commercial limit" (LCL). These limits—calculated using probability distribution analysis[34]—lie outside normal historic statistical variations and are rare occurrences.[35] He will also apply this statistical apparatus to the noncommercials while studying its longs and shorts. One signal he looks for at their market extremes is a divergence of the fund net position from price, even though the funds are characteristically trend-followers, providing much of the financial fuel for the move.[36]

Like Williams and Briese, Upperman's attention is on the market extremes in the net positioning data, and (like them) he is also aware that while extreme net commercial readings are almost always present at significant market turning points, they don't always produce significant trend changes. Most of the time such readings are necessary but not sufficient to take action, since an extreme market reading can remain for weeks or even months before the market turns. To handle this problem, Upperman relies on an overall trading strategy he calls Individual Market Participation Analysis (IMPA). The IMPA system consists of four parts: (1) the commercials holding an extreme position as determined by proprietary statistical tools; (2) a similarly opposing position in the noncommercials and/or nonreportables; (3) certain price-based technical indicators, such as a proprietary RSI diverging appropriately and atypical moving average lengths; and (4) seasonal studies (if applicable) with price-based patterns (such as his Plunger Pattern) indicative of a new trend.[37]

The COT Report Indicators of Jamie Saettele

Like the other experts, especially Williams whom he credits with the idea, Saettele acknowledges the importance of watching the commercials at extremes. But he notes that for the most part the net positioning of the commercials and noncommercials move inversely to one another. Consequently, he combines the net commercial and noncommercial data into an indicator he calls the Composite COT, constructed by subtracting the net commercials from the net noncommercials. While this indicator can be effective, it can be improved by giving it fixed boundaries that are created by a ranking system based on a percentile calculation of the lookback period (52 weeks is recommended, with 26 and 13 weeks for shorter-term signals). This indicator, he calls the COT Index,[38] correlates positively with price, so that a reading of 0 means that the noncommercials are extremely short while the commercials are very long and vice versa. Its problem (noted by Saettele) is the by-now familiar one that extreme readings of 0 and 100 are often too familiar and frequently premature, resulting in ongoing excess readings while the market continues to trend.

A third indicator results, this time by considering noncommercial long positions as a percentage of total noncommercial positions. An illustration can be obtained from the COT report of the euro FX futures back in Table 12.2. We see there that the noncommercials are long 42,987 and short 59,435. Thus, 42,987 / (42,987 + 59,435) = 0.419—that is, 42 percent of the noncommercials are net long in the second week of December 2009. This resulting dataset (the percent long ratio or Speculative Ratio Index) is charted as another oscillator-like indicator alongside the Composite COT, the benefit being that the percent long ratio is a better timing filter for adjudicating market tops and bottoms identified by the Composite COT. As noted, the percent long ratio is constructed from net noncommercial data, though the same indicator can be derived from commercial net positioning. The latter version is called the Commercial Ratio Index.

MIDAS and COT Report Timing

At this juncture, then, we know where current expertise places the emphasis in reading the COT report, and we also understand more about the key indicators used on these data, which (with the exception of Briese's COT Movement Index) focus on market extremes. As also noted, the major problem with these indicators is in their timing of the extremes, for even though they can identify them well, they can't always identify their ends. With this in mind, it's now time to consider how we might use the MIDAS tools in relation to these findings.

At first sight, it may seem that we've run into a problem insofar as the majority of these techniques focus on net positioning data. Recall that the MIDAS tools cannot process negative numbers. There is, however, a solution. In uptrends we know that the bulk of the commercials will be net short, whereas in downtrends they will be net long. The situation will be reversed for the noncommercials. Therefore it will be often necessary when using the MIDAS tools to switch from the commercials to the noncommercials, depending on the direction of the price trend. Readers might have a concern about this because of the weight given by deeper levels of expertise in Williams, Upperman, and Briese to commercial net positioning data. To alleviate this concern, all of the following topfinder/bottomfinder curves are processed with noncommercial data and compared with the indicators listed above processed with commercial data. As we'll see, the results are extremely good.

Before proceeding, readers should note that on occasions it may be that neither commercial nor noncommercial data can be used because there are simply too many negative numbers. If so, readers are again advised to use total open interest data, which, as we've seen, also produce extremely reliable results. Thus, it's always possible to use MIDAS tools with the COT report.

Comparing the Commercial Net Positioning Indicators with MIDAS using Noncommercial Net Positioning Data

Let's make a start with Figure 12.8, which is a weekly chart of continuous rough rice futures. The indicator in the topmost window is the COT Index, which we already examined when I constructed it out of total open interest data. Here it is created from commercial net positioning data in the middle pane (with noncommercial data beneath). The focus of the chart is the parabolic uptrend between the two outer vertical lines. Notice first that the COT Index gives a buy signal as it drops below the 80 level fairly soon after the trend accelerates (remember that the noncommercial COT Index works inversely). It then drops below the 20 level for a potential sell signal midway through the acceleration at the middle vertical line, potentially shaking out

FIGURE 12.8 Weekly continuous rough rice futures with COT Index and topfinder.

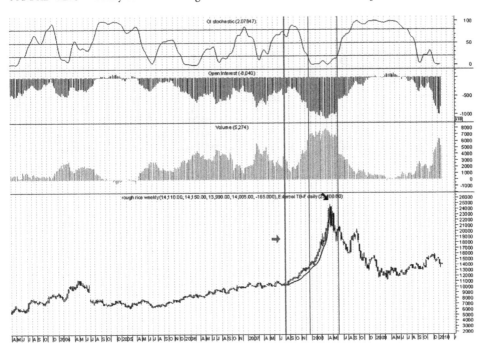

Source: eSignal, Metastock and COT Collector. www.esignal.com, www.equis.com, www.cotcollector .com.

many traders unless they had additional filters. The sell signal is then confirmed later when the index breaks above the 20 level midway through the downtrend at the third gray line.

Here, then, we have a clear illustration of that same market timing problem discussed earlier in a potential premature close of the trade when the COT index moves rapidly below the 20 level. Yet for the topfinder using noncommercial net positioning data there is no such problem. The topfinder was fit to several minor pullbacks at a cumulative net positioning reading of 185,000 and terminated on the last bar of the trend (black arrow). For trade management purposes, the trade could've been closed (or a short position opened) on the break of the low of this candlestick (following trade-management principles discussed in Chapters 1 and 3), with a stop being placed just above its high.

Our next chart, Figure 12.9, replaces the COT Index with the second indicator Williams introduces. He calls it "commercial net positioning as a percentage of total open interest" (i.e., the commercial long position divided by the total open interest, or the commercial short position divided by the total open interest). The rationale behind it is to get clear on how changes in total open interest are related to the net positioning of the commercials. We then know whether an uptrend in total OI

FIGURE 12.9   Weekly continuous corn futures with several TB-Fs and Williams's commercial net shorts as a percentage of total open interest.

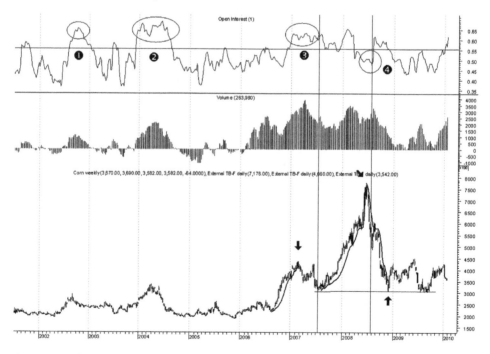

Source: eSignal, Metastock and COT Collector. www.esignal.com, www.equis.com, www.cotcollector .com.

is being caused by the noncommercials and nonreportables adding longs while the commercials are decreasing their longs, or vice versa. In a downtrend we'd look for opposite confirming data. When charted, this indicator is not an oscillator with fixed boundaries, so overextended areas are identified by reviewing the previous movements of the indicator. When using the version that divides the commercial short positioning by the total OI, Williams observes that when the indicator gets to 55 percent of all market selling action, a top has been close at hand.

In Figure 12.9 I have recreated this indicator in the top pane of a weekly chart of continuous corn futures, with net positioning of the noncommercials in the middle pane. As can be seen by the areas above 55 percent labeled (1), (2), and (3), when short selling has risen above 55 the market has declined, albeit the same timing problem afflicts this indicator. To see this, look at the excess selling area marked by (3). After 2007 the indicator pretty much stays above the 55 percent level until mid-2008. However, during this time two topfinders are launched on accelerated portions of the uptrend, the first in mid-2006 terminating at the end of the trend in early 2007 (first arrow), and the second at the first vertical black line in mid-2007 and expiring again precisely in mid-2008 (second arrow). Notice on the expiration of the second topfinder that commercial short selling had been around the 50 percent level for several months (see the area marked (4)). Only the topfinder gave the precision we were looking for. Finally, as the parabolic move rapidly terminated, a bottomfinder was launched that once again accurately caught the end of the parabolic downtrend terminating at a fairly predictable support level of 3,000. At the time of the bottom, the percent ratio index was giving a reading at the same level, 50 percent.

To obtain sell signals, the reverse version of this indicator must be created. That is, the commercial long position must be divided by the total open interest. I won't chart this indicator here for space reasons.

Let's continue applying net noncommercial data with the TB-F curves by examining Figure 12.10. This weekly chart of the continuous Japanese yen futures contains Williams's final indicator and is a duplication of the first chart he uses to illustrate it, including the same buy signals (vertical lines) when it crosses the 50 line and rises to the 70–80 level. This indicator was created to solve the issue of whether we analyze the long or the short side of the commercial positioning data. Here Williams takes the longs of the commercials and subtracts the shorts. The resulting dataset is then divided by the total open interest, as before. Finally, the original COT Index stochastic formula is applied to the result with a 26-week lookback period. Williams calls the indicator WILLCO, short for Williams Commercial Index. Again, because this indicator is based on commercial data its high readings (around 70–80) mean users look for reasons to go long and vice versa. This is opposite to how the stochastic is normally interpreted, as emphasized before. Note, too, on this chart the area I have circled. Here the indicator has dipped below the 10 level, warning of a potential sell-off, which is exactly what occurs throughout 2005.

Now let's take a look at this indicator alongside the MIDAS topfinder/ bottomfinder curves. Figure 12.11 is a weekly chart of continuous orange juice futures. The middle pane is the net noncommercial data being used by the

FIGURE 12.10 Weekly chart of continuous Japanese yen futures, which duplicates the same WILLCO buy signals in the vertical lines.

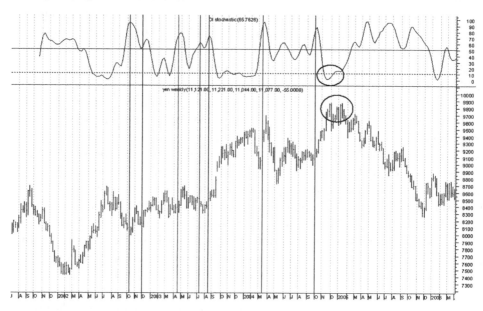

Source: eSignal, Metastock and COT Collector. www.esignal.com, www.equis.com, www.cotcollector .com.

FIGURE 12.11 Weekly chart of orange juice continuous futures with the WILLCO index and three TB-F curves.

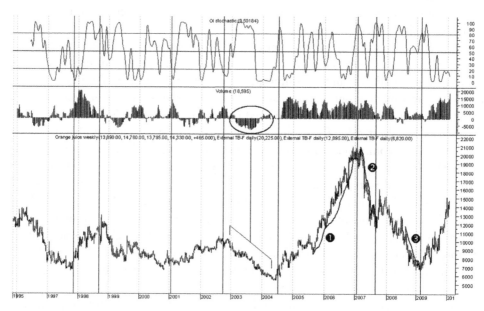

Source: eSignal, Metastock and COT Collector. www.esignal.com, www.equis.com, www.cotcollector .com.

topfinder/bottomfinder curves, while the upper pane is the WILLCO oscillator processing commercial data. I have placed vertical bars where the oscillator gave sharp buy and sell signals when it moved beyond the 80 and 20 levels respectively. Its 26-week lookback period explains this and it explains, too, why it oscillates so much, often producing buy and sell signals long before ongoing trends have ended. This could be remedied by changing the lookback period, but that is highly relative to a trader's own trading preference. Note the downtrend between late 2002 and mid-2004 where the noncommercial data are negative. As noted, negative readings produce anomalies in the MIDAS curves and, where necessary, we need to switch to commercial data or total OI. There are three TB-F curves on this chart labeled (1), (2), and (3). The first one is fit to the first pullback and captures the top precisely where WILLCO captures it. The second TB-F also captures the first leg of the downtrend alongside a WILLCO buy signal. Finally, the third TB-F also does the same accurate job alongside another timely buy signal by WILLCO. Here, using the TB-F curves with noncommercial data produces robust calls alongside a very successful indicator using commercial data.

The next indicator in the earlier discussion was Briese's COT Movement Index, which I want to look at last due to its unique status among the COT indicators as an identifier of the ends of pullbacks in ongoing trends. This sounds a lot like the function of a standard MIDAS support/resistance curve, which is why I'll set it aside and continue with end-of-trend indicators.

The next indicator, Saettele's Composite COT, is another end-of-trend timing tool, constructed by subtracting the net commercial data from the net noncommercial data. Its limitation is that it lacks boundaries, making it harder to detect when a market is at an extreme. His solution is an indicator he calls the COT Index, which unlike the stochastic-like oscillator discussed by Williams and Briese, is created by a percentile ranking of the data over 52 weeks (or 26/13 weeks for shorter signals). Yet as Saettele observes, this indicator's signals still aren't immune to familiar timing problems at market extremes. As a remedy, he proposes a third indicator that takes noncommercial long positions as a percentage of total noncommercial open interest (see the prior discussion for details). This resulting indicator, which he calls the percent long ratio or Speculative Ratio Index, is charted as another oscillator-like indicator alongside the Composite COT, with the latter acting as a filter for the former. (The percent long ratio can also be created from Commercial net positioning data, which he calls the Commercial Ratio Index.)

Figure 12.12 is a weekly chart of NYMEX crude oil continuous futures containing four windows above the lower price pane. The first above it is the untreated Composite COT with no fixed upper and lower boundaries. The next one is the Speculative Ratio Index—interestingly, although Saettele uses this index as a filter for the percentile COT Index, it too lacks boundaries, so the only way of introducing them is to look back over previous data to see at what levels turns are typically located (see the dotted lines). Here they're set at 80 and 20, though Saettele mentions the 90 level as an important one. In this chart I have actually normalized the Speculative Ratio Index by

FIGURE 12.12 Weekly chart of continuous NYMEX crude plus raw and normalized COT data.

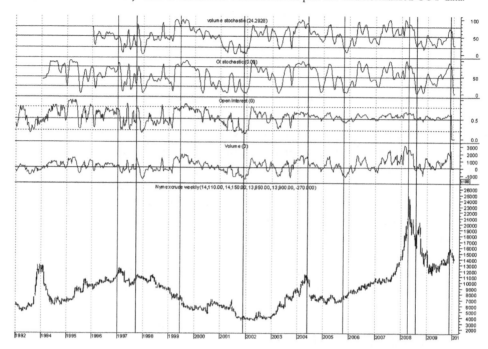

Source: eSignal, Metastock and COT Collector. www.esignal.com, www.equis.com, www.cotcollector
.com.

running it through the same stochastic formula. The result is the indicator third up from the price pane. Finally, the top indicator is a normalized version of the Composite COT. As noted, Saettele uses percentile rankings to create the COT Index from the Composite COT. Here, however, I've run the Composite COT through the same stochastic formula.

As can be seen from the vertical bars, the two normalized indicators do a pretty good job of identifying the main market turns, though this is a very long-term weekly chart, and there are going to be many resulting oscillator fluctuations in ongoing trends. Here the lookback period for the oscillators is three years. This would be reduced at least to 52 weeks and probably much lower to time turns in the intermediate (two to nine months) trend. Aside from the two suggestions as to how we might normalize the data, it isn't possible to launch TB-F curves in Figure 12.12 because the volume and open interest columns in the Metastock chart contain data for the Composite COT and Speculative Ratio Index. By now in any case we have seen enough proof that combining the MIDAS TB-F curves with total open interest and noncommercial net positioning data produce extremely good results.

This brings us back to the idea that COT data aren't exclusively used to time major market tops and bottoms. For example, Stephen Briese's indicator, the COT

Movement Index, has an important role to play in catching the ends of pullbacks in ongoing trends. As noted earlier, it's based on the popular rate of change (ROC) formula, so is the difference between the current reading of the COT Index and its reading over a newly selected lookback period (Briese chooses six weeks). Extremes on the COT Movement Index are marked at the ± 40 levels. Briese's rules are:

1. During a correction from a prevailing uptrend, a +40 point movement in the COT Index within a six-week period often marks the end of a corrective pullback and the resumption of the major uptrend.
2. During a reaction in a prevailing downtrend, a −40 point movement in the COT Index within a six-week period frequently marks the end of a price reaction and the resumption of the established downtrend.
3. The failure of a ±40 point COT Movement Index signal to restart the prevailing trend is a tip-off to a major trend change.

In Figure 12.13, a weekly chart of COMEX silver continuous futures, the middle pane is the by-now familiar COT Index created with the standard stochastic formula. Above it is Briese's COT Movement Index with the ± 40 levels.

FIGURE 12.13 Weekly chart of continuous silver futures with the COT Index in the middle pane and the COT Movement index in the upper pane.

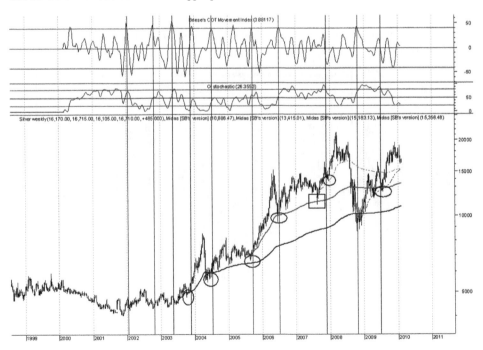

Source: eSignal, Metastock and COT Collector. www.esignal.com, www.equis.com, www.cotcollector. com.

The 10 vertical lines highlight Briese's first rule for the COT Movement Index. There are no clear instances of the second rule because there is no significant downtrend on the chart. With regard to each of these signals at a pivot bottom, I have either launched a standard MIDAS support curve from it or found that an already launched curve from a previous signal-related pivot catches it. The only exception is the major pivot bottom highlighted by the square in late 2007—this was caught by MIDAS but not by the Movement Index. While of course the COT Movement Index is here processing commercial net positioning data, the MIDAS support curves, like the TB-Fs earlier, are processing noncommercial net positioning data.

Finally, in an article referred to earlier, Kathy Lien identifies another type of trade setup using the COT report she calls a flip in market positioning. Although Lien advocates the use of noncommercial data and looks for this setup on them, they can easily be applied to commercial data. Basically, a flip occurs when the noncommercial net positioning either crosses up through the zero line or down through it. Figure 12.14 is an illustration of this approach with the histogram (and its scale on the left) the noncommercial net positioning and the gray line the weekly continuous wheat futures. Now if we look at this chart, we can see that the noncommercials are relative latecomers to the trend at the zero line, as indicated by the vertical gray lines. All in all, because of the lag problem this doesn't seem to be a great timing tool and we're better off sticking with the oscillator analyses examined earlier.

FIGURE 12.14 Weekly chart of continuous wheat futures with noncommercial net positioning data scaled on the left side.

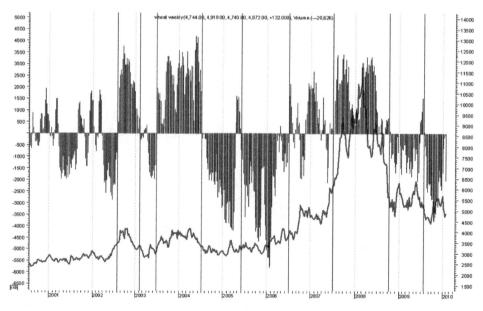

Source: eSignal, Metastock and COT Collector. www.esignal.com, www.equis.com, www.cotcollector .com.

FIGURE 12.15 Continuous wheat futures with noncommercial net positioning in the middle pane and commercial net positioning in the upper pane.

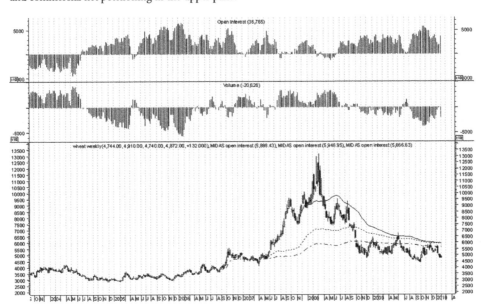

Source: eSignal, Metastock and COT Collector. www.esignal.com, www.equis.com, www.cotcollector .com.

I turn finally in this chapter to Figure 12.15, which is a reminder that while the MIDAS TB-F and standard S/R curves will work consistently with total open interest data, they won't always work with the net positioning data for the reason given earlier, namely that negative numbers won't process in the MIDAS calculations.

In Figure 12.15 the middle pane contains the noncommercial net positioning while the upper window contains the commercial net data. It has been impossible most of the time in this chart to launch standard MIDAS S/R curves using noncommercial net positioning data, because for so much of the time the data are in minus territory. As a result, the few standard support curves on this chart have been created using commercial net positioning data. When a MIDAS user wishes to launch one of the curves from a region associated with a persistent set of negative net positioning values, he must resort instead to total open interest, standard volume, or indeed nominal MIDAS curves, as discussed in Chapters 13 and 14.

Additional Reading

Seasonality is important when interpreting COT report data regardless of which indicator is being used. For readers who wish to deepen their knowledge the following books are a starting point:

Bernstein, J. *Key Date Futures Seasonals, the Best of the Best in Seasonal Trades.* New York: MBH Commodity Advisors, 1995.

Hirsch J. A., and J. L. Person. *Commodity Trader's Almanac 2010* (Almanac Investor Series). Hoboken, NJ: John Wiley & Sons, Inc., 2009.

Jiler, W. L. 1985. "Analysis of the CFTC Commitments of Traders reports can help you forecast futures prices." In *CRB Commodity Year Book*, ed. Walter L. Emery et al., 50T–58T. New Jersey: Commodity Research Bureau, 1985.

Momsen, J. *Ultra-Reliable Seasonal Trades.* New York: Windsor Books, 1999.

Momsen, J. *Superstar Seasonals: 18 Proven-Dependable Futures Trades for Profiting Year after Year.* New York: Windsor Books, 2004.

Schwager, Jack, and Steven C. Turner. *Futures: Fundamental Analysis.* New York: John Wiley & Sons, Inc., 1995.

Shaleen, K. H. "Analyzing the Commitments of Traders report." In *The CRB Commodity Yearbook*, ed. Anne K. Ingles et al., 17T–42T. New York: John Wiley & Sons, Inc., 1996.

Smith, C. *Seasonal Charts for Futures Traders.* New York: John Wiley & Sons, Inc., 1987.

Williams, L. *Sure Thing Commodity Trading: How Seasonal Factors Influence Commodity Prices.* New York: Windsor Books, 1987.

Summary

- When confronted with price-volume relationships of the type discussed in Chapter 11, open interest can be used with MIDAS curves instead of "nominal curves."
- Despite the relatively low-key treatment of total open interest among current expertise on the COT report, it is sometimes essential to use it with the MIDAS tools when related volume trends aren't conducive to timing pullbacks so accurately. Here open interest curves work far better.
- Curves created from total open interest are the only option when the MIDAS analyst is confronted with persistent negative numbers in the net positioning data. When total open interest is used with the MIDAS tools, it's highly dependable, and its signals are as good as any using the net positioning data.
- There is a tendency in current expertise on the COT report to favor commercial over noncommercial net positioning data and a number of important oscillator indicators have been developed for them. These oscillator indicators suffer from the usual timing problem at market tops and bottoms, and the TB-F curves are an important help when timing market extremes.
- Despite a lot of negative numbers being generated in commercial net positioning data, the MIDAS curves produce robust and highly dependable signals when used with noncommercial net positioning data and occasionally commercial net positioning data.
- Although such treatments have not been included here for space reasons, other more refined datasets can also be used with the MIDAS curves, provided they don't

produce too many negative numbers. An example would be the dataset in Saettele's Composite COT or Williams' WILLCO indicator.

- Current expertise on the COT report leans almost exclusively towards the development of indicators that measure the market extremes of the net commercial data. The exception is Briese's COT Movement Index as a tool to measure exhaustion points in smaller countertrends in ongoing trends. Here the standard MIDAS support/resistance curves add an important extra dimension to COT report analysis outside of the emphasis on extreme market positioning. To this extent, Briese's indicator and the standard MIDAS S/R curves are unique in COT report analysis.

CHAPTER 13

Price Porosity and Price Suspension

The Causes of these Phenomena and Several Partial Solutions

Andrew Coles

> "[P]orosity" . . . is the term I use to characterize situations when a "bounce" from a support or resistance level is not "clean" in the sense that some relatively small penetration occurs before the expected trend reversal. Perhaps "elasticity" would be a better term than porosity, since the [support/resistance] level can be imagined to have some "give" rather than being rigid. Or one could just say that the Midas method is after all a simple approximation to a more complex and less deterministic reality.
>
> —Paul Levine[1]

The phenomena of price porosity and suspension (a related problem not identified by Levine) in relation to the standard MIDAS support/resistance curves occur so often that it's important not only to understand them but also to explore a few solutions. In the second half of Chapter 1 it was stressed how porosity would be one of the main factors forcing a clarification of trade re-entry criteria when using the standard S/R curves. Several related issues were also discussed in Chapter 3. In addition, the porosity problem has been the backdrop to several related discussions by Hawkins in Chapters 2 and 9. This chapter will explain what causes porosity and suspension as well as explore several ways of dealing with it. As we'll see, the cause of these phenomena is not a by-product of an underlying indeterminacy in price behavior, as Levine assumed, but largely a symptom of the way MIDAS curves are calculated in relation to the high/low range. They also occur as a result of changing price-volume relationships. We saw an example of this intraday in Chapter 10 when looking at volume surges in the cash FX markets associated with the overlap beween the Asian and London sessions and the London and United States sessions. On these occasions, significant divergences can occur between standard volume-based MIDAS curves and their nominal curve counterparts.

Porosity and Suspension Illustrated

Let's remind ourselves graphically of what porosity is. Figure 13.1 is a 5m chart of the Xetra DAX March 2010 futures. A standard MIDAS support curve is launched from the long black candlestick that creates the lowest point in the sharp one-hour downtrend before price reverses and continues moving up into the next day. However, notice that at the two higher lows, circled price penetrates the MIDAS support curve by several points before responding to it. It does this twice in the first highlighted low and then again in the second one. This is the phenomenon of price porosity. It occurs on all chart timeframes and on all degrees of trend, and it will be present regardless of the format used to chart price.

Levine never identified the related phenomenon of price suspension but I first wrote about it in my articles on intraday applications of MIDAS curves in 2008 when I used the adjective "levitation."[2] If we go back to the same chart and view it again in Figure 13.2, we can see a new higher low (circled) that prints a mini-triple bottom prior to price turning higher.

FIGURE 13.1   5m chart of Xetra DAX March 2010 with price porosity in the two circled lows.

Source: eSignal and Metastock. www.esignal.com and www.equis.com.

FIGURE 13.2   5m chart of Xetra DAX March 2010 with price suspension or "levitation" in the
newly circled low.

Source: eSignal and Metastock. www.esignal.com and www.equis.com.

Notice that all of the reversal candlesticks associated with this mini-triple bottom,
reverse not on the MIDAS curve but a few points of chart whitespace above it.
Sometimes the gap between the MIDAS curve and the reversal bars that define the
levitation can be wider, just as the porosity can be much deeper than the instances
highlighted in Figure 13.1. Price suspension, then, is like two "like" poles of a magnet
repelling one another without actually coming into contact.

Identifying the Cause of the Two Phenomena

In the majority of cases, both phenomena are linked to the same cause. When Levine
created the MIDAS support and resistance curves, his choice of input was the average
price, which he calculated by adding today's high and low and multiplying by 0.5.
It's not clear whether this was an arbitrary choice or the result of deliberation; equally
possible is that Levine was influenced by the original VWAP methodology from which
the MIDAS system is an adaptation.

As we saw in Chapter 1, there's more than one way of calculating the daily VWAP,
but the basic formula is to multiply the price and volume at each time interval and
then divide by the total volume:

$$\Sigma(Pn * Vn)/\Sigma(Vn)$$

where

P = price of instrument traded
V = volume traded
n = number of trades

The averaging methodology in this approach would be an obvious influence on Levine's adjustment of it to create the MIDAS formula and, as a result, it's likely that he gave little weight to considering what the implications would be for MIDAS curves using the average price of each bar. As an alternative he might have considered what traders call the "typical price." Typical price calculations are the basis of several well-known indicators such as the Money Flow Index and the Commodity Channel Index and are calculated by the (High + Low + Close) / 3. However, in practice typical price calculations don't produce results that differ markedly from average price calculations.

Where significant differences do emerge is when we consider the values associated with the so-called true range of a price bar. The true range of a bar is defined as the greatest of the following:

- The current high minus the current low, or
- The absolute value of the current high less the previous close, or
- The absolute value of the current low less the previous close.

The latter two conditions shouldn't concern us here because they're based on interbar relationships while MIDAS requires an actual bar from which to launch. This leaves the first option; that is, the high and the low values of a given bar.

With the first option in mind, let's go back to Figures 13.1 and 13.2 and add two new MIDAS support curves launched from the low and the high of the same bar. Figure 13.3 is the same 5m DAX chart with the same black support curve being the original (H + L)*0.5 curve we looked at in the previous two charts. The lower grey support curve is calculated using the low price, and the upper dotted curve, the high.

In the highlighted circles, notice that the support curve launched from the low price is the actual support level for price pullbacks that are otherwise described as porous in relation to the original average price curve. Notice too with respect to the highlighted rectangle that the support curve launched from the high price is the actual support level for the price pullbacks. Here there is no price suspension.

Solving the Problem of the Two Phenomena

Now that we've identified one of the main causes of these two related phenomena, there are several ways that we might tackle the problem. The following options also include discussions by Hawkins in Chapters 2 and 9 that readers might have missed.

FIGURE 13.3 The same 5m DAX chart with two additional curves launched from the low and high price values.

DAX March 10 (5,772.50, 5,777.50, 5,771.00, 5,772.50, +0.50), I-Midas Coles High, I-MIDAS-Coles (5,533.86), I-Midas Coles High (5,538.72), I-Midas (Coles) low (5,529.00)

Source: eSignal and Metastock. www.esignal.com and www.equis.com.

Option #1: Using the High and Low

The first obvious solution is to add the two high and low curves of Figure 13.3 to the default "average price" MIDAS curve I've been using throughout this book. Indeed, one might suggest removing the "average price" curve and using a MIDAS support curve calculated with the low price in uptrends and one calculated with the high price in downtrends. This is actually Hawkins' preferred choice. Indeed, in Chapter 2 he argues that porosity is greatly reduced when the average price is replaced in uptrends by the low price and vice versa in downtrends.[3] I agree with Hawkins here, though as I've illustrated in Figures 13.2 and 13.3, curves with the low price in uptrends are then susceptible to what I've called the "price suspension" or "levitation" problem, with high price curves in downtrends facing the same problem. Figure 13.4, a 60m chart of the yen September 2010 futures, is a quick illustration of this problem. The solid black curve uses the low price and points (1) and (2) illustrate how it successfully resists the pullbacks while the dotted curve with the average price is subject to porosity. However, points (3) and (4) highlight where the average price curve successfully resists price while the high price curve is subject to price suspension. Since the price porosity and price levitation problems are literally two sides of the same coin, it's up to the reader whether he'd prefer Hawkins' solution to one side of it or the average price to the other.

The alternative is always to plot a set of three curves on every trend involving the high, low, and average price. But there are two drawbacks. First, it leads very quickly

FIGURE 13.4   60m chart of yen September 2010 futures illustrating price porosity and suspension
depending on which type of curve is used.

Source: eSignal and Metastock. www.esignal.com and www.equis.com.

to chart clutter; second, for day traders the memory resources required to calculate
so many curves create capacity problems and charts can literally grind to a standstill.
However, this can be an option in cases where traders might be watching a key test
of support or resistance using one or a small number of curves, especially on a higher
chart timeframe.

Option #2: The Choice of Launch Point

In a separate discussion in Chapter 2, Hawkins showed that porosity can sometimes
occur depending on the pivot from which a curve is launched and then advocated
launching a curve as far to the left of a trend reversal area as possible.[4] In Figure 2.15
he gave an example on a daily chart; here I'll provide an illustration on an intraday
timeframe. Figure 13.5 is a 5m chart of the euro FX September 2010 futures. The
arrows highlight a double bottom before a new uptrend begins. The first (black)
curve is launched from the first bottom and captures the pullback highlighted in a
strong candlestick reversal pattern; the second (dotted) curve launched from the second bottom is subject to porosity. In general, reversal patterns consisting of a double
or triple bottom should be subject to the same approach: the MIDAS analyst should
start his curves as far to the left as possible. Continuation patterns should also be
treated in a similar fashion, with the emphasis placed on the far left side of the correction. Again this solution to the porosity problem wouldn't be a solution to the price
levitation problem.

FIGURE 13.5   5m chart of euro FX September 2010 futures with a double bottom.

Source: eSignal and Metastock. www.esignal.com and www.equis.com.

Option #3: Switching to a Higher Timeframe

Reversal patterns such as double and triple bottoms are minority patterns. Most of the time there is a single swing high or low from which to launch a standard MIDAS curve. Again in Chapter 2 Hawkins observes that when a curve is subject to porosity on one timeframe a solution is to step up to a higher timeframe where the porosity disappears.[5] Once more, let's illustrate this observation on two intraday charts. Figure 13.6 is a 5m chart of the EUREX Bund September 2010 futures with a resistance curve launched from a swing high just before 4:00 P.M. There are two examples of porosity clearly indicated on this chart. The second is a perfectly formed–mini head and shoulders.

In contrast, Figure 13.7 is a 60m chart of the same period. Here there's no porosity. In the first pullback only the high of the candlestick penetrates the resistance curve, while in the second there's a clear engulfing candlestick reversal pattern.

However, it's important to understand what's going on in the switch to higher timeframes when using the average price calculation in S/R curves. It's tempting to assume that the curves themselves are different, but this would be an optical illusion based on the fact that the range of a higher timeframe bar or candlestick is simply going to encompass the range of several smaller bars that had strayed beyond the original curve on the lower timeframe. In Chapter 2 Hawkins emphasizes that he uses the low price in uptrends and the high price in downtrends. His research suggests that in relation to different timeframes there is a small but genuine displacement between the curves, resulting in a porosity that's genuine and not illusory. However, when

FIGURE 13.6   5m chart of EUREX Bund with two instances of porosity.

Source: eSignal and Metastock. www.esignal.com and www.equis.com.

FIGURE 13.7   60m chart of the EUREX Bund September 2010 futures with the porosity removed.

Source: eSignal and Metastock. www.esignal.com and www.equis.com.

using the average price there is no objective difference between curves on different timeframes. Interestingly, a classic reversal pattern on a lower timeframe such as a head and shoulders also produces a larger reversal pattern on a higher timeframe (in the case of Figure 13.7 a classic candlestick engulfing pattern). Finally, it's important to stress again that stepping up to a higher timeframe doesn't solve the related problem of price levitation.

Option #4: Keeping an Eye on the Spread

Another solution is one I've used, since as emphasized I still favor using the average price in MIDAS S/R curves rather than Hawkins' high and the low. According to this solution, a simple spread would be taken of the average price curve and a high or a low price curve and then multiplied by two in order to get a "price reversal window." As a simple illustration, Figure 13.8 is a 5m chart of the DJ Eurostoxx 50 September 2010 futures showing a two-day uptrend. The solid black curve is the average price, the lower grey curve is the low price, and the upper dotted curve is the high price. At point (1) price is porous in relation to the average price curve but is supported by the low price curve. At point (2) price is caught by the average price curve. At point (3) price levitates above the average curve and is supported by the high price curve. In the upper pane there's a spread calculation between the average and low price curves multiplied by two. For much of this time, this price reversal window is six futures

FIGURE 13.8   5m chart of DJ Eurstoxx 50 September 2010 futures with a modest "price reversal window" that would be far larger on daily and weekly charts.

Source: eSignal and Metastock. www.esignal.com and www.equis.com.

points, meaning that 3 futures points either side of the average curve defines the area where price would be expected to reverse. I don't use this indicator intraday but do use it on the daily and weekly charts where the price reversal window can be very large. For example, in a volatile market such as the DAX futures the reversal window can easily be as much as 150 to 200 index points; this is a very significant margin for estimating reversal points.

Option #5: Calibrated Curves

Calibrated Curves were the subject of Hawkins' Chapter 9 and a large part of their rationale is to alleviate the problem of price porosity and suspension. Here again briefly is an intraday illustration. Figure 13.9 is a 5m chart of the September 2010 Australian dollar futures with a two-day downtrend. The first MIDAS resistance curve is launched from the start of the downtrend at point (1); it then displaces quickly from price and the price reversals are levitating below it. The second MIDAS resistance curve is launched at point (2); price is porous in relation to it, as can be seen from the circled pullbacks later. Another standard resistance curve was launched from the swing high at the arrow but it too wasn't very effective. Accordingly, a calibrated curve is launched from an insignificant pivot at point (3) and it naturally calibrates to the first swing high in the rectangle. The next swing high isn't porous because the large candlesticks are actually engulfing candlesticks. Beyond these two pullbacks, the curve also goes on to capture the next two swing highs circled on the following trading day.

FIGURE 13.9   5m chart of Australian dollar September 2010 futures with two standard MIDAS resistance curves and a calibrated curve.

Source: eSignal and Metastock. www.esignal.com and www.equis.com.

FIGURE 13.10 5m chart of British pound September 2010 with the MIDAS Displacement Channel capturing the porosity on the swing lows.

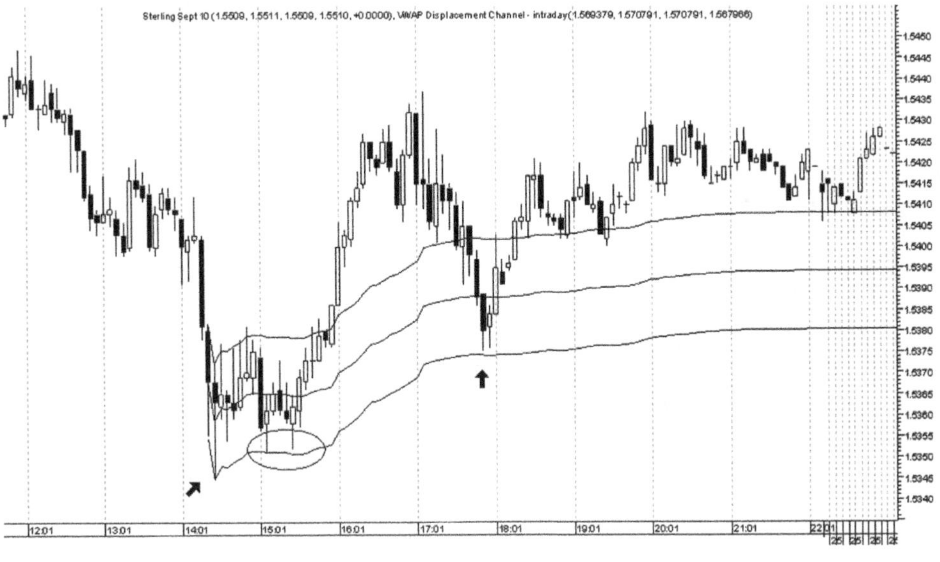

Source: eSignal and Metastock. www.esignal.com and www.equis.com.

Option #6: Using the MIDAS Displacement Channel for Price Porosity and Suspension Problems

The MIDAS Displacement Channel (MDC) is the subject of the next chapter so I'm not going to waste space here introducing it. Its primary use is for sideways markets, while a secondary use is to catch swing highs in uptrends and swing lows in downtrends, thus complementing a standard curve's support role in an uptrend and resistance role in a downtrend. Its tertiary use is to deal with the problem of price porosity and suspension. This topic is dealt with thoroughly towards the end of Chapter 14, so here I'll only provide a brief illustration. Figure 13.10 is a 5m chart of British pound September 2010 futures. The MDC on this chart consists of a standard MIDAS support curve (middle) surrounded by a lower and upper band. The indicator is launched from the first arrow and the ringed area shows immediate porosity in relation to the standard (middle) curve. The lower curve is then fixed to this porous low at a displacement of 0.090 percent so that it catches the next porous swing low at the second arrow. Readers will find the MDC discussed thoroughly in the next chapter.

One of the main benefits of tackling the porosity and suspension problems with the MDC is that it's capable of handling much larger instances of these phenomena due to the fact that the bands are so easily adjusted.

Option #7: Watching Price-Volume Trend Relationships

In Chapter 11, I drew attention to the importance of price-volume relationships in connection with the plotting of MIDAS curves and created four rules that a MIDAS

FIGURE 13.11 5m chart of British Pound September 2010 futures with a standard MIDAS support curve (black) and a no-volume ("nominal") curve (dotted)

Source: eSignal and Metastock. www.esignal.com and www.equis.com.

analyst should be aware of. One of those rules was **Rule #2**, namely that a rising price trend plus decreasing volume pulls standard MIDAS support curves down from the price trend. In Figure 13.11, another 5m chart of the British pound September 2010 futures, we see an instance of this rule as the declining volume is emphasized in the three period (20 minute) moving average. Because of this sharply declining volume trend, the standard MIDAS support curve (black) has displaced well away from the pullbacks in the price uptrend, thus creating a price levitation problem. On the other hand, the "nominal" curve inputted with a nominal one unit of trading volume adequately captures these pullbacks because its algorithm isn't influenced by the declining volume. Here we've illustrated the price-volume relationship with an instance of price levitation; however, price porosity illustrations are just as easy to come by. Readers who haven't read Chapter 11 are advised to do so before working with these price-volume relationships.

Summary

- The phenomenon of price porosity has an opposite tendency I have named "price suspension" or "levitation."
- For the most part these phenomena are not, as Levine supposed, the result of an underlying indeterminacy in price behavior. They occur largely because of the high/low range problem; that is, the difference in range with regard to a price bar as this affects the MIDAS calculation going forward.

- Where low price curves are calculated for uptrends and high price curves for down-trends, the porosity is very much reduced. However, low price curves are then often subject to the price levitation problem in uptrends, and high price curves suffer the same drawback in downtrends.
- Several methods have evolved to deal with the porosity problem and to some extent its levitation counterpart, including:
  - The high/low option
  - The choice of launch point
  - The switch to higher timeframe charts
  - Keeping an eye on the spread
  - The use of calibrated curves
  - The MIDAS Displacement Channel
- When porosity and levitation aren't being directly affected by the range, they're being affected by various price-volume relationships as these relationships were discussed in Chapter 11. The solution here is to be thoroughly aware of how volume impacts price trends and thence to choose carefully between standard MIDAS S/R curves and their nominal counterparts.

CHAPTER 14

A MIDAS Displacement Channel for Congested Markets

Andrew Coles

I briefly introduced the MIDAS Displacement Channel in the final section of Chapter 3 on how to capture the day's high and low using MIDAS.

In this chapter, I introduce this indicator and explain its role first and foremost in congested markets and then in trending markets and other chart contexts.

As we saw in Chapter 1, behind the MIDAS approach there's a thorough philosophy of what drives market prices. To recap, this philosophy can be reduced to five basic tenets that are implicit in Paul Levine's lectures:

1. The underlying order of price behavior is a fractal hierarchy of support and resistance levels.
2. This interplay between support and resistance is a coaction between accumulation and distribution.
3. This coaction, when considered quantitatively from raw price and volume data, reveals a mathematical symmetry between support and resistance.
4. This mathematical symmetry can be used to predict market tops and bottoms in advance.
5. Price and volume data—the volume weighted average price—subsequent to a reversal in trend, and thus to a major change in market (trader) sentiment, is key to this process of chart prediction.

The Problem: Mean Reversion in Sideways Markets

While there's no obvious flaw in the logic that binds these five principles, there's one overriding weakness associated with the final tenet of what follows the end of a trend and a significant change in market sentiment.

This weakness can be seen in the large number of occasions in his lectures when Paul Levine identifies the ends of trends as significant trend reversals. Yet of course this need not be the case; the end of a trend can equally herald a resting phase in market activity. While market resting phases create problems for standard MIDAS S/R curves, it's possible to create a new MIDAS-based indicator to cope with it. This indicator is the subject of the present chapter.

Technicians describe resting phases as sideways moving markets defined by clear support and resistance boundaries. These phases are subdefined in terms of various patterns, the most common being flags, pennants, triangles, and rectangles. According to market observation, markets trend only 25 percent of the time. Consequently the ends of trends—and the attendant change in trader sentiment—only lead to a genuine trend reversal in perhaps one in four chart patterns.

The significance of this for the MIDAS approach can be understood by looking at the following two charts. First, Figure 14.1 is by now a familiar textbook example of what the fifth tenet takes for granted. Here we have a significant trend reversal, with the first MIDAS resistance curve, R1, launched from it. Then, as the trend

FIGURE 14.1   5m chart of Exetra DAX December 2009 futures.

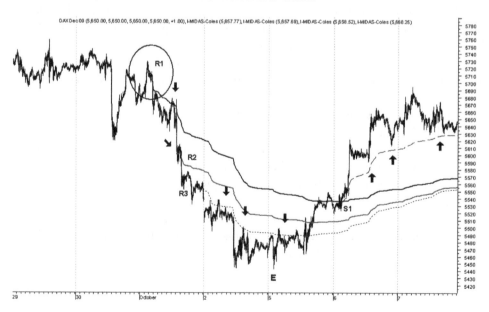

Source: eSignal and Metastock. www.esignal.com and www.equis.com.

develops, the swing highs (the smaller changes in sentiment subsumed in a larger bearish psychology) are captured by MIDAS curves and/or are ideal launch points for further MIDAS resistance curves. The downtrend ends at the point labeled "E" and a new MIDAS support curve, S1, is launched halfway up the new uptrend.

Now contrast Figure 14.1 with Figure 14.2. Here we have an uptrend ending on the close of November 9, 2009 marked by a capital E. Thereafter the market goes into a sideways corrective phase on the 10th until 5:30 P.M., when it starts a rally from within the area highlighted by the rectangle, gaps up the following day, and continues.

Now the end of the uptrend at E doesn't herald a change in trend; instead, it ushers in an untidy pattern that lasts for a significant portion of the trading day. Notice that the standard MIDAS curve (dotted line) launched at 20:51 on the 9th immediately moves into the center of this corrective phase, rendering it ineffective until it stops the rally on the close of the 10th. Its centered position within the broader price range is highlighted by the upper and lower black boundary curves I come to in a moment.

The problem, then, is that to be continuously effective MIDAS curves require the end of a trend to usher in the start of another instead of a corrective phase. When this doesn't occur, MIDAS curves struggle to locate subsequent swing highs and lows in sideways moving markets with anything like the constancy they achieve in genuinely trending markets.

FIGURE 14.2 5m chart of Exetra DAX December 2009 futures.

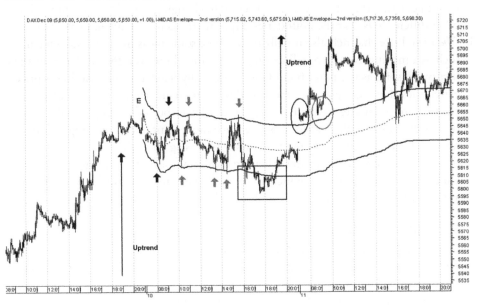

Source: eSignal and Metastock. www.esignal.com and www.equis.com.

The Solution: Applying a Displacement Channel to Sideways Markets

Paul Levine believed that his MIDAS curves worked because the price and volume readings marking the start of a change in trend (and for him in market sentiment) are intimately linked with subsequent changes in price and volume readings. The important question is what additional associations there are between these same price and volume data when they are adjusted in certain critical ways for sideways moving markets.

Several methods have emerged for containing a price series when it is sideways moving—or indeed trending—and it will be helpful to begin with a few definitions before discussing a VWAP-based solution for sideways markets.

1. *Trading bands.* Trading bands surround a price series by being created above and below a measure of central tendency. Typically this would be a moving average or a linear regression line. The bands are constructed by a variety of techniques. Bollinger Bands, for example, use standard deviation, while Jon Andersen's Standard Error Bands use standard error. The resulting bands increase and decrease their proximity to the central tendency continuously based on changing price volatility.

2. *Envelopes.* The main difference between trading bands and envelopes is that envelopes move at a fixed displacement from a measure of central tendency such as a moving average. For example, the Moving Average Envelope, which emerged in the mid-1970s, projects an upper and lower boundary by adding and subtracting a fixed percentage (usually 3 to 4 percent) to a moving average. Unlike trading bands, the boundaries cannot deviate from the central tendency because there is nothing in their calculation that allows them to respond to changing volatility conditions. The other difference is that the boundaries duplicate the central tendency calculation.

3. *Channels.* Price channels also usually incorporate some measure of central tendency such as a moving average or a linear regression line. However, they differ from the first two insofar as the outer boundaries are visually fixed at upper and lower price extremities. For example, the standard deviation channel uses a linear regression channel and then creates the fixed upper and lower boundaries by visually identifying the initial highs and lows of the price movement and projecting two lines forward from these initial highs and lows. There is again nothing in the construction of the boundaries that allows them to change according to changing volatility. Unlike envelope boundaries, which are typically nonlinear, channel boundaries are a form of linear trend line above and below the central tendency.

In locating a method to contain a price series using the MIDAS methodology, significant results can be achieved when using a combination of the channel and envelope methodologies. One simple indicator I've called the MIDAS displacement channel is a hybrid combining elements from price envelopes and price channels.

Theoretically, what the MIDAS displacement channel (MDC) shows is that there are far more proximate associations of support and resistance levels than the fractal nature of the MIDAS system initially reveals.

We can take a first glance at the MDC by reexamining Figure 14.2 and the solid black boundary curves. The upper black boundary has been fitted to the first immediate swing high of the correction marked with the black arrow at a displacement from the standard MIDAS curve of 0.32 percent, while the lower one has been fitted to a swing low that occurs an hour before (lower black arrow) at a displacement of 0.33 percent. Once the boundary curves have been fitted to these initial swing highs and lows on either side of the standard (dotted) MIDAS curve, we can see from the subsequent gray arrows how effectively the MDC contains price in terms of the upper and lower boundaries.

The congestion ends with a porous price move highlighted in the black box. Price then rallies into the close, terminating on the standard MIDAS curve. The following day it gaps above the upper channel while finding support on it. Soon afterwards there's a throwback to this upper channel support before the trend resumes.

MIDAS Displacement Channel Methodology

Let's halt here briefly and expand on the methodology outlined in the previous paragraph. Here in two quick steps is the procedure for applying the MDC.

1. On a standard MIDAS curve moving to the middle of a sideways (congested) price movement, an MDC is launched from a swing high/low marking the start of the movement. The upper boundary is fixed to the first swing high after (or at) the launch point and the lower to the first swing low. This fixing methodology is similar to the TB-F curves insofar as that indicator too is anchored to the trend by fixing it to the first significant pullback.
2. Inspired by the price envelope methodology, this fixing of two upper and lower curves is carried out by a percent displacement from the original MIDAS curve. Percent displacements are user-adjusted until there is a visual fit to the first relevant swing high and low after the launch point of the MIDAS curve.

Trading Implications of the MDC

Any indication that price is reversing against the upper or lower band will imply that it will move back at least as far as to the standard MIDAS curve or else to the opposite band. If price breaks out, this is usually a highly significant occurrence because it indicates a resumption of or change in the trend. As indicated in Figure 14.2, when price does break out the outer boundary will often reverse its support/resistance role. The reader will see these trading features of the MDC illustrates throughout the charts in this chapter.

Additional Forecasting Implications

Figure 14.3, a 5m chart of the Xetra DAX December 2009 futures, contains another two instances of the MDC channel marked by (1) and (2) on the chart. The first

FIGURE 14.3   5m chart of Exetra DAX December 2009 futures.

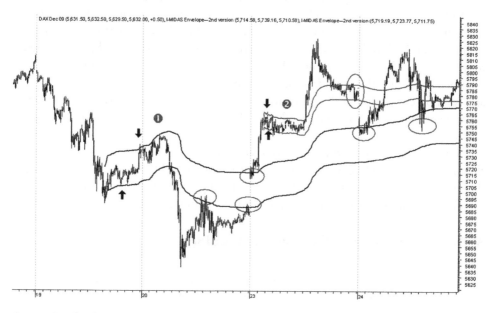

Source: eSignal and Metastock. www.esignal.com and www.equis.com.

larger one is fitted at the black arrows at 0.43 percent and 0.07 percent, and the second smaller one is fitted at the black arrows at 0.08 percent and 0.13 percent (the standard MIDAS curve is blanked out in both instances because it is playing no effective role). However, Figure 14.3 shows in addition that the curves of the DMC can often go on to play significant roles in capturing subsequent swing highs and lows. With regard to the first MDC, the gray ovals highlight this on two occasions during November 20. Moreover, on November 23 the market gaps up on the upper MDC band and finds key support on it twice on November 24, with the second support being porous. Likewise, the second DMC created to capture the smaller congestion on November 23 also captures the closing price level on the same trading day. On the 24th price gaps down onto the upper curve of the first MDC and, as noted, also finds further support there later in the trading day, albeit with one of the bounces being porous.

Additional Benefit: Applying the MDC to Trending Markets to Capture Swing Highs in Uptrends and Swing Lows in Downtrends

A MIDAS critic might make the lesser complaint that just as a standard MIDAS S/R curve fails to identify significant swing highs and lows in sideways markets, it also fails to capture the swing highs in normally trending rising markets and the swing lows in normally trending falling markets. This would be a fair assessment. In contexts where the end of a trend leads to a genuine trend reversal, we have seen in Figure 14.1 that standard MIDAS S/R curves do an exceptional job of capturing the swing lows in uptrends and the swing highs in downtrends. Yet traders would also benefit from a curve which captures *both* sides of an uptrend and a downtrend.

Figure 14.4 is a 5m chart of the German EUREX Bund December 2009 futures. It's a busy chart extending over 14 trading days from November 11 to 30 and of critical importance for anyone day trading the Bund futures. To appreciate the significance of what the MDC captures, we need to break the chart down into segments according to what is accomplished by each MDC.

1. The first MDC (black curves) is launched at the point on the chart labeled (1) on the far left. Because the standard MIDAS curve moved to the center of the range, it is blanked out. The upper curve is fitted at the gray arrow at 0.25 percent while the lower one is fitted to the first swing low at 0.17 percent. Between them they go on to capture all of the subsequent swing highs and lows in the price range, albeit with some price porosity.
2. The second MDC (gray curves) is launched on the 16th when price breaks through the upper band of the first MDC. The second MDC's lower band is redundant (as lower bands obviously often are in uptrends), but the upper band is fitted at the gray arrow at a displacement of 0.34 percent. The standard MIDAS curve of an MDC is retained in an uptrend. Here it quickly conjoins with the upper band of the first

FIGURE 14.4 5m chart of EUREX Bund December 2009 futures, spanning 14 days.

Source: eSignal and Metastock. www.esignal.com and www.equis.com.

MDC and goes on to capture several swing lows of the uptrend until it displaces downwards from price on the 19th. During this time, however, the upper curve of the second MDC continues to resist price very impressively between November 16 and 20.

3. The third MDC (dotted black curves) is launched on November 20 because price began to displace upwards from the second MDC on the previous day. Here again the lower curve is blanked out, and the standard curve and the upper curve remain on the chart. The upper curve is fitted at the gray arrow at a displacement of 0.20 percent. Thereafter it again captures all of the intraday highs for the next three days, while the standard MIDAS curve captures the intraday low of the 25th as price begins an accelerated trend requiring the application of a topfinder.

4. Finally, a fourth MDC (gray curves) is launched from the swing low on the 27th in the upper right of the chart. The upper curve is fitted at the gray arrow at a displacement of 0.23 percent and captures the two swing highs of the 30th.

These results produced from the upper curves of the three MDCs are remarkable and would be of extreme interest to a day trader, since they capture the intraday swing highs every day for 10 straight days, albeit with a small amount of porosity here or there.

Figure 14.5 is an intraday downtrend in the CME euro Globex FX December 2009 futures. The first MDC (black curves) is launched at point (1) and fitted to the swing low at the gray arrow at a displacement of 0.10 percent. This time the upper

FIGURE 14.5   5m chart of CME Euro Globex FX December 2009 futures.

Source: eSignal and Metastock. www.esignal.com and www.equis.com.

curve is blanked out. There is a lot of porosity with the standard curve, but the lower one does a good job of containing the trend. The second MDC is launched at point (2) when price breaks below the lower band of the first MDC. It's then fitted at the gray arrow at a displacement of 0.14 percent. The standard MIDAS curve conjoins with the lower curve of the first MDC for a period of time. The lower curve captures the swing lows effectively. When price does break down, there's a brief throwback before the trend resumes.

Second Benefit: Applying the MDC to the Problem of Price Porosity

As we saw in the previous chapter, "porosity" and "elasticity" are terms Levine used to describe cases where price penetrates a MIDAS S/R curve marginally before responding to it. Rather than illustrate this with another chart, we can go back immediately to Figure 14.5 and look at the porosity of price in relation to a standard MIDAS curve between points (1) and (2).

The problem with this phenomenon is that price can penetrate an S/R curve more deeply, so it is sometimes difficult to conclude whether we have a genuine case of porosity because the percentage seems too great. This can obviously affect trading confidence.

We can avoid the problem of porosity in an uptrend by using the lower (support) band, and we can avoid the problem of porosity in a downtrend by using the upper (resistance) band.

Figure 14.6 is a 5m chart of the CME Globex British pound FX December 2009 futures with a very gradually rising trend over three trading days. The two outer black curves comprise the MDC; the inner dotted line is a standard MIDAS support curve. Price is porous in relation to the standard curve from the very first bar highlighted by the gray arrow on the left. At this first bar the lower support curve of the MDC is fitted at 0.08 percent. Subsequently over the next few days price is porous in relation to the standard curve on another seven occasions highlighted by the black arrows. All of them are captured by the marginally displaced lower curve of the MDC.

Figure 14.7 is another 5m chart of the euro FX December 2009 futures contract, this time demonstrating the use of the MDC to eliminate porosity in a gradually declining downtrend. As can be seen, price is porous in relation to the standard MIDAS resistance curve (dotted black line) from the outset, so the upper curve of the MDC is fitted to the first sign of porosity at the gray arrow at a displacement of 0.10 percent. I have also retained the lower curve on the chart fitted at the lower gray arrow at a displacement of 0.22 percent.

After the upper curve is fitted to the first porous pullback, it then captures all of the remaining swing highs in the downtrend before price hesitates and then breaks out at the gray oval on the far right side. As regards the lower band, it can be seen in the gray boxes that price can produce porous pivot areas even in relation to the MDC curves. This in turn could be eliminated by producing a variation of the MDC

FIGURE 14.6 CME Globex GBP FX December 2009 futures.

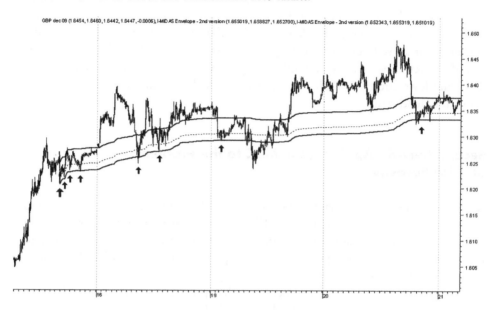

Source: eSignal and Metastock. www.esignal.com and www.equis.com.

FIGURE 14.7 5m chart of CME Globex Euro FX December 2009 futures.

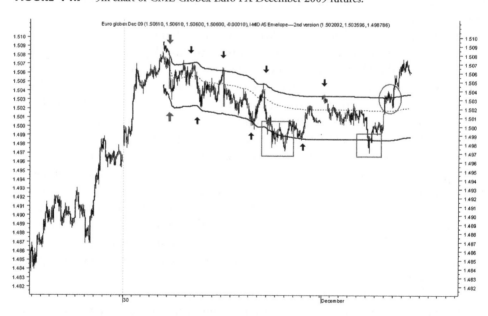

Source: eSignal and Metastock. www.esignal.com and www.equis.com.

with two outer curves instead of one. I am, however, content with the version being outlined in this chapter.

Comparing the MDC with the Moving Average Envelope

It was emphasized earlier that there are significant differences between the MDC and the moving average envelope as well as some similarities. First, like the MA envelope there's an average price calculation in MIDAS.[1] Second, there's also the technique of deploying user-defined percentages to displace a central line above and below itself. However, Figure 14.8 reveals some major differences. The latter is a 1m chart of the Xetra DAX December 2009 contract with a 20-period exponential moving average and envelopes plotted at a conventional setting of 0.20 percent. The chart is broken up into three phases: (1) marks the uptrend, (2) marks the gradual downtrend, and (3) marks the accelerated downtrend. In all three phases the reader will see the problem immediately: a fixed setting of 0.20 percent fails to capture the swing lows in phase (1) while in this same phase the swing highs are continuously porous. In phase (2) the setting fails to capture the swing highs or the swing lows, and in phase (3) the opposite occurs to phase (1): The swing lows are porous and the swing highs are too far away from the upper band.

Figure 14.8 reveals just how crucial it is in band analysis not only to adjust the upper and lower bands separately, but also to adjust them to the near-term price action. The suggestion is to do this as soon as there is a new swing high or low, since the

FIGURE 14.8   1m chart of Xetra DAX June 2009 futures.

Source: eSignal and Metastock. www.esignal.com and www.equis.com.

likelihood is that this will set a precedent for similar price behavior, as we have seen in most of the chart illustrations in this chapter.

Levine was critical of moving averages because they've taken over any interval of time from the past to the present, meaning that they have no direct connection to the underlying psychology of the market. By contrast, the fifth tenet of the MIDAS approach highlighted at the start of this chapter makes clear that the average must be taken over a fixed period of similar psychology; that is, a period subsequent to a reversal in trend. For this reason he would have been critical of any central line (and thus of any boundary instrument derived from it) that did not respect what was for him the crucial change in market psychology. This point is given added substance by the fact that the MIDAS approach not only incorporates an average price but also volume. Volume too plays a critical role in Levine's view that an indicator must capture the ongoing changes in market psychology.

The MDC in Relation to Topfinder/Bottomfinder (TB-F) Curves

At the time of this book's writing I do not have a version of the MDC based on the TB-F algorithm. Its justification of course would not be to capture swing highs and lows in sideways markets because TB-F curves are only used on accelerated phases of uptrends and downtrends. However, with regard to these accelerated phases it would certainly be helpful to have a version of the MDC that captures the swing highs in uptrends and the swing lows in downtrends.

The MDC in Relation to the MIDAS Standard Deviation Bands

The MIDAS Standard Deviation Bands (MSD, for short) are the subject of the next chapter. In the section "Comparing the MSD with the MIDAS Displacement Channel" the pros and cons of using the two indicators are discussed.

Features of the MDC in Relation to Other Boundary Indicators

1. Unlike most other boundary indicators, the MDC requires a launch point reflective of a change in underlying market psychology. Only the Raff Regression Channel incorporates a fixed launch point.
2. Unlike other boundary indicators the MDC incorporates volume.
3. Unlike other boundary indicators its bands are adjusted individually, not in parallel, so that there may be a significant difference, say, between the distance between the central curve and the upper channel and the same curve and the lower one.
4. Unlike some boundary indicators—such as the Donchian Channel, the Raff Regression Channel, and the Standard Deviation Channel—the bands of the MDC are nonlinear.
5. Finally, unlike other band indicators the displacement of both of its bands is under constant review. This adjustability has definite price forecasting implications.

Summary

- The main pretension of the MIDAS approach is that it is an independent all-encompassing system of market forecasting. However, due to the end of a trend not always presaging the start of another (a key assumption in Paul Levine's philosophy), its biggest weakness has always been the inability of MIDAS curves to forecast support and resistance in sideways markets. Here the MDC can replace a standard MIDAS S/R curve to create a new and effective means of identifying subsequent areas of support and resistance in congested markets.
- The MIDAS system's lesser derivative problem is that it cannot forecast rising market tops in uptrends and declining market bottoms in downtrends. The MDC eliminates these problems insofar as the upper curve in an uptrend and the lower one in a downtrend effectively create a reliable trending price channel.
- The MDC eliminates the problem of porosity/elasticity. This phenomenon is often indicative not of a mild penetration by price but of a genuine swing high or low slightly beyond the vicinity of a standard MIDAS S/R curve, which then sets a precedent for further price swings at corresponding levels.
- The MDC is compared with the MIDAS standard deviation bands in the next chapter.
- Finally, because the calculation and methodology of the MDC distinguishes it from other boundary indicators, it offers an exclusive perspective on boundary-based support and resistance approaches to analyzing price activity.

CHAPTER 15

MIDAS and Standard Deviation Bands

Andrew Coles

Volume Weighted Average Price (VWAP) standard deviation bands began their gradual evolution into hybrid MIDAS standard deviation bands in July 2007. Two Trade-Station forum members, dbntina and boxmeister, created the code for two standard deviation bands to be added to original VWAP code supplied by TradeStation in 2003. Later in July 2007 the trading platform Ninja Trader added a third standard deviation band, but more importantly it fundamentally modified the VWAP bands so that they could be anchored to a starting point, thus converting the original VWAP bands into hybrid MIDAS standard deviation bands. Two months later in September 2007 the trading platform Investor/RT also created the MIDAS standard deviation bands, albeit with two bands instead of three. In August 2009 Bob English of The Precision Report also anchored the original VWAP bands to create the first TradeStation version of the hybrid MIDAS bands. Finally, in November 2009 the two-band version of the hybrid MIDAS bands was created in the Ensign Windows charting system.

The term *hybrid* is used in this account of the bands' development because, as discussed in Chapter 1, although anchoring marks a theoretical distinction between standard VWAP and MIDAS curves, the original MIDAS algorithm is a modification of the VWAP formula, and this results in a curve that can often be slightly displaced from a standard VWAP curve.

The bands themselves are created by adding a standard deviation calculation to create the upper bands and subtracting it to create the lower ones. The standard deviation is between the closing price and the VWAP curve (close – VWAP), and the result is computed on a cumulative basis from the start of the indicator's launch. The bands are then dispersed by means of a multiplier. Thus,

- upper band = VWAP formula + standard deviation * multiplier
- lower band = VWAP formula – standard deviation * multiplier

Initially, Equis advised that this indicator couldn't be created in Metastock. However, with a little perseverance I was able to come up with something in the Metastock script. To my knowledge, the result is the first combination of the standard deviation bands with the MIDAS formula in place of the standard VWAP formula. Moreover, it's also the first time a version of the indicator has appeared in Metastock.

The main focus of this chapter will be introducing the indicator on a variety of intraday charts. Towards the end of the chapter it'll also be worthwhile to compare it with the MIDAS Displacement Channel, which was the subject of Chapter 14.

Like the MIDAS Displacement Channel (MDC), the MIDAS standard deviation bands (or MSDBs for short) can be applied in all market conditions, whether trending or congested.

The MIDAS Standard Deviation Bands in Sideways Markets

Let's make a start by taking a first look at the bands in a sideways market. Figure 15.1 is a 5m chart of the DAX September 2010 futures over three trading days. Until the vertical line, the market is drifting sideways while gradually expanding its range; after the line it expands its range to the downside. The heavy black line in the middle of the indicator is the original MIDAS support curve launched from a moderately sized low on August 22. Above and below it are three standard deviation bands. The circled areas highlight where the standard MIDAS support curve supports and then resists

FIGURE 15.1 5m chart of DAX September 2010 futures with the standard deviation bands using the MIDAS formula.

Source: eSignal and Metastock. www.esignal.com and www.equis.com.

price. The arrows highlight areas where the bands above the central MIDAS curve resist price and where the ones below support it.

What readers familiar with band indicators will notice straightaway about the MSDBs is that it they are continuously expanding due to the cumulation function in their calculation. Other band indicators that also deploy a mechanism to capture volatility, such as Bollinger Bands and Standard Error Bands, don't continuously expand in the same way and also contract sharply during periods of reduced volatility. Likewise, other related forms of indicator such as price envelopes and price channels either have fixed (linear) outer boundaries or else have nonlinear boundaries that follow the nonlinear movement of the central tendency upon which they're based without expansion or contraction. Moving average envelopes are a good example of the latter. Readers can consult the previous chapter for a refresher on the basic differences between bands, envelopes, and channels. Thus, the MSDBs really are unique among band/channel/envelope indicators because of their continual expansion.

Another aspect readers may notice in Figure 15.1 is that there's occasionally a little price porosity and suspension when price interacts with the bands. These two phenomena were covered in Chapter 13. As we saw there, the reason for the presence of these two phenomena can be traced to two factors. First, the original MIDAS curve is being plotted here with the average price; it was explained in Chapter 13 that alternatives such as the low price in uptrends and the high price in downtrends can reduce the phenomena in various ways. Second, the standard deviation is based on the standard MIDAS curve being subtracted from the closing price. Instead, we could use the average price or indeed the low price in uptrends and the high price in downtrends. This choice too would have a bearing on the extent to which the MSDBs are affected by porosity and suspension.

The MIDAS Standard Deviation Bands in Uptrends and Downtrends

There's absolutely no reason for the application of the MSDBs being restricted to sideways markets. Figure 15.2 is a 5m chart of the DJ Eurostoxx 50 September 2010 futures again showing three trading days. The market until the vertical line is in an uptrend with the emphasized middle curve again a standard MIDAS support curve between the outer bands. In the uptrend two of the bands resist price while in the downtrend the first lower band, which by now has expanded considerably, supports the downtrend on two key occasions, although in the first instance there is price suspension.

So far, we've taken a pretty broad perspective when using this indicator inasmuch as the market action analyzed has ranged over several trading days. For more active day trading, there's no reason why the indicator can't be applied to lower-timeframe charts such as the 2m or 1m. Figure 15.3 is a downtrend on a 1m chart of the DAX September 2010 futures with the heavy black curve being the original MIDAS resistance curve. The circled areas highlight where the two bands beneath the original MIDAS curve have supported price.

FIGURE 15.2 5m chart of DJ Eurostoxx 50 with three trading days.

Source: eSignal and Metastock. www.esignal.com and www.equis.com.

FIGURE 15.3 1m chart of DAX September 2010 futures illustrating a seven-hour downtrend with the standard deviation bands.

Source: eSignal and Metastock. www.esignal.com and www.equis.com.

FIGURE 15.4 1m chart of the DAX September 2010 futures with a smaller multiplier creating narrower volatility bands.

Source: eSignal and Metastock. www.esignal.com and www.equis.com.

Band Adjustment for Shorter Timeframe Analysis

As Figure 15.3 highlights, the MSDBs can be applied to lower timeframes as well as higher ones. In the examples so far, the bands' multiplier has multiplied them to wider levels of volatility. Narrower multipliers would be required when working with the bands on smaller segments of trends. Figure 15.4 is another 1m chart of the DAX September 2010 futures showing a much smaller segment of a downtrend with the band multipliers reduced.

The MSDBs and Narrowing Volatility

There will be times, regardless of whether the market is moving sideways or trending, when volatility will decrease and the market will get narrower. In such circumstances the bands are effective only in the earlier part of their plot as they expand from the first bar and catch the initial highs and lows; thereafter, as price narrows, the curves will have little further effect. Figure 15.5 is a 2m chart of the DAX September 2010 futures with a large pennant-shaped formation. The bands in the early part of the plot do the job expected; however, after the lower arrow the price range narrows considerably, and the lower bands are ineffective. After the upper arrow the price range also keeps narrowing, and the only other potential interaction with the bands is circled. Volatility bands such as Bollinger Bands or Standard Error bands would not be subject to this limitation.

FIGURE 15.5   2m chart of DAX September 2010 futures with a large pennant-shaped price movement with narrowing volatility.

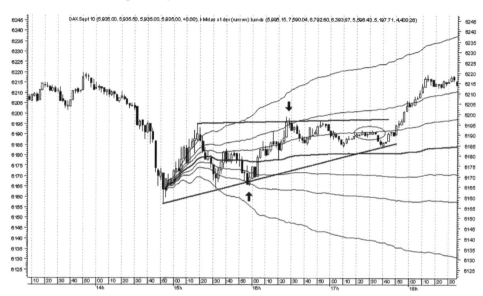

Source: eSignal and Metastock. www.esignal.com and www.equis.com.

Comparing the MSD with the MIDAS Displacement Channel

It's an issue that all admirers of band/channel/envelope indicators sooner or later face, namely how to avoid the charge that setting the multiplier will always be an arbitrary affair. This is an issue that faces Bollinger Bands, certain channel indicators, as well as envelope techniques such as the Moving Average Envelope. Indeed, an illustration of the failings of the latter with this precise point in mind was shown in Figure 14.8 in Chapter 14.

It's at this point that it's worth contrasting briefly the MSDBs with the MIDAS Displacement Channel (MDC), which was the subject of Chapter 14. The obvious difference between these two indicators is that the MDC fixes its outer boundaries meaningfully to the first pivot points on either side of the standard MIDAS curve.[1] In the previous chapter I mentioned that certain channel indicators such as the Standard Deviation Channel also incorporate this methodology.

Let's briefly take the same chart to illustrate both indicators and compare them. First, Figure 15.6 is a 3m chart of the DJ Eurostoxx 50 September 2010 futures over four trading days with the MIDAS Displacement Channel (MDC). The heavy black curve is the standard MIDAS support curve. The first lower band at arrow (3) is fixed at a displacement of 0.28 percent. The next-lower one is redundant because there's no lower swing low to which it can be fixed. The first upper band at the first black arrow is fixed to the swing high at 0.40 percent but it doesn't have much of a role to play apart from supporting price at the first ringed area. However, as soon as price breaks

FIGURE 15.6 3m chart of DJ Eurostoxx 50 September 2010 futures with the MIDAS Displacement Channel, the subject of the previous chapter.

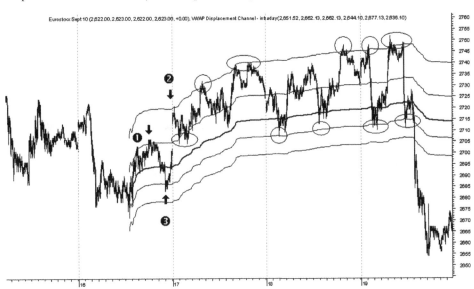

Source: eSignal and Metastock. www.esignal.com and www.equis.com.

through it to form a new swing high, the second curve is fitted to it at a displacement of 0.80 percent. As we can see, it's extremely effective in resisting the upper levels until price finally breaks down through the MDC. I didn't illustrate the MDC in the previous chapter with a second tier of bands because of the difficulty of obviating Metastock's limitation of six user inputs, though there are ways of getting around this in Metastock's code.

In contrast to Figure 15.6, Figure 15.7 is the same 3m DJ Eurostoxx chart with the MDC removed and the MSDBs replacing it. As usual, the thick black curve is the standard MIDAS support curve. Notice that in contrast to the curves of the MDC the MSDB curves fan out very quickly as a result of the cumulative feature applied to standard deviation. The result is that the MSDBs don't capture (at least in this chart) as many price reversal points as the bands of the MDC. I've ringed the areas where the bands successfully interact with price, but as the trend develops the bands move further away from it. The upper arrow highlights where the MSDBs caught the swing high to which the upper band of the MDC was fixed and likewise for the corresponding lower arrow. By definition, these were fixing points and hence not caught by the curves of the MDC.

Alternatives to Standard Deviation

There are alternatives to calculating the MSDBs aside from using standard deviation. Figure 15.8 is a 5m chart of the DAX September 2010 futures with a three-day

FIGURE 15.7   The same 3m chart of the DJ Eurostoxx 50 September 2010 futures illustrating the MIDAS standard deviation band (MSD).

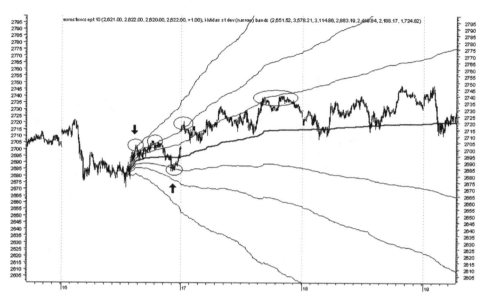

Source: eSignal and Metastock. www.esignal.com and www.equis.com.

FIGURE 15.8   5m chart of DAX September 2010 futures with variance.

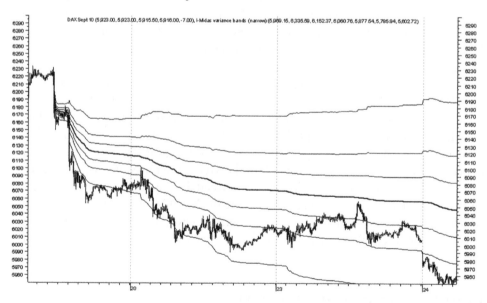

Source: eSignal and Metastock. www.esignal.com and www.equis.com.

downtrend. Here standard deviation is replaced by variance in the basic calculation and the thick black curve is again a standard MIDAS resistance curve.

Figure 15.9 is another 5m chart of the DAX September 2010 futures, this time with standard deviation being replaced by the r-squared calculation. Bands will need adjustment as different formulae are used to calculate the bands.

A third method of producing the standard deviation bands has been proposed by Bob English of The Precision Report, whose other contributions to the MIDAS method will be discussed in more detail in the second half of Chapter 17. The result is a version of the indicator he calls the Accelerated MIDAS (AM) Fan.

English has proposed a small incremental increase for the upper bands and a decrease for the lower ones to the standard MIDAS S/R formula. This is done by a factor F in the numerator of the original MIDAS formula alongside the original multiplication of the price and volume of the current bar.[2] Like other versions of the standard deviation bands and the MIDAS Displacement Channel, the size of F will depend on the chart timeframe and is calibrated to fit a subsequent high or low. An F greater than 1 will produce an accelerated curve to the upside, whereas an F less than 1 will produce a decelerated curve to the downside. Thus, by including a range of F factors for each bar both below and above 1, it's possible to create a form of Gann-style MIDAS-based Fan. Figure 15.10 is a 3,000 volume chart[3] of the euro FX September 2010 futures where each bar consists of 3,000 contracts. The solid line is the original

FIGURE 15.9 5m chart of DAX September 2010 futures with r-squared.

Source: eSignal and Metastock. www.esignal.com and www.equis.com.

FIGURE 15.10 3,000 volume chart of the euro FX September 2010 futures with the accelerated/decelerated MIDAS (ADM) Fan.

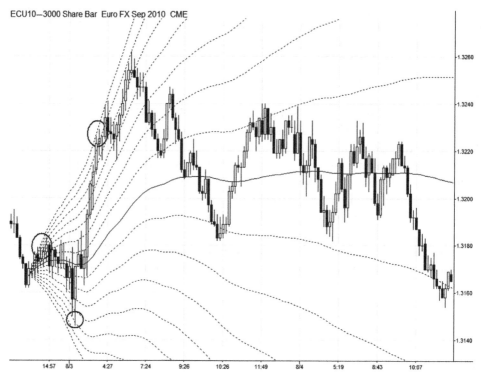

Source: TradeStation. www.tradestation.com.

MIDAS curve, with seven accelerated/decelerated MIDAS (ADM) bands on each side of it. Each band was created using a multiple of 0.00005 and, importantly, this factor was selected because it calibrates price at the three areas circled.

Turning to Figure 15.10, after an initial thrust upwards between the second and third areas circled, price began to retrace, but the price high of the initial thrust was the second most outer ADM band. The first leg of the downside correction was supported on the band above the original MIDAS curve, followed by the MIDAS curve itself, and then the first band below it. Subsequently price rallied back up to the first ADM band above the original curve. Thereafter, price meandered around the original MIDAS curve before falling back to the ADM band below the curve that had held price previously and by now had displaced further from the original curve.

Trading with the MIDAS Standard Deviation Bands

As noted in Chapter14 when discussing the MDC, the same support and resistance strategies with Japanese candlesticks can be deployed.

Setting Price Targets

With the MDC, the expectation when price reaches one of the bands is for it to move back at least as far as to the central MIDAS curve or else to move all the way through the indicator to one of the bands on the other side of the MIDAS curve. Alternatively price will break out and new price targets external to the bands can be established. However, reversal price targets within the bands back to the central MIDAS curve or to bands on its other side cannot be so easily guaranteed with the MSDBs due to the fact that the latter's bands are continually fanning out. Therefore a more proximate and realistic price target would be the next-nearest band to the one that price is reversing on. If price breaks through that band instead of reversing on it and there's a band beneath or above it, this band must be considered to be the next price target, albeit if this next band is already far from price then other price targets must be utilized.

Working with Several MSDBs Simultaneously

As with MIDAS curves generally, there's no reason why multiple MSDB indicators can't be used at the same time. Figure 15.11 is a 2m chart of the DJ Eurostoxx September 2010 futures with two MSDB indicators plotted simultaneously. It's not easy to work with more than one MSDB indicator in black and white charts because there are so many curves; on colored charts the task is a lot easier. The first MSDB indicator is launched from point (1) in the bottom left of the chart, and it does an

FIGURE 15.11 2m chart of the DJ Eurostoxx September 2010 futures over a full trading day with two MDCs launched from points (1) and (2).

Source: eSignal and Metastock. www.esignal.com and www.equis.com.

exceptional job of capturing the swing highs and lows as the uptrend develops, with the most impressive support and resistance appearing at the two arrows when the market moves dramatically to the upside and then swings wildly to the downside. Despite the volatility, the first MSDB captures the ends of the swings extremely well.

The second MSDBs indicator is launched from point (2) and is plotted with heavy black curves to try and differentiate it from the first one. One of its curves highlighted in the gray sloping rectangle does another exceptional job of capturing the swing highs in the uptrend before price tails off on the following trading day.

Summary

- Over the past few years VWAP standard deviation bands have evolved into hybrid MIDAS standard deviation bands. In this chapter the VWAP formula is replaced by the MIDAS formula to ensure that these bands are genuine MIDAS standard deviation bands.
- Despite the uncertainty, it's possible to program this indicator in the Metastock scripting language and this chapter has seen the first instance of the indicator in Metastock.
- The indicator can be applied to all market conditions—sideways as well as to uptrends and downtrends.
- When applying the indicator to smaller segments of trends, or in lower intraday timeframes, the multipliers must be reduced so that the bands become narrower. If they aren't, they'll be measuring larger segments of the trend that might be inappropriate for an active day trader.
- Care must be taken when markets are narrowing because in such circumstances the MSDBs will only capture the earlier pivots. The longer the market narrows, the less effective the MSDBs will be as its bands continually fan out.
- The MSD can be usefully compared with the MIDAS Displacement Channel when the pros and cons of each indicator are more easily identifiable.
- The MSDBs can be created with other methods of measuring volatility, including variance, r-squared, and standard error. It can also be created using alternative dispersion techniques such as the fanning technique in Bob English's version.
- Price targets are less easy to establish in the MSDBs than in the MIDAS Displacement Channel because the fanning out of the curves in the MSDBs means that price is less likely to travel all the way back to a proximate curve and certainly less likely to travel back across the central MIDAS curve to one of the bands on the other side. There are exceptions and Figure 15.10 is a good example with respect to the first MSDB indicator launched from point (1). Indeed, the two arrows highlight how easily extreme intraday volatility is captured by the MSDBs.
- It's possible to work with multiple MSDB indicators on any timeframe in colored charts.

CHAPTER 16

Nominal–On Balance Volume Curves (N-OBVs) and Volume–On Balance Curves (V-OBVs)

Andrew Coles

It has been emphasized in various chapters in this book how important On Balance Volume (OBV) was to Paul Levine's conception of the MIDAS method. In this chapter I want to introduce a new type of curve based on the On Balance Volume indicator called a Nominal–On Balance Curve (N-OBV) and its variant, the Volume–On Balance Curve (V-OBV).

This curve creates an entirely new perspective on the familiar role of standard MIDAS S/R curves as providing forecasting and market timing information based on the familiar notion, introduced in Chapter 1, of a price series being a fractal hierarchy of support and resistance levels. This new perspective is possible because an OBV plot can be looked upon as having the same fractal trend characteristics as a price series while simultaneously diverging from it in virtue of the role that the OBV indicator plays in relation to price. We'll summarize that role immediately in a brief introduction to OBV before illustrating the curve on various cash and futures markets.

On Balance Volume for the Uninitiated

On Balance Volume was first introduced in the early 1960s by Joe Granville and was one of the first indicators to measure positive and negative volume flow.[1] The basic idea behind the indicator is that volume precedes price and this notion emerges in the

371

use of the indicator in three important ways that are briefly illustrated in the following list. The construction of the indicator is straightforward:

1. If the close of the current bar is greater than the close of the previous bar, the current bar's volume is added to the previous bar's OBV value.
2. If the close of the current bar is less than the close of the previous bar, the current bar's volume is subtracted from the previous bar's OBV value.
3. If there's no change between the close of the current bar and the previous one then the OBV line is unchanged.

The OBV line is formed from the cumulative total of the volume additions and subtractions. The Accumulation/Distribution Line, which is also sometimes known as the Intraday Intensity Index,[2] and Williams's Accumulation/Distribution are variations of the basic philosophy behind OBV, and the MIDAS indicator I'm proposing could also be plotted with these two indicators.

Based on the idea that volume (or money flow) precedes price, the OBV indicator has traditionally been used for two types of signal, though a third robust signal has also now become associated with it.

The first type of signal is confirmatory. For example, if price is in an uptrend and this uptrend is also duplicated by the trend in the OBV, it means that volume is heavier on the rising bars and hence OBV is confirming price. In downtrends, this situation would be reversed.

The second type of signal is a disconfirmation. For example, if price is in an uptrend but the volume is lighter on the rising bars, the OBV line will decline in relation to the upside price trend and will thus produce a classic negative divergence pattern. Again this situation would be reversed in a downtrend to produce a positive divergence. As this explanation indicates, the numerical value of OBV isn't important; what's important is the direction of the line in relation to the price trend.[3]

A third use to which the OBV line is put is in relation to price breakouts from areas of consolidation. Very often the OBV line will break out of its corresponding area of consolidation a considerable time before a price breakout; thus, OBV will forewarn of an impending directional move out of the price congestion.

Briefly, we can illustrate all three of these uses of the OBV in Figure 16.1, a 15m chart of the Australian dollar September 2010 futures over 12 trading days. At point (1) we see the downtrend in the OBV line confirming the price downtrend. In fact, whereas the price trend produces two false breakouts from its trend line, the OBV plot does not, thus highlighting its disconfirmatory role. At point (2) we see the OBV line break down through its support several hours before price breaks its own support line, as emphasized by the vertical line. After breaking down, price also misleadingly throws itself back across the support (now resistance) line, potentially creating a false signal; in contrast, the OBV line stays well below the breakdown point in the area circled. Finally, at point (3) the OBV line diverges positively while price goes on to make a new low, thus disconfirming the price move.

FIGURE 16.1 15m chart of Australian dollar futures over 12 trading days with an OBV line in the upper pane. Its three signals are highlighted at points (1), (2) and (3).

Source: eSignal and Metastock. www.esignal.com and www.equis.com.

When Paul Levine used OBV, he used its confirmatory and disconfirmatory signals in relation to standard MIDAS S/R curves. Quite simply, if the OBV line was confirming a price trend, Levine assumed that a given S/R curve would hold price and a bounce to a new high or low was likely; if the OBV line was disconfirming price, a given S/R curve would be unlikely to hold price and a trend reversal would be assumed with a price target being the next proximate S/R curve. In Figure 16.2, our last chart of this introductory discussion of the OBV, we see an illustration of this in relation to a standard MIDAS support curve. Figure 16.2 is a 15m chart of the German Bund September 2010 futures over 12 trading days with a large negative divergence in the OBV in the upper pane. Price breaks the MIDAS support curve briefly in the first pullback circled before breaking it permanently in the second area circled.

Nominal–On Balance Volume Curves

As indicated in the introduction to this chapter, the impressive feature of the OBV line and its variants, such as Accumulation/Distribution (Intraday Intensity Index) and Larry Williams' version, is that they manage to create the three types of signals highlighted in the previous section while being an independent time series with a fully trending fractal structure. It's this aspect of the OBV line that makes it so conducive

FIGURE 16.2   15m chart of the EUREX Bund September 2010 futures over 12 trading days.

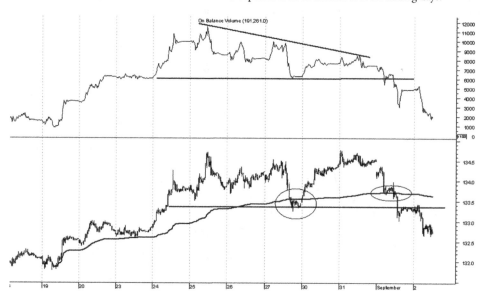

Source: eSignal and Metastock. www.esignal.com and www.equis.com.

to the application of MIDAS curves in relation to the various types of confirmatory and disconfirmatory associations it has with price.

Aside from the fact that a nominal OBV curve (or N-OBV, for short) is plotted on an OBV time series and not on a price series, it also differs in terms of its algorithm. For instead of an actual volume feed from the market, it takes a nominal "1" unit of cumulative volume (discussed in Chapters 6, 10, and 11). It also differs in virtue of the fact that the average price (or the low or the high price) is replaced in the algorithm by the OBV calculation (or indeed the calculation in the A/D formula or Williams's version).

Let's take a first look at this indicator in Figure 16.3, a weekly chart of the S&P 500 continuous futures from 1992 to the present. If we look first at the price plot we see the familiar tech bubble high of 2000, the decline between 2000 and 2003, the credit boom of 2008, the subprime crash of 2009, and the market's upside trajectory since.

In the lower pane, a standard MIDAS support curve (solid) is launched from the 1994 low alongside a nominal curve (dotted) launched from the same date. Because the volume trend was rising so sharply in the lead-up to the 2000 high, the standard curve is pulled up towards price due to **Rule #1** outlined in Chapter 11. Another standard support curve (long dashes) is launched from the 2003 bottom. As we can see, none of these three curves comes anywhere near either the 2003 bottom or the 2008 bottom. Contrast the action in the lower pane with the top pane. The plot here is the OBV line with the N-OBV (solid) launched from the same 1994 low and

FIGURE 16.3 Weekly chart of S&P 500 continuous futures from 1992 to the present with nominal and standard MIDAS support curves in the lower pane and an N-OBV curve plotted on OBV in the upper pane.

Source: eSignal and Metastock. www.esignal.com and www.equis.com.

fully capturing the 2003 low. What's more, a second curve (dashed) launched from the 2003 low captures the first 2004 pullback as well as the all-important 2008 crash bottom (albeit with a little price suspension). This will be an important curve to watch on any significant future downside movement.

Figure 16.4 is a 15m chart of British pound September 2010 futures showing two months of price activity. This is an excellent chart to illustrate the power of the N-OBV curve. In the lower pane, the swing highs marked (1), (2), and (3) remain far above the three standard MIDAS resistance curves; moreover, the peak at (2) even breaks a conventional down trend line, highlighting an overall price pattern that is far out of reach of the standard curves. However, in the top pane the OBV line does not confirm the second price peak while creating a smooth downward trend of lower highs. The first two peaks are caught by the main N-OBV curve launched from the far left, while the third is resisted by a second N-OBV curve launched from the second peak. On the right of the upper pane, there's also a positive divergence in progress, with the OBV line now hitting the first N-OBV curve. If there's a breakout to the upside, it'll be confirmed first by the OBV breaking its N-OBV curve and not by price breaking through its standard resistance curves in the lower pane.

Figure 16.5 is a daily chart of continuous oats futures from 1992 to the present. The rectangle in the lower price pane highlights a price pattern, Paul Levine called

FIGURE 16.4 15m chart of September 2010 British pound futures over two months.

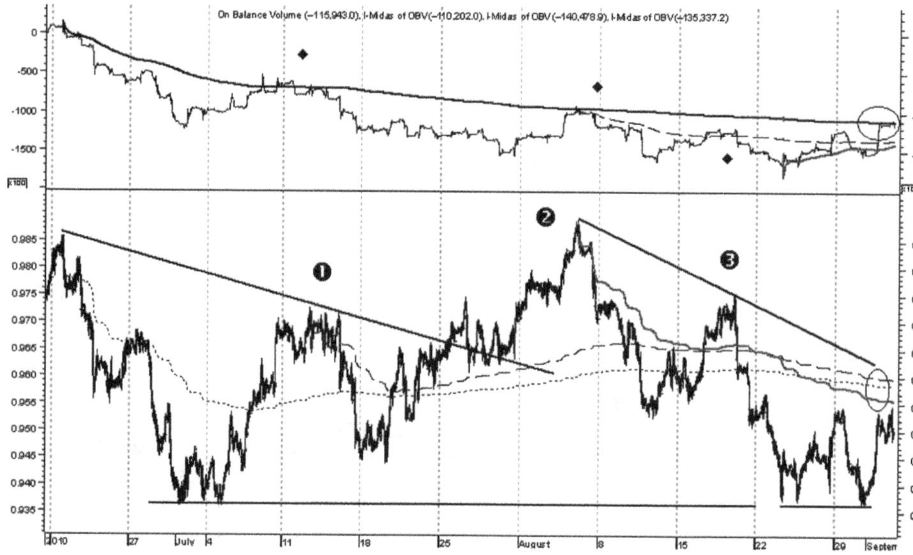

Source: eSignal and Metastock. www.esignal.com and www.equis.com.

FIGURE 16.5 Daily chart of continuous oats futures.

Source: eSignal and Metastock. www.esignal.com and www.equis.com.

it a "foothills" pattern—prior to a much steeper acceleration in price, since it resembles a series of rolling hills on the western approach to the Sierra Mountains in California with which Levine was familiar. Foothills are extremely common in the commodities markets because of their cyclical nature. Often one sees these patterns prior to price suddenly taking off in the main upside segment of the cycle before declining just as sharply. The problem is that foothills aren't always easy to chart with MIDAS support curves because their pullbacks tend to be deep; as a result, MIDAS support curves (usually S1 or S2) often move through the middle of them, thus preventing early opportunities to join the trend. In Figure 16.5 we see just this problem in the lower pane as first S1 and then S2 drift aimlessly through the foothills. By contrast, OBV's trending confirmation of what will become a parabolic uptrend means that the same curve, S1, in its guise as an N-OBV curve creates an unambiguous opportunity to join the trend early.

In sum, then, N-OBV curves work so well because while OBV lines trend fractally they also confirm and disconfirm price activity and also provide early warning signals in contexts such as breakouts and breakdowns from congested areas. In all three of these cases, N-OBV curves can be appended to swing highs and lows that are positioned very differently on price charts and hence can create buy and sell patterns and indications of price direction when the associated patterns on a price chart are very different.

The Dipper Setup

Although there are several confirmation and disconfirmation patterns that are identifiable, one disconfirmation pattern I particularly like occurs at market tops and bottoms when the OBV produces a negative and positive divergence respectively. This allows an N-OBV (or V-OBV) curve to be launched from the highest or deepest swing low of the OBV in order to catch the actual price high and low. Here's an illustration of this pattern I call the dipper. Figure 16.6 is a 15m chart of euro September 2010 futures showing a seven-day price uptrend in the lower pane with the highest price high at point (1). In the top pane, the high at point (1) is actually a lower high on the OBV and thus amendable to an N-OBV launched from the OBV's highest high as highlighted in the circle. In the rectangle we also see other highs of the uptrend caught by the N-OBV as the negative divergence in the OBV proceeds.

Volume–On Balance Volume Curves

I'm going to say very little about Volume–On Balance Curves (V-OBVs) because they share the same principles with N-OBVs. The difference is that while N-OBVs take a nominal "1" as input to the volume component of the algorithm, V-OBVs take the actual volume feed.

FIGURE 16.6   15m chart of euro September 2010 futures with a seven-day uptrend.

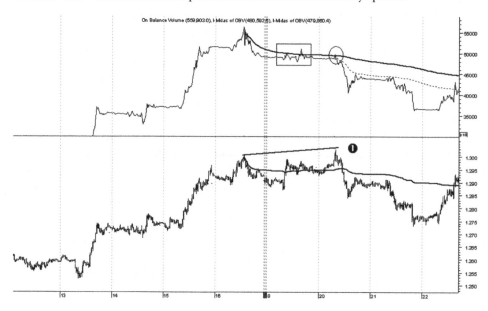

Source: eSignal and Metastock. www.esignal.com and www.equis.com.

Let's illustrate a V-OBV curve alongside an N-OBV. Figure 16.7 is a daily cash chart of the Sydney All Ordinaries index from 2003 until the present. We see immediately in the lower price pane a standard MIDAS support curve (solid) launched from the 2003 low and being pulled up by the volume trend (not shown). Below it (dotted curve) we see a nominal support curve. In the top pane plotting with OBV, we see an N-OBV as the long dashed curve. Notice that there's a fair amount of price suspension in relation to it and the 2008–2009 crash. By contrast, the V-OBV catches the bottom perfectly because volume is pulling the curve up towards price. (Again, consult Chapter 11 for an in-depth examination of the relationship between price and volume in the plotting of MIDAS curves.)

Further Chart Illustrations

I complete this chapter with a few more charts (Figures 16.8–16.11) without chart commentary save for the brief descriptions that follow. In each case, standard MIDAS S/R curves will be plotted on the lower price pane with their shortcomings evident. The latter should be contrasted with the successful combination of the OBV line and the N-OBV and V-OBV curves in the upper pane.

FIGURE 16.7   Daily cash chart from 2003 to the present of the Sydney All Ordinaries illustrating a V-OBV curve (solid) in the top pane and an N-OBV curve (long dashes).

Source: Metastock. www.equis.com.

FIGURE 16.8   Henry Hub Natural Gas continuous futures with several foothills plus an advanced breakdown of support on the far right of the chart. The OBV curves are N-OBVs.

Source: eSignal and Metastock. www.esignal.com and www.equis.com.

FIGURE 16.9   NYMEX continuous copper futures with foothills and a major low resembling the positioning of the curves in the S&P 500 continuous futures. The OBV curves are N-OBVs.

Source: eSignal and Metastock. www.esignal.com and www.equis.com.

FIGURE 16.10   South African rand continuous futures with price resistance at 0.140 being explained by R2 and R3 N-OBV curves. In the coming months it'll be interesting to see whether the combination of OBV's disconfirmation and the N-OBV resistance curves suppress the rand for a further significant downside move.

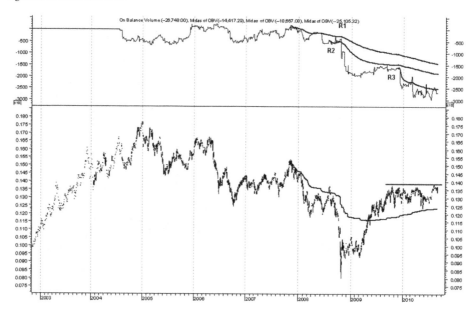

Source: eSignal and Metastock. www.esignal.com and www.equis.com.

FIGURE 16.11 Daily cash chart of China's SSE Composite with a V-OBV in the upper pane, albeit with some price suspension.

Source: eSignal and Metastock. www.esignal.com and www.equis.com.

Summary

- Granville's OBV and its variants such as Chaikin's Accumulation/Distribution and Williams' Accumulation/Distribution are independent time series that resemble a price series in so far as they possess fractal trend characteristics.
- The main signals of the OBV are confirmations and disconfirmations of price trends as well as early warning indications of price breakouts. These signals establish the independence of OBV and its variants from price. This independence, combined with OBV's fractal trend characteristics, means that it's an excellent subject for MIDAS curves when attempting to obtain a deeper underlying insight into price direction that's often absent on price charts.
- A standard MIDAS S/R curve can be plotted on an OBV line using the OBV calculation and either using an actual cumulative volume feed from the market or a nominal "1" unit of trading volume cumulatively applied.
- The result is the positioning of MIDAS S/R curves that can't be duplicated on a price plot and hence a positioning that very frequently reveals deeper underlying areas of support and resistance that are impossible to locate when applying standard MIDAS S/R curves on a price chart.

Summary

CHAPTER 17

Extensions, Insights, and New Departures in MIDAS Studies

Andrew Coles

It goes unnoticed to most people who read Paul Levine's lectures that Levine himself had begun exploring ways in which new techniques could be created from the MIDAS method. It has already been mentioned several times in this book that he was happy to combine MIDAS with other technical tools, such as conventional trend lines, the MACD, Bollinger Bands, and On Balance Volume.[1] However, he had also begun exploring the possibility of developing new MIDAS indicators. For example, in Lecture 9 he imagined MIDAS as part of a sophisticated neural network running over a daily database of stocks. As part of this network, he envisaged three additional indicators:

1. An "OBVR" ratio calculated by dividing On Balance Volume by its maximum reading
2. A "DIST" (= "distension") ratio as a normalized measure of how close price is to a given MIDAS curve
3. A "SPRD" (= "spread") or volatility measurement as a means of ensuring that the stock in question is volatile enough for a sufficient reward

I'll begin this chapter by looking briefly at Levine's DIST indicator, for although when charted in real time it appears flawed, it inspires the creation of two additional volume-based oscillators that do provide useful perspectives when charting MIDAS S/R curves and that probably produce more consistent measures than the original underlying indicator upon which they're based.

After this discussion, the second half of the chapter will focus on a number of recent contributions to the MIDAS method by Bob English, an active day trader in the United States who writes a daily market timing newsletter called The Precision

Report (www.precisioncapmgt.com) as well as economic and trading commentary for various publications. English was introduced to the MIDAS method by members of a private trading group in 2009 and since then has become an active student of the MIDAS approach, using it daily in his analysis, market commentary, and trading.

MIDAS Curves and Volume-Based Oscillators

Levine's formula for DIST is (P-S1)/(PMax-PMin), where P is the closing price, S1 is a MIDAS curve, and PMax and PMin are the highest and lowest prices of the period. DIST was intended as a normalized overbought/oversold oscillator measuring how close the latest price is to S1 (or R1), which usually for Levine is the most significant curve on the chart. Levine was vague about the oscillator's function, but presumably an oversold reading would coincide with the end of a price pullback to S1, while an overbought condition would signify the risk of the start of a pullback to the curve (readings would be reversed for R1).

Unfortunately, when the raw formula is programmed into Metastock the result isn't normalized (centered). However, by altering it slightly we do end up with the oscillator in Figure 17.1. Figure 17.1 is a 15m chart of the euro FX September 2010 futures with a MIDAS resistance curve acting in a primary role over two days. In the pane above there's a normalized (bounded) oscillator of the type Levine had in mind.

First, readers will notice that the indicator produces one good divergence signal and that in the circled areas it goes overbought at a time when price reapproaches the

FIGURE 17.1   15m chart of euro FX September 2010 futures.

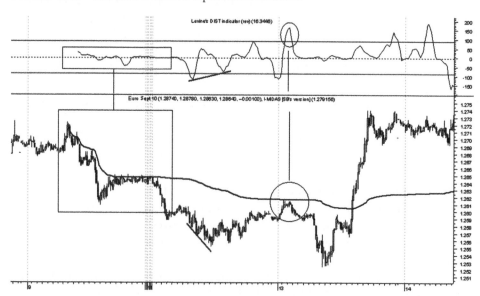

Source: eSignal and Metastock. www.esignal.com and www.equis.com.

resistance curve. However, the bulk of the interaction between price and the resistance curve in the rectangle before the curve displaces is missed by the oscillator, since it never reaches overbought levels associated with the price pullbacks to the curve. However there's a deeper problem, especially for short-term traders such as day traders. One aspect of the problem is that there's always a continuous displacement of price from primary MIDAS curves, leading to a quick redundancy for the indicator. Second, on any given chart there'll be a multitude of S/R curves running simultaneously, leading to a hypothetical plethora of such oscillators all anchored to various curves. This isn't feasible. It would be far better if we could develop a volume-based oscillator that's universally applicable to any S/R curve being plotted.

Because Levine regarded the role of OBV as critical alongside MIDAS, a useful starting point would be an adaptation of the basic OBV indicator. The philosophy behind OBV is that OBV changes precede price changes, thus confirming or disconfirming price moves.[2] Disconfirmation, in the form of divergences, means that a trend change is likely. The OBV indicator is also often used in the context of breakouts, since OBV breakouts usually precede price breakouts. I discussed the OBV in the previous chapter, but here again for the uninitiated is an example of these two signal types in Figure 17.2, a 5m chart of the September 2010 Canadian dollar futures. First, a two-day correction breaks down on the OBV at least half a day before the trend line is broken by price in the area circled and highlighted by the vertical line. Second, the end of the downtrend is signaled again by at least a half a day by OBV not proceeding to new lows while price creates several new lower lows before eventually turning up.

FIGURE 17.2   5m chart of Canadian dollar futures with OBV in the upper pane.

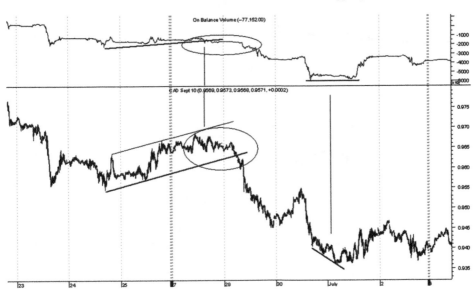

Source: eSignal and Metastock. www.esignal.com and www.equis.com.

Paul Levine liked to use the OBV indicator as a means of measuring the strength of the trend. This in turn would provide background information on the likelihood of a MIDAS S/R curve holding price. The problem is that OBV is hit-or-miss: sometimes it will produce excellent timely warnings while at other times it will provide no advance information. Figure 17.3 is another 5m chart of the Canadian dollar futures. Here we have a MIDAS support curve being respected by a rising price trend. However, the price trend ends at the high circled while the OBV continues making new highs. The signal is misleading because it implies that the MIDAS support curve will continue supporting price, whereas the new downtrend is accentuated by our being able to launch a MIDAS resistance curve.

We can take inspiration from Levine's ideas on volume-based oscillators by creating a bounded (normalized) oscillator of On Balance Volume in virtue of running it through the stochastic formula. The result is an impressive indicator that avoids the two objections to Levine's bounded oscillator raised earlier. First, the "Stoch-OBV" produces very consistent overbought and oversold levels, unlike Levine's oscillator, which struggled to establish such levels in Figure 17.1. Second, the Stoch-OBV is applicable to all MIDAS S/R curves simultaneously. Recall that the problem with tagging an oscillator to a MIDAS S/R curve is that the curve soon displaces, making the oscillator redundant. Moreover, with a multitude of curves on a chart a plethora of oscillators would be required, making the enterprise needlessly complex if not redundant. A better option would be to create a catch-all oscillator that applies to all curves. The Stoch-OBV accomplishes this.

FIGURE 17.3   The same 5m chart of the Canadian dollar futures with OBV in the upper pane.

Source: eSignal and Metastock. www.esignal.com and www.equis.com.

Figure 17.4 is a 5m chart of the September 2010 DAX futures showing a downtrend and an uptrend over two trading days separated by a V-shaped bottom. Two MIDAS resistance curves resist the downtrend, and three support curves support the uptrend. The upper pane houses the Stoch-OBV. The reader can follow the normalized overbought and oversold areas corresponding to pullbacks to the resistance and support curves respectively, while very small divergences in the indicator also forewarn of the ends of the trend. The oscillator can apply to multiple curves simultaneously and its overbought and oversold levels are timely and unambiguous. I actually prefer this indicator to the familiar price-based stochastic.

For more noteworthy divergences, whose function would be to forewarn of whether a curve will hold, we can create a MACD of the OBV indicator, the "MACD-OBV." Figure 17.5 is a 5m chart of the British pound September 2010 futures with a MACD-OBV in the upper pane. The price plot has two support curves, S1 and S2, and the actual OBV indicator in gray (highlighted by the arrow). Notice that in the first box OBV makes a higher high alongside price, while the MACD-OBV warns of the trend's end by diverging. As a result, neither S2 nor S1 holds price. In the second box OBV makes a new low alongside price; thus, only the MACD-OBV again warns of the trend's end.

The final chart of this section is Figure 17.6, a 5m chart of the Eurex Bund September 2010 futures with the MACD-OBV in the middle pane and Stoch-OBV at the top. While the Stoch-OBV continues its normalized overbought/oversold readings in relation to price bounces off the curves and pullbacks to them, the MACD-OBV does an excellent job of producing the divergences. As we can see, in every case where

FIGURE 17.4   5m chart of the September 2010 DAX futures with the Stoch-OBV in the upper pane.

Source: eSignal and Metastock. www.esignal.com and www.equis.com.

FIGURE 17.5 5m chart of British pound September 2010 futures with MACD-OBV in the upper pane.

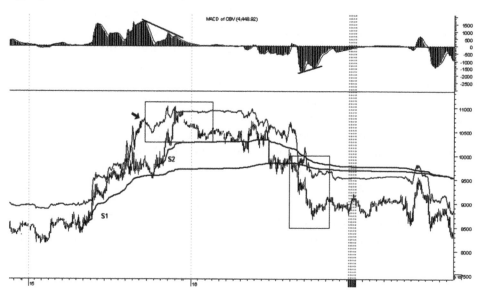

Source: eSignal and Metastock. www.esignal.com and www.equis.com.

FIGURE 17.6 5m chart of Eurex Bund September 2010 futures with the Stoch-OBV in the upper pane and the MACD-OBV in the middle. The OBV indicator is plotted as the gray curve alongside price in the lower pane.

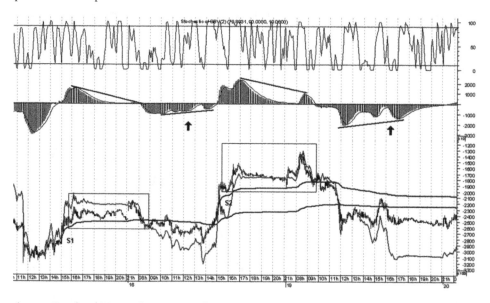

Source: eSignal and Metastock. www.esignal.com and www.equis.com.

the OBV, plotted on the chart as the gray line, misleadingly confirms new price highs and lows, the MACD-OBV diverges. In the first box price breaks down through S1, but this was predicted by the large negative divergence in the MACD-OBV. In the second box price breaks S2, but this too was predicted by the MACD-OBV. The two black arrows highlight two further divergences that aren't replicated in the actual OBV indicator.

In sum, then, Paul Levine was correct to suggest that a bounded oscillator would be useful for stable and consistent overbought and oversold readings and that some additional indicator would be useful for divergences, but his initial proposals fell a little short of what we were looking for. We can take inspiration from his initial suggestions by evolving Granville's OBV into a useful bounded and centered oscillator respectively, which I've referred to as the Stoch-OBV and MACD-OBV.

Correlation Analysis as an Effective Overbought/Oversold Oscillator

There's room in this chapter for a short section on another indicator I've found to be useful as a replacement for Levine's DIST oscillator. Like the Stoch-OBV oscillator it too has the advantage of working extremely well even when a primary curve has displaced from price. However, unlike the Stoch-OBV this indicator *is* tagged to a particular MIDAS curve as Levine intended with the DIST oscillator. Figure 17.7 is a 5m chart of the DAX September 2010 futures showing a five-day downtrend. A

FIGURE 17.7 5m chart of DAX September 2010 futures with a correlation analysis (upper pane) between the primary resistance curve launched at (1) and the closing price.

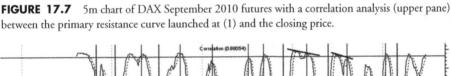
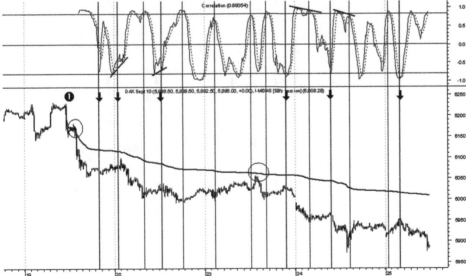

Source: eSignal and Metastock. www.esignal.com and www.equis.com.

primary MIDAS resistance curve is launched from the start of the trend highlighted by (1). As expected, it quickly displaces from price and only interacts with it on two further occasions highlighted by the circles. In the top pane there's a 25-period correlation analysis between the primary curve and the closing price plotted with an 8-period moving average (dotted line) and bound between the +0.8 percent and –0.2 percent positive and negative correlation levels respectively.

Despite the fact that the primary resistance curve displaces from price immediately, the correlation analysis consistently produces good signals. Indeed, what I've found with this indicator is that a positive correlation between the closing price and a MIDAS curve of +0.8 percent and above marks out oversold levels and that a negative correlation between the close and a MIDAS curve of –0.2 percent consistently identifies overbought levels. The latter levels on this chart are highlighted by the gray vertical lines with the black arrows, while the oversold levels are marked by the black vertical lines. The indicator will also often produce small positive and negative divergences at market extremes, as also highlighted on the chart.

Traders wishing to try this indicator should note that the conditions in an uptrend are reversed. Figure 17.8 is a 5m chart of the Swiss Market Index September 2010 futures with a three-day uptrend. The primary support curve is launched from (1) and displaces quickly from the price, only interacting with it again at the two circled pivots. The same robust overbought and oversold levels are identified, this time, however, with oversold levels corresponding to negative correlations of –0.2 percent and overbought levels with +0.8 percent and above. The latter are highlighted by the gray vertical

FIGURE 17.8   5m chart of Swiss Market Index September 2010 futures with a three-day uptrend.

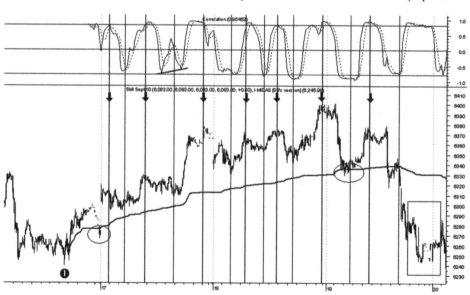

Source: eSignal and Metastock. www.esignal.com and www.equis.com.

lines with black arrows. Only towards the end of the 19th in the rectangular area does an oversold market correspond to a positive correlation above the +0.8 percent level.

The Contributions of Bob English

As noted in the introduction to this chapter, Bob English is an active day trader and author of The Precision Report (www.precisioncapmgt.com). He became acquainted with the MIDAS method in early 2009 and since then has become an active student of the MIDAS approach, using it daily in his various market analyses.

English has made a number of contributions that have expanded or evolved the MIDAS method, and samples of his work are outlined here.

Simplifying MIDAS Calculations with Volume Charts

As noted in Chapter 7, one of Hawkins's motivations for using equivolume charts is the smoothing effect they have on MIDAS curves. English finds that volume charts also produce a similar effect for day trading. Volume charts are available on many trading platforms and are so-called because each price bar contains the same amount of volume.[3] One advantage of this is that price action is much smoother during periods of relatively high volume; another is that subminute price action becomes more evident for traders with extremely short trading time horizons. Occasions of particularly high volume, such as blow-off tops and selling climaxes, can distort time-based bars severely, and this in turn can have a knock-on effect on the plotting of MIDAS curves.

Figure 17.9 is of the September 2010 S&P 500 e-mini futures and displays a time-based 1m chart on the right and on the left a chart where each bar consists of 5,000 contracts. The latter reveals intraminute detail not in evidence in the time-based chart.

Volume-based charts have their drawbacks, including their limitations as regards conventional trend line analysis and low-volume environments, but English maintains that their use simplifies MIDAS calculations due to the fact that volume is constant for each bar. Because of this, a MIDAS user can simply assume that each bar equates with 1 unit of trading volume. Hence, to all intents and purposes MIDAS curves plotted on volume charts are nominal curves, which were the detailed subject of Chapters 6, 10, and 11.

Volume bars also result in a simplification of the procedure for calculating the TB-F curves. We can recall from Chapter 4 that once D is known as a result of fitting the TB-F to the appropriate pullback, the value of the TB-F curve for each bar is found by means of the following procedure:

1. Calculating the parabolically-related volume amount e:

$$e = \Sigma V_n * [1 - (\Sigma V_n / D)] \tag{17.1}$$

FIGURE 17.9   1m time-based chart of the September 2010 S&P 500 e-mini futures and, on the left, a 5,000 contract chart.

Source: TradeStation. www.tradestation.com.

where ΣV_n is the cumulative volume from the beginning of the curve to the current bar.

2. Iterating backwards to the point where e equals the cumulative volume of the iterated (displaced) bars.

3. Dividing the displaced price * volume by e, such that:

$$TBF = [\Sigma(P_n * V_n) - \Sigma(P_e * V_e)]/e \qquad (17.2)$$

However, with a volume chart the volume is directly proportional to the number of bars traversed; thus, it's possible to solve for D precisely at the first pullback bar. This is because at the first pullback bar e will be equal to the sum of the prices of a specified number of displaced bars divided by the price of the pullback bar, P_n. Hence, for the special case of a pullback bar:

$$e = (\Sigma P_n - \Sigma P_m)/P_n \qquad (17.3)$$

Thus, to find D we must first find the bar m that makes this equation true. Accordingly, e is calculated for each bar i starting at bar 1 until bar m ($m < n$) is found that satisfies Equation 17.3. When implementing a topfinder, for each bar i less than m, e will be a fraction less than the number of displaced bars between i and n. At bar m, e will be equal to the number of displaced bars between m and n. In practice, at bar *m*, *e* is nearly always a fraction greater than the integer it is supposed to equal (it goes from negative to positive between $m - 1$ and m), and a little interpolation may be required for TBF curves with shallow pullbacks. When implementing a bottomfinder, the reverse is true, and m is found when the difference between e and the number of displaced bars between i and n goes from positive to negative.

Once m is known, it is now a simple matter to solve for D by rearranging Equation 17.1, substituting n for ΣV_n (because volume always equals 1) and substituting m for $\Sigma V_n - e$:

$$D = n^2/m \qquad (17.4)$$

MIDAS Averages and Delta Curves

It has been acknowledged on several occasions in this book that MIDAS curves do have their limitations just like any other technical indicator. Where these limitations arise, there is a responsibility to provide solutions to them so long as they are robust and consistent. Examples in this book include calibrated curves, nominal curves, OBV-based curves, the MIDAS Displacement Channel, the MIDAS Standard Deviation Channel, and here a solution by English to the problem posed for MIDAS curves by deeper pullbacks in range-bound markets and steeply moving price trends that aren't accelerating sufficiently for the application of a TB-F curve.

Deeper pullbacks present a problem to MIDAS curves because normally-plotted MIDAS curves are subject to whipsawing price movements (though the problem is far less severe than in the case of traditional moving averages). On the other hand, steeply moving price trends can create difficulties because, as mentioned, while they're not accelerating sufficiently for the conventional application of a TB-F curve, their speed of ascent or descent still gives rise to a great deal of displacement in relation to standard MIDAS S/R curves unless a multitude of standard S/R curves are launched. While the latter is possible, English suggests two adjustments to standard S/R curves to cope with these two conditions.

First, a standard MIDAS S/R curve is charted and then the average of this standard S/R curve is plotted. Next, a third curve is plotted equidistant from the standard MIDAS S/R curve on its other side. English calls the former curve the MIDAS Average Curve and the latter the MIDAS Delta Curve. English observes that the MIDAS Average Curve (or MAC, for short) is particularly important in longer-timeframe charts. Figure 17.10 is a monthly chart of the cash S&P 500 index showing the past decade, with the MAC the long dashed line, the MIDAS Delta Curve (MDC) the short dashed curve, and the solid curve a standard MIDAS resistance curve.

The three curves on this chart are nominal curves, meaning that volume is set to a nominal one for each bar, as this idea was introduced in Chapters 6, 10, and 11. Methodologically, English will plot both nominal and standard MIDAS S/R curves from major turning points, as this idea was also recommended in Chapter 11. Here standard S/R curves are omitted to avoid clutter.

FIGURE 17.10 Monthly cash chart of the S&P 500 showing the movement of the index over the past decade.

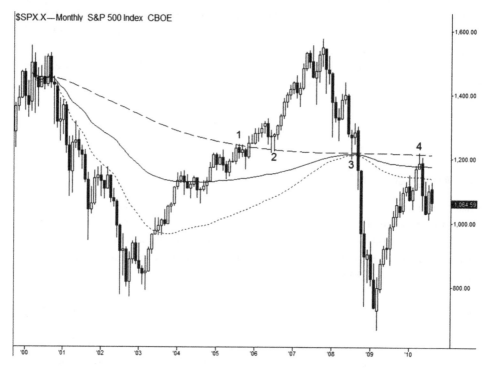

Source: TradeStation. www.tradestation.com.

Attention should focus first on the MDC which, as intended, didn't displace from the sharp post-tech bear market between 2000 and 2003 and also helped signal its end when price broke up through it in mid-2003. During the uptrend that terminated in 2008, price hesitated at the standard MIDAS curve and then again at the MAC at point (1). The MAC then became support at point (2). Point (3) marked an important point insofar as all three curves converged to form support. It was here, after the Lehman bankruptcy in September 2008, that the market decline turned into an all-out crash. Moving forward, point (4) has been particularly important in this analysis in relation to the market rise since early 2009. Would the market be held by this amalgam of the three curves, or would it break through? In April 2010, the amalgam held the market, albeit the MDC and standard MIDAS curve were porous in relation to price and only the MAC interacted with price to produce a classic Japanese candlestick reversal pattern.

Briefly, Figure 17.11 is a daily cash chart of Goldman Sachs from October 2007 to the present. Here the MACs have been bolded to highlight their powerful support and resistance roles, most recently upon the convergence of two of them in August 2010 just below the 160 price level. At the time of this writing, price is consolidating between the MACs launched from the October 2007 high and the March 2009 low.

FIGURE 17.11 Daily cash chart of Goldman Sachs with the MACs highlighted in bold.

Source: TradeStation. www.tradestation.com.

Detrended MIDAS curves

The first part of this chapter focused on volume-based oscillator analysis of price in relation to a MIDAS S/R curve or set of S/R curves. Inspired by Pascal Willain's Active Boundaries approach,[4] English has also developed an oscillator-style indicator he calls the Detrended MIDAS Curve (or DMC, for short) that's similar in concept to the MIDAS Displacement Channel. The indicator is based on the percentage price deviation from a given MIDAS S/R curve. One of the interesting features of the resulting indicator is that trend lines and horizontal support and resistance lines can be applied to it that will function as price inflection points.

We can take a look at this indicator in Figure 17.12, a long-term monthly cash chart of the Dow Jones Industrial Average since 1930. Many of the standard MIDAS support curves are launched from the 1932 low to illustrate the long-term persistence of MIDAS curves (both standard and nominal), and the reader should compare these plots to those discussed by Hawkins in Chapter 6. The indicator in Figure 17.12 was first plotted in September 2009, during which time English speculated that downward trend lines on the far right would prove formidable resistance over the coming two years and possibly for much longer. It's also notable that the two lowermost horizontal

FIGURE 17.12 Long-term monthly cash chart of the DJA from 1930 illustrating the very long-term application of nominal and standard MIDAS support curves with the Detrended MIDAS Curve in the lower pane.

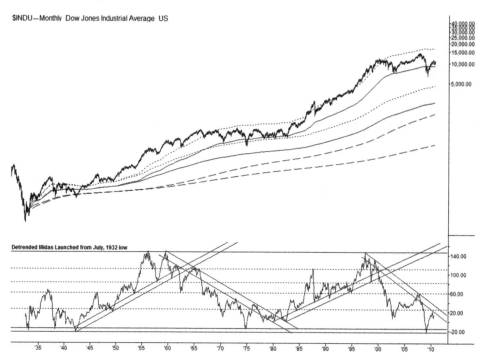

$INDU—Monthly Dow Jones Industrial Average US

Source: TradeStation. www.tradestation.com.

support lines served as support in 1933, 1938, 1942, 1974, and then again most recently in 2008.

The DMC in Figure 17.12 is based on one of the standard MIDAS support curves, not a nominal one. For several decades price has displaced from the MIDAS Average Curves (see previous section and the long dashed curves in the present chart), while the standard MIDAS curves have kept up well with price due to the ongoing increase in the volume trends (see Chapter 11 for a detailed discussion of this point). On the other hand, the MIDAS Delta Curves (see previous section) have provided support and resistance on numerous occasions, and price breaches have been important signals in both directions.

In this book, the DMC is illustrated on a single very long-term chart of the DJIA. However, it can be applied to any chart timeframe to provide timely insight into support and resistance levels and indicator-based trend line analysis.

Active Boundaries and "Reverse VWAP"

As noted earlier, Active Boundaries is a concept founded by Willain and in essence is the price detrended VWAP measured over a fixed amount of volume, where the finite volume is the Active Float, that is, the number of actively traded shares of a company.[5] Here English extends the notion of Active Boundaries into the MIDAS method to develop a market timing technique with the help of what he calls "Reverse VWAP."

The notion of VWAP measured over a fixed amount of volume is similar to the basis of the Detrended MIDAS indicator, as indicated earlier, albeit the latter also utilizes the MIDAS formula and not the basic VWAP formula.[6] One major difference is that the DMC is anchored from an initial predetermined bar, while Active Boundaries are not. Instead, to determine an Active Boundary for a given bar, one must iterate backwards until the predetermined volume (the Active Float) is reached. The next step is to calculate the VWAP over the iterated bars, followed by a calculation of the percentage price deviation from the VWAP at the bar from which the backward iteration began. Essentially, we are measuring how far price is able to stray from a specially calculated average, expecting mean reversion at those extremes where the indicator has reverted in the past.

The absence of a fixed starting point might appear to disqualify this approach from lending itself to further evolution into a MIDAS-inspired technique. However, there is a broad parallel with MIDAS insofar as an Active Boundary implies a fixed amount of volume that needs to be recalculated periodically in relation to market responses to new traders and strategies. Broadly, this idea is in line with Levine's requirement of how a MIDAS curve should be calculated, as noted in Chapter 1:

> We have not yet specified the interval over which the averages are to be taken. In fact, it is this choice of averaging interval which uniquely distinguishes the MIDAS method. . . . Our "message" is that instead of "moving" averages, one should take fixed or "anchored" averages, where the anchoring point is the point of trend reversal.[7]

As noted above, the Active Float is an estimate of the number of actively traded shares for a company. Because active traders tend to enter and exit the market according to their own persistent patterns of trading,[8] their average percentage profit and loss, as expressed by Active Boundaries, will tend to reverse at these same percentage amounts. Indeed, Willain answers the question of why trends persist by drawing partly on this notion:

> Trends exist because members of the group of active shareholders have concurrent levels of long-term expectations regarding the stocks' future price movements, but divergent short-term expectations. It is the average of their long-term expectation that helps to form a price trend, and it is the average of their short-term expectations that moves the stock price within the trend's boundaries. Active Boundaries, since they are measuring a range of expectations, are an excellent tool for monitoring a trend.[9]

While the method was created for equities analysis, it's possible to generalize it for all liquid markets and, in line with tenet one of Levine's philosophy of price movement in Chapter 1, it's possible to introduce a hierarchy of Active Boundaries of progressing volume amounts that's consistent with the underlying philosophy of the MIDAS approach.

As opposed to searching for a single level, English uses a technique he calls "Reverse VWAP" to establish multiple Active Boundaries of progressing volume. The "Reverse VWAP" method works as follows. First, from a given bar, iterate backwards while calculating the VWAP along the way until, in most cases, a bar is reached in relation to which the VWAP is equal to its price. In other words, a VWAP or MIDAS curve launched from this prior bar would act as support (or resistance) once the original bar to the right had been reached.[10] Once the bar equal to the VWAP is reached through backward iteration, the method continues to iterate backwards until other bars are found that satisfy the same condition. While this procedure continues, the method also keeps track of the volume between the various bars equal to the VWAP as well as the periodic percentage price deviations from the VWAP.

The resulting analysis reveals the movement of price in relation to various trading strategies as the price movement meanders between equilibrium and extreme price levels. Ultimately the analysis will establish the volume amounts to be used in the Active Boundaries indicators. Figure 17.13 is a 15m chart of the euro FX September 2010 futures, with the lower part of the chart revealing the volume between each successful backward iteration leading to VWAP reversion plotted from each bar.

The horizontal lines in Figure 17.13 are manually drawn and, as noted above, identify certain volume increments that persist and thus stand out.[11] Figure 17.13 only covers a brief time period, but the higher volume levels identified can persist for months, while it's the lowest volume levels (indeed, those that are actually measured on subminute volume charts) where English finds the earliest warning signs of a price change significant to a much larger trend turnabout appropriate to higher-timeframe

FIGURE 17.13   15m chart of euro FX September 2010 futures with the resulting "Reverse MIDAS" volume levels at the bottom of the chart.

Source: TradeStation. www.tradestation.com.

chart analysis. This idea is in line with Levine's notion of a fractal hierarchy of support and resistance in tenet one discussed in Chapter 1, but the idea is also confirmed in markets dominated by high frequency trading algorithms that, by some estimates, account for 70 percent or more of volume in certain markets. Indeed, in the days leading up to the May 6 "2010 Flash Crash" the Active Boundaries indicator set to 10,000 contracts (actually a low number) and applied to the S&P 500 e-mini futures was giving readings not seen since the post-Lehman collapse.

If we return to the euro FX futures, we'll see in Figure 17.14 that the volume levels in the lower half of the chart are marked by the volume levels of 31,000 and 460,000. These levels will be used as the levels in the Active Boundaries indicator in the last part of this discussion. Figure 17.14 has switched to a 1,000 volume chart (see English's first section for volume charts), his preferred choice for day trading this market. The chart demonstrates the consistent reversal points predicted by the two instances of this indicator in Figure 17.14.

Depending on the market, English uses up to three volume indicators on the same chart, each with a volume an order of magnitude higher than the last (for example, 10,000, 100,000, 1,000,000). The actual volume amount can vary (+/– 10 percent) without causing much of a difference in the indicator. Figure 17.14 is essentially

FIGURE 17.14 1,000 volume intraday chart of the euro FX September 2010 futures with volume levels of 31,000 and 460,000.

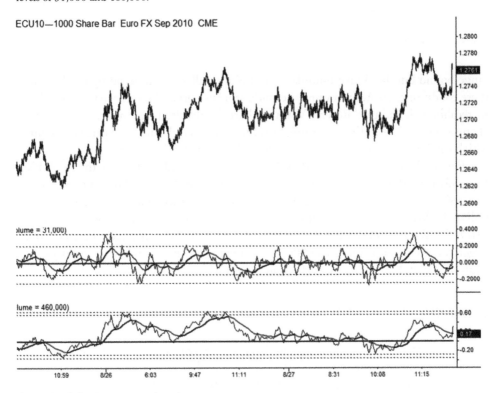

Source: TradeStation. www.tradestation.com.

FIGURE 17.15 Another 1,000 volume intraday chart of the euro FX September 2010 futures with the Active Boundaries horizontal support and resistance curves plotted alongside price and alongside standard MIDAS S/R curves and TB-F curves.

range-bound but the Active Boundaries technique still works in trending markets. In these conditions, the Active Boundaries indicator support and resistance levels need to be recalibrated, and the "Reverse VWAP" chart should also be monitored to identify changes. From time to time, abnormal readings will precede an actual price breakout, which can be an important clue as to a possible major trend change.

Finally, Figure 17.15 is another 1,000 volume intraday chart of the euro FX September 2010 futures. It illustrates that the Active Boundaries horizontal support and resistance levels can be plotted directly onto the price chart. The result is not unlike the MIDAS Displacement Channel. Here they're charted along with standard MIDAS S/R curves plus TB-F curves. The Active Boundaries indicator based on the larger volume amount (here 160,000) is retained beneath the chart because it yields additional useful information, such as momentum.

Summary

- During the writing of his lectures Paul Levine was beginning to explore new ways of combining the MIDAS method with other technical indicators and was also starting to explore ways of creating additional indicators from within the MIDAS approach.

- One such experimental indicator was the "DIST" indicator. Although when plotted in real time it appears to have several imperfections, we can retain the emphasis on volume in the MIDAS approach and convert the OBV indicator to do the job Levine intended.
- The "Stoch-OBV" indicator isn't tagged to a particular curve, so it doesn't suffer from displacement nor require multiple copies. It creates robust overbought and oversold signals. The "MACD-OBV" is an unbounded oscillator that produces better divergences than the original OBV plot. As such, it offers a credible alternative to patchy divergence signals in the original OBV line. This approach doesn't undermine the N-OBV and V-OBV curves in the previous chapter because they are exploiting a different aspect of the OBV line, namely its fractal trend characteristics.
- Correlation analysis with a particular MIDAS curve retains Levine's original idea and again creates very reliable short-term market exhaustion signals.

Bob English, a U.S. day trader and author of The Precision Report (www. precisioncapmgt.com), among other commitments, has actively explored the MIDAS method and developed a number of indicators and techniques based on it.

- For simpler calculations resulting in smoother curves, English uses volume charts in a way that parallels Hawkins' reliance on equivolume charts.
- English's MIDAS Average Curves and MIDAS Delta Curves are effective in range-bound markets and accelerating markets respectively. MDCs are applicable when the market isn't accelerating sufficiently for the application of a TB-F curve.
- English often detrends MIDAS S/R curves to produce an oscillator with identifiable market exhaustion points and that is capable of further technical analysis such as trend line application.
- Based on Willain's notion of Active Boundaries, English has developed a technique he calls "Reverse VWAP" whose underlying methodology partly resembles the anchoring methodology in the MIDAS approach. "Reverse VWAP" uncovers important volume levels associated with fractal hierarchies of support and resistance, and can be used for future market timing purposes as well as for monitoring early signs of more significant changes in trend.

APPENDIX A

Programming the TB-F

David G. Hawkins

The topfinder-bottomfinder (TB-F) indicator turns out to be rather challenging to program. It requires using for-next loops (or, "do loops" as they're often called), which are not part of the high-level scripting languages of many of the standard technical analysis (TA) software packages, such as MetaStock. So, for those platforms, it has to be programmed in one of the full-featured programming languages, such as C++, and then attached as a plug-in to a TA program. We have had this done for a MetaStock plug-in, and that's what is being used for most of the illustrations in this book. I also advised the programmer at StockShare Publishing, LLC on how to do this, and they produced a plug-in that works nicely with their program.

There are a few TA platforms, such as Tradestation and eSignal, whose indicator scripting languages are robust enough to allow programming of the TB-F.

The TB-F is so unusual, both in its concept and application, that considerable explanation is necessary for anyone to program it. I won't show the details of how to program the TB-F, but instead will describe some of the peculiarities and pitfalls of programming the TB-F so that, with these descriptions in hand, any competent programmer may succeed. There are three particular issues that need elucidation—The Starting Point Ambiguity, the need for do loops, and the right way to account for the location of the e-point in the calculation of the points on the TB-F curve.

Moving Averages and the Starting Point Ambiguity

This first issue applies equally to both the standard Midas S/R curves and the TB-F. This issue, which I call the Starting Point Ambiguity, relates to how one treats the price bar that is designated as the starting point of one of these curves; namely, should this bar be included in the calculation of the curve? The correct answer is yes.

Since a standard Midas S/R curve is a variant of the well-known volume weighted moving average, the S/R curves are easy to program with the high-level indicator scripting languages that come with most TA software packages. I've done it, and everyone I know who has attempted it has gotten it right, not falling to the wrong side of the Starting Point Ambiguity. The standard TA indicator scripting languages include the first bar of a curve in its calculation by default. But, for some reason, every professional programmer with whom I have worked in creating a plug-in to do both the S/R curves and the TB-F has gotten it wrong, and has resisted doing it the right way. In 1995, right after Paul Levine[1] published his two articles on the TB-F, I engaged a programmer to write both the S/R curves and the TB-F into an Excel spreadsheet using Visual Basic. He did a beautiful job, except, he got the Starting Point Ambiguity wrong. I could not convince him of it, finally accepting what he wrote, and thereafter always had to offset the designated starting point by one bar to get it to do what I knew it should do. More recently, while working with the programmers for both the MetaStock and the StockShare plug-ins, I insisted that they do it right, and they did.

Probably, the confusion has something to do with the difference between some conventions within professional programming and the way that technicians understand things in TA. So, coming from the TA side, let me demonstrate exactly what is needed, and leave it to the programmers to figure out how to do it right. I'll start from the simplest of moving averages, and work up finally to the TB-F. Much of the following will be elementary to readers who are familiar with technical analysis. But I'm putting this all here, very pedantically, so that programmers may see how technicians view things.

The Simple Moving Average (SMA)

By definition, an N period SMA is the mean of the prices (usually the closing prices) of the most recent N bars. For example, let's assume we have a data file of 300 days of daily bars of a security, and thus a chart of 300 price bars. The first bar is called bar number 1, the second is bar number 2, and so on, and the last bar is bar number 300. Now, let's calculate and plot the 10-period SMA. To start, you sum the (closing) prices of the first 10 bars, number 1 through 10 *inclusive*, and divide by 10. This is the value of the first point of the SMA curve, which is plotted at the 10th day on the chart. The second point on the SMA curve is the mean of the prices of bars numbers 2 through 11 inclusive, plotted at the 11th day, and so on for each succeeding point. The last point on the SMA curve, plotted at the 300th day, is the mean of the prices of bars number 291 through 300 inclusive.

The code for the ten-period SMA, using a typical indicator scripting language such as MetaStock's, is

$$sum(C, 10)/10$$

which automatically includes the first of the 10 points in the calculation.

The Two Meanings of "Starting Point"

There are two different ways that technicians use the phrase, "starting point," which sometimes causes confusion. In the above example of a 10-period SMA on a chart of

300 price bars, the starting point of the curve is the first point of that curve, which appears at the 10th day on the chart. There is only one SMA curve, and thus only one starting point of that curve. But sometimes, we use "starting point" to refer to the first price bar used in the calculation of any one point on the curve. For instance, the starting point for the calculation of the last point on the curve, a point that appears at day 300, is at bar number 291. The starting point for the calculation of a point on the curve moves, always being $N - 1$ bars earlier than the point being calculated. So, it's important to distinguish between "the starting point *of the curve*" and "the starting point *of the calculation of a point on the curve.*"

The Volume Weighted Moving Average (VWMA)

The VWMA is like the SMA except that, before the summation, each bar's price is first multiplied by its volume. Then, the summation is divided by the sum of the volumes of the N bars. The MetaStock script for a 10-period VWMA is:

$$sum(C * V, 10)/sum(V, 10)$$

that also automatically includes the first of the 10 points in the calculation.

Notice that both the SMA and the VWMA are "moving" averages in the sense that the starting point for the calculation of the points on the curve moves forward in time just as the points on the curve do, but with a fixed lag of $N - 1$ periods.

A Midas S/R Curve

A Midas S/R curve, by definition, is a fixed starting point moving average of the volume weighted price. Unlike all other moving averages in TA, with a Midas S/R curve, "the starting point of the curve" and "the starting point of the calculation of a point on the curve" are one and the same point, and it does not move.

For example, if we start a Midas Support curve right at the first bar of the chart, then the starting point for the curve is at bar 1, *and* the starting point for the calculation of *every* point on the curve is also at bar 1. Let's say we're calculating the point on this S curve at day number 4. (Remember, we calculate S curves with low prices, not closes.) Then, the height of the fourth point on the S curve is:

$$(L_1 * V_1 + L_2 * V_2 + L_3 * V_3 + L_4 * V_4)/(V_1 + V_2 + V_3 + V_4)$$

where the subscripts refer to the bar numbers. Obviously, the first bar's data are included in the calculation of the curve.

From the foregoing, it's obvious that the height of the second point on the S curve would be:

$$(L_1 * V_1 + L_2 * V_2)/(V_1 + V_2)$$

and the height of the first point would be:

$$L_1 * V_1/V_1$$

which equals L_1, the low of the first price bar. So, the first point on the S curve is coincident with the low of the first price bar, *but thereafter, beginning with the second point, the S curve separates from the price bars.*

Now, finally, we're able to address the Starting Point Ambiguity problem. When programmers have erred on the Starting Point Ambiguity, their second point of the S curve always comes out to be the low of the second bar, meaning that their erroneous S curve stays coincident with the price bars' lows for the first *and* the second points of the curve, before separating.

The TB-F

The TB-F curve is like the S/R curve except that the starting point for the calculation of the points on the curve moves, but not in the same way that it moves in the VWMA. If you start a topfinder curve from the same bar that you're also starting an S curve, then the first point on each of the two curves will have exactly the same value, the low of that first bar. But starting with the second bar, the two curves begin to diverge, *neither one of them being at the low of the second bar.* When programmers err with the Starting Point Ambiguity, their second point on the TB-F curve is coincident with the second price bar, not separate from it.

The Need for Do Loops

As described earlier, the starting point for the calculation of a point on a TB-F curve is located to the left of the plotted point by a cumulative volume distance given by the formula for e. The value of e is set at zero at the first point on the curve, gradually increases to one-quarter of D at the middle of the curve, then declines back down to zero at the last point on the curve. Reminder, in all that I'm writing here, the horizontal axis of the chart is linear in cumulative volume, not time, and both e and D are values of cumulative volume. The words *distance*, *length*, and *duration* always refer to an amount of cumulative volume measured along the horizontal axis, not time.

When starting the calculation of a particular point on the TB-F curve, the first step is to evaluate e from the formula, and then locate the point on the horizontal axis that is a distance e to the left of the curve point being calculated, a location that I'm calling the e-point. Then, the height of the current curve point is calculated as the volume weighted average of all the prices located from the e-point up to the current curve point, *inclusive.*

The problem comes because e is a continuous variable, calculated from a closed form expression, whereas the price bars are located at discrete points along the horizontal axis. The e-point essentially never lands right on the location of one of the price bars. It lands somewhere between two points. In calculating the curve point, you must use all of the prices from the e-point up to the current curve point, inclusive. So, you have to discover between which two price bars the e-point is located. This is accomplished with a do loop, which starts at the current price bar and steps to the left, one bar at a time, until it finds the first price bar whose cumulative volume location is less than the e-point's.

The So-Called Interpolation

This section addresses Levine's[2] rather cryptic instructions on how to take into account the e-point location in the calculation of the TB-F. Figure A.1 shows the SPDR Gold Shares, ticker GLD, monthly bars, from October 2008 through the middle of January 2010. I've deliberately chosen one of those rare examples, which has only one significant

FIGURE A.1   GLD, monthly, Oct. 2008 to mid Jan. 2010.

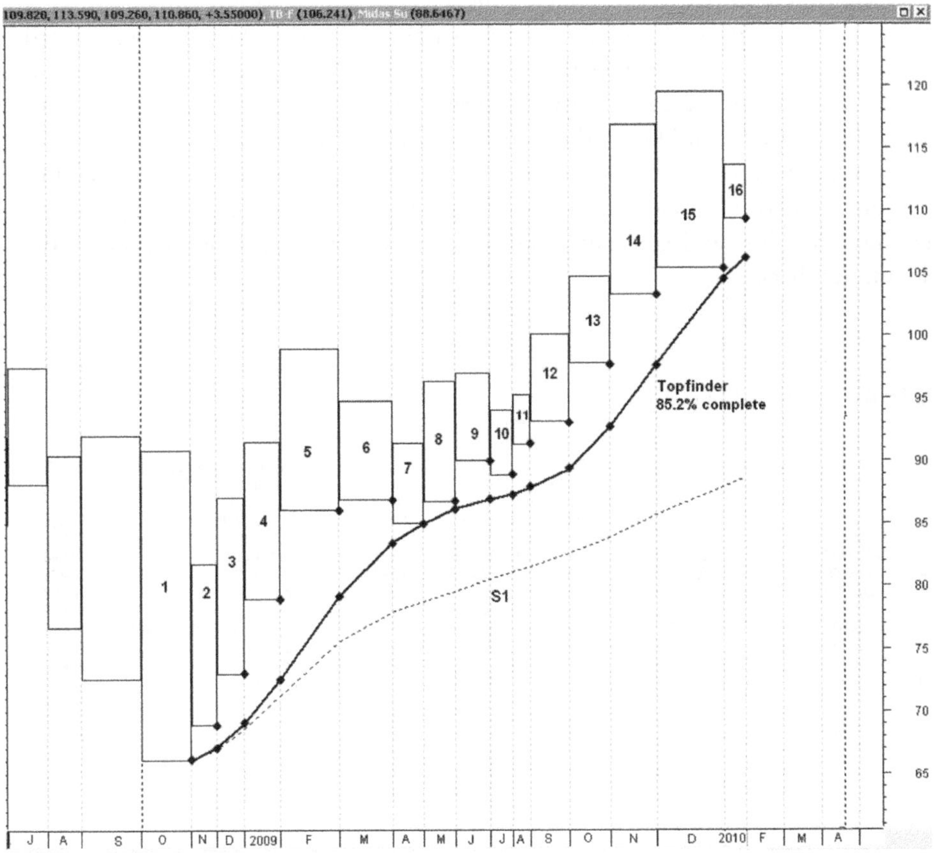

Data source: Reuters DataLink.

pullback and a very small number of price bars, only 16, so that the proper treatment of the e-point is very significant. On an example such as this, even a small error in taking the e-point into account will produce a sizable distortion to the shape of the TB-F curve, which will be immediately recognizable. I'm presenting this example in detail so that it may be an exercise for you to use to check the validity of your program for the TB-F.

This chart was generated in MetaStock, using our TB-F plug-in, and displayed as an EquiVolume chart. Unfortunately, the way MetaStock labels the horizontal axis can be confusing. They put the letter for the month to the right of the price bar instead of directly under it, so I have edited the display here, shifting the letters to be directly under their corresponding price bars. The bar marked 1 is the October 2008 bar, 2 is the November bar, and so on. I've also added a solid tick mark on the lower right corner of each price box; this is the relevant data point, its height being the low price of the month and its horizontal location relative to the preceding point representing all of the volume of that month. I've also put tick marks on the TB-F curve to emphasize that this really is a broken line graph, not a smooth curve. The fact that it looks quite smooth testifies to the success of this plug-in in correctly calculating the heights of those points. The dotted vertical line on the left marks the location of the beginning of this accelerated uptrend, and the one on the right is placed at the location projected by the fit of the TB-F to be where the trend will end. In fitting the curve, I iterated D, the total duration of the event, until the curve exactly touched the pullback at price box no. 7. That value of D turned out to be 61,200,000 shares.

Now let's go into detail about how to calculate the TB-F for one point, the seventh point on the curve. (The fact that this happens to be the fitting point is not significant; the same procedure and considerations apply to every point.) Table A.1 shows the relevant numbers.

TABLE A.1   Data for Figure A.1

Bar no.	Date	Low Price	V	S1	d	e	Location of e-point, d-e	Interpolated Volume	TB-F
1	10/31/08	66	4,338,672	66.0000	4,338,672	4,031,089	307,583		66.000
2	11/28/08	68.81	2,235,817	66.9556	6,574,489	5,868,216	706,273		67.071
3	12/31/08	72.91	2,419,069	68.5572	8,993,558	7,671,922	1,321,635		68.998
4	1/30/09	78.87	3,089,867	71.1943	12,083,425	9,697,654	2,385,770		72.472
5	2/27/09	86	5,035,921	75.5496	17,119,346	12,330,588	4,788,758		79.156
6	3/31/09	86.83	4,601,219	77.9392	21,720,565	14,011,693	7,708,871		83.500
7	4/30/09	84.92	2,689,227	78.7083	24,409,791	14,673,878	9,735,914	2,347,511	84.922
8	5/29/09	86.692	2,708,423	79.5057	27,118,214	15,101,915	12,016,300		86.153
9	6/30/09	89.95	2,997,568	80.5452	30,115,783	15,296,169	14,819,614		86.956
10	7/31/09	88.82	2,041,711	81.0706	32,157,494	15,260,363	16,897,131		87.336
11	8/31/09	91.28	1,547,934	81.5395	33,705,427	15,142,424	18,563,004		87.807
12	9/30/09	93.06	3,275,949	82.5600	36,981,376	14,634,608	22,346,768		89.317
13	10/30/09	97.74	3,579,645	83.8997	40,561,021	13,678,726	26,882,295		92.659
14	11/30/09	103.25	4,035,009	85.6505	44,596,030	12,099,202	32,496,828		97.665
15	12/31/09	105.312	5,696,395	87.8775	50,292,425	8,963,536	41,328,889		104.560
16	1/15/10	109.26	1,876,855	88.6467	52,169,279	7,698,140	44,471,139		106.241

D = 61,200,000

Here, d is the cumulative volume location of each price point along the horizontal axis; e is calculated from the formula, and the next column shows the location of the e-point on the horizontal axis.

The bar 7 row is bolded as we're going to calculate the TB-F at that location. Notice that the e-point is at 9,735,914. Bar rows 3 and 4 are also bolded to call attention to the fact that our e-point is located somewhere between price points 3 and 4, 3 being at about 9 million and 4 at 12 million; the do loop in your program should have identified this.

To calculate the TB-F, one must sum the products of price and volume, L ∗ V, for all the price data from the 7th point back to the e-point. Figure A.2 shows this more clearly. Here I've removed the price boxes, leaving just the low price points, and the

FIGURE A.2   Figure A.1 in more detail and labeled with cumulative volume.

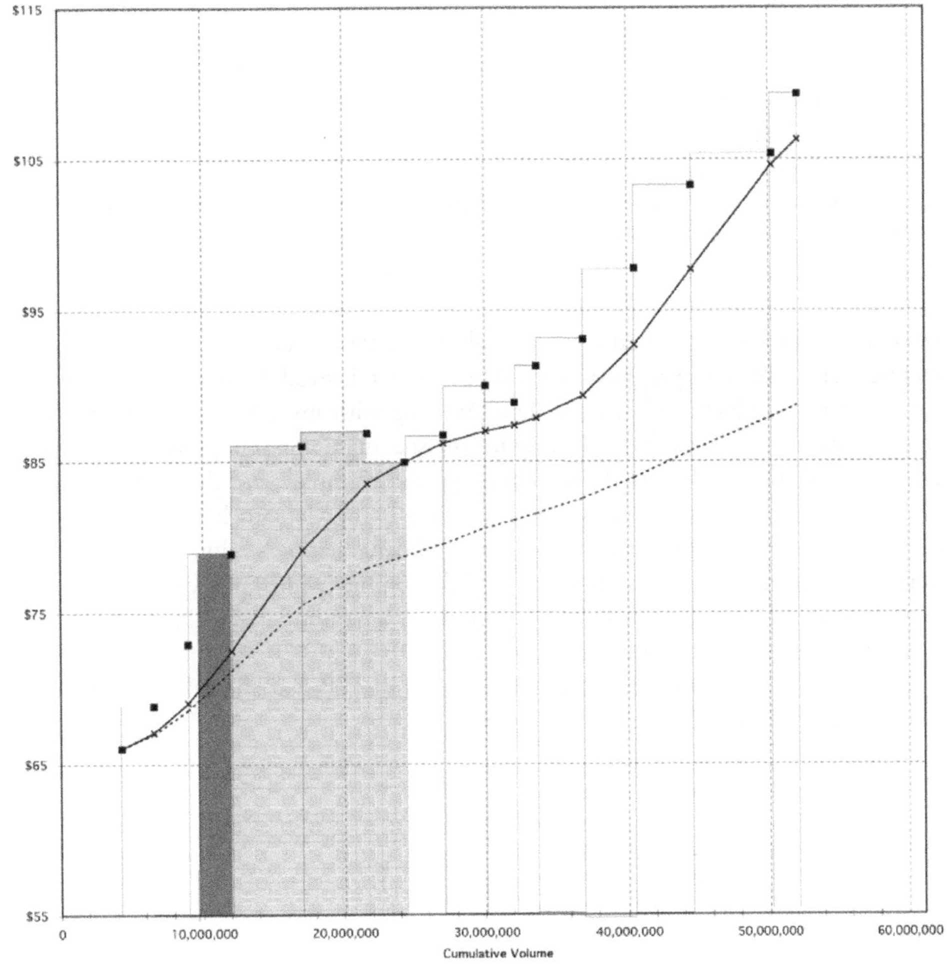

Data source: Reuters DataLink.

horizontal axis is explicitly labeled in cumulative volume. The e-point is just a little under 10 million, about a quarter of the way from the third to the fourth price points. The rectangles here are not the price boxes, but rather are the L ∗ V boxes for each data point, and they actually extend all the way down to price zero. The area of each rectangle is the L ∗ V product for that data point.

Starting from our plotting point, the seventh one, and moving to the left, the seventh, sixth, and fifth L ∗ V boxes are included in the summation *and* that part of the fourth box that's to the right of the e-point, shown in dark gray. The entire fourth L ∗ V box has a width of about 3.1 million, but the width of the dark gray rectangle is 2,347,511, which I'm calling the "interpolated volume." That dark gray rectangle is taking the place of the full fourth one in the summation, keeping the same price as point 4.

After the summation of the areas of those shaded rectangles is done, that sum is divided by the total volume between the seventh point and the e-point inclusive, and the result, 84.922, is the value of the height of the TB-F curve at the seventh point.

In Paul Levine's[3] fifteenth article, he made some vague remarks about how to do what I've just described here. He talked about using only the volume that I've identified as the width of the dark gray rectangle here, but then he seemed to be saying that the price data as well as the volume need to be somehow interpolated between the third and fourth prices; yet it's not clear if that's exactly what he meant. Then he ends the discussion by copping out with the following sentence, which is my favorite out of all of his articles: "Here I'll have to leave you to your own devices since to help you set up such calculations would carry us beyond the scope of these articles."[5]

When I first started working with programmers on the TB-F, I thought that the dark gray rectangle's height had to be literally interpolated between the neighboring two price values. But, the programmers did not do that, instead doing what I've shown above, and the results have been excellent. Starting with my 1995 spreadsheet, I've compared its calculations (after adjusting for the starting point ambiguity) with those that Levine[5] showed in his articles for some specific examples, and the results match to four significant figures. Similarly, our TB-F plug-in for MetaStock gives exactly the same values as my spreadsheet does. So, I'm confident that we've done the so-called interpolation correctly, which is, finding the right volume (width) of the e-point's box, the dark gray one, but no price interpolation. If we were not correct, the TB-F curve in this example would not be so smooth.

In Table A.1, I've supplied the correct values of the TB-F at all of the points. You should compare your program's results to these.

APPENDIX B

MetaStock Code for the Standard MIDAS S/R Curves

Andrew Coles

The token MetaStock code below is for the adjustable (O, H, L, C, Average Price) version of the standard MIDAS support/resistance curves for intraday and higher time-frame charts. The application to intraday charts differs due to the need for hour and minute functions. I've refrained from supplying further code here because of the tedium for the reader in having to retype the code and there are also risks of syntax errors. Instead, most of the code is available on our web site, www.midasmarketanalyis.com, where it is simply a matter of copying and pasting.

Readers interested in the nominal curve versions of the standard S/R curves should replace the "v" (volume) in the formula below with 1.

Standard MIDAS S/R Curves for Daily and Higher Timeframe Charts*

```
sm:=Input("starting month",1,12,1);
sd:=Input("starting day of month",1,31,1);
sy:=Input("starting year",1980,2100,2000);
start:= sd=DayOfMonth() AND sm=Month() AND sy=Year();
x:=Input("Price Field, 1=O,2=H,3=L,4=C,5=MP()",1,5,4);
y:=If(x=1,O,If(x=2,H,If(x=3,L,If(x=4,C,If(x=5,MP(),0)))));
ab:=y*V;

denom:= If(Cum(V)-ValueWhen(1,start,Cum(V))=0,1,Cum(V)-
    ValueWhen(1,start,Cum(V)));
If(BarsSince(start),(Cum(ab)-ValueWhen(1,start,Cum(ab)))/
    denom,MP())
```

Standard MIDAS S/R Curves for Intraday Charts*

```
sm:=Input("starting month",1,12,1);
sd:=Input("starting day of month",1,31,1);
sy:=Input("starting year",1980,2100,2000);
sh:=Input("hour", 1,24,1);
se:=Input("minute",0,60,0);

start:= sd=DayOfMonth() AND sm=Month() AND sy=Year() AND
    sh=Hour() AND se=Minute();
x:=Input("Price Field, 1=O,2=H,3=L,4=C,5=MP()",1,5,4);
y:=If(x=1,O,If(x=2,H,If(x=3,L,If(x=4,C,If(x=5,MP(),0)))));
ab:=y*V;
denom:= If(Cum(V)-ValueWhen(1,start,Cum(V))=0,1,Cum(V)-
    ValueWhen(1,start,Cum(V)));
If(BarsSince(start),(Cum(ab)-ValueWhen(1,start,Cum(ab)))/
    denom,MP())
```

---

*Metastock code for the MIDAS standard S/R curves.

TradeStation Code for the MIDAS Topfinder/Bottomfinder Curves

Bob English

Bob English is an active day trader in the United States who writes a daily market timing newsletter called The Precision Report (www.precisioncapmgt.com), as well as economic and trading commentary for various publications. English was introduced to the MIDAS method by members of a private trading group in 2009 and since then has become an active student of the MIDAS approach, using it daily in his analysis, market commentary and trading. Some of his developments are discussed in Chapter 17, "Extensions, Insights, and New Departures in MIDAS Studies." To reciprocate the generosity of the trading community, he offers the following Trade-Station implementation of the TBF algorithm, which can be ported to any platform that supports backwards iteration.

TradeStation Implementation of Paul Levine's Topfinder/Bottomfinder (TBF)

This work is licensed under a Creative Commons Attribution-ShareAlike 3.0 Unported License http://creativecommons.org/licenses/by-sa/3.0/2010, Bob English (www.precisioncapmgt.com).

```
Input: Vol_D(0),          //Input Volume ("D" from Levine's
                          //formula)

       TBF_Price(L),      //Bar Price to use; suggest "L" for
                          //TopFinder and "H" for BottomFinder;
                          //Alternatively, "(H+L+C)/3"
```

```
                                      //may be used for an average price
             MyVolume(Ticks),         //Bar Volume information to use;
                                      //suggest "Ticks", or "1"
                                      //if no volume information
                                      //"Ticks" yields total volume,
                                      //and "Volume" yields only
                                      //up volume on intraday charts
             StartingDate(1120101),   //Start Date in TradeStation date
                                      //format: YYYMMDD, where YYY
                                      //is years since 1900
                                      //Example date is January 1, 2012
             StartingTime(1530),      //Start Time in military time with no
                                      //punctuation; example time is 3:30 pm
             StartColor(Yellow),      //Color of TBF curve will start with
                                      //StartColor and end with EndColor...
             EndColor(Red);           //...and changes according to %
                                      //D completion
Vars: running(false),                 //whether or not TBF calculation has
                                      //started and not ended
             pv(0),                   //cumulative price * volume
             vol(0),                  //cumulative volume
             _D(0),                   //variable that holds input volume, D
             pvInt(0),                //interpolated pv
             j(0),                    //loop iterator
             e(0),                    //same as Levine's "e" variable
             eT(0),                   //temporary copy of "e" used for
                                      //iteration
             tbf(0),                  //current calculated price of TBF curve
             pct_D(0);                //percent completion of TBF curve

//begin at user specified date and time
if (date = StartingDate and time = StartingTime) or running then begin

             running = true;

             pv = pv + TBF_Price * MyVolume;      //add current bar's price *
                                                  //volume to cumulative total
             vol = vol + (MyVolume);              //running total of volume

             //begin calculation of TBF price
             if Vol_D <> 0 then begin
                        _D = Vol_D;               //store copy of input volume

                        e = vol * (1 - vol / _D);    //calculate "e" per
                                                     //Levine's formula
                        //if "e" greater than zero, continue to
                        //calculate TBF price
                        //otherwise, TBF is completed
                        if e > 0 then begin
                                   eT = e;                    //temporary
                                                             //copy of "e"
```

```
                                 j = -1;                    //used for iteration
                //iterate backwards until the cumulative
                //displaced volume is greater than or
                //equal to "e"

                while eT > 0 begin
                        j = j + 1;
                        eT = eT - MyVolume[j];
                end;

                //If displaced volume is greater than "e"
                //(nearly always),
                //an interpolated pv amount is calculated
                //for "j" bars ago using only that part of
                //"j" bar's volume needed to make cumulative
                //displaced volume equal to "e".
                //Note that at this point, "eT" is negative
                //and contains the partial volume
                //of "j" bars ago that should be excluded.
                if eT < 0 then pvInt = TBF_Price[j] *
                (MyVolume[j] + eT) else pvInt = 0;

                tbf = (pv - pv[j] + pvInt) / e;    //calculate
                                                   //TBF curve
                                                   //price for
                                                   //this bar
                pct_D = vol / _D * 100;            //calculate
                                                   //percent TBF
                                                   //completion
                plot1(tbf, "TBF");
                //Set Plot Color based on gradient between two
                //Input colors
                SetPlotColor(1, GradientColor(pct_D, 0, 100,
                //StartColor, EndColor));
            end
        else running = false; //TBF curve is completed; do
        //not run anymore
    end;
end;
```

Notes

Introduction

1. Darell Jobman, "Has Technical Analysis Kept Up with the (Dow) Jones?" *Futures Magazine* 35, no. 3 (February 2006); Jean Folger, "Day-Trading: Then and Now," *Futures Magazine* 35, no. 15 (December 2006); Tom Busby, "A Day in the Life of a Day Trader," *Futures Magazine* 30, no. 13 (October 2001); Diane Rochon, "Technical Analysis Behind Closed Doors," *Active Trader* 2, no. 9 (October 2001); Brendan McGlone, "Lessons from Pit-Traded Markets," *Futures Magazine* 38, no. 9 (September 2009).
2. J. Sweeney, "Product Review: WinMidas, ver 2.1," *Technical Analysis of Stocks & Commodities* 16, no. 14 (1998).
3. G. Reyna, "Volume Weighted Average Price for Support and Resistance," *Technical Analysis of Stocks & Commodities* 19, no. 5 (2001).
4. See the section "MIDAS S/R Curves with Moving Averages" in Chapter 3 of Bo Yoder, *Mastering Futures Trading: An Advanced Course for Sophisticated Strategies That Work* (New York: McGraw-Hill, 2004); and S. W. Bigalow and D. Elliott, "Day Trading with Candlesticks and Moving Averages," *Futures Magazine* 23, no. 14 (November 2004).

Chapter 1 MIDAS and Its Core Constituents

1. "Plunge in US Equities Remains a Mystery," *Financial Times*, May 8–9, 2010. See also Jeff Poor, "CNBC's Bartiromo: 'That Is Ridiculous. This Really Sounds like Market Manipulation to Me.'" Available at www.businessandmedia.org/articles/2010/20100506174136.aspx. Bruce Krasting, "The Yen Did It?" Available at http://seekingalpha.com/article/203603-the-yen-did-it?source=hp_wc.

   Over the subsequent week other explanations emerged, including an intermarket sweep order (see Matt Phillips, "Accenture's Flash Crash: What's an 'Intermarket Sweep Order,'" available at http://blogs.wsj.com/marketbeat/2010/05/07/accentures-flash-crash-whats-an-intermarket-sweep-order/); a large purchase of put options by the hedge fund Universa Investments (*Wall Street Journal* May 11 story); as well as a vast sale of 75,000 e-mini contracts, which alone were worth $4 billion (see Michael Corkery, "SEC Chairman Admits: We're Outgunned by Market Supercomputers," available at http://blogs.wsj.com/deals/2010/05/11/sec-chairman-admits-were-outgunned-by-market-supercomputers/).

The issue is currently under investigation by the Securities and Exchange Commission and Commodities Futures Trading Commission prior to scheduled hearings before the House Financial Services Subcommittee on Capital Markets. But the problem was compounded further by automated superfast networked computer systems that linked not only stock indices but also other markets, including the currencies and bonds markets.

2. Ronald D. Oral, "SEC, CFTC Blame Algorithm for 'Flash Crash.'" Available at www.marketwatch.com.

3. http://moneyterms.co.uk/vwap/.

4. See, for example, Grant Johnsey, "Insights on . . . Volume Weighted Average Price." Available at www-ac.northerntrust.com/content/media/attachment/data/white_paper/0603/document/ntgil_whitepaper_transmgmt.pdf. In his article, Johnsey raises several criticisms he believes hinders the VWAP from being a truly effective benchmark.

5. G. Reyna, "Volume Weighted Average Price for Support and Resistance," *Technical Analysis of Stocks & Commodities* 19, no. 5 (2001).

6. If using this latter method a trader wished to discover the average price at which an instrument had traded during a specific period, he'd average the sum of the average prices and volume weight over the period.

7. See, for example, http://ezinearticles.com/?Day-Trading-Software-VWAP-Calculation-Differences—Iterative-VWAP-Versus-Cumulative-VWAP&id=831607.

8. This observation is based on a number of online formula expressions for calculating the VWMA. In print, formula expressions for the VWMA can be found, for example, in B. Dormeier, "Buff Up Your Moving Averages," *Technical Analysis of Stocks & Commodities* 19, no. 2 (2001); and in B. Dormeier, "Between Price and Volume," *Technical Analysis of Stocks & Commodities* 25, no. 7 (2007).

9. Thom Hartle, "A Guide To Conquering the Trading Markets: Kevin Haggerty," *Technical Analysis of Stocks & Commodities* 17 (August, 1999).

10. Bob English's discussion can be found at www.precisioncapmgt.com/tag/anchored-vwap-bands/ under the discussion, "Using Prior Day's Closing VWAP as Support/Resistance."

11. http://traderfeed.blogspot.com/2009/02/using-vwap-to-determine-structure-of-.html. See also www.brettsteenbarger.com. In the same discussion Steenbarger adds that early moves that fail to break resistance or support will often return to the VWAP, suggesting a trade opportunity. Successful breakouts imply a rejection of the VWAP; consequently, it can be treated as a moving stop for the resulting trade with the trend. Steenbarger is the author of a number of trading books, his most recent being *The Daily Trading Coach* (Hoboken, NJ: John Wiley & Sons, 2009). For similar applications of the VWAP see also Brian

Shannon at http://alphatrends.blogspot.com and www.alphatrends.net/; and Brian Shannon, *Technical Analysis Using Multiple Timeframes* (Centennial, CO: LifeVest Publishing Inc, 2008).

12. The system, outlined in 2007 by a trader on the Traders Laboratory forum with the username "jperl," starts here: www.traderslaboratory.com/forums/f6/trading-market-statistics-i-volume-histogram-1962.html.

13. The emphasis is Levine's. At the beginning of Article 8 he continues: "In the preceding article we identified the theoretical support/resistance (S/R) level with the VWAP at which the stock or commodity had changed hands during an as-yet-unspecified interval of time." Levine's notes are now available at a number of web-hosting domains and investment management sites. One example is www.stocksharepublishing.com/MIDAS/MIDAS_Lessons.htm.

14. Levine, Article 8.

15. Andrew Coles, "The MIDAS Touch, Part 2," *Technical Analysis of Stocks & Commodities* 26, no. 10 (2008).

16. For further discussion of these aspects, see Chapter 3.

17. Levine, Article 11, p. 21; see also Article 18, p. 37: "Finally, the fractal character of the S/R hierarchy is clearly demonstrated, since this 11 year MIDAS chart is indistinguishable in its morphology from the many year-long charts we've seen in the various articles."

18. H. E. Hurst, "The Long Term Storage Capacity of Reservoirs," *Transactions of the American Society of Civil Engineers* 116 (1951).

19. See B. Mandelbrot, "Statistical Methodology for Non-Periodic Cycles: From the Covariance to R/S Analysis," *Annals of Economic and Social Measurement* 1 (1972); B. Mandelbrot and J. Wallis, "Robustness of the Rescaled Range R/S in the Measurement of Noncyclic Long Run Statistical Dependence," *Water Resources Research* 5 (1969); and A. W. Lo, "Long-Term Memory in Stock Market Prices," *Econometrica* 59 (1991). Mandelbrot's work was later collected in B. Mandelbrot, *The Fractal Geometry of Nature* (New York: W. H. Freeman, 1982); and later still in B. Mandelbrot, *Fractals Scaling in Finance* (New York: Springer, 1997). A survey of the work on the development of this field can also be found in W. A. Brock and P. J. F. de Lima, "Nonlinear Time Series, Complexity Theory and Finance," in *Handbook of Statistics*, vol. 14, ed. G. S. Maddala and C. R. Rao (Amsterdam: Elsevier Science Publishing, 1996).

20. Peters had published his work initially in the *Financial Analysts Journal*. See E. E. Peters, "Fractal Structure in the Capital Markets," *Financial Analysts Journal* 45, no. 4 (1989); and E. E. Peters, "R/S Analysis Using Logarithmic Returns," *Financial Analysts Journal* 48, no. 3 (1992). But it's more likely that Levine's attention was captured by Peters's two books. See E. E. Peters, *Chaos and Order in the Capital Markets* (New York: John Wiley & Sons, 1991) and E. E. Peters, *Fractal Market Analysis: Applying Chaos Theory to Investment and Economics* (New York: John Wiley & Sons, 1994).

21. See in particular J. Feder, *Fractals* (New York-London: Plenum Press, 1988).

22. Einstein, "Über die von der molekularkjnetischen Theorie der Wärme geforderte Bewegung von in ruhenden Flüssigkeiten suspendierten Teilchen," *Annals of Physics* 322 (1908); and Peters, *Fractal Market Analysis*, 55.

23. It's beyond the scope of this chapter to discuss this methodology in detail. Interested readers can pursue it in a wide variety of resources online, or they can look at the work of Peters or work cited below.

24. Apart from works cited earlier, Mandelbrot has written a popularization of the Hurst techniques applied to the financial markets for *Scientific American*. See B. Mandelbrot, "A Fractal Walk Down Wall Street," *Scientific American*, February 1999; and also in his *The (Mis)Behaviour of Markets* (London: Profile Books, 2004).

25. Aside from Peters, there is far too much literature to cite here, but see for example Mehmet Horasanli (Istanbul University), "Rescaled Range Analysis and Predictability of Stock Market Indices," *Ekim* (2007) for a discussion of the NYSE, FTSE, Nasdaq, Xetra DAX, Nikkei, and Xutum (Istanbul); and M. D. McKenzie, "Non-Periodic Australian Stock Market Cycles: Evidence from Rescaled Range Analysis," School of Economics and Finance, RMIT University, Melbourne, Australia. See http://onlinelibrary.wiley.com/doi/10.1111/1475-4932.00032/abstract. See also Bo Qian, and Khaled Rasheed, "Hurst Exponent and Financial Market Predictability," Department of Computer Science, University of Georgia. See www.cs.uga.edu/~khaled/publications.html.

26. The articles discussed in the previous footnote arrive at various Hurst exponents for the markets they examine. In their book *A Non-Random Walk Down Wall Street* (Princeton, NJ: Princeton University Press, 1999), Andrew Lo and Craig MacKinlay do not find long-term memories in the stock market returns they analyzed. See especially Chapter 6, "Long-Term Memory in Stock Market Prices." See also B. N. Huang and C. W. Yang, "The Fractal Structure in Multinational Stock Returns," *Applied Economics Letters* 2 (1995). However, these are minority findings and they have been criticized for using insufficient data. See, for example, McKenzie, "Non-Periodic Australian Stock Market Cycles," in the University of Melbourne paper.

27. Peters, *Fractal Market Analysis*, 61.

28. See, e.g., ibid., 4ff.

29. Ibid., 16.

30. D. Saupe, "Random Fractal Algorithms," in *The Science of Fractal Images*, ed. D. Saupe and Heinz-Otto Peitgen (New York: Springer Inc, 1988). Elements of this chapter are also discussed in the article "Estimating the Hurst Exponent" at www.bearcave.com/misl/misl_tech/wavelets/hurst/index.html.

31. For an example of real-time Hurst estimates in the forex market, see Abe Cofnas, "The Misbehaviour of Forex Markets," *Futures Magazine* 34, no. 4 (2005).

32. Radha Panini, "From Nile to NYSE," *Technical Analysis of Stocks & Commodities* 25 (February 2007); and Radha Panini, "Trading Systems and Fractals," *Technical Analysis of Stocks & Commodities* 25 (March 2007). See also Erik Long,

"Making Sense of Fractals," *Technical Analysis of Stocks & Commodities* 25 (March 2003).

33. Levine, Article 11, p. 21. See also Levine, Article 18, p. 37: "Finally, the fractal character of the S/R hierarchy is clearly demonstrated, since this 11 year MIDAS chart is indistinguishable in its morphology from the many year-long charts we've seen in the various articles."

34. This isn't merely because the fractal conception Levine posits relies on nonrational emotional responses by traders and investors, but also because Levine's model of accumulation and distribution is based on access to different levels of information and different responses to it. See, e.g., Article 14.

35. However, as Peters, in *Chaos and Order in the Capital Markets* and in *Fractal Market Analysis,* and many others preceding him, including Mandelbrot, have pointed out, there are far too many large changes at all degrees of trend for this normal curve to be associated with these distributions. In particular, the bell-shaped curve actually tapers off into much fatter tails than the normal distribution allows for. This indicates that exceptional higher sigma events occur with far more frequency than the traditional theory allows. The fat tails actually scale according to a power law.

36. See in particular Chapter 3.

37. As Peters in *Chaos and Order in the Capital Markets* and in *Fractal Market Analysis* acknowledges, the Fractal Market Hypothesis is based in turn on the Coherent Market Hypothesis of Vaga insofar as it assumes that the market can experience different states, some of which can lead to stable and unstable conditions. It also owes a debt to the K-Z Model of Larrain inasmuch as the latter assumes that market crises can occur when investors on the longer timeframe lose faith in fundamental information. See T. Vaga, "The Coherent Market Hypothesis," *Financial Analysis Journal*, Dec./Jan. 1991; and M. Larrain, "Empirical Tests of Chaotic Behaviour in a Nonlinear Interest Rate Model," *Financial Analysis Journal* 47 (1991).

38. www.iitm.com/articles/What-is-a-Trading-System.html. See also Van K. Tharp, *Trade Your Way to Financial Freedom* (New York: McGraw-Hill, 2006); and *Super Trader: Make Consistent Profits in Good and Bad Markets* (New York: McGraw-Hill, 2009).

39. S. Nison, *Japanese Candlestick Charting Techniques* (New York: Simon & Schuster, 1991).

40. See also Stephen Bigalow, "Dynamic Doji Is a Clear Trend Reversal Signal," *Futures Magazine* 34, no. 3 (Feb. 2005).

Chapter 2   Applying Standard MIDAS Curves to the Investor Timeframes

1. Alexander Elder, "Triple Screen System Provides Logical Approach to Trading," *Futures Magazine*, April 1986; *Trading for a Living* (New York: John Wiley & Sons, 1993); *Come Into My Trading Room* (New York: John Wiley & Sons, 2002).

2. Paul Levine, "Introducing the MIDAS Method of Technical Analysis (1): The MIDAS Chart," 3. Available at http://public.me.com/davidghawkins.

3. Ibid.

4. Richard W. Arms Jr., *Profits in Volume* (Columbia, MD: Marketplace Books, 1971).

5. Paul Levine, "Introducing the MIDAS Method of Technical Analysis (1): The MIDAS Chart."

6. Arms, *Profits in Volume*.

7. Richard W. Arms, Jr., *Profits in Volume*; *The Arms Index (TRIN)* (Columbia, MD: Marketplace Books, 1989); *Volume Cycles in the Market* (Salt Lake City, UT: Equis International, 1994); *Trading Without Fear* (New York: John Wiley & Sons, 1996).

8. Levine, "Introducing the MIDAS Method of Technical Analysis."

9. Paul Levine, "Introducing the MIDAS Method of Technical Analysis (4): Anatomy of a Bull Move." Available at http://public.me.com/davidghawkins.

10. Levine, "Introducing the MIDAS Method of Technical Analysis (4): Anatomy of a Bull Move," 4.

Chapter 3   MIDAS Support and Resistance (S/R) Curves and Day Trading

1. See Andrew Coles, "The MIDAS Touch, Part 1," *Technical Analysis of Stocks & Commodities* 26, no. 9 (2008); and Andrew Coles, "The MIDAS Touch, Part 2," *Technical Analysis of Stocks & Commodities* 26, no. 10 (2008).

2. See Martin J. Pring, *Technical Analysis Explained* (New York: McGraw-Hill, 2002), Chapters 1 and 2.

3. Compare for example the moving averages system advocated by Bo Yoder, *Mastering Futures Trading: An Advanced Course for Sophisticated Strategies that Work* (New York: McGraw-Hill, 2004).

4. We have already seen in one or two charts earlier that 38.2 percent seems to be a key Fibonacci displacement level for MIDAS S/R curves. This association is discussed more thoroughly in the second part of this chapter in the sections on Elliott Wave and Fibonacci retracements.

5. I have no qualms about popular U.S. futures contracts and their e-mini counterparts. Readers will find them discussed extensively in relation to day trading in John F. Carter, *Mastering the Trade* (New York: McGraw-Hill, 2006), especially in Chapter 4. Here I merely draw attention to certain popular European futures contracts alongside other well-known currency futures.

6. Exchange rates during the compilation of this table were as follows: GBP/USD, 1.45; GBP/EUR, 1.183; GBP/CHF, 1.6709; USD/CHF, 1.15; EUR/USD, 1.22.

7. Comparative volatility readings for these futures contracts taken in March 2007 can be found at http://daytrading.about.com/od/marketprofiles/a/ProfileSMI .htm.

8. As noted in Chapter 1, sometimes porosity can force re-entry considerations. See also Chapter 13.

9. See for example Stephen Bigalow, "Dynamic Doji Is a Clear Trend Reversal Signal," *Futures Magazine* 34, no. 3 (February 2005).

10. Very new traders shouldn't assume that the system here is some magic bullet for instant trading profits. Without a carefully laid out plan no trading enterprise will survive let alone flourish. On setting up a trading business see, for example, Jean Folger "Getting Down to Business," *Futures Magazine* 35, no. 11 (2006); Mark Cook, "Be an Idiot, Not a Moron," *Active Trader* 3, no. 5 (May 2002); and Christine Birkner, "Getting Started in Trading," *Futures Magazine* 38, no. 2 (February 2009). For common newcomer mistakes, see Paul M. King, "Eight Practices for Long-Term Success," *Futures Magazine* 37, no. 3 (March 2008).

11. See again Carter, *Mastering the Trade*, 59–60 and 69–74, for an extensive list of liquid futures contracts.

12. I say "for the most part" because there will be one additional setup to be discussed below.

13. For more on this technique see David A. Baker "Playing the Flip Side," *Active Trader* 2, no. 8 (September 2001).

14. Andrew Coles, "The MIDAS Touch, Part 2," *Technical Analysis of Stocks & Commodities* 27, no. 10 (2008).

15. See, for example, Chapter 4 of Kathy Lien, *Day Trading & Swing Trading the Currency Market*, 2nd ed. (Hoboken, NJ: John Wiley & Sons Inc, 2009); and "Strategy 7—News Straddling" in Grace Cheng, *7 Winning Strategies for Trading Forex* (Petersfield: Harriman House Ltd, 2007). Longer treatments can be found in Peter Navarro, *If It's Raining in Brazil, Buy Starbucks: The Investor's Guide to Profiting from Market-Moving Events* (New York: McGraw-Hill, 2004); and Ashraf Laidi, *Currency Trading and Intermarket Analysis* (Hoboken, NJ: John Wiley & Sons, 2009). As an invaluable reference volume see especially Evelina M. Tainer, *Using Economic Indicators to Improve Investment Analysis*, 3rd ed. (Hoboken, NJ: John Wiley & Sons, 2006); Richard Yamarone, *The Trader's Guide to Key Economic Indicators* (New York: Bloomberg Professional, 2007); and "Making Sense of the Market Puzzle," *Active Trader* 3, no. 4 (April 2002).

16. As a selection, see Bo Yoder, *Mastering Futures Trading: An Advanced Course for Sophisticated Strategies That Work* (New York: McGraw-Hill, 2004); Oliver Velez and Greg Capra, *Tools and Tactics for the Master Day Trader: Battle-Tested Techniques for Day, Swing, and Position Traders* (New York: McGraw-Hill, 2000); Greg Capra, *Intra-Day Tactics Course Book* (Marketplace Books, 2007); S. W. Bigalow and D. Elliott, "Day Trading with Candlesticks and Moving Averages," *Futures Magazine* 23 (September 14, 2004); A. Cofnas, "Visualizing Price Direction in Forex," *Futures Magazine* 31, no. 10 (August 2002); S. Bigalow "Getting Your Kicks with Candlesticks," *Futures Magazine* 34, no. 7 (June 2005); Leslie K. McNew, "Simple System, Big Profits," *Futures Magazine*, 34, no. 14 (November 2005); Les McNew, "Trading the Plan," *Futures Magazine* 35, no. 1 (January 2007);

Kira McCaffrey Brecht, "The Face of Trading: Adult Education," *Active Trader* 4, no. 6 (June 2003); Jeff Greenblatt, "Better than Average," *Futures Magazine* 37, no. 12 (November 2008).

17. Yoder, *Mastering Futures Trading*. See also Don Wright, "Profiting with Pivots," *Futures Magazine* 35, no. 14 (November 2006); and Dennis D. Peterson, "What Are Pivots?" *Technical Analysis of Stocks & Commodities* 20, no. 4 (April 2002).

18. See also Michael Kahn, "Trading Intraday Selling Climaxes," *Active Trader* 2, no. 6 (July 2001).

19. See Carter, *Mastering the Trade*; and John L. Person, *A Complete Guide to Technical Trading Tactics, How to Profit Using Pivot Point, Candlesticks, & Other Indicators* (Hoboken, NJ: John Wiley & Sons, 2004). For additional discussion of weekly and monthly pivots as well as daily, see John Person, "Better Tactics for Breakout Traders," *Futures Magazine* 33, no. 6 (May 2004); and Christopher Terry, "Pivot Levels and the Power of Commonality," *Technical Analysis of Stocks & Commodities* 22, no. 1 (January 2004).

20. For the interview, see www.camarillaequation.com/interview.html.

21. Interested readers can still find the entry on page 2 of the original thread here: www.trade2win.com/boards/trading-software/5637-camarilla-equation-calculator-2.html.

22. See, for example, www.earnforex.com/pivot-points-calculator; www.pivotpointcalculator.com/; www.mypivots.com/Investopedia/Details/42/camarilla-pivot-points; www.livecharts.co.uk/pivot_points/pivot_points.php; http://atr-forex.com/forex-fx-technical-analysis/camarilla-pivot-points-calculator.php.

23. See J. Peter Steidlmayer and Steven B. Hawkins, *Steidlmayer On Markets, Trading with Market Profile* (Hoboken, NJ: John Wiley & Sons, 2003); John J. Murphy, "Technical Analysis of the Financial Markets," New York Institute of Finance (1999); J. Gopalakrishnan, "Market Profile Basics," *Technical Analysis of Stocks & Commodities* 17 (December 2002); Robin Mesch, "Reading the Language of the Market using Market Profile," in *New Thinking in Technical Analysis, Trading Models from the Masters*, ed. Rick Bensignor (Princeton, NJ: Bloomberg Press, 2000); Robin Mesch, "Deconstructing the Market: The Application of Market Profile to Global Spreads," in *Breakthroughs in Technical Analysis, New Thinking from the World's Top Minds*, ed. David Keller (Princeton, NJ: Bloomberg Press, 2007); Robin Mesch, "Tracking 'Price Acceptance' with Market Profile," *Active Trader* 10, no. 11 (November 2009).

24. See Mesch, "Reading the Language of the Market using Market Profile."

25. Gopalakrishnan, "Market Profile Basics."

26. See Bill Williams and Justine Gregory-Williams, *Trading Chaos: Maximize Profits with Proven Technical Techniques*, 2nd ed. (Hoboken, NJ: John Wiley & Sons, 2004). See also the online article www.tradingfives.com/articles/elliott-wave-fractals.html; and www.tradingfives.com/articles/elliott_oscillator.htm.

27. See the first half of Chapter 16 for improvements.

28. D. W. Davis, "Daytrading with On-Balance Volume," *Technical Analysis of Stocks & Commodities* 22, no. 1 (2004).

Chapter 4 The MIDAS Topfinder/Bottomfinder on Intraday Charts

1. Again I add the proviso that the necessary condition can be relaxed only if the user of the MIDAS curves is not using a uniform combination of high/high, low/low, or midprice/midprice. Since I use a combination of high/low and midprice for the TB-F and standard MIDAS S/R curves respectively, I can downgrade Levine's necessary condition to a sufficient condition. In my 2008 article in S&C I also used the midprice for standard S/R curve calculations and all of the code submitted by the various trading platforms also used the midprice. It's likely therefore that most users of standard S/R curves are using the midprice, albeit (as indicated) Hawkins advocates using the high and low prices and also ensured that this option is available in the StockShare Publishing trading platform.
2. For more on this idea, see Gerald Marisch, "Gann vs Geometric Angles," *Futures Magazine* 33, no. 15 (December 2004).
3. For the Fractal Dimension Index, see again Erik Long, "Making Sense of Fractals," *Technical Analysis of Stocks & Commodities* 25 (March 2003); Radha Panini, "From Nile to NYSE," *Technical Analysis of Stocks & Commodities* 25 (February 2007); and Radha Panini, "Trading Systems and Fractals," *Technical Analysis of Stocks & Commodities* 25 (March 2007).
4. For more on this technique, see David A. Baker "Playing the Flip Side," *Active Trader* 2, no. 8 (September 2001).
5. Tom DeMark, "Applying TD Sequential to Intraday Charts," *Futures Magazine* (April 1997). See also Tom DeMark, "Trading With a Magnifying Glass," *Futures Magazine* (May 1996); Tom DeMark, "Trend Setups and Market Hiccups," *Futures Magazine* (December 1997); Tom DeMark, "*Active Trader* Interview—Tom DeMark: Objectively Speaking," *Active Trader* (November 2001); Tom DeMark and Rocke DeMark, "Absolute Price Projections," *Active Trader* (July 2004); Lindsay Glass, "DeMarking Trend Exhaustion Zones," *Active Trader* (July 2002). See also Tom DeMark, *The New Science of Technical Analysis* (New York: John Wiley & Sons, 1994); Tom DeMark, *New Market Timing Techniques* (New York: John Wiley & Sons, 1997); and Tom DeMark, *DeMark on Day Trading Options* (New York: McGraw-Hill, 1999).
6. See Jason Perl, "Jason Perl of UBS—*Active Trader* Interview," *Active Trader* (October 2008); and Jason Perl, *DeMark Indicators* (New York: Bloomberg Market Essentials, 2008).
7. John J. Murphy, *Technical Analysis of the Financial Markets* (New York: New York Institute of Finance, 1999), 338.

Chapter 5 Applying the Topfinder/Bottomfinder to the Investor Timeframes

1. Paul Levine, "Introducing the MIDAS Method of Technical Analysis (12): TOPFINDER I" (1995). © 1995 Paul Levine. Available at http://public .me.com/davidghawkins.

2. Ibid.

3. Paul Levine, "Introducing the MIDAS Method of Technical Analysis (14): Computing TOPFINDER I" (1995). © 1995 Paul Levine. Available at http://public.me.com/davidghawkins.

4. Alexander Elder, "Triple Screen System Provides Logical Approach to Trading," *Futures Magazine* (April 1986).

5. Carl Swenlin, "Blog on Stockcharts" (2007). Available at http://blogs.stockcharts.com/chartwatchers/2007/04/index.html (accessed October 14, 2010).

6. Richard W. Arms Jr., *Volume Cycles in the Market* (Salt Lake City, UT: Equis International, 1994).

Chapter 6   Applying MIDAS to Market Averages, ETFs, and Very Long-Term Timeframes

1. Harry J. Dent Jr., *Our Power to Predict* (Mill Valley, CA: BRC Publications, 1989); *The Great Boom Ahead* (New York: Hyperion, 1993), Figure 6.6-5, p. 153; *The Roaring 2000s* (New York: Simon & Schuster, 1998); *The Roaring 2000s Investor* (New York: Simon & Schuster, 1999); *The Roaring 2000s* (New York: Simon & Schuster, 2008).

2. Cecilie Rohwedder, "Deep in the Forest, Bambi Remains the Cold War's Last Prisoner," *Wall Street Journal*, November 2009, A1.

3. Dent, *The Roaring 2000s*.

Chapter 7   EquiVolume, Midas and Float Analysis

1. Richard W. Arms Jr., *Profits in volume* (Columbia, MD: Marketplace Books, 1971); *Profits in Volume*, 2nd ed. (Columbia, MD: Marketplace Books, 1998); *Volume Cycles in the Stock Market* (New York: Equis International, 1994); *Trading without Fear* (New York: John Wiley & Sons, 1996).

2. Paul Levine, "Introducing the MIDAS Method of Technical Analysis (12): Topfinder I" (1995). © 1995 Paul Levine. Available at http://aaiibos.com.

3. Steve Woods, *Float Analysis* (Columbia, MD: Marketplace Books, 2002).

4. Richard W. Arms Jr., *Profits in Volume* (Columbia, MD: Marketplace Books, 1971).

5. Arms, *Profits in Volume*, 115; *Profits in Volume*, 2nd ed.

6. Arms, *Volume Cycles in the Stock Market*.

7. Arms, *Profits in Volume*.

8. Levine, "Introducing the MIDAS Method of Technical Analysis (12): Topfinder I."

9. Woods, *Float Analysis*.

10. Arms, *Profits in Volume*, 2nd ed.

11. Ibid.

12. Ibid.
13. Steve Woods, *Precision Profit Float Indicator* (Columbia, MD: Marketplace Books, 2000); *Float Analysis* (Columbia, MD: Marketplace Books, 2002).
14. Woods, *Float Analysis*.
15. Ibid.
16. Arms, *Volume Cycles in the Stock Market.*
17. Ibid.
18. Ibid.
19. Arms, *Profits in Volume* (1971).
20. Levine, "Introducing the MIDAS Method of Technical Analysis (12): Topfinder I."
21. Woods, *Precision Profit Float Indicator*; *Float Analysis*.
22. Arms, *Volume Cycles in the Stock Market.*

Chapter 8   Putting It All Together

1. Alexander Elder, "Triple Screen System Provides Logical Approach to Trading," *Futures Magazine* (April 1986); *Trading for a Living* (New York: John Wiley & Sons, 1993); *Come Into My Trading Room* (New York: John Wiley & Sons, 2002).
2. Richard W. Arms Jr., *Profits in Volume* (Columbia, MD: Marketplace Books, 1971); *Profits in Volume*, 2nd ed. (Columbia, MD: Marketplace Books, 1998); *Volume Cycles in the Stock Market* (New York: Equis International, 1994).
3. Steve Woods, *Precision Profit Float Indicator* (Columbia, MD: Marketplace Books, 2000); *Float Analysis* (Columbia, MD: Marketplace Books, 2002).
4. Arms Jr., *Profits in Volume*; *Profits in Volume*, 2nd ed.; *Volume Cycles in the Stock Market.*

Chapter 9   Standard and Calibrated Curves

1. Paul Levine, "Introducing the MIDAS Method of Technical Analysis, The Internet Articles" (1995). © 1995 Paul Levine. Available at http://public .me.com/davidghawkins.

Chapter 10   Applying the MIDAS Method to Price Charts without Volume

1. A. Elder, *Trading for a Living* (New York: John Wiley & Sons, 1993), 167.
2. For the benefits, see James Mooney, "Forex Futures vs. Cash Forex—Trading in the Then or Now?" 33, no. 6 (May 2004).
3. Unlike ETFs, ETNs are debt instruments with maturity dates of up to 30 years. Holding an ETN to maturity would entitle the holder to a cash payout, though ETNs are intended for shorter-term trading and investing.

4. Readers will recall from earlier chapters, especially Chapter 3, that the secular-term trend is the next-largest trend up from the primary trend, which lasts between nine months and two years.

Chapter 12   MIDAS and the CFTC Commitments of Traders Report

1. See for example an online study by Kathy Lien entitled "Forecast the FX Market with the COT Report" for www.investopedia.com; Grace Cheng, *7 Winning Strategies for Trading Forex* (Petersfield, UK: Harriman House Ltd, 2007); and Jamie Saettele, *Sentiment in the Forex Market* (Hoboken, NJ: John Wiley & Sons, 2008).
2. See Larry Williams, *Trade Stocks & Commodities with the Insiders* (Hoboken, NJ: John Wiley & Sons, 2005); Floyd Upperman, *Commitments of Traders* (Hoboken, NJ: John Wiley & Sons, 2006); and Stephen Briese, *The Commitments of Traders Bible* (Hoboken, NJ: John Wiley & Sons, 2008).
3. This is labelled "aggregate" by eSignal and is denoted by the symbol #OI.
4. John J. Murphy, *Technical Analysis of the Financial Markets* (New York: New York Institute of Finance, 1999).
5. For volume and open interest in intraday applications, see Matthew Reynolds, "Intraday Trading with the Herrick Payoff Index," *Futures Magazine* 34, no. 13 (October 2005).
6. www.cftc.gov/marketreports/index.htm.
7. More fully, the definitions are as follows:
   Producer/Merchant/Processer/User A "producer/merchant/processor/user" is an entity that predominantly engages in the production, processing, packing, or handling of a physical commodity and uses the futures markets to manage or hedge risks associated with those activities.
   Swap Dealers A "swap dealer" is an entity that deals primarily in swaps for a commodity and uses the futures markets to manage or hedge the risk associated with those swaps transactions. The swap dealer's counterparties may be speculative traders, like hedge funds, or traditional commercial clients that are managing risk arising from their dealings in the physical commodity.
   Money Manager A "money manager," for the purpose of this report, is a registered commodity trading advisor (CTA); a registered commodity pool operator (CPO); or an unregistered fund identified by CFTC. These traders are engaged in managing and conducting organized futures trading on behalf of clients.
   Other Reportables Every other reportable trader that is not placed into one of the other three categories is placed into the "other reportables" category.
8. Stephen Briese, *The Commitments of Traders Bible* (Hoboken, NJ: John Wiley & Sons, 2008).

9. Larry Williams, *Trade Stocks & Commodities with the Insiders: Secrets of the COT* (Hoboken, NJ: John Wiley & Sons, 2005); and Floyd Upperman, *Commitments of Traders: Strategies for Tracking the Market and Trading Profitably* (Hoboken, NJ: John Wiley & Sons, 2006). For a succinct discussion, see also Yesenia Salcedo, "Trading off 'commercials'," *Futures Magazine* 33, no. 6 (May 2004); and Jon Andersen, "The Commitment of Traders Report," *Technical Analysis of Stocks & Commodities* 20, no. 4 (April 2002).

10. Interestingly, a recent 21-year study of the relationship between the American Association of Individual Investors and the S&P 500 suggests that the dumb money isn't so dumb after all. See David Bukey, "Trading the Market's Mood," *Active Trader* 10, no. 6 (June 2009).

11. See the discussion in Williams, *Trade Stocks & Commodities with the Insiders*, Chapter 5.

12. Briese, *The Commitments of Traders Bible*, 37.

13. Ibid., 39. Briese points out that it is rare for the commercials to stop buying before prices hit a bottom or to see them stop selling before prices hit a top. Sometimes, however, this does occur and he uses the term "commercial capitulation" to describe these rare events. This is the only time when it is safe to buy when the commercials are buying and to sell when they are selling.

14. Upperman, *Commitments of Traders*, 6.

15. Briese, *The Commitments of Traders Bible*, 31.

16. See Table 12.2 for the Spreads subcolumn beneath the Noncommercials.

17. Briese, *The Commitments of Traders Bible*, 34.

18. www.investopedia.com/articles/forex/05/COTreport.asp?v.

19. Cheng, *7 Winning Strategies for Trading Forex*, Chapter 5.

20. J. Saettele, *Sentiment in the Forex Market: Indicators and Strategies to Profit from Crowd Behavior and Market Extremes* (Hoboken, NJ: John Wiley & Sons, 2008), 91.

21. Ibid., 92.

22. Ibid., 92.

23. See Williams, *Trade Stocks & Commodities with the Insiders*, Chapter 4.

24. This is the same name actually given to the indicator by Stephen Briese. See Briese, *The Commitments of Traders Bible*, Chapter 6.

25. Williams, *Trade Stocks & Commodities with the Insiders*, 89.

26. Cheng, *7 Winning Strategies*, 91–92.

27. Williams, *Trade Stocks & Commodities with the Insiders*, 4.

28. Upperman, *Commitments of Traders*, 8. In Chapter 7, Upperman writes that the commercials have information regarding the fundamentals not known by anyone else; hence, they represent the "knowledgeable money" (p. 7). He calls the noncommercials the "smart money" and fuel for the trend (p. 80).

29. Briese (2008), Chapter 3, 32.

30. Williams (2005), Chapter 10, 99.

31. Briese, *The Commitments of Traders Bible*, 63.

32. Ibid., 75.
33. Upperman, *Commitments of Traders*, 6.
34. What this seems to boil down to is a normal distribution mean weighted towards more recent years combined with a formula which generates a number of standard deviations from the mean.
35. Upperman, *Commitments of Traders*, 32–33.
36. Ibid., 37.
37. Ibid., 42. Plungers are end-of-day price patterns that show signs of market capitulation. See also Chapter 6 (p. 81). Upperman will use 10- and 18-day moving averages on his daily charts and 4- and 9-week moving averages on his weekly charts. They produce results similar to a 20- and 45-day moving average. He also uses a 200-day moving average for longer-term study.
38. Although sharing the same name, this indicator is not to be confused with the stochastic-style indicator used by Williams in *Trade Stocks & Commodities with the Insiders* and Briese in *The Commitments of Traders Bible* and also called the COT Index.

Chapter 13   Price Porosity and Price Suspension

1. Paul Levine, "Introducing the MIDAS Method of Technical Analysis (5)." Available at https://public.me.com/davidghawkins.
2. See Andrew Coles, "The MIDAS Touch, Part 1," *Technical Analysis of Stocks & Commodities* 26, no. 9 (2008); and "The MIDAS Touch, Part 2," *Technical Analysis of Stocks & Commodities* 26, no. 10 (2008).
3. See in particular his discussion under the subheading, "What Price Should be Used?" and Figure 2.3.
4. See the discussion under the subheading, "Special Start Points—The Left Side."
5. See the discussion under the subheading, "Same Launch Point, Different Time-frames" and Figures 2.13 and 2.14.

Chapter 14   A MIDAS Displacement Channel for Congested Markets

1. It's true that there is only an average price in MIDAS and not a moving average, but a moving average could easily replace the average price in the formula, resulting merely in a smoother curve.

Chapter 15   MIDAS and Standard Deviation Bands

1. However, in principle there's no reason why the standard deviation bands could not also be made sensitive to the first meaningful pullbacks while still incorporating the cumulative function for their expansion.

2. For a refresher on the MIDAS formula, readers should consult the section "The Formula Difference" in Chapter 1.

3. For more on volume charts see the second half of Chapter 16.

Chapter 16   Nominal-On Balance Volume Curves (N-OBVs) and Volume–On Balance Curves (V-OBVs)

1. See Joe Granville, *Granville's New Key to Stock Market Profits* (New Jersey: Prentice Hall, 2000); and for intraday applications of the OBV, see D. W. Davis, "Daytrading with On-Balance Volume," *Technical Analysis of Stocks & Commodities* 22, no. 1 (2004). See also Thom Hartle, "Indicator Insight: On Balance Volume," *Active Trader* 4, no. 3 (March 2003).

2. For more on this indicator, see John Bollinger, "Volume Indicators Revisited," *Active Trader* 3, no. 3 (March 2002).

3. See, for example, the chart school section of http://stockcharts.com.

Chapter 17   Extensions, Insights, and New Departures in MIDAS Studies

1. See Article 10. Levine's notes are now available at a number of web-hosting domains and investment management sites. One example is www .stocksharepublishing.com/MIDAS/MIDAS_Lessons.htm.

2. See Joseph E. Granville, *New Strategy of Daily Stock Market Timing for Maximum Profit* (New York: Simon & Schuster, 1976); and D. W. Davis, "Daytrading with On-Balance Volume," *Technical Analysis of Stocks & Commodities* 22, no. 1 (2004).

3. For practical purposes, each bar has slightly more than the specified volume amount because orders come in blocks. However, the overage remains nearly constant over time, so we say the bars are equal volume.

4. Pascal Willain, *Value in Time: Better Trading Through Effective Volume* (Hoboken, NJ: John Wiley & Sons, 2008). Available at www.effectivevolume.eu.

5. For more on the concept of Active Float and its application in trading strategies, see Steve Woods, *Float Analysis: Powerful Technical Indicators Using Price and Volume* (Hoboken, NJ: John Wiley & Sons Inc, 2002). See also Hawkins in Chapter 7.

6. Willain does not discuss the MIDAS method in his book.

7. Levine, Article 8.

8. See Willain, *Value in Time*, for a much deeper exploration of this point.

9. Ibid., 81.

10. Note that because price can displace permanently from a MIDAS curve, it's possible that the search will not be successful.

11. This identification procedure can also be determined algorithmically.

Appendix A

1. Paul Levine, "Introducing the MIDAS Method of Technical Analysis," Articles 12 and 14, TOPFINDER I (1995). © 1995 Paul Levine. Available at https://public.me.com/davidghawkins.
2. Ibid.
3. Levine, Article 15.
4. Levine, Article 14.
5. Levine, "Introducing the MIDAS Method of Technical Analysis," The Internet Articles.

About the Authors

Andrew Coles

Andrew Coles, PhD, graduated with a First Class Honors degree and a Henry Neville Gladstone Exhibition from King's College (KQC), University of London. He holds a master's degree and a doctorate in the early history of Philosophy and Science and is a former Postdoctoral Research Fellow of the British Academy. During his graduate and postdoctoral years, he worked at a number of institutions, including King's College, the Institute of Classical Studies, and Oxford University. He has a diploma in technical analysis from STA–UK and from the International Federation of Technical Analysts (IFTA). He is also a Certified Financial Technician (CFTe). With a solid publication background in his former academic field, including a book for Oxford University Press, he has published widely on technical analysis topics and trading and is an active trader running a private investment fund.

David G. Hawkins

David Hawkins' degrees are in Physics from Brown University, specializing in electro-optics. He has worked as a college instructor, moving into industry as a design engineer, project manager, and eventually into sales and marketing. Throughout he has nurtured an avid interest in the stock market, particularly in applying mathematical techniques to technical analysis.

In 1995 he started learning the MIDAS method of analysis from its founder, fellow physicist Dr. Paul Levine, and quickly incorporated these techniques into his software and his trading. Since Levine's passing, David Hawkins has further expanded upon the MIDAS techniques and has coupled them with other technical analysis tools.

David Hawkins is an active member of the Boston chapter of the American Association of Individual Investors (AAII), where he co-leads the New England Stocks Group. Over the years he has given numerous presentations to various AAII groups on the MIDAS method and other technical analysis topics. He has published articles on the Thrust Oscillator, the Volume Weighted MACD, and other volume-related indicators, and has co-written, with Andrew Coles, three articles on the MIDAS topfinder/bottomfinder.

David Hawkins has served as a consultant to several technical analysis software developers on how to code the topfinder/bottomfinder algorithm.

Index

Accelerated trends, 162–163, 188

Accumulation/distribution line, 372

Active boundaries, 396–400

Arms, Richard W., 32, 219. *See also* Price projection; Volume Leads to Volume principle; Volume Periodicity

Band analysis, 355–356

Bands, trading, 348, 361

Bar counting, 156

Base breakouts, 251–253

Bavarian deer herd phenomenon, 214–215

Behavioral economics, 214–215

Bollinger Bands, 361

Breakout strategies, 99–100

Briese, Stephen, 304, 307, 314. *See also* COT Index; COT Movement Index

Calibrated curves, 257–267, 340–341

Calling bottoms, 249–251

Camarilla equation, 100–105

Candlestick displays, 168–169

Candlevolume displays, 34–35, 168–169

Cash FX markets, 269–284
cash FX tick data vs. futures volume data, 270–275
daily/weekly, 277–283
MIDAS S/R curves, 270–273, 277–280
options for higher timeframe charts, 275–283
replacing with futures markets or currency ETFs/ETNs, 276–277
TB-F curves, 273–275, 280–283

Channels, 348. *See also* MIDAS Displacement Channel (MDC); Price channels

Cheng, Grace, 307

Commercial net positioning as a percentage of total open interest, 320–322

Commercials, 306

Commercial vs. noncommercial positioning data, 312–315

Commitments of Traders (COT) report. *See* COT (Commitments of Traders) report

Commodity Futures Trading Commission (CFTC), 302–303

Composite COT, 323–325

Consolidations, 188, 226–227

Contrarian plays, 93–96

Contrarian trading, 153

Conventional trend lines, 117–119

Correlation analysis, 389–391

COT (Commitments of Traders) report, 297–298
Composite COT, 323–325
Disaggregated COT, 303
indicators of Larry Williams, 315
indicators of Stephen Briese, 316–317
Legacy COT, 303–307
overview, 302–303
timing, and MIDAS, 318–319
total open interest, 307–312

COT Index:
Saettele, 323–325
Williams/Briese, 315–317, 318–319

COT Movement Index, 316, 323, 325

Day trading:
MIDAS as standalone system, 68–82
MIDAS with other technical indicators, 82–121 (*see also specific indicators*)
multimarket day trading system, 73–82
overview, 61–62
summary, 120–121
trend lengths and chart timeframes, 63–68

Dead cat bounce, 55–57

DeMark, Tom, 155. *See also* TD Sequential analysis

Demographic analysis, 209–214

Dent, Harry, 209, 215

Detrended MIDAS Curves, 395–396

Dipper setup, 377

Disaggregated COT (Commitments of Traders)
    report, 303
Displacement, of MIDAS S/R curves, 83–88.
    See also MIDAS Displacement Channel
    (MDC)
Distortions, 4–5
DIST ratio, 383, 384–389
Do Loops, 406–407
Down gap start point, 55–57
Downtrends:
    from trading range, 41–43

Efficient Market Hypothesis (EMH),
    19–20
Elder, Alexander, 29, 269. See also Triple Screen
    Trading System
Elliott Wave (EW) Oscillator, 113–117
Elliott Wave Theory, 83–86, 153–154
End-of-trend analysis, 155
English, Bob, 8, 367, 391–400
    Active Boundaries and Reverse VWAP,
        396–400
    Detrended MIDAS Curves, 395–396
    MIDAS Average Curves and Delta Curves,
        393–395
    use of volume charts, 391–393
Entry setups, 46–48
Entry signal, 22–23, 71
Envelopes, 348, 361
EquiVolume charting, 32–35, 167–168,
    219–223
Exchange traded funds (ETFs):
    and cash FX markets, 276–277
    with MIDAS S/R curves, 202–205

Fibonacci retracement, 85, 87–88, 156–159
15m to 60m trend on 1m chart, 67–68
Flash Crash of 2010, 4
Flip in market positioning, 326
Float Analysis, 227–230
Foothill pattern, 40–41, 377
Foreign Exchange markets. See Cash FX markets
Formulas, MIDAS SR curves, 9–14
Fractal Dimension Index (FDI), 18, 139–140
Fractal market analysis, 13–20, 83–86
Futures markets, 276–277. See also Open interest
FX markets. See Cash FX markets
FXMarket Space, 270

Growth booms, 210–211
Guaranteed VWAP executions, 5

Haggerty, Kevin, 8
Hierarchy of MIDAS Curves, 43–46
Highest R/lowest S start point, 57–59
Historical data/analysis, 209–214, 215–217
Hurst, H.E., 14–15
Hurst exponent, 14–17, 26

Inflation adjustment, 209–211
Initial Public Offering (IPO) start point, 53–55
Intermediate-term trend, 62–64
Interpolation, 407–410
Intraday Intensity Index, 372

Launch points, 336–337
Left Side start point, 50–53
Legacy COT report:
    key players in, 304–307
    trader categories, 303–306
Levine, Paul:
    insights governing MIDAS methodology, 126
    philosophy of price movement, 9–14
    on price porosity, 331
    reasons for VWAP formula modification, 11
Levitation. See Price suspension
Lien, Kathy, 307, 313
Long-term timeframes, 205–218
    demographic analysis in, 209–214
    historical data/analysis, 209–214, 215–217
    inflation adjustment with, 209–211
    volume data with, 205–209

MACD-OBV, 387
Mandelbrot, Benoit, 14–15
Market filter, 21–22
Market indices:
    with TB-F curves, 201–202
    use of MIDAS S/R curves with, 195–198
Market Profile, 105–113
Maturity booms, 210–211
Mean reversion, 346–347
Metastock:
    codes for the Standard MIDAS S/R, 411–412
    and MIDAS Standard Deviation Bands
        (MDSBs), 260
MIDAS:
    conflation with VWAP techniques, 8–9
    differentiation from VWAP, 9–14
    five basic tenets of, 345
    and fractal market analysis, 13–20
    as standalone trading system, 20–21
MIDAS Average Curve (MAC), 393–395

MIDAS Delta Curve (MDC), 393–395
MIDAS Displacement Channel (MDC), 348–357
  applying to sideways markets, 348–349
  compared to MIDAS Standard Deviation Bands (MSDBs), 364–365
  compared to other boundary indicators, 356
  comparison to moving average (MA) envelope, 355–356
  forecasting implications, 349–350
  methodology, 349
  for price porosity and suspension problems, 341
  and TB-F curves, 356
  trading implications of, 349
  used to create a reliable trending price channel, 350–353
MIDAS S/R curves:
  and On Balance Volume (OBV), 378–381 (*see also* On Balance Volume (OBV))
  base breakouts, 251–253
  basic behavior of, 31–32
  calling bottoms, 249–251
  capturing high/low of the day, 119–120
  cash FX tick data vs. futures volume data, 270–273
  contrarian plays with, 93–96
  and conventional trend lines, 117–119
  daily/weekly cash FX markets, 277–280
  for day trading (*see* Day trading)
  demographic analysis and, 209–214
  detrended curves, 395–396
  displacement of, 83–88
  down gap/dead cat bounce, 55–57
  Elliott Wave Theory, 83–86
  for entry setups and triggers, 46–48
  and equivolume charting, 32–35
  with ETFs, 202–205
  and Fibonacci retracement, 85, 87–88, 156–159
  foothill pattern, 40–41, 377
  formula, 9–14
  and Fractal market analysis, 13–20, 83–86
  hierarchy of, 43–46
  highest R/lowest S start point, 57–59
  historical data/analysis, 209–214, 215–217
  IPO start point, 53–55
  Left Side start point, 50–53
  with long-term timeframes, 205–218
  with market indices, 195–198
  and Market Profile, 105–113

and mean reversion in sideways markets, 346–349
Metastock codes, 411–412
with moving averages, 88–96
nominal, 291–294
with open interest, 300–302 (*see also* Open interest)
and pivot point techniques, 96–105
porosity in, 263–266
prices used, 35
ratio analysis, 294–296
real-time fractal dimension and, 17–19
Rg curve, 55–56
rules for price/volume trend relationships, 286–290
special start points, 50–59
Standard/calibrated, 257–267
and starting points, 405–406
supplementary displacement, 92–93
support becoming resistance/resistance becoming support, 35–39
TB-F curves (*see* TB-F curves)
and TD Sequential analysis, 154–156
timeframes of launch points, 48–50
tracking trends with, 43–46
trading range turning into downtrend, 41–43
trend following, 239–248
uptrend vs. trading range, 39–40
use of multiple, 13–14
use with other technical indicators, 82–119
and volume-based oscillators, 384–389
volume-free, 193–198, 277–280
and volume/momentum indicators, 113–117
where to launch, 10–13
MIDAS Standard Deviation Bands (MSDBs), 356, 359–370
  adjustment for shorter timeframe analysis, 363
  alternatives to standard deviation, 365–367
  compared to MIDAS Displacement Channel (MDC), 364–365
  evolution from VWAP deviation bands, 359–360
  and narrowing volatility, 363–364
  porosity and suspension and, 361
  setting price targets, 369
  in sideways markets, 360–361
  trading with, 368–370
  in uptrends and downtrends, 361–362
MIDAS Topfinder/bottomfinder indicator. *See* TB-F curves
Momentum indicators, 113–117

Momentum trading. *See* Trend following
Moving average (MA) envelopes, 355–356, 361
Moving averages, 88–96
Multimarket day trading system, 73–82
Multiple pullbacks, 170–178
Multiple trend and timeframe analysis, 62–68
Murphy, John, 156, 157, 298

Nested TB-F curves, 178–180
Net positioning data, 312–318, 319–327
    commercial net positioning as a percentage of
        total open interest, 320–322
    commercial vs. noncommercial, 312–315
    Composite COT, 323–325
    COT movement index, 316, 323
    and negative numbers, 311, 312, 319,
        326–328
    WILLCO, 316, 322–323
Nominal curves, 291–294
Nominal-On Balance Volume Curves
    (N-OBVs), 371, 373–377
    chart illustrations, 378–381
    the dipper setup, 377
Noncommercials, 307
Nonreportables, 305–306

On Balance Volume (OBV), 113–117. *See also*
    Nominal-On Balance Volume Curves
    (N-OBVs); Volume-On Balance Volume
    Curves (V-OBVs)
    MACD-OBV, 387
    overview, 371–373
    Stoch-OBV, 386–387
    with TB-F curves, 153–154
One-to-two-day trend on 15m charts, 65–66
Open interest, 297–329
    changes in, explained, 298–299
    choosing appropriate category, 307
    commercial vs. noncommercial positioning
        data, 312–315
    Commitments of Traders (COT) report,
        302–307
    MIDAS S/R curves with, 300–302
    orthodox interpretation of, 299
    overview, 298–299
    rule for, 301
    total open interest, 307–312
Overhead Consolidation, 188

Panini, Rada, 18
Peters, Edgar, 19–20

Pivot point techniques, 96–105
    Camarilla equation, 100–105
    trading floor pivots, 97–100
Porosity. *See* Price porosity
Price channels, 348, 361
Price envelopes, 348, 361
Price manipulation, 4–5
Price porosity, 263–266, 331–333
    calibrated curves, 340–341
    cause of, 333–334
    choice of launch point, 336–337
    high/low option, 335–336
    and MIDAS Displacement Channel (MDC),
        341, 353–355
    with MIDAS Standard Deviation Bands
        (MDSBs), 361
    Paul Levine on, 331
    solutions for, 334–342
    spread monitoring, 339–340
    switching to higher timeframe charts,
        337–339
    and volume-trend relationships, 341–342
Price projection, 219–227
Price suspension, 331–342
    calibrated curves, 340–341
    cause of, 333–334
    high/low option, 335–336
    and MIDAS Displacement Channel (MDC),
        341
    with MIDAS Standard Deviation Bands
        (MDSBs), 361
    spread monitoring, 339–340
Price-volume trend relationships:
    four rules for use in plotting MIDAS Curves,
        286–296
    and price porosity and suspension problems,
        341–342
Primary-term trend, 62–63
Prior directional price bias, 107–109
Profit-taking exits, 25
Protective stop, 23, 72
Pullbacks, multiple, 170–178

Quinn, Edward S., 32

Rangebound strategies, 98–99
Ratio analysis, 294–296
Real-time fractal dimension, 17–19
Re-entry strategy, 23–24
Relative strength, 294–296
Rescaled/Range (R/S) analysis, 14–15

Reverse VWAP, 396–400
Rg curve, 55–56
Rohwedder, Cecilie, 214
Rules for price/volume trend relationships,
    286–294

Saettele, Jamie, 307, 310, 317
Saupe, Dietmar, 16
Secular-term trend, 62–63
Setup conditions, 22, 71
Shiller, Robert, 209, 217
Short-term trend, 62, 64–65
Sideways markets, 346–349
    applying MIDAS Displacement Channel
        (MDC) to, 348–349
    MIDAS Standard Deviation Bands (MSDBs)
        in, 360–361
Signals over timeframe of interest, 25
Simple moving average (SMA), 404–405
Spending Wave, 215–216
Spread monitoring, 339–340
Standard curves, 257, 260–267. *See also* MIDAS
    S/R curves
Standard deviation, 365–367. *See also* MIDAS
    Standard Deviation Bands (MSDBs)
Standard Deviation Bands. *See* MIDAS Standard
    Deviation Bands (MSDBs)
Standard Error Bands, 361
Starting Point Ambiguity, 403–406
"Starting point" meaning, 405
Steenbarger, Brett, 8
Stochastic indicators, 113–117
    Stoch-OBV, 386–387
    and total open interest, 309–310
Stop loss, 23
Supplementary displacement, 92–93
Suspension. *See* Price suspension
Swenlin, Carl, 186

TB-F curves, 125–160, 161–189
    accelerated price trend in relation to
        algorithm, 134–135
    accelerated trends, 162–163
    and On Balance Volume (OBV), 153–154
    basic program, 162
    in Candlestick charts, 168–169
    in Candlevolume charts, 168–169
    cash FX tick data vs. futures volume data,
        273–275
    compared to original MIDAS formula,
        126–127

compared to price projection, 223–224,
    225–226
completing before end of trend, 144–145
in contrarian trading, 153
daily/weekly cash FX markets, 280–283
and different timeframes, 180–185
discovery process of, 163–165
Do Loops, 406–407
and Elliott Wave (EW) Oscillator, 153–154
end of, 187–188
engineering aspects of, 135–159
in Equivolume charts, 167–168
and Fibonacci retracement, 156–159
fitting D to pullback, 136–145
fitting to multiple pullbacks, 170–178
and Fractal Dimension Index (FDI), 139–140
getting into trend with, 150–152
implications of working with, 145–149
interpolation, 407–410
launching, 128–132, 136
with market indices, 201–202
and MIDAS Displacement Channel (MDC),
    356
nested, 178–180
overrunnning the trend, 143–144
overview, 125, 161–167
parabolic nature of *e*, 133–134
problems with bottomfinders, 185–186
programming, 403–410
quantitative features of algorithm, 126–135
relation of D to *e* in algorithm, 132–133
role of D in formula, 127–128
and the simple moving average (SMA),
    404–405
Starting Point Ambiguity, 403–406
and TD Sequential analysis, 154–156
and total open interest, 311–312
Tradestation codes for, 413–415
trading with, 150
uniqueness of, 161–162
using, 165–166
volume-free, 280–283
and volume/momentum indicators, 153–154
with WILLCO, 322–323
TD Sequential analysis, 154–156
Timeframes:
    trend relationships between, 62–68
    Triple Screen Trading System, 29–31
Topfinder/bottomfinder indicator. *See* TB-F
    curves
Total open interest, 307–312

Trade equity timing, 109–113
Trade management options, 109–113
Tradestation codes for the TB-F, 413–415
Trading bands, 348
Trading floor pivots, 97–100
Trading range:
    distinguishing from uptrend, 39–40
    turning into downtrend, 41–43
Trading system:
    components of, 20–26
    defined, 20
    need for more than one, 25
Trend following:
    13 steps for, 239–240
    analysis, 245–248
    example, 240–245
Trend lines, conventional, 117–119
Trend tracking, 43–46
Triggers, 46–48
Triple-nesting, 178–179
Triple Screen Trading System, 29–31
Two- to six-hour trend on 5m or 3m/2m charts,
    66–67

Upperman, Floyd, 314, 317
Uptrends, distinguishing from trading range,
    39–40

Volume. See also Price-volume trend relationships
    equivolume charting, 32–35
    MIDAS S/R curves, 193–198, 277–280
    TB-F curves, 280–283
    and TB-F curves, 280–283

Volume-based oscillators, 384–389
Volume charts, 391–393
Volume data:
    and ETFs, 202–205
    with long-term timeframes, 205–209
    MIDAS S/R curves without, 193–195
    validity of, 198–200
Volume indicators, 113–117
Volume Leads to Volume principle, 219–221.
    See also Volume Periodicity
Volume-On Balance Volume Curves (V-OBVs),
    371, 377–381
Volume Periodicity, 230–237, 249
Volume reporting, 269–270
Volume trends. See Price-volume trend
    relationships
Volume Weighted Average Price (VWAP):
    conflation with MIDAS curves, 8–9
    differentiation from MIDAS curves, 9–14
    guaranteed VWAP executions, 5
    initial motivations for, 4–5
    standard calculations, 5–8
    standard deviation bands, 359–360
    support/resistance curve placement, 10–13
    trading applications of, 8–9
Volume Weighted Moving Average (VWMA),
    405

WILLCO (Williams' Commercial Index), 316,
    322–323
Williams, Larry, 298, 308, 309–310, 314. See also
    WILLCO (Williams' Commercial Index)
Woods, Steve, 22. See also Float Analysis

Printed and bound by CPI Group (UK) Ltd, Croydon, CR0 4YY

16/04/2025

14658509-0005